ACCOUNTABIL

ACCOUNTABILITY

POWER, ETHOS AND
THE TECHNOLOGIES
OF MANAGING

ROLLAND MUNRO

Reader in Accountability
Department of Management
Keele University, UK

JAN MOURITSEN

Professor of Accounting
Copenhagen Business School
Denmark

INTERNATIONAL THOMSON BUSINESS PRESS
I ⓣ P An International Thomson Publishing company

London • Bonn • Boston • Johannesburg • Madrid • Melbourne • Mexico City • New York • Paris
Singapore • Tokyo • Toronto • Albany, NY • Belmont, CA • Cincinnati, OH • Detroit, MI

Accountability: Power, ethos and the technologies of managing

Copyright ©1996 R. Munro and J. Mouritsen

First published by International Thomson Business Press

 A division of International Thomson Publishing Inc.
The ITP logo is a trademark under licence

British Library Cataloguing-in-Publication Data
A catalogue record for this book is available from the British Library

First edition 1996

Typeset in the UK by J&L Composition Ltd., Filey, N. Yorkshire
Printed in the UK by the Alden Press, Osney Mead, Oxford

ISBN 0-412-62560-1

International Thomson Business Press
Berkshire House
168–173 High Holborn
London WC1V 7AA
UK

International Thomson Business Press
20 Park Plaza
14th Floor
Boston MA 02116
USA

http://www.thomson.com/itbp.html

Contents

List of contributors

Thomas Ahrens has just completed his doctoral studies at the London School of Economics and is now a lecturer at the University of Southampton. He is interested in the interpretive study of management accounting practice and has completed research in Britain and Germany, drawing on ethnographic methods.

Richard J. Boland, Jr is Professor and Chair, Department of Information and Decision Systems and Professor of Accountancy at the Weatherhead School of Management, Case Western Reserve University, Cleveland, Ohio. He is the Editor-in-Chief of the research journal *Accounting, Management and Information Technologies* and is Co-Editor of *Series in Information Systems* for John Wiley & Sons.

Carla Carnaghan is a PhD student at the University of Alberta, Canada, teaching financial accounting and working on her dissertation. Her main research interest is judgement and decision making in financial disclosure. Publications include a co-authored paper, 'A Profile of Contemporary Accounting Research' in *Contemporary Accounting Research*.

Barbara Czarniawska-Joerges holds a chair in management at Lund University, Sweden. Her research focuses on control processes in complex organizations. She has published books and articles in the area of business administration in Polish (her native language) as well as in Swedish and English.

Mike Gibbins is the Winspear Professor of Accountancy, University of Alberta and is currently Honorary Visiting Professor at the University of New South Wales, Australia. He was editor of *Contemporary Accounting Research* (1992–95) and has published articles on judgement and accountability in *The Accounting Review, Journal of Accounting Research* and *Accounting Organizations and Society*.

Keith Hoskin is Professor of Management Accounting at Manchester School of Management, UMIST. Much of his academic career has been spent as a lecturer in education at Warwick University, but his historical interests have led him increasingly to a study of accounting and management history.

Seppo Ikäheimo is an Assistant Professor at the Turku School of Economics and

Business Administration. His research is in the area of stock market communication, including financial disclosure management, shareholders' use of information and consequent stock market reactions.

Sten Jönsson is Professor of Accounting and Finance at the School of Economics and Commercial Law, University of Gothenberg. He is currently on leave to conduct research on comparative management for GRI – an institute affiliated with the Gothenburg University. He is Editor of the Scandinavian Journal of Management.

Katrine Kirk is a PhD student at Copenhagen Business School where she is writing a dissertation on flexibility and organizational control. Her research interests are managerial control technologies and their implications for the constitution of organizational identity.

Kristian Kreiner is an Associate Professor in the Department of Organization and Industrial Sociology, Copenhagen Business School. His current research interests include technology management, project management, high tech organizations, cross-border and cross-cultural R&D collaboration.

Richard Laughlin joined the University of Essex as Professor of Accounting in September 1995. He has over 60 publications in accounting, management, organization and political refereed journals, books and conference proceedings. Most of these are related to methodological issues and to understanding the organizational and human effects of changes in accounting, finance and management systems in organizations and society.

John Law is Professor of Sociology at Keele University and a member of the Department of Sociology and Social Anthropology, and the Centre for Social Theory and Technology. He has written widely on technology and science, organization and social theory. His major publications include *Organizing Modernity, Shaping Technology, Building Society* (edited with Wiebe Bijker) and *A Sociology of Monsters* (editor)

Simon Lilley is a lecturer in the Department of Management at Keele University, having previously been Lecturer in Organization Behaviour at the University of Glasgow. His publications cover a range of management topics including the 'new' managerialism, time and management information systems. He is the co-author of *Changing Managers and Managing Change*, recently published by CIMA.

Brendan McSweeney is Lecturer in Accounting and Finance at Warwick Business School, University of Warwick and Academic Director of its post-graduate International Management Programme. He has published over one hundred articles and book chapters, and is joint author of two books. His published research covers various aspects of the interface between management and accounting.

Jan Mouritsen is Professor of Accounting at Copenhagen Business School. His interests include management control systems, technology, the new manufacturing environment, organizational immaterial capabilities, multinational firms and new managerialism in the public sector.

Rolland Munro is a Reader in Accountability in the Department of Management at Keele University. He is also a founding member of the Centre for Social Theory and

Technology. He has written widely on belonging, identity work and organization culture, as well as writing on the relations between managing and accounting from his studies of large companies.

Fabrizio Panozzo is currently Visiting Associate at Templeton College, Oxford, although he normally earns his living by teaching financial accounting at Ca'Foscari University, Venice. He has been attracted by various marginal areas in the field of management, ranging from the epistemological status of strategic studies to the use of accounting in loosely coupled organizations.

John Roberts is a lecturer at the Judge Institute of Management Studies, University of Cambridge. His research, based in sociology and organizational behaviour, has spanned a variety of topics: power and identity, accounting and accountability, strategic decision making processes and the growth of high technology firms. He has published papers related to all these issues.

Ulrike Schultze is a PhD candidate in the Information and Decisions Systems Department at the Weatherhead School of Management, Case Western Reserve University, Cleveland, Ohio. Her thesis research is an ethnographic study of knowledge work. Recent publications include 'From Work to Activity: Technology and the Narrative of Progress' in *Information Technology and the Transformation of Work* (eds Orlikowski, Walsham and Jones).

Hugh Willmott is Professor of Organizational Analysis in the Manchester School of Management, UMIST. He is working on a number of conceptual and empirical projects with a common theme of the critical examination of the changing organization and management of work in modern society. His most recent books include: *Critical Management Studies* (co-edited with Mats Alvesson); *Skill and Consent* (co-edited with Andrew Sturdy and David Knights); *Making Quality Critical* (co-edited with Adrian Wilkinson); *Making Sense of Management: A Critical Introduction* (co-authored with Mats Alvesson).

Preface

An errant Home Secretary. A careless social worker. Overpaid bosses. This is the spectacle of accountability. Case by case we follow the chase, with the tabloid press promising to find a scapegoat. This public hounding of individuals is often dramatic and results in the same call: 'Make people more accountable.'

Today almost everyone accepts this call to make people more accountable. Indeed, who could oppose? Who could be against accountability? As a consequence, enormous changes have spread into all walks of life: in our government, in our hospitals and in our schools; and in the office, the shop, or factory floor. Promises are now given in a plethora of contracts, customer codes and citizens' charters. That's before things go wrong. Afterwards, disciplining is conducted against our 'own' individual performance measures. Each of us is becoming suspended in these intricate webs of other people's promises and pseudo-market prices.

Responsibilities, once general and communal, are becoming increasingly specific and individual. But surely this 'individuating' of the buck hardly adds up to a cultural revolution? How important is all this blaming work? Does it do any more than touch the skin of society? At the time we planned this book most of the authors had completed sufficient detailed research across a wide range of organizations, public and private, large and small, to think that today's clamour for 'more' accountability cannot be so easily satisfied. Or so easily dismissed.

There is another view. Since the sixties, groups of researchers have shown how accountability is *already* situated in organizational life. Rather than think of account-ability as a 'lack', an absence into which new technologies of managing can enter unimpeded, it is also possible to understand accountability in terms of ethos. Giving each other 'accounts' is an everyday and all pervasive process of mundane expressions and mutual understandings. Just so. People already settle matters with each other. People already know who is to call on whom for an account. And over what.

Or do they? As others have pointed out, the giving and receiving of accounts is 'most extraordinary'. Among the many reasons for thinking this is that our identities are created by the mundane things that we say and do; and by how these are heard, seen, or felt. This emphasis would also pay close attention to non-discursive aspects of accountability, such as gestures, movements of the body and even everyday artefacts that begin to accompany persons – such as a squeaky-clean curriculum vitae, a proven track record of fund-raising, an unblemished marriage, or a penchant for carrot juice. A further reason for taking the transaction of accounts more seriously is that we tend to overlook the extent to which this continuous exchange of accounts may be shaping our lives more generally. A mundane, taken-for-granted, and matter-of-fact presentation of accounts can easily efface just how crucial their absence or presence may be in opening up specific opportunities and in shutting down other conditions of possiblilty.

In our view it is critical to see accountability as more than a background against which day-to-day decisions are being made. Indeed, we argue, it is perhaps the very accountabilities themselves that are being continuously created, negotiated, challenged and decided. Who is to take the credit? And who is to carry the can? How? And when? These are effects that are never finally settled, but are always involved in forming and reforming social relations. For example, in taking up the case of the manager who monitored nurses' performance through their christmas cards, we wonder what these were supposed to say. That too few cards meant not enough client care; or that too many cards implied too much time being spent on patients?

At a time of upheaval and change there is an enormous potential to direct and change accountabilities. This would fit with the fashionable rhetoric of democratizing the workplace, with talk of empowerment and the like. So this idea of 'more' accountability might be one way of understanding the advent of the new technologies of managing; as a story of organizational change. But there are other possibilities. For example, a vast increase in performance indicators might be directed more at maintaining senior management's propensity for extracting credit and divesting blame. And talk of empowering at a time of job insecurity may help instal a consciousness of dependency, inducing people to be more grateful for their position, no matter how lowly. A story of changing cultures might be also a complex pattern of subtle and crude forms of influence learning to co-exist.

Instead of just assuming that accountability is being pressed into all walks of life, the critical point is to see *differences* in accountabilities that are emerging. This is the ambition of this book: to understand how new forms of accountability emerge within a heightened presence of new, and old, technologies of managing. Different forms of accountability are permeating our relations. But what are these forms? How are they different? And what ramifications follow, especially for such topics as the self, networks, local communities and large or small organizations?

1 Alignment and identity work: the study of accounts and accountability

Rolland Munro

Getting into accounts

Imagine Susie. She is on her way to see Tom. Over the last month he has been listening to her ideas about a quality initiative she is about to run in her department. Only, not in the last few days. Just ahead of her launching details of the quality initiative to her staff, she has found it difficult to get hold of Tom. She's left a number of messages headed 'quality' on the e-mail, as yet without response.

In the corridor to his room, she meets Harold, the head of another department, coming the other way.

> 'Hi, how are you?'
> 'Oh, fine. I've just been discussing the output charts with Tom.'
> 'Output? Oh, the output charts. I'd forgotten all about them!'
> 'Well, I thought he had too, but he's just been over mine with a fine tooth-comb.'
> 'So how was it?'
> 'Yeah, well seems OK. He seemed happy enough. Well, better get back.'
> 'Yeah, great. Maybe see you later.'

Susie goes on down the corridor. But although she hesitates outside Tom's room, she doesn't go in. Instead, she takes the long way round the other stairs and goes back to her department. She avoids looking at June, who's been hoping to find out over lunch whether her idea on quality is getting a green light. Instead, she calls to Steve to get out the output charts for the last six months. When these arrive ten minutes later, she turns to June and excuses herself, saying 'Sorry, June, something's come up'.

Harold and Susie's brief meeting is drawn from my ethnography of a highly prestigious company conducted over the years 1987–1992. We could just see this incident as Harold getting one over on Susie. But I want to resist such quick readings and, in the rest of this chapter, I will attempt to explain why I see this exchange as crucially implicated in accountability today. As a first pass at understanding what is going on, however, we can list the several **accounts** which are exchanged. For example, Harold recounts what has passed between him and Tom as 'discussing the output charts'. And, in turn, Susie reports that she had 'forgotten all about' these. Further, in his expression 'with a fine toothcomb', Harold lets Susie know that Tom has examined the output charts very carefully. Finally, in response to Susie's direct question, Harold also adds that Tom 'seemed happy enough'.

A particular feature of our book is that exchanges, such as Susie and Harold's, make up much of the research material for the various chapters, but first I want to stress that we are not directly concerned with studying what are called face-to-face conversations, at least as a subject in their own right. Considered simply in terms of the 'machinery of conversation' (Zimmerman and Boden, 1991), Susie and Harold's exchange seems merely mundane. The opening and closing salutations are there. There is a rapid 'turn-taking', familiar in what might seem to be no more than incidental chat. And, although these are less clear, there are plenty of attributions of what sociologists call 'agency': for example, in Harold calling the output charts 'mine', rather than calling them the department's; and in Susie saying '*I'd* forgotten all about them' (emphasis added).

Instead, the authors of the various chapters treat conversations in the workplace as media for accounts. The spoken word is only one form of media, albeit a ubiquitous one, in which accounts are elicited. Other media, especially numerical inscriptions such as accounting numbers or production statistics, abound and enter pervasively into this process. The point here goes beyond recognizing that 'indexing' these matters has long permeated everyday talk in organizations. However mundane accounts look, researchers mistake the nature of accountability if they imagine what is involved somehow inheres in the words or numerals themselves.

The crucial point is that accounts, whatever their form, are always pre-figured. This is not just to say that only some accounts count. It is to add that any distribution of particular materials and devices, sometimes known as **intermediaries**, is likely to play a considerable and possibly decisive part, both in eliciting accounts and in shaping their form. For example, as Harold's accounts imply, the mysterious 'output charts' constitute an occasion for Tom calling Harold to account. They also elicit what seems to be an unsolicited 'confession' from Susie.

Much of this book is about materials and devices like these 'output charts'. As much as they discuss more informal modes of account-giving, such as everyday conversations, the contributors to this book also draw on formal modes of accounting: human resource management, project formation, manpower planning, financial reports, management information systems and budgeting. For the authors, accountability is never just a question of its participants moving each other about in face to face confrontations. Inanimate scraps of paper or silent computer print-outs, albeit implicitly, seem to elicit accounts from people as they go about their work.

As researchers, we are interested in how these materials and devices enter into accountability relationships. And, as intermediaries, we want to include them as part of our understanding of accountability. In the various chapters, therefore, we will be moving between accounts as stories, explanations and reasons for conduct on the one hand and accounts as coded representations, records, often in the form of numbers, on the other hand. But far from wanting to keep these apart, as is usually the case, the authors draw attention to the ways in which each mode actively mediates the other, in a continuous fashion.

So here is a further reason for wishing to distance ourselves from what has been called in the psychology literature, discourse analysis and in the sociology literature, conversation analysis. The problem is that other forms of accounting, such as the numericals created and produced under the rubric of costs or profits, tend to be kept separate from everyday conversation and become relegated to 'context'. The danger here is that any distribution of intermediaries is seen as lying outside 'the social'; existing in another world from that of talk, perhaps in a world of pure action, or in a physical world of 'technical' things. This stance, we suggest, is blind to how forms of materials and devices, even words, enter into accountability relations.

The position adopted in this book is that, far from being somewhere 'out there', context is that which is always being created and reproduced through accounts. If this is so, then the aforementioned distribution of intermediaries also does not lie 'outside'. Distributions of materials and devices are as much an *effect* of the giving and calling for accounts, as they are integral to the business of producing and consuming accounts. It is this insight that stops Susie and Harold's exchange of accounts from being as 'everyday' as each is making it sound. As we will see, a world in which quality is important is being exchanged for a world in which quantities remain the name of the game. But before I talk more about this, some definitions are helpful.

Key concepts

This book is about accountability. What gives accountability a special interest to researchers of contemporary organizations, is that accountability itself forms a subtext – and more recently, often the explicit text – of current government and business agendas. Accountability can be understood in terms that not only make it conducive to the study of 'ethos', but in ways that implicate it at the very centre of a massive struggle over power. Who is to get the cream and who is to carry the pain, are vitally integrated with questions of who takes the credit and who carries the can.

Chief executive officers tend to think of accountability in terms of 'outcomes'; as something their company or institution needs to 'get', rather than as something people already do. If only people would be accountable, the argument goes, then the company could turn away from the dead hand of command and control, the state where people wait to be told what to do. People could be 'empowered'; that is, given 'discretion' and left to get on and 'do things' without instructions. Consequently, senior managers have been ready to spend vast sums either attempting to buy in accountability through management training, or manufacture it by re-engineering the organization culture.

Much of the emphasis on accountability here focuses on measurement of individual performance. We appear as a society obsessed with targets and outcomes and, expressed in the vernacular of management accounting or statistical process control, these technologies look to have become **obligatory passages** for the processes of accounting. In the management accounting literature, for example, a rich vein of study has emerged around the notion of **centres of calculation**. Although much more is involved in these concepts of obligatory passages and centres of calculation, at least as they appear in the work of Michel Callon, Bruno Latour and John Law, one important effect of measurements being set as targets is the creation of lines of 'visibility' into which participants are drawn by being held accountable – as individuals – for meeting these targets.

A very different, if less fashionable, version of accountability comes from the work of psychologists and sociologists, who define accountability as the capacity to give an account, explanation, or reason. In this 'process' view accountability is already, and endlessly, going on: the giving of accounts is that in which everyday activities subsist. Whether in what we say, or by what we do, we are always giving explanations and reasons for our conduct. I say, for example, that I am helping to edit this book because I think it will become a seminal text; or you explain that you are reading this particular chapter only because you will be examined on it. These are accounts and we exchange perhaps hundreds of these daily.

Accountability, in this view, involves more than a study by psychologists and sociologists of expressions that are circulated in discourse. Accountability pivots instead on an analysis of the **methods** by which participants engage in accountability relations. This is one key concept which requires discussion, but an equally important and related concept should be mentioned alongside the matter of methods. This concept, arising from the sociology literature, is that of **membership**. According to Garfinkel (1967), members of the same grouping have methods by which they sanction other members' conduct.

The implications of this view are, however, surprising. What is easily overlooked is that such arrangements entail membership never being settled, but remaining provisional. Membership, in its inclusion and exclusion of others as 'members', enters into the sanctioning process as both medium and outcome. Inevitably, therefore, inclusion and exclusion of membership appears then to be one of the 'methods' by which participants sanction each other. For this very important reason, we will continue to use the term **participants** as well as members. While membership is often what is at stake in accountability processes, anyone who enters into a giving or calling for accounts may be understood to be a participant.

The unlikely bed-companions of top managers and sociologists hardly explains the widespread interest in accountability – taking place in the office, the factory, the hospital, schools and even in the home. However, it is the potential for relating these different notions of accountability that forms much of the rationale for this book. To help indicate some of the direction of study here two, interrelated, aspects of accountability can be mentioned. We call the first of these two aspects **alignment**. Alignment is a difficult concept to define, but it reflects a concern over the 'line' which accounts, when considered together, offer a participant. For simplicity's sake, you might consider this as the 'story-line', or 'narrative', that is on offer. Nevertheless, it is important to appreciate that there is never just a single story-line on offer. Accounts involve an intricate, and continuous, process of embedding accounts in other accounts, one in which a multiplicity of readings is always possible. For example, we have already suggested that Harold and Susie's exchange of words might also be read as incidental chat.

The second aspect which enlivens the study of accountability is the concept of **identity work**. Like alignment, identity work is not easy to define and, indeed, we shall spend much of the rest of this chapter explicating these two terms. For the moment, it is perhaps sufficient to say that identity work is concerned with the self-portrait that is being painted through a participant giving, and asking for, accounts. Again, in terms of identity, a multiplicity of readings are possible. However, some of these will be stabilized, or ruled out, through the story-lines that emerge out of the processes of alignment. For example, any appearance of helplessness offered initially in Susie's remark 'Oh, the output charts. I'd forgotten about them!' is countered the next moment by her confident 'So how was it?' question.

Clearly, there is a two-way flow here. First, the 'line' which is being followed may be elicited precisely by a concern of participants to put up one form of identity, rather than another. Second, identity work helps set up the conditions for a stable alignment of accounts. And these together help set limits to interpretability, even if the limits are not always strict. For example, we might consider it bizarre of Harold, should we subsequently discover that he has walked away with the image of Susie as a giraffe. We will return in a moment to more likely interpretations.

Seeing through accounts

Exchanges of everyday accounts, such as that of Susie and Harold, are often perceived as being no more than talk. It is the notion of action, understood as that which is opposed to talk, which dominates today. Action, in the form of 'macho management', the 'one minute manager', being 'pro-active', or in 'managing by wandering around' is currently in ascendency. And notions of action run central, not only to the work of many social theorists, for example in the work of Anthony Giddens, but are central to popular culture. For example, in the genre of 'action movies' (who ever wanted to see an 'account movie'?) and also in the strictures we swap one with another – 'just *do* it!'.

So what is so special about accounts? Harold Garfinkel, a leading ethnomethodologist, stresses that the peculiar feature of organizing work is the attempt to make itself 'tell-able'; that is, account-able:

> Any setting organizes its activities to make its properties as an organized environment of practical activities detectable, countable, recordable, reportable, tell-a-story-about-able, analyzable – in short *accountable*.
>
> (Garfinkel, 1967: 33, emphasis in original)

The argument here is that work is nothing more than making readable. Work is not ever organized instrumentally, as some would have it and as it is treated in many management textbooks. It is organized to be 'read' by other members, including oneself. Accountability is about making the invisible visible.

This feature of organizing is easily overlooked by researchers and is perhaps unexpected, until one understands how organizing work is made visible, both to the self and to others. To illustrate the emphasis here, we can begin with a story from Gilbert and Mulkay's (1983) study 'In search of the action'. Briefly, Gilbert and Mulkay had finished their fieldwork on a particular group of biochemists, when they discovered that someone else had interviewed the same group of scientists some years before. The previous researcher had wanted to create a difference between 'truth-telling action' and 'political action'. So he had looked at the accounts of the scientists, ostensibly to understand what sort of 'action' was 'going on'. For him, the definitive version of 'what was going on' was 'political action' as scientists made, for example, strong claims about what he called 'the control of collegiate competition'. Thus, from a reading of these accounts, he had argued that, contrary to well-established ideas of scientists acting to tell the truth, scientists often engaged in 'political action'.

All that Gilbert and Mulkay had to do to dispute this definitive version was to point out that other scientists gave very different accounts of the action; and even the same participants offered blatantly different versions of ostensibly the same events. So Gilbert and Mulkay either have to dismiss the scientists as liars, or re-examine their accounts for a different explanation. By looking closely at one aspect of what they call patterning and what we are calling alignment, they were able to show that examples of political action occur in accounts of scientific error; and, conversely, that such examples are conspicuously absent in stories about the discovery of truth. So, in this version, politics no longer takes on the shape of an underlying reality, but can be seen now as a particular device that is incorporated, selectively, as part of the methods by which scientists *construct* their accounts.

Of course, for others, terms like action or reality might sound much more interesting than accounts, if these are to be understood only as mere talk. So as editors, perhaps we'd better be clear where we are coming from. Our position is that we are always in accounts. There is no hard and fast separation of talk and action. For all practial purposes of research, there may be much that lies outside accounts, but there isn't anything that we can *point* to outside accounts. A description of reality, whether offered in words or presented in numerals, is no more than that: an account.

In restricting ourselves to accounts we are not suggesting, against social theory and popular culture, that action is a figment of imagination. The restriction is better understood as a methodological device to remind us that any access to 'viewing' action is always mediated by accounts. A second story which illustrates this theme arises out of a class in which the set book was *In Search of Management* by Tony Watson. After a few weeks of closely reading a chapter a week, the class was asked: what did the managers do? They made profits, of course, came the reply. No, I said, we can't see them doing this. What, I wanted to know, could we actually *see* managers doing? This question elicited a truly amazing array of accounts of different actions by managers. But, no, I repeated, we can't actually see any of this. All we can see is the managers giving accounts. If we follow managers about and see what they do, that's what they do. They give each other accounts. That *is* how they 'get things done'.

Of course, if giving each other accounts constitutes their 'action', this paints a very different picture from the current hype over 'managing by doing'. But I want to make a different point. This is that we need not doubt for a moment the veracity of what students said, as accounts of what *they* had seen. Clearly the managers' accounts, as transported to them in the form of Tony Watson's text, acted like a camera lens for them to visualize managers in action. The extraordinary detail in which they described managers in action certainly took me by surprise. Their competence in using accounts as a lens for action was stunning. But just as stunning was the extent to which they had shut out this as a process for making the invisible visible. They didn't consider that they had summoned up the picture of managers in action from the accounts; what shocked them was the realization that, in order to see managers in action, they had effaced the fact of these being accounts altogether.

This effacement of accounts takes us back to Gilbert and Mulkay's study. For they are also worried about something else, something they see as generic to research. The previous researcher's shift from accounts to action struck Gilbert and Mulkay (p. 11) as a fairly typical research ploy, which they characterize as: 'take the participants' statements at face value as accurate accounts of what is really going on'. By presenting interview accounts, not as accounts, but as what Raffel (1979) calls 'records of events', the typical researcher effaces the material of the research. We are invited to see the action and forget we are only 'seeing' through accounts.

So here is the main problem, researchers, just like the students, might want to stage an argument about what 'is really going on'. But they have no warrant to leave the domain of accounts. All the researcher has, like the reader, is accounts. This point is not intended to stop research in its tracks. Rather, as Gilbert and Mulkay point out, all we need throw out is the idea that we can 'see' (with more data, more observations) a final and definitive version of action. The great advantage of sticking to accounts is that they let us see how constructs like 'action', or 'reality' are just part of the methods by which participants frame their accounts.

Aligning accounts

But is an analysis of accounts of interest to anyone other than a management researcher or the sociologist? Yes, if the arguments of this book are correct. On this vital point, if on no other, we could hardly disagree more with Gilbert and Mulkay, who assert that only 'occasionally' are patterns in the ways participants portray action 'a matter of concern to the participants themselves' (p. 24). In the terms that frame the debates in this book, alignment is a key activity of participants in either the giving or the reading of accounts.

In raising this matter of alignment, it hardly needs to be said that we are assuming that accounts do not just occur haphazardly. Accounts follow and flow from each other in ways that go beyond mundane conventions, such as salutations and turn-taking. So much so, that what is being said at one moment has to be understood as **indexing** what has been said, either a moment before, or what might yet be said some time later. However, this flow is not always transparent: some accounts might seem so self-evident as to be left unsaid and their presence can only be retrieved through their being indexed. For example, in meeting a casual passer-by out on a walk, I might say 'Fine day!', without feeling any need to preface the remark by first saying, 'I'm now going to talk about the weather'. At least in England, the expression 'Fine day!' indexes a discussion of the weather. But these matters of context are never settled. For example, whatever the taken-for-grantedness, the same remark hurled at a traffic warden might index a quite different sort of discussion.

As we have already mentioned, accountability involves the study of how accounts happen to line up – or indeed are made to line up. The main point is that the way in which accounts line up is 'expressive' of a participant's position; and is thus open to processes of surveillance and sanctioning. So this feature of accounts is of interest to all participants, albeit in different ways, since their very participation in accounts depends upon their reading, and understanding, of alignment.

To see what is being discussed under the concept of alignment, let's go back to the exchange between Susie and Harold:

> 'Hi, how are you?'
> 'Oh, fine. I've just been discussing the output charts with Tom.'
> 'Output? Oh, the output charts. I'd forgotten all about them!'
> 'Well, I thought he had too, but he's just been over mine with a fine tooth-comb.'
> 'So how was it?'
> 'Yeah, well, seems OK. He seemed happy enough. Well, better get back.'
> 'Yeah, great. Maybe see you later.'

The way accounts line up here cannot be taken for granted. Not all accounts align, at least in ways that participants might readily expect they might. Notice, for example, that Harold's reply to Susie's confession does not quite follow suit as a confession. He might have said that he had forgotten all about the output charts as well. But he doesn't do this. His account implies quite something else. He displaces Susie's forgetting into a matter of Tom's forgetting. 'I (Harold) thought that he (Tom) had [forgotten] *too*' (emphasis added). That is, a lack of earlier attention by Tom had (also) suggested to Harold that Tom had forgotten about the output charts. In this way, Harold can be read as affirming to Susie that she had good cause to forget all about them.

His response offers therefore a different form of alignment. He can be understood as affirming Susie's conduct within what Barbara Czarniawska-Joerges calls a 'logic of appropriateness'. For example, one way of looking at Harold's response is that he is (positively) sanctioning Susie's forgetting as rational and reasonable. In this way, Harold can also be understood as supplying researchers with a condition of possibility (i.e. Tom's inattention) for understanding Susie as having 'forgotten all about them'. It is not inappropriate to suppose that one of Susie's methods for not 'forgetting' things is through her study of Tom's accounts. Or indeed, as we have already seen, when she can't get it from the horse's mouth, through her study of the accounts of her fellow managers.

And Harold's accounts accomplish something else. Susie can study his account to see how it represents alignments over *identity*. Indeed, his account, rather succinctly, re-presents existing alignments: it offers a different picture from how previous alignments over identity may have seemed. We can see how participants are lining themselves up by noting differences in the accounts. Harold's account first marks a distance between himself and Susie. As we have noted, he is not admitting to being one of those who 'forgot' the output charts. So he is different to Susie here.

What is more, this difference carries a further resonance. For, although before it might have seemed over quality, that Susie was in line with Tom's priorities, this is no longer the case. Harold's account implies that, in being in line with Tom over the output charts, he is now *as one* with Tom. Over the output charts, they are the same. So this is the new alignment. Tom and Harold are on one side, and Susie is on the other. Although any (negative) sanctioning is left implicit, the implication in Harold's account is that it is now Susie who is out of line. In going on past Tom's door and back to her department to examine her own output charts, it is also clear that this matter is not lost on Susie.

It is very much a theme of this book that no media for account-giving can be cut up and isolated for separate study. As researchers, we cannot decide that a practice is *either* the object of study for sociology *or* the object of study for management. Methodologically, we refuse to accept current academic arrangements that partition the sociologists as listening to the conversations, while management researchers study the design of new systems of reporting. Rather, as ethnographers, we follow people when they pore over the accounting numbers, as much as we follow their interchanges in the corridors. So perhaps we should follow Susie as the output charts call her back towards them?

Intertextuality and identity

When one mode of accounting speaks from and through another, we call this inter-textuality. This is the idea that no one context of interpretation is sealed off from another. For example, Susie's spontaneous confession over 'forgetting' the output charts appears to elicit the vital matter for Susie: how to pursue her quality agenda. Harold's report of Tom going through the output charts with a 'fine toothcomb' suggests to her that it is the output charts, not her quality agenda, that are aligned with Tom's current priorities. She is now in a position to understand why she's not been able to get his attention. Drawing on Harold's accounts, she can assume Tom has switched attention away from her quality programme back to output numbers. This is why she passes the door, she feels the time is not right to raise her agenda.

A general finding of our research is that modes of accounting are always interdependent. Conversation can never be separated off, and delimited from other accounting media. Each technology or media draws on and sustains the other. Admittedly, studying some media often gives meagre results. For example, sitting by Susie, watching her look at the department output charts, one only gets glimpses of what's going on. This sort of interaction, between a person and the rubric on the paper is certainly hard to follow; the conversation seems internalized, with only occasional grunts, nods or finger movement helping the researcher trace what is going on. Perhaps we should stand back for a moment and consider how the researcher can best proceed here?

As a minor problem, my interrupting Susie to ask what it is she thinks she's 'up to' would switch her out of one interaction into another (that of being interviewed by the ethnographer). The specific problem here is that interview accounts are likely to be influenced by my intervening, and hence disrupting, a different form of interaction with its own accounting logic. This said, the more general problem for researchers is to take care to stay with the material of the research and not separate off Susie's 'real' intentions as being different in any way from those expressed in her accounts. Intentions, like action, are another stylistic device. Access to her 'real' intentions is difficult, even for Susie when accounting to herself, for herself. However hard Susie tries, she cannot go beyond accounts to guarantee what it was she was *actually* 'up to'.

On the argument of intertextuality, what someone is 'up to' is likely to have some transparency to other participants. For example, whatever Susie thinks she's up to, something is transparent enough for June to keep her distance and disappear off to lunch. June can immediately read that Susie is busy with other priorities. Just as Susie got the message from Tom to keep away until she has her house in order, so June can infer that the time is not ripe to press Susie. Something has 'come up' and her agenda has to wait. (And it is once again *her* agenda; for, as June will not fail to notice, the quality programme is back to being June's agenda – at least temporarily – until Susie reclaims it as hers, no doubt when Tom is ready to re-claim it – and transmute it – as his).

Perhaps now we should stress the advantages of not separating everyday conversations from intermediaries? The intrigue in conducting research extends to the problem of working out what is happening *to* participants – as an effect of their interaction with material. In her interaction with the output charts, Susie may be in the process of switching identities – at least partially and at least temporarily. As June experiences it, Susie plus output charts is not the same as Susie plus the quality agenda. The latter creates room for June in a way that the former has not (until perhaps June changes *her* identity).

This *motility* in Susie's identity – as she 'tries on' different readings of the output charts and sees how they fit – is hard to observe. It is possibly analogous to the way we suspect people's identities move about in conversation; one moment with us, the next moment against. Watching Susie, my surmise is that, as yet, her involvement with the output charts is very tentative. Susie is not sure about her relations with these output charts – of the ways in which they are calling her to account. She seems to be looking at the output charts, but as much in order to let them 'tell' her what it is that she should be looking for. Yet, she can't go very far. Instead of magnifying her as a 'competent' manager, as yet they diminish her. She cannot align yet with what they are 'telling' her, either by getting their accounts in line with hers, or her accounts in line with theirs. So, for the moment, they appear as having a different and separate identity. They are still the department's output charts; they are not yet hers, in a way that Harold talks freely about *his* output charts.

And perhaps all that she can accomplish by way of identity for the moment is a line of reasoning that says that her end of the month numbers should be going up. Of course, but by how much? To answer this second problem, Susie needs to check her 'line' by taking it back to a different accounting media. Indeed, once she has got hold of a rough idea of the relative scale of the numbers, she might visit Harold again in order to compare her numbers to his. If they align with hers, if they seem comparable, she can guess that her numbers may be all right with Tom. Her numbers may be already in line with his expectations.

But Susie has also to consider the downside of this move and its potential ramifications as an exchange of accounts. If her numbers look dreadful against Harold's, she could lose face *as a manager* to Harold. And, worse, she may not be getting what it is they 'tell'; or at least in the same way in which Harold, as their self-appointed 'spokesperson', feels they tell.

And the danger does not stop with Harold. Intertextuality abounds. Just as there is an interplay between different media of accountability, so the spaces in which account-giving take place must be considered as leaky. Harold's reading of her figures may not stay with Harold. This is not only because, when forced on a later occasion to account for his own numbers, he is likely to resort to comparisons with hers. Susie also has to watch what she lets others like Harold see because Harold, unwittingly or not, is always helping make, and break, her reputation.

Other people do not just supply information; they also, as Anthony Cohen has suggested, supply 'selves'. In that there is always an undecidability over the question of 'who are you to me?', participants are, simultaneously, engaged in settling these issues through 'identity work'. People are not to be imagined as only engaged in a perpetual exchange of information. There is an intertextuality between information gathering and identity work.

Multiple memberships

The methods by which participants go about getting and giving accounts has to be considered as much a matter of lining up identity, as it is instrumental to gain information. Let's go back to the earlier interchange. There is a nice contrast between Harold's 'seemed happy enough' response to a direct question and the way in which Susie elicits Harold's 'fine toothcomb' account as a response to her confession. As already commented, the more vital matter for Susie is to find out about Tom's commitment to the output charts. Finding out how Harold is scoring with Tom is a lesser concern.

Consider, speculatively, one possible turn the conversation might have taken if Susie had asked a more direct question first, prior to her 'confession'.

> 'I've just been discussing the output charts with Tom.'
> 'Oh, how was that?'
> 'OK. He was just looking at them.'
> 'I'd forgotten all about the output charts,'
> 'He just went over them with me. Are you going in to see him?'
> 'Yeah, but it's about something else, the quality initiative I'm running.'

This sequence inverts the positioning of ambiguity in the original text. Instead of Susie appearing as someone who doesn't know, she is positioning Harold as someone who should know. (After all, 'he was there'.) However, Harold's imagined response would leave Susie with *less* knowledge about Tom's current interests. For Harold adds ambiguity in his response. 'Just looking' is not quite as revealing as 'fine toothcomb'. But, in that Harold gains more material, there are other possibilities. We can, for example, imagine how the conversation might continue, with Harold returning the direct question by asking if Tom is still interested in Susie's quality initiative? This could put Susie in a quandary, should she attempt to deceive Harold, or admit that she's engrossed in something that Tom isn't?

The danger of giving a false account is that Susie could lose *membership*, her inclusion as belonging to a group of department heads. If her accounts become perceived as untrustworthy, Harold, together with the other department managers, could exclude her from the regular exchanges which up-date each other on Tom's current concerns. Such an exclusion would likely prove fatal to any chances of promotion and could seriously disrupt her current ability to manage her department. Possibly it is just such an apperception of consequences that prevents Harold from 'siding' with Susie and pretending that he had forgotten all about the output charts. (The corollary is that Harold's refusal to do this will facilitate him being identified with the output charts; and I will return to this matter again in a moment.)

Rather than lose face as a person, someone whose accounts cannot be trusted, the lesser danger is to lose face as a manager. At least that is the ethos in this particular company. In another organization, the positions might be reversed: losing face as a manager might invite more sanctions than losing face 'as a person'. In Susie's company, she's better off to admit that she's out of line with what are (putatively) current priorities. Admitting this might also let her off the hook of having committed her-self, in front of Harold, of still going to see Tom. This is no light matter, since, from what she now knows from Harold's accounts, calling on Tom would give him the opportunity to raise the matter of the output charts with her. Indeed, her call would provide an opportunity for Tom to elicit an account from Susie that she has 'forgotten' all about something that he now sees as his current priority.

In fact, none of this happens. Susie's competence with accounts saves her from some of these dangers. Instead of pressing Harold for an account, she relies on the spontaneous advantage of having caught him on the way back from Tom's room. Harold is only too ready to give an account of himself. He knows a failure to do so would create an opportunity for Susie to speculate with the other department heads about why he has been meeting with Tom.

Intermediaries and identity work

Cut off, as mentioned earlier, as Harold is from an account which insinuates that he had forgotten the output charts, Harold's accounts expose him to being identified as standing for them. On this occasion (and it is in line with other occasions witnessed by the ethnographer), Harold's accounts identify him as someone engaged with the agendas associated with the output charts. In terms of all the different possible agendas in the company, it is where he 'stands'. It is not too fanciful to say that in the eyes of Susie, and no doubt Tom as well, Harold stands for the output charts. He has become their **spokesperson**. We can go back now and see how he answers Susie's opening salutation:

'Hi, how are you?'
'Oh, fine. I've just been discussing the output charts with Tom.'

Harold doesn't explain that he is fine because he no longer has a cold, or because his wife has just had a baby. Instead, he moves directly to the output charts. His alignment with the accounts of this particular intermediary are one of the 'methods' by which he can be identified.

In the way that the accounts line up, Harold appears happy that they, the output charts, are *symbolic* of him. This might seem odd. Surely as a person, Harold is much more than someone who stands for the output charts? Surely he wants to be seen, as has already been suggested, as a person to be trusted and so on? Well, of course, but on the analysis we have presented, all the department heads do this. Indeed, everyone in the company protects their image as trustworthy. This is not only taken for granted as mandatory in the ethos, it is this very taken-for-grantedness that helps produce and reproduce the ethos.

As we have remarked, people in other organizations may do it differently. But when everyone is the same, trustworthiness is mundane and will not, of itself, give one identity. It may grant one membership, but it does not distinguish one among one's fellow members. It does not mark one out *as* different. Managers, as the saying goes, also have to make their mark. So this is how we can see Susie and Harold: as aligning their accounts (strategically) with corporate agendas. In aligning herself with the quality agenda, Susie positions herself to act as a spokesperson for quality measures. In aligning himself with the output charts, Harold is acting as their spokesperson.

And it is surely apposite to suggest also that Susie and Harold's knowledgeability must also extend to knowing that they are being read in this way. As discussed earlier, reading the patterning of accounts is of consummate interest to participants. Through the way accounts line up, participants are attuned to picking up on how others may be forming impressions of them. Further, they are likely to pick up any specific reading of their own identity. And, if and when they do, they can either go along with it, re-marking by their accounts their alignment in different ways, or attempt to refuse it by realigning their identity to other agendas.

What we have been drawing out here is that sanctioning, as usually understood, goes beyond a nod and a wink over expressions. This work of attaching oneself to material such as corporate agendas, and going along with, or refusing, the effects of people's readings of these attachments, or detachments, is part of members' methods and is what we have been calling identity work. The point being that identity is something that is *added* to participants, or subtracted, in order to account for their inclusion or exclusion from membership.

In this view, for all practical purposes, participants treat each other as having no 'core' self. There is a lack of self, or at least a lack of transparency, that is remedied only by making one's manoeuvres visible (i.e. account-able) in ways that enable others to make *attributions* over identity. In so far as participants line up their accounts as part of their methods for making attributions over identity, sanctioning is also likely to be intense in the form of affirming or contesting such attributions.

However much serendipity helps form an alignment in accounts, the interest in research is over whether the identity work of social actors helps sustain, or changes, existing readings. It is this aspect of identity work that makes the actual exchange of accounts between Susie and Harold intensely interesting. Just look at how the alignment is being reshaped as networks of accountabilities. Harold's account suggests that the previous alignment of interests between June, Susie and a quality programme, and between Susie, Tom and a quality programme and (drawing on the research material from which the current vignette has been chosen) between Tom, the CEO and a quality programme, has broken down.

Now new networks, new alliances have to be formed – however momentarily – around the output charts. These intermediaries, at least for the moment, appear to have been made into an obligatory passage. In order to regain her access to Tom, or re-establish her standing with her fellow managers, Susie has to make herself 'visible' through the output charts. Susie has to submit to the discipline of the output charts and get her numbers up. Even if she will not change her identity altogether, she has at least to augment it. Only once these output charts are working for her – accounting for her *as* a good manager – will she be able to risk raising the quality agenda again.

In summary, the processes of accountability, properly understood, provide a clear explanation of how ethos comes to be produced and reproduced. Ethos appears as both a medium and outcome of the exchange of accounts. In the example to hand, Harold and Susie rendered their accounts in ways that enabled them to appear as trustworthy; only in this way could they preserve their membership of the account-giving group. But, as we also saw, participants simultaneously render their accounts in ways that gave them room for manoeuvre and made them *different*. Through their accounts, they seek to manage identity work in ways that cover both groupings: first, as 'colleague', in ways which they have to efface themselves as the same; and, second, as 'manager', in ways which mark their identity as different.

Approach of the book

Each of us is involved, daily, in the mundane process of giving accounts. So a reasonable expectation of those studying something so mundane is that we, as experts, should be able to provide quick answers. But, indeed, this is part of our point. That quick answers are just too quick. The mundane is seldom just ordinary. If we 'intend' in accounts more than we 'deliver' (the conventional separation of thought and action discussed earlier) then, as Jacques Derrida suggests, we also have to be understood as delivering in accounts more than we intend.

On the argument of intertextuality, mundane accounts supply windows into other relations. The mundane processes of everyday account-giving allow Susie to 'know' what Tom is up to, without going to the horse's mouth. But they do not, for example, stretch to explaining why accountability has come to be so closely associated with hierarchy. They do not go as far as explaining, say, why each of us seems more ready to account to strangers, than we ever might be to our kith and kin. And they do not explain how participants like Tom become treated as **centres of discretion** in ways that enable others to switch agendas without, it seems, ever being given a single instruction.

So this is our position. When accountability is performed as a mundane process, this tells us no more than that participants are likely to be highly competent in this aspect of their giving of accounts: that of keeping them mundane. It does not give us the title to expect that the methods for giving accounts are widely understood and discussed. Indeed, we would argue strongly the opposite. Membership often depends exactly on an effacement of its methods. In our family lives we want the expression of love, not a discourse on the methods for loving. In our places of work, we want to feel the friendliness of our colleagues, not have them account to us about the techniques they deploy to keep on-side with us. However avidly we might read about the methods in *Cosmopolitan*, or the weekend magazine, discussing methods gets bracketed off as the peculiar practice of academics.

So methods are a matter of effacement. They are deleted from everyday accounts. And perhaps this is how they should be left. But two points also need to be made here. First, we might experience ourselves as 'editing' the text, but in any giving of accounts we are supplying material to others for identity work. So the text is also editing us. Second, researchers are not only nosy people, asking awkward questions, or detectives dusting out skeletons from their cupboards. Sometimes they are also intrigued when mundane matters seem to be being turned into economic or political weapons.

Certainly, this is what we think is happening to accountability. It is on the move. The picture of accountability as a remnant of community processes, quietly removed from the market logic into the backwaters of family life, has been irrevocably upturned. By becoming implicated in a new managerialism that has swept through all forms of institutional life, accountability has become more than a topic that is central to much contemporary research. It is what is being made visible. There is not only a production and reproduction of practice, as Garfinkel understood in his emphasis on ethos. There is also, simultaneously, a 'rendering apart' of practice that is invoking new forms of power.

As we will go on to discuss in various chapters, a 'rendering apart' also gives participants additional opportunities to *manoeuvre* by including other participants *as* members, in particular ways, rather than others. As managers of universities, large companies, tennis clubs, governments and scientific research laboratories keep telling each other. 'We have to be *seen* to be doing the right thing.' We are all making ourselves accountable, as a self, as an institution, as a partner. So perhaps something that is becoming so ubiquitous, and so pervasive, can't be that simple anymore!

Indeed, within business and other institutional organizations, account-giving is undergoing what amounts to a near revolution. Charged by notions of 'empowerment', 'ownership of decisions', 'team-building', 'corporate values' and a more 'demo-cratic workplace', there are at work specific attempts to alter and direct account-giving in ways that may yet prove productive for organizations.

For many of the so-called excellent companies, this has amounted to deliberate attempts to re-engineer accountability within the organization. Although perhaps not often successfully, different technologies have been introduced in ways that discipline people to align with officially approved corporate values and written codes of conduct. For other institutions, and sometimes the same companies, change agendas have been marked by an attempt to recover accountability, as if it had somehow been lost through a putative absence of markets, or from feather-bedding middle-management and the like.

All this is happening at the very time when understanding about the nature of power, and the way it works, are also undergoing change. These ideas about power will be discussed further in the book, but they have generated a new set of technologies of managing. Technologies of managing, such as total quality management, manpower planning, project management and budgeting, are different from the old technologies of work study. Almost as if in response to critiques of traditional sociology, the individual has become centrepiece; the 'men are dragged back in' in ways that position accountability no longer at the fringes of management, but at the core.

These considerations have led us as researchers to develop an approach in a number of ways that mark it off from ethnomethodology, at least as conventionally understood. First, as we have already mentioned, there is the matter of intertextuality. While Garfinkel occasionally touches on matters that transcend membership boundaries, his discussion usually proceeds as if contexts were sealed off, recursively, as a conse-quence of the accounting procedures. This is an important insight in that clearly accounts are often presented *as if* contexts were independent. However, it is equally important not to overlook what Howard Becker called 'leakages' from one accounting space to another.

The contributors to this book explore the extent to which people, in their accounting procedures, systematically attempt to present their accounts in ways that acknowledge that their accounts 'build' context, but *also* take account of a propensity for leakage. We have already met a number of occasions on which Susie and Harold appear cut off from giving accounts that would not sustain across time and space. For example, Harold might find it difficult to insinuate that he has not pursued the matter of output charts.

An awareness of intertextuality, then, necessarily forms part of a member's compe-tence. This, by now, should be clear. But there is a twist to the issue that is of particular importance to understanding the process of account-giving in the contemporary workplace. One is never just included, or excluded, as a member of an organization. One is included, or excluded, through a *multiplicity* of identities. For example, we have already seen, Susie and Harold are at work maintaining their identities *as* trustworthy persons, *as* good managers, *as* engaged in quality agendas or *as* engaged in output charts.

The possibilities for membership are multiple in ways that are often overlapping, but, as in the vignette of Susie and Harold, sometimes not. It is this second emphasis, perhaps more than any other, that distinguishes the contribution of this book not only from much other work in ethnomethodology, but also, as will be clear in Chapters 4 and 5, from much work in social psychology, particularly when accountability is studied in the laboratory. What is of interest in studying accountability in the field is seeing how and when methods vary. And, in their helping accomplish an ethos, say, of winners and losers, how identity work becomes turned on, and against, each other.

Outline of the book

We have organized the chapters of the book around the question we are making central to our enquiry: '**Who is accounting to whom, over what?**' This question is seldom as straightforward as it sounds. Indeed, it is a *questioning* of relations here that develops different understandings that form several different spaces for examining this question as 'units of account'. Each unit of account corresponds to a unit of analysis by the different authors and opens up a set of different positional arrangements (indexed by 'who', 'whom' and 'what') in which the authors can focus on the accountability relations.

The chapters of the book are arranged in five sections, each section addressing a different unit of account. A unit of account can be defined as a space in which the account-giving is being staged, or foregrounded. The five possibilities for staging accounts on which we focus are:

1 the self;
2 encounters in networks;
3 manoeuvres in networks;
4 centres of calculation; and
5 centres of discretion.

These five units of account are now discussed briefly in turn, with further explanation being given at the beginning of each section.

The self

The first unit of account involves a staging of accounts as 'the self'. Here identity work is turned inwards. The key idea involves the notion of an **index**. The self draws on the accounts of others as material and resources for its own construction. In aligning all this heterogeneous material into a self, the self needs to create identity and difference through 'indexing': that is, separating out material, say, as 'hers', or as 'mine', or even 'ours'. The exact moves are as follows:

1 Self is imagined as drawing distinctions between 'itself' and 'others'.
2 To do this, it incorporates material as 'mine' or 'hers', sometimes 'ours'.
3 Self reshuffles this material, seeing how it looks as 'mine' rather than 'hers'.
4 Accordingly, the self takes up different positional arrangements: sometimes looking at 'self', as is portrayed by 'others'; sometimes looking from the 'self' as it is portrayed by 'others'; and, recursively, acting as a 'spokesperson' for each of these versions of the self.

We summarize the recursive quality in these three positional arrangements for the self as: '**the self accounting to the self, for the self**'.

Encounters in networks

The next unit of account involves the staging of accounts as encounters in networks. The analysis here covers much the same argument over relations as in the previous section, but here the identity work is turned 'outwards'. So the focus shifts to seeing how networks become indexical to participants' accounts. The key idea is that accountability is managed in ways that accomplish **multiple memberships**. In framing accounts in ways that create new allegiances, and dissolve difference, participants help create and reproduce networks of memberships.

1 Participants' accounts enrol each other as 'members'.
2 To do this, participants attribute accounts as 'ours', or 'theirs'.
3 But members are understood to be already enrolled by other sets of accounts.
4 Accordingly, accounts become framed so as to address networks of memberships.

We summarize these three positional arrangements – participants, others and members – as **participants accounting to others, as putative members**.

Manoeuvres in networks

The next unit of account involves the staging of accounts as manoeuvres in networks. The analysis here is similar to encounters in networks, but this time the questioning turns to ask how identity work is accomplished within networks. The key idea is participants enrol materials and devices, known as intermediaries. They do not appeal to people directly *as* members, but perform as **spokespersons** for the intermediaries. Thus, the networks which emerge are temporary, as much as they are multiple. Allies, such as the press or shareholders, stay enrolled only as long as the common intermediaries, say, profit announcements, are enrolled. Questions in this unit of account thus turn into: Who gets to speak on behalf of which technologies? And under which circumstances?

1 Participants' accounts enrol intermediaries as manoeuvres.
2 To do this, participants elect themselves as 'spokespersons' for intermediaries.
3 These manoeuvres attract other spokespersons as 'members', albeit temporarily.
4 Accordingly, manoeuvres, to be understood, have to be seen as accomplishing membership in temporary networks that straddle across more stable networks.

As in the previous arena, networks are assumed to open up, or close, in response to an interplay of accountability pressures. In addition to participants and members, the three positional arrangements in this unit of account include being spokespersons. We can formulate this as: **participants accounting to members, as spokespersons**.

Centres of calculation

The next unit of account involves the staging of accounts as if these were addressed to centres of calculation. The key idea here is that of an **obligatory passage**. Intermediaries are fixed into place by being made the obligatory passage for the giving of accounts between participants. The analysis is similar to that of manoeuvres in networks, but there we emphasized the ways in which technologies are drawn on for manoeuvres over identity in the form of membership. The corollary of this is that sometimes it is identity that can be manoeuvred, with coercive effect. Typically, management accounting numbers become the obligatory passage through which accounts are given. These create lines of 'visibility' and, hence, the possibility of centres of calculation.

1 Intermediaries are drawn on by participants to form their accounts.
2 To ensure this, intermediaries are interposed *between* participants as accounts.
3 Intermediaries are difficult to manoeuvre as they are pre-aligned in networks.
4 Lined up as a 'precession' of accounts, intermediaries create lines of visibility, imputing a centre of calculation. So arranged, accounting numbers are more likely than not to *prevent* membership and sustain relations of hierarchy.

In this unit of account, the three positional arrangements are participants, others and intermediaries. While intermediaries, usually in the form of accounting numbers, are drawn into accounts, they are treated *as if* they spoke for themselves. Accordingly, this unit of account foregrounds an analysis of **participants accounting to each other, through intermediaries**.

Centres of discretion

The final unit of account involves the staging of accounts in what we call centres of discretion. There are many ideas in this section, but a key idea is **distribution**. So what is distributed? The answer turns out to be not only, as we saw in the previous unit of account, materials and devices in the form of obligatory passages, but also **discretion**. In the previous unit of account we assumed there was one dominant regime of intermediaries. Now we want to be more careful and allow for the effects that follow from *multiple* distributions of intermediaries. This is to say that we need to place management accounting among the multiplicity of other control technologies that exist to see how discretion has also been re-distributed in networks that lionize some participants as having discretion and diminish others as having none.

1 Arrange a distribution of intermediaries to be drawn into participants' accounts.
2 Multiply the number of distributions by adding different sets of intermediaries.
3 Assign the different distributions of intermediaries to different spokespersons.
4 Defer discretion for 'activating' intermediary accounts to select participants.
5 Accordingly, any activation of intermediary accounts manoeuvres into position networks of spokespersons who defer discretion to the select participants.

It is clear from the third unit of account that prescribing a technology for account-ability is insufficient to radiate any durable power effects. Even the prescription of accounting numbers, merely creates more discretion, more room for manoeuvre. Only by making a technology an obligatory passage, via the fourth unit of account, can certain manoeuvres be curtailed and others encouraged. But which manoeuvres should be encouraged and which discouraged? How could we know? Given the 'undecid-ability' here, centres of discretion can be created in order to sustain, simultaneously, the motion of 'keeping things happening' alongside a process of deferral in 'wait and see'. In view of this double positioning, we can think of the analysis in this unit of account foregrounding the **distribution of obligatory passages and discretion**.

At this point, the reader might like to know which unit of account is best? However, we provide this set of five units of account not as a shopping list, but as an expression of our commitment to preserve a plurailty in research on accountability. Rather than seeking to know which unit of account is best, it seems more important to see how each may be working simultaneously. But this is not how it seems. So it is also important to appreciate how work in each arena appears to delete work in others. However much we try to see accountability by grouping the units of account together, we never can. As John Law suggests in Chapter 14: just as there is no single 'object' in accountability, so too accountability can never collapse to a single 'discretionary point' from which to arbitrate one arena as more important than another. All the units of account are important for any serious student of contemporary managing.

References

Garfinkel, H. (1967) *Studies in Ethnomethodology*, Prentice Hall, New Jersey.

Gilbert, G.N. and Mulkay, M. (1983) In Search of the Action, in G.N. Gilbert & P. Abell, *Accounts and Action: Surrey conferences on sociological theory and method I*, Gower, Aldershot, pp. 8–34.

Raffel, S. (1987) *Matters of Fact: a sociological inquiry*, Routledge & Kegan Paul, London.

Zimmerman, D.H. and Boden, D. (1991) *Talk and Social Structure: studies in ethnomethodology and conversation analysis*, Polity Press, London.

Part One

The self

The unit of account in this section is the self. The main focus is the alignment of the self as a self. As with using the index to a book, the self has access to a composite set of materials through reference to different sources. So there need be no single self, no single source of self.

The image here is the way in which an entity can reference this same material, but sometimes indexed as hers, sometimes seen as mine. The authors thus examine how the accounts of others come to be drawn upon as material and device to create the appearance of a centre of consciousness. Of course, this depiction of the self sounds a little clumsy. We are much more used to thinking of the self as almost complete in itself; as something unitary, which only occasionally, and temporarily, feels divided. Perhaps this commitment to a reflexive self is best caught in the motif: the self accounting to the self, for the self.

In all the chapters in this section, the reflexive self becomes an arena for alignment of accounts. For Hugh Willmott, in Chapter 2, this alignment of accounts attempts to respond to, and overcome, the dialectics of a subject-object split in which there is both an 'I' (e.g. a putative centre of consciousness) and a 'Me' (what others identify as the 'I'). This position draws on the argument of the American pragmatist, George Herbert Mead. In that the sense of being a discrete, autonomous individual is not innate, but is learned through processes of giving and receiving accounts. An 'I' is acquired that is understood to be in charge of, and responsible for, the conduct of the 'Me'. Thus, instead of examining the ready-made world of 'subjects', who give us accounts about 'objects' (including themselves), Willmott's argument is that we need to examine how our conduct, and indeed sense of agency as 'sovereign', is mobilized by frameworks of accountability.

Substantially, this is the issue which occupies John Roberts in Chapter 3. While he goes on to discuss the importance of dialogue, primarily he is concerned to explicate how the different frameworks of accountability produce different selves. Unlike social forms of accountability, hierarchical forms of accountability produce a solitary self, reminiscent of

Descartes's sovereign self. As such, the solitary self might seem to escape the notion of a unit of an account as relational, but Roberts is committed to a relational view of selfhood. Quoting Merleau-Ponty, he argues a view of the individual that is 'compounded through and through of relationship'. Thus, although hierarchical forms of accountability individuate the self, and turns it inward, they also produce a mirror-like effect that is caught in Roberts's phrase 'accounting for the self, to the self'.

In taking individuals somewhat more for granted, Richard Boland and Ulrike Schultze begin Chapter 4 rather differently. Following the work of the social psychologist Jerome Bruner, they posit two modes of cognition, 'narrative' and 'paradigmatic'. For Boland and Schulz, therefore, accountability comes in either a narrative, or a paradigmatic form. They show convincingly that forms of conversation on e-mail are textured by this dual mode of accounting. This suggests to the authors that formal and informal encounters always draw on both modes of accountability. Since in his previous chapter he shows the hierarchical and the social as interdependent, this is not a conclusion to which Roberts would object. Boland and Schultze notice, however, an important asymmetry in that the paradigmatic mode closes up issues (black-boxes them) and the narrative mode helps keep them open. This feature of opening up issues might be another way of looking at what is important to Roberts about dialogue.

Although the next three sections will go on to foreground a more familiar picture of participants, either as engaged in identity work, involved in manoeuvres, or entrapped as agents reporting to centres of calculation, some form of self-reference is ever present. In this respect, Boland and Schultze's position is that it is the ability of accounts to tell – i.e. to narrate events in a meaningful order rather than the ability to talk – i.e. to express (maybe trivially) in spoken words, that makes a responsible self and socializing forms of accountability possible. To the editors, this position clarifies the main thrust of what is being argued in Willmott's and Roberts' chapters. The argument makes more or less the point made in the Introduction: that accounts have to be aligned and that the 'reflexive self' has to be considered as a principle arena in which a performance of this alignment takes place. However, the reader is faced with a choice over whether this capacity to narrate is innate to an individual, Bruner's view, or whether it is acquired in the process of becoming an individual, Mead's view.

2 Thinking accountability: accounting for the disciplined production of self

Hugh Willmott

Introduction

Accountability has two intertwined aspects. One is universal; the other is historical. Accountability – in the sense of rendering intelligible some aspect of our lives or our selves – is a distinctive and pervasive feature of what it is to be human. Human beings are continuously involved in making and giving accounts to others, and to ourselves, about who we are, what we are doing, etc. This universal aspect of accountability is a condition of our participation in any social world. The universal aspect of accountability enables our experience in the world to be rendered intelligible to others and to ourselves. For example, it enables me to produce the following 'accounts' of accountability.

However, as human beings, we participate in particular social worlds. Universal processes of accountability do not float free of historically and culturally distinctive frameworks of accountability. We are inescapably within historically specific, and often discordant, frameworks of accountability. It is these frameworks that identify and articulate our sense of who and what we are.

It is worth stressing that frameworks of accountability are not restricted to formal accountability systems, such as annual statements of accounts to shareholders (principals) provided by corporate executives (agents) or procedures (e.g. regular elections) developed to render politicians responsive to electorates. Formal accounting systems are always embedded in already established frameworks of accountability that make such systems relevant and meaningful. As Mouritsen (1994: 4) has argued, formal accounting systems:

> may or may not be called forth in systems of accountability. Their calling forth depends on people deploying their potentiality to support or raise issues through controlling interpretations of accounting results . . . Accounts are thus produced in and contextualised by systems of accountability.

To repeat, accountability is a widespread phenomenon that occurs whenever people strive to account for their experience-in-the-world.

Accountabilities arise in relation to diverse discourses, including those relating to age, gender, ethnicity and employment. These accountabilities operate to position us in terms of being, for example, middle aged, male, white and unemployed. Our experience is rendered accountable through the (shifting) meanings that such categories convey or whatever categories we strive to replace them with.[1]

Frameworks of accountability differentiate people in terms of their status, access to resources, responsibilities, etc. In work organizations, people are often represented as managers or as workers. In universities, academic staff are differentiated from administrative staff and students. Underpinning these divisions are sundry material and symbolic means of securing compliance with the particular meanings and values that are privileged by these frameworks. In work organizations, workers are charged by managers with the responsibility for clocking in on time and are penalized for poor timekeeping; and managers are held accountable for the timekeeping of their staff. In universities, students are ascribed responsibility for submitting assignments by the due date, a responsibility enforced by a variety of rewards and punishments. However, the range of human actions that are accountable is extensive, and certainly flows well beyond the confines of so-called formal institutions such as universities, factories or government.[2]

Many commentaries on accountability are preoccupied with the description, classification and analysis of the components and workings of accountability structures and systems (see, for example, Gray *et al.*, 1987). In contrast, this chapter offers a series of reflections upon accountability as a universal and historical property of social relations. It offers a loosely connected series of reflections upon the two meanings of accountability – universal and historical – sketched above. The intention of this chapter is not to provide a well integrated, authoritative statement on accountability but rather to present a number of more or less self-contained meditations that may enrich and extend established ways of thinking about accountability.

Thinking about accountability 1: the universal and the historical

Accountability is endemic to our lives. As human beings, we are continuously engaged in the activity of making sense of the world, including the sense of self in the world, by giving and receiving accounts.

At social gatherings or parties, a typical question is 'What do you do?', not least because more probing questions about age, gender, politics or religion are usually deemed to be too self-evident or too sensitive. Such enquiries anticipate and expect some kind of account of self – such as 'I'm a student' or 'Well, actually, I'm unemployed'. In modern societies, statements about the type of employment offer a barometer of status: one that is also deemed to provide a relevant indicator of other affiliations. As the response is given, the speaker is positioned in some historical social space – such as the space occupied by the connotations attaching to 'merchant banker', 'housewife', 'computer analyst' which is subsequently expanded or qualified by additional accounts that elaborate and elucidate this positioning process.

When coming within the orbit of the influence of particular frameworks of accountability, human beings find themselves constructed within, and accountable to, the disciplines that accompany these frameworks. For example, in modern societies, men and women are understood to be separate from nature whereas, reportedly, the Canaque[3] do not and cannot distinguish the body from nature. Nor do the Canaque conceive of the body as the site of the self.[4] Arguably, a compelling explanation of such differences is to be found not in an aberrant genetic make-up of the Canaque but rather, in the distinctive frameworks of accountability that fix, albeit precariously and temporarily, our experience in the world in historically and culturally different ways.

From this it follows that our own modern, western commonsense understandings cannot sensibly be adopted uncritically as a firm foundation for making sense of our world. Instead of assuming the analytical adequacy, or self-evident authority of notions such as 'person', 'ego' and 'individual', it is necessary to address how the sense of such notions, which are important conditions of possibility for systems and processes of accountability, is produced and sustained within particular power-knowledge relations (Pollner, 1987).

Willy nilly, accounts have their effects. They act 'to produce subjects of a certain form, to mould, shape, and organize the psyche, to fabricate individuals with particular desires and aspirations' (Rose, 1988: 196). The giving of accounts has consequences for how subjectivity is organized as well as influencing the way others perceive and relate to the person giving the account. Through the medium of these accounts, the capabilities and possibilities of those that they identify are routinely shaped, guided and appraised.

> It takes little imagination to grasp the importance of giving an account of our lives . . . all of us at least some of the time seek to render our lives intelligible to ourselves and to others . . . giving an account is one activity in which we *come to be* as selves and particular kinds of communities through forms of discourse that shape, guide and judge life . . .
>
> (Schweiker, 1993: 233–4, emphasis in original)

Not to offer a socially recognizable and acceptable account in response to the question 'What do you do?' – for example, to stare at the questioner blankly or to reply with some (apparently unrelated) observation about the Children of God – is to invite (or provoke) hostility and sanction (Garfinkel, 1967). However, what 'counts' as acceptable is itself a contextually-dependent matter of accountability. Whilst it is likely that staring blankly will provoke hostility, it may not necessarily be taken as a sanctionable threat to the 'good sense' (and identity) of the questioner. Instead, it may be heard playfully, as an ironic riposte to such a ritualistic question. Processes of accountability and their outcomes are invariably subject to interpretation and negotiation; they are never wholly predetermined.

Even where formal systems of accountability are seemingly tightly defined, processes of accountability are often complex and problematical precisely because, in practice, the meaning of what we say and do is potentially open to multiple interpretations. The response, 'God told me that I had more important work to do' when a student is asked to explain the absence of an assignment may be successfully construed as buffoonery or parody which gains the sympathy and indulgence of the teacher. At the very least, the offering of this account, if skilfully done, may gain the indulgence of the teacher or make the strict imposition of a sanction seem churlish or over-zealous (see Gouldner, 1954). The skilful use of humour, in particular, is a powerful weapon in the hands of those who are skilled at deploying it to demonstrate, and thereby deflate, the arbitrary, socially constructed quality of apparently authoritative conventions and their associated demands.

What about the discussion of accountability presented so far? Does it strike you as an acceptable account? The notion of accountability is often formulated, or accounted for, in a rather narrow and technical way. As a consequence, earlier references to parties, students and humour may well seem rather fanciful or irrelevant. However, such judgements presume a shared understanding that discussions of accountability should focus primarily upon the design and operation of systems of accountability (as if these operate independently of the social relations through which these systems are established and maintained). As a consequence, little or no attention is given to how the operation of these systems is necessarily impeded as well as facilitated, distorted as well as warranted, by moral and political relations. For example, if the weekly reports prepared by a plant manager are deemed to be ineffective in promoting required levels of performance, conventional understandings of accountability are more likely to diagnose such failings in terms of inadequacies of the reporting systems or imperfections in the design of the report that in relation to moral and political pressures upon plant managers to produce acceptable accounts (and to 'fiddle' these if necessary). The intent of this chapter is to question this proclivity and, more constructively, to sketch some alternative ways of thinking about accountability that may *inter alia* be relevant for appreciating how the design and operation of 'formal' accountability systems is embedded within broader frameworks of accountability.

Thinking about accountability 2: accountability, identity and power

Accountability is at the centre of human relations and interactions. In everyday life, people continuously mobilize accounts as they render the world accountable, and as they render themselves accountable to others. Of all contemporary social scientists, Garfinkel (1967: 1) has articulated this understanding most fully and subjected the phenomenon of everyday accountability to detailed investigation. By 'accountable', Garfinkel has in mind:

> . . . such matters as the following. I mean observable-and-reportable, i.e. available to members (of groups) as situated practices of looking-and-telling. I mean, too, that such practices consist of an endless, on-going, contingent accomplishment; that they are carried on under the auspices of, and are made to happen as events in, the same ordinary affairs that in organizing they describe; that the practices are done by parties to those settings whose skill with, knowledge of, and entitlement to the detailed work of that accomplishment – whose competence – they obstinately depend upon, recognize, use, and take for granted; and *that* they take their competence for granted itself furnishes parties with a setting's distinguishing and particular features, and of course it furnishes them as well as resources, troubles, projects, and the rest.

In other words, Garfinkel highlights the pervasive nature of accountability practices through which human beings render the world, including themselves, 'observable-and-reportable' in those ways that are commonsensical to other members who share this way of accomplishing a commonsense world. For Garfinkel, as for other analysts influenced by phenomenological forms of analysis (or accountability), the world exists only in the ways that we account for it: the social world is, in this sense, 'an endless, on-going, contingent accomplishment'.

If all human beings were to deny or abandon these everyday accountability practices, the intersubjective world would collapse into the void of solipsism; and without continuous demonstrations of this accountability, people would not be recognized (or accounted for) as (socially) competent members of society. Instead, they would be identified (or accounted for) as persons who had apparently taken leave of their (common) senses.[5]

Social institutions are inherently precarious, at least when compared with natural processes, because their continuation relies upon the willingness of human beings to subscribe to, account for, and (re)enact, their existence.[6] This thesis is graphically illustrated by Garfinkel (1967) in a series of breaching experiments.[7] Garfinkel asked his students to violate commonsense background understandings in the course of everyday interactions – such as asking professors, at the beginning of lectures, to clarify their request to 'make a start' or to ask what tools are needed to fabricate 'a start'. Such experiments, I want to argue, are very helpful in revealing not only the pervasiveness (and importance of social interaction) of everyday processes of account-ability, but for disclosing the normative force that underpins and powers the reproduction of the routines of everyday life – a force that usually becomes evident only when the disruption of routines is met with strenuous efforts to restore the reality of normal appearances, such as the self-evident, commonsense meaning of 'making a start'.

In Garfinkel's experiments, the violation of established understandings and expectations was met by attempts to restore normality by making strenuous efforts to repair breaches in the familiar world. In one experiment, Garfinkel asked his students to spend a period of between 15 minutes to an hour in their family homes behaving as if they were boarders. Students were instructed to act out this assumption by conducting themselves in a very circumspect and polite fashion, thereby breaching taken for granted, commonsensical understandings about normal, casual interaction in the home. In four-fifths of the cases, Garfinkel (ibid: 47) reports that:

> . . . family members were stupefied. They vigorously sought to make the strange actions intelligible and to restore the situation to normal appearances. Reports were filled with accounts of astonishment, bewilderment, shock, anxiety, embarrassment, and anger, and with charges by various family members that the student was mean, inconsiderable, selfish, nasty, or impolite.

Garfinkel continues:

> . . . Family members demanded explanations: What's the matter? What's gotten into you? Did you get fired? Are you sick? What are you being so superior about? Why are you mad? Are you out of your mind or are you just stupid? (ibid)

Various pleas, threats and stratagems were then introduced by parents and siblings in a bid 'to restore the situation to normal appearances' (ibid).

In such experiments, the (common)sense of the naturalness of everyday life was shown to be conditional upon the reproduction of everyday processes of accountability; and the contents of this 'everydayness' were shown to be held in place by the normative impulse to defend and reproduce the world taken for granted that is the product of such everyday processes. Or, as Garfinkel (ibid: 53, emphasis added) puts it, 'the features of the real society are produced by persons' motivated compliance with these background expectancies'. What are routinely assumed to be the natural facts of life' are also 'through and through moral facts of life' (ibid: 35). Garfinkel's experiments serve to demonstrate how social reality is a moral and political order.

Giving an account is a political act because it either confirms or unsettles whatever happens to be taken for granted as the world of normal appearances. In doing so, processes of accountability contribute to the continuation or disruption of the practices that they serve to sustain. In general, it is morally unremarkable and acceptable to confirm established background understandings, just as it is morally problematical and troublesome to breach them. However, whilst Garfinkel was concerned to expose the existence of everyday accountability processes by disrupting their reproduction, his interest in breaching the world of normal appearances did not extend to the question of why motivated compliance exists, or how it is shaped within historical and cultural institutions. To address these questions, it is necessary to understand the significance of identity and power in the reproduction of social life.

First, the issue of *identity*. Like other social institutions the sense of identity developed by human beings is a precarious construction, dependent upon the reproduction of discourses and practices that affirm its reality. Earlier it was noted that to have practices accounted for – as male, British and/or a manager, for example – is to be positioned within social space in a distinctive way. An array of signs is mobilized in ways that serve to enable and constrain the possibilities of identity and action. Not only are these signs loaded with meanings – about what it is to be masculine or British – but they are invariably infused with a strong normative content, in the form of expectations, that accommodate and reward conformity as they resist and sanction deviation. Making the connection between accountability, the interpretive schemes that endow the world with meaning and the normative order(s) that infuse these schemes, Giddens (1984: 30) has suggested that

> The idea of 'accountability' in everyday English gives cogent expression to the intersection of interpretive schemes and norms. To be 'accountable' for one's activities is both to explicate the reasons for them and to supply the normative grounds whereby they may be 'justified'.

The intersection of interpretive schemes and norms does not occur in the abstract. Instead, this intersection is enacted by embodied beings whose sense of identity is either confirmed or denied through processes of accountability. When identity is problematized, there tends to be an emotional, self-disciplining compulsion to restore normal appearances (e.g. by removing what is perceived to be the source of the disruption). For example, in Garfinkel's breaching experiments, parents felt compelled to demand an explanation of their children who were behaving with exceptional politeness and formality, and thereby locate a remedy that would restore their sense of normality. This (conservative) compulsion to preserve the established order is interpreted by Giddens in terms of the functional capacity of the world-taken-for-granted, produced by the commonsense monitoring of action, to hold down sources of anxiety. So long as the world-taken-for-granted can be maintained, it can be relied upon as a firm foundation for ontological security.

> The reflexive monitoring of action draws upon and reproduces forms of tacit and discursively available knowledge: *continuity of social reproduction involves the continual 'regrooving' of established attitudes and cognitive outlooks* holding down potential sources of anxiety . . .
>
> (Giddens, 1979: 128, emphasis in original)

However, whilst it is important to appreciate how accounts are embedded in continuing processes of self-formation, it is equally important not to assume the adequacy or naturalness of our commonsense assumptions about human agency (Willmott, 1986). For it may be that reliance upon preserving normal appearances to 'hold down potential sources of anxiety' is *productive* of existential insecurity (as it is inevitably subject to disruption) rather than an effective remedy for it (to be discussed below).

Second, there is the issue of *power*. Whether or not the individuals' senses of identity are secured by complying with a particular routine, they may well be concerned about the implications of failing to do so. For example, students may be indifferent or even antagonistic to the identity ascribed to the 'diligent student' but will submit the coursework on time because they believe that this will be advantageous in terms of the material and symbolic value of obtaining a qualification. Here, compliance occurs because it is understood by each student to be empowering within the prevailing structure of power relations (put crudely, gaining the qualification opens doors), and not because failure to submit the essay would be experienced as personally demeaning or shameful. Conversely, questioning authority – for example, by refusing to regurgitate the authority of lecture notes, perhaps with minor deviations or embellishments to demonstrate a degree of creativity and independent thinking – is more likely to close doors inasmuch that such refusals can be perceived as subversive of the prevailing structure of power relations.

Established structures of power operate to impede communication as acceptable rationalizations of 'failure' are produced instead of a more open discussion of problems (e.g. students produce excuses for that late submission of coursework that are accepted by the authorities, or managers provide carefully worded explanations of variance). Equally, the recipients of these accounts may not openly question their plausibility even though they suspect their veracity because, to do so, disrupts the normal appearances upon which they also are psychologically dependent. These structures of power can make it difficult to relate the ineffective operation of formal accountability systems (e.g. accounting for the submission of late coursework) to the embeddedness of these systems in relations of power and domination that unintentionally foster deviation (e.g. students are unnecessarily alienated from their studies) and reward deceit (e.g. students are tacitly encouraged to 'play the game' rather than divulge unacceptable reasons for the late submission of coursework). Unhappily, the taken for granted use of established accountability systems can make it difficult for the lecturer to recognize and change how accounts, or excuses, presented by students are shaped as much (and more) by what is deemed to be acceptable and excusable within the complex of power relations (e.g. illness, lack of books, stolen notes, etc.). This may serve to hone the skills of students in manipulating bureaucratic organizations but it impedes the development of students' capacity to recognize and communicate their own understandings (e.g. boredom with the subject, forgetfulness, expecting to 'get away' with it) of why the coursework had not been produced. Indeed, these power relations may make it very difficult for students (or managers) to reflect critically upon a commonsense tendency to blame the lecturing staff (or divisional managers) or to blame themselves rather than to understand the problem as symptomatic of a perverse and oppressive complex of relations where deceit and self-deception become normalized.[8]

Issues of power and identity are interrelated (Knights and Willmott, 1985). Impregnated within the giving of accounts are the power relations – of domination and resistance – that reproduce or transform our sense of self-identity. The dynamic process of developing a sense of self-identity, which may become apparent when this sense is impugned, occurs as we become accountable, and account for ourselves, in terms of historically and culturally contingent, power-invested meaning(s) – such as the meanings associated with being 'male', being 'a student' or being 'a manager'. It is likely, for example, that the desire to obtain the material (e.g. income) and symbolic (e.g. status) benefits associated with gaining a good degree is meaningful for the student in terms of the sense of identity (e.g. as a high flyer) that the individual has acquired and internalized. Likewise, any feelings of shame and guilt, associated with a failure to make the best of a learning opportunity, are fuelled within relations of power when a positive value is ascribed to the acquisition of particular kinds of knowledge. It is the combination of the dimensions of identity and power that explains why enforced responsibility operates to render individuals accountable for the routine reproduction of whatever is deemed culturally and historically to be normal and expected.

Thinking about accountability 3: a case of management control

The reflections upon accountability presented in the previous sections are now elaborated through a more detailed examination of an example of accountability in which a parent is seeking to render a child accountable for expenses incurred as a student:

> 'if I say to my child – "here's $2,000 towards your education, please spend it on your education and, oh, by the way, please give me receipts and other documentation and data which will demonstrate to my satisfaction that you have employed the money in an economical manner most conducive to your education . . . that is, for the purposes I intended" – I have introduced the fundamentals of "accountability". It now behoves the child, and myself, to create systematic processes which will absolutely assure both of us that the money was well spent for the purpose intended in a most efficient and effective manner'.
> (Brown-John, 1993: 63)

The meaning of accountability is here equated narrowly with the use of accounting procedures (the collection of receipts) that are deemed to demonstrate, and thereby enforce, the responsible use of the funds provided to purchase education. In effect, the parent is establishing a means of monitoring how these funds are spent in a way that serves to confirm both the identity of the parent and the (paternalistic) structure of power relations.

The example also illustrates how those with access to resources (e.g. parents) are able to make others' (continuing) use of these resources conditional upon demonstrated compliance with the purposes intended by those in possession of the resources. Systematic processes are identified as the preferred means of ensuring that resources are consumed by the child in the way that the parent deems to be responsible – that is, in a way that 'demonstrate(s) to my satisfaction that . . . the money was well spent for the purpose intended in a most efficient and effective manner' (ibid). In this example, the accountability procedures associated with the $2,000 budget for education involve an exercise of power in which the parent plays upon the dependence of the child in a way that simultaneously structures and limits the possibility of communication between them – the ultimate threat being the refusal to provide the child with further resources if satisfactory evidence of the efficient and effective expenditure of resources is not supplied. In the following discussion of this example, I generalize the argument by referring to the parent as the principal, and the child as the agent. The agent could equally be the production manager who is accountable to the principal, the divisional manager, for a budget of $10,000,000. It is therefore not difficult to interpret this as a case of management control.

Three points arising from the example are worthy of comment. *First*, an assumption is being made by the principal that it is possible (as well as desirable) to create procedures that will 'absolutely assure' that the money is spent in a 'manner most conducive to your education' (ibid). Yet, as noted earlier, it is questionable whether any system can deliver such absolute assurances as there is invariably scope for creative accounting and diverse forms of subterfuge. In any event, systems of accountability are themselves costly in terms of time and money (and therefore could arguably be charged against the $2,000 budget, though it is doubtful whether the agent could successfully charge the parent for the time spent in collecting and processing the receipts!). In any event, from the standpoint of the principal, systems of accountability can be rendered counter-productive by their unintended consequences. Their introduction by a principal may, for example, signal to the agent a lack of confidence and trust and thereby weaken any (moral) obligation to go beyond mere compliance with a request from the principal. In turn, this may dissolve any qualms the agent may have about supplying false receipts and other documentation and data that seemingly provide satisfactory evidence of the responsible use of the allowance. When the principal (inadvertently) sends signals that indicate distrust of the agent, the agent may be more inclined to fiddle receipts, provide misleading documentation, etc. *and* feel morally justified in doing so.

Second, it seems possible, and perhaps likely, that a concentration on formalized accountability processes may devalue or even supplant what is arguably the more fundamental and important concern: the kind of education that is being sought and bought. In the above illustration, a focus upon the accountability of means (i.e. the

$2,000) seems to displace discussion that could offer reassurances that the ends (i.e. the type of education) had been carefully chosen. Although we are not given further details, it would seem that the principal is more concerned to establish a system for monitoring expenditures than to develop a dialogue about the kind of education that is to be bought with the money.

Third, the example illustrates how accountability processes can be enabling as well as constraining for those who are obliged to account for their actions. In this example, the agent can be seen to derive some benefit from the existence of systemic processes in so far as these reduce uncertainty about how the agent is to be held to account, and whether the agent will continue to enjoy the patronage (and perhaps also maintain the respect) of the principal (see du Gay, 1994). Without such a system, the agent would be at greater risk from the whim of the principal who could simply dismiss all efforts made by the agent to demonstrate accountability as irrelevant or insufficient.

The example also illustrates the extent of the embeddedness of the formal system in a wider pattern of accountabilities – for example, the positioning of the parent as a person who, commonsensically, has a responsibility and associated accountability for the child and is therefore entitled (if not expected) to provide for the child's education. The three specific points drawn from the example highlight the complexity and precariousness of formal accountability processes as well as the pitfalls associated with narrowing its meaning to the design and operation of a set of procedures that seemingly provide a clear and reliable way of defining and policing specific responsibilities. Except where the agent is frightened into conformity or captivated by the charisma of the principal, a likely consequence of introducing such a formal system of accountability is the risk of a spiralling, vicious circle of control and deceit (Knights and Roberts, 1983; Roberts, 1984). Whenever the agent deviates, consciously or inadvertently, from the requirements of the principal, the lack of trust makes it more likely that the agent will conceal or dissemble this deviance (e.g. by obtaining false receipts) or communicate variances in a highly selective and partial way. To the extent that the scope for deception and dissembling is anticipated or detected by the principal, the probable response is the development of more extensive and penetrating systems of surveillance – for example, by checking the authenticity as well as the existence of the receipts and documentation that the agent provides. Interpreting this as further evidence of the principal's lack of trust, the agent may then be prompted to devise more sophisticated, less easily detectable, forms of deceit.

The spiral can be avoided or reversed in two ways. Either the principal secures the total submission of the agent who becomes an automaton, passively complying with every instruction of the principal. Loyalty, albeit dog-like, is achieved. In which case, the agent is mindlessly obedient, accepting the authority of the principal as absolute: the agent fulfills the requirements of the parent by collecting and supplying the necessary receipts and documentation. However, as an automaton, the agent is even less likely to make informed choices between alternative forms of educational provision or indeed to participate in such education except as an undiscriminating consumer. The alternative is to rebuild respect and trust. This does not involve the removal of accountability as this is a universal feature of human existence. Rather, it necessitates relying less heavily upon a narrow conception of accountability that perversely undermines the normative foundations upon which it depends (Roberts, 1991).

Instead of simply telling the agent how much money is to be received, and how expenditure is to be accounted for, the principal could have discussed the nature and size of the contribution to the agent's education as well as the question of the scope of the agent's accountability. However, whilst a more open and dialogical approach is potentially possible, established relations of power and associated conventions in modern society frequently operate to frustrate and distort moves in this direction. To avoid a romantic, idealized vision of what may be possible, it is important to remember that the design and operation of systems of accountability tends to reflect and reproduce the relations of power in which they are embedded. It is not just that dialogue is an unusual form of interaction between principals and agents or that the prevailing, 'normal' accountability procedures are symptomatic of the structure of power relations. It is also that moves to develop a more dialogical approach necessarily carry with them what has been termed 'the slime of history'. Change never starts with a 'clean sheet'.

In the $2,000 budget example, the system of accountability reflects and sustains an authoritarian relationship between principal and agent: the principal dictates what is to happen. But the accountability system also reflects and reproduces the premium placed upon individualism in modern society, and the lip-service that is paid to self-determination. Note that the principal does not purchase the education for the agent but 'allows' the agent to exercise 'responsible autonomy' (Friedman, 1977) in determining how the budget is to be spent. Indeed, the formal system of accountability makes it possible for the principal to contemplate this exercise of discretion because the provision of receipts provides a method of management control. The system favoured by the principal enables him or her to save the time and opportunity cost of making the purchases for the agent, though the principal reserves the right to withdraw further funding if the accounting information indicates that the agent has failed to use these funds in acceptable ways.

Thinking about accountability 4: conditions of possibility for the production of disciplined selves

As in the previous example of parent-child relations, employees are routinely located within the social space of a hierarchy of superordinates to whom they are accountable for their performance. Intertwined with this hierarchical structure there are often lateral processes of communication and accountability (as there are between siblings) – most usually between employees positioned at a similar level within the hierarchy but sometimes (and often selectively) between individuals occupying different positions. As Munro and Hatherly (1993: 379) have suggested, in relation to the increased attention being given to time-competition and flexibility,

> . . . the new strategies . . . imply a fundamental shift away from the dyadic structure of the firm . . . towards an 'enabling' focus upon lateral flows designed to minimise requirements for managerial intervention.

The relationship between hierarchical and lateral forms of accountability is not necessarily antagonistic. Hierarchical accountability may be developed to formalize and defend systems of lateral accountability, as in the case of Total Quality Management where lateral accountability within teams is promoted and defended by top-down monitoring (Wilkinson and Willmott, 1995). Likewise, lateral accountability may be invoked to support and regenerate sluggish systems of hierarchical accountability – the strengthening of Corporate Culture (Willmott, 1993) or the creation of teamworking (Ezzamel and Willmott, 1995) being examples of how mutual accountability to core values has been identified as a means of boosting performance without sacrificing systems of hierarchical accountability.

Holding individuals or groups of employees accountable for their conduct would make no rational sense if human behaviour were understood to be the product of some external force or the hidden hand of Providence. The plausibility and rational defensibility of the idea of accountability depends upon making the assumption that human beings are able to act somewhat autonomously or, at the very least, exercise some degree of discretion, or control, over their conduct. That this is so is suggested by the absurdity of claiming that tigers, rather than zoo keepers, are accountable for the visitors they devour, or that dogs, rather than their owners, are accountable for the pavements that they foul. In each case, it is assumed that zoo keepers and dog owners could have acted otherwise to protect the public from the animals for which they are ascribed responsibility. In the previous section, the very possibility of allocating a budget of $2,000 to be spent upon education rested upon the assumption that the child was capable of taking responsibility and exercising a degree of control over its use (albeit that this moral appeal is simultaneously backed up and undermined by the use of a formal monitoring process that required the child to produce receipts and other relevant documentation and data).

In short, accountability is possible because human beings are endowed with a capacity to identify themselves as centres of consciousness that can engage in (seemingly) self-determined activity. Through processes of social interaction, human infants are expected, and are induced by others, to develop a sense of subject-object separation in which there is both an 'I' (e.g. a putative centre of consciousness) and a 'Me' (what others identify as the 'I'). Or, as Mead (1934: 138) makes this argument,

> The individual experiences himself (sic) as such, not directly, but indirectly, from the particular standpoints of other(s) . . . he enters his own experience as a self or individual, not directly or immediately, not by becoming a subject to himself, but only in so far as he first becomes an object to himself just as other individuals are objects to him or in his experience; and he becomes an object to himself only by taking the attitudes of other individuals towards himself.

The sense of being a discrete, autonomous individual is not innate but, rather, is learned, or socially constructed, through processes of social interaction in which it is regarded as normal to become an object to oneself. To repeat, this process of representing human experience as the responsibility of a centre of consciousness (usually located in the brain, and often likened to the novice rider of an unruly, passionate horse) is not 'direct or immediate'. Rather, it is slowly acquired as the infant identifies with the way that others relate to him (or her) as an object of their experience – a process of identification that is facilitated by the sense in which others appear as discrete objects, or individuals, to the infant.

Through the process of self-formation an 'I' is acquired that is understood to be (at least partially) in charge of, and responsible for, the conduct of the 'Me'. This 'Me' is identified by others as the responsibility of the 'I' who does things – such as the academic who writes a chapter about accountability or the architect who makes a model of a building. The 'I' thus imbued with some degree of responsiblity for the conduct of the self, though the extent of this responsibility varies according to the powers that are attributed to other forces (e.g. fate, witchcraft or God). The 'I' becomes accountable to others for whatever aspects of the 'Me' that are deemed to be in its charge.[9]

Blum and McHugh (1974: 102) argue that the very possibility of producing and interpreting mundane accounts, including the attribution of responsibility and account-ability to an autonomous agent, is predicated upon what they term 'a deep structure' of culturally and historically specific understandings about what human beings are, what responsibilities they carry, etc., and not just about what kind of account is admissible or goes unchallenged within a particular context or system of accountability (see also Gerth and Mills, 1953: 116). Characterizing the medium and outcome of these understandings as 'mundane reason(ing)', Pollner (1974; 1987) suggests that modern, western accounting practices and frameworks of accountability are 'composed of a network of interrelated, mutually defining terms for specifying both subject and object' (Pollner, 1987: 128). The 'mundane idiom' for rendering the world accountable, Pollner contends,

> . . . includes all the terms whose meaning implicates or is implied by an objective world. Thus the mundane idiom includes not only variants for the real world such as 'reality', 'out there', and the 'object' but the variants of the subjectivity that is deemed to stand over and against (and within) the world such as the 'subject', 'person' or 'knower' (ibid).

The Cartesian ascription of autonomy to human agents is reproduced and legitimized in the work of major social theorists, such as Giddens, who routinely borrow from (the mundane idiom of) commonsense the understanding that 'actors . . . draw upon rules and resources in a diversity of action contexts' (Giddens, 1984: 25) in ways that reproduce (or transform) their relationships. Despite a strong acknowledgement of the way that agents are also constituted through their involvement in the mobilization of rules and resources, the idea of the human agent as a sovereign subject who acts to mobilize resources is taken for granted. To the extent that an examination of the social construction of this sense of sovereignty is excluded or marginalized within such analyses, the authority of commonsense is uncritically accepted.

By focusing attention upon the mundane idiom, Pollner invites us to adopt a more sceptical and analytic stance so that commonsense ideas can be better appreciated as an historically and culturally constructed set of conventions rather than a natural, author-itative or universal phenomenon. Instead of examining the ready-made world of 'subjects' who give accounts about 'objects' (including themselves), Pollner invites us to appreciate how these historically and culturally specific distinctions are accomplished and the associated entities are designated, reproduced and transformed (or dissolved, see Preston, 1988). The sense of self as a sovereign agent, for example, is then under-stood to be a product of particular cultural memberships rather than a condition of the acquisition of this membership. From this it follows that, contra commonsense, our conduct, and indeed our sense of agency, is mobilized by frameworks of accountability rather than as is commonly believed that we, as sovereign human agents, mobilize the contents of these frameworks.

Concluding remarks

There is a delightful irony in the task of writing about accountability. To produce an account of accountability involves invoking the universal capacity of human beings to render their world (including their actions) accountable.[10] But the content and presentation of this account has been at once enabled and constrained by a historically specific framework for making sense of accountability – such as the framework that makes a distinction between universal and historical aspects of accountability, the distinction that can be made between hierarchical and lateral accountabilities and, of course, the use of 'I' to assign authorship.

Writing the chapter has involved a challenge to extend the frameworks in which both current analysis and practice of accountability finds itself. For the reader, your reading of my account – whether positive or negative, engaged or dismissive – is sustained by the particular frameworks of accountability that you have invoked. It is to be hoped that a greater appreciation of the accomplished and conditioned aspects of accountability processes will encourage further critical engagement, one that may make it easier to problematize both the authority of accounts and the authority of whatever frameworks of accountability are invoked to make sense of them.

The invitation of this chapter has been to inform the study of accountability with an appreciation of the central presence of reflexivity, identity formation and the dynamics of power relations in their diverse manifestations. If we are to be faithful to the understanding with which I began – that the meaning attributed to such concepts is the product of historically and culturally contingent regimes of truth and forms of accountability – then the coherent, analytic response to this understanding is to study our accounts of the world as the product of specific regimes. The implication being that we should pay greater attention to accounts, accounting and accountability while abandoning ideas of accounts as more or less faithful reflections of reality, or as an unproblematically reliable resource for producing social scientific knowledge.[11]

Notes

1. For example, in the process of identifying and discussing 'accountability' diverse frameworks may be constructed and mobilized, as is evident from the variety of treatments, or accounts, of accountability to be found in this volume.
2. And, indeed, within these spheres, different kinds of accountability have been identified, such as accountabilities relating to policy, programmes, probity or legality (Stewart, 1984).
3. Melanesians of New Caledonia, known in French as the Canaque, whose accounts of their experience in the world are reported and interpreted by Leenhardt (1979) and summarized by Pollner (1987: 135 et seq.).
4. 'The Melanesian is unaware that the body is an element which he himself (sic) possesses. For this reason, he finds it impossible to disengage it. He cannot externalize it from his natural,

social and mythic environment. He cannot isolate it. He cannot see it as one of the elements of the individual' (Leenhardt, 1979: 22 quoted in Pollner, 1987: 136).

5. Accountability is foundational to social existence because it is what constitutes our (common) sense of the world, including the (socially mediated) sense that we make of ourselves as we mobilize 'forms of tacit and available knowledge' (Giddens, 1979: 128). However, as phenomenologists from Husserl to Garfinkel have repeatedly argued, this universal process (which enables what is sensed to be familiar and commonplace to be rendered familiar and commonplace) is neither widely recognized nor, relatedly, is it addressed as a topic of enquiry. This observation is elaborated later in the paper in relation to Pollner's work.

6. Giddens (1984), for example, rightly stresses the central importance of reflexivity in the reproduction and transformation of social institutions. However, despite a recognition of the necessity of treating terms like 'purpose' and 'intention' with caution, he equates reflexivity with purposiveness. That is to say, he attributes the content and direction of reflexivity and intentionality to the powers of a sovereign agent. The alternative, which is germane to this chapter and developed in a later section, is to appreciate how the commonsensical attribution of reflexivity to a sovereign agent is itself a truth-effect produced through particular forms of social interaction and accountability. See also note 5.

7. As Garfinkel (1967: 38) notes, these studies 'are not properly speaking experimental. They are demonstrations, designed, in Herbert Spiegelberg's phrase, as aids to a sluggish imagination'.

8. The relations are perverse in so far as such systems operate to deflect responsibility; and they are oppressive in so far as knowledge of this deflection cannot be openly admitted.

9. The use of terms such as 'I', 'Me' and indeed 'Self' conjures up the idea of some core of agency or 'me-ness' that remains the same. Upon reflection, however, it is more coherent to say that the sense of a core amounts to no more than the effects of ingrained habits and routines of mind and body that, regardless of the context, effectively confine experience within familiar boundaries. It is the sense of solidity and continuity produced by these socially organized habits that is routinely identified as the core of 'self' (Preston, 1988).

10. In order to give an account, it is necessary to avert one's gaze from the reflexive process that enables accounts to be given. Only when the account has been devised is it possible, by means of a reflective glance, to address, and account for, a process that was assumed in order to produce the account. The reflective glance (or turn) reminds us of the foundational quality of accountability and its constitutive presence in the giving of all accounts. But direct consideration of the reflective conditions of its own possibility is necessarily suspended as claims about the foundational quality of accountability are articulated.

11. As Bittner (1965) rightly points out, we are obliged to borrow commonsense notions in order to analyse social phenomena. The problem arises when the analytical adequacy of commonsense understandings and concepts is taken for granted. For at this point, unreconstructed commonsense understandings are deployed to do the work of analysis. As Bittner articulates the difficulty: 'When the actor is treated as a permanent auxiliary to the enterprise of sociological inquiry at the same time as he (sic) is the object of its inquiry, there arise ambiguities that defy clarification' (ibid: 240).

References

Bittner, E. (1965) The Concept of Organization. *Social Research*, **32**(3) pp. 239–55.

Blum, A. and McHugh, P. (1971) The Social Ascription of Motives. *American Sociological Review*, **36**, (February) pp. 98–109.

Brown-John, C.L. (1993) Accountability Re-visited. *Optimum*, **23**(4) pp. 64–8.

du Gay, P. (1994) Colossal Immodesties and Hopeful Monsters, *Organization*, **1**(1) pp. 125–48.

Ezzamel, M. and Willmott, H.C. (1995) Using Accounts to Blast Changes Through: From Particularism to Holism in Cost and Quality Control, paper presented at the 12th EGOS Colloquium, University of Istanbul, Istanbul, July.

Friedman, A. (1977) *Industry and Labour; Class Struggle at Work and Monopoly Capitalism*, Macmillan, London.

Garfinkel, H. (1967) *Studies in Ethnomethodology*, Prentice-Hall, Englewood Cliffs, New Jersey.

Gerth, H. and Wright Mills, C. (1953) *Character and Social Structure: A Psychology of Social Institutions*, Harcourt, Brace and World, New York.

Giddens, A. (1979) *Central Problems in Social Theory*, Macmillan, London.

Giddens, A. (1984) *The Constitution of Society*, Polity, Cambridge.

Gouldner, A.W. (1954) *Patterns of Industrial Bureaucracy*, Free Press, New York.

Gray, R.H., Owen, D.L. and Maunders, K.T. (1987) *Corporate Social Reporting: Accounting and Accountability*, Prentice-Hall, Hemel Hempstead.

Knights, D. and Roberts, J. (1983) Understanding the Theory and Practice of Management Control. *Employee Relations*, **5**(4) pp. 3–43.

Knights, D. and Willmott, H.C. (1985) Power and Identity in Theory and Practice. *Sociological Review*, **33**(1) pp. 22–46.

Knights, D. and Willmott, H.C. (1989) Power and Subjectivity at Work: From Degradation to Subjugation in Social Relations. *Sociology*, **23**(4) pp. 1–24.

Leenhardt, M. (1979) *Do Kamo*, University of Chicago Press, Chicago.

Mead, G.H. (1934) *Mind, Self and Society*, University of Chicago Press, Chicago.

Mouck, T. (1994) Corporate Accountability and Rorty's Utopian Liberalism. *Accounting, Auditing and Accountability Journal*, **7**(1) pp. 6–30.

Mouritsen, J. (1994) Marginalising the Customer: Customer-Orientation, Quality and Accountability. Working Paper, Copenhagen Business School.

Munro, R.J.B. and Hatherly, D.J. (1993) Accountability and the New Commercial Agenda. *Critical Perspectives on Accounting*, **4**(4) pp. 369–95.

Pollner, M. (1974) Mundane Reason. *Philosophy of the Social Sciences*, **4** pp. 35–54.

Pollner, M. (1987) *Mundane Reasoning: Reality in Everyday and Sociological Discourse*, Cambridge University Press.

Preston, D.L. (1988) *The Social Organization of Zen Practice; Constructing Transcultural Reality*, Cambridge University Press.

Roberts, J. (1984) The Moral Character of Management Practice, *Journal of Management Studies* **21**(3) pp. 287–302.

Roberts, J. (1991) The Possibilities of Accountability. *Accounting, Organizations and Society*, **16**(4) pp. 355–70.

Rose, N. (1988) Calculable Minds and Manageable Individuals. *History of the Human Sciences*, **1**(2) pp. 179–200.

Schweiker, W. (1993) Accounting for Ourselves: Accounting Practice and the Discourse of Ethics. *Accounting, Organizations and Society*, **18**(2/3) pp. 231–52.

Stewart, J.D. (1984) The Role of Information in Public Accountability in *Issues in Public Sector Accounting*, (eds A. Hopwood and C. Tomkins) Philip Allen, Oxford.

Wilkinson, A. and Willmott, H.C. (eds) (1995) *Making Quality Critical*, Routledge, London.

Willmott, H.C. (1986) Unconscious Sources of Motivation in the Theory of the Subject: An Exploration and Critique of Giddens' Dualistic Models of Action and Personality. *Journal for the Theory of Social Behaviour*, **16**(1) pp. 105–22.

Willmott, H.C. (1990) The Dialectics of Praxis: Opening Up the Core of Labour Process Analysis in *Labour Process Theory* (eds D. Knights and H. Willmott) Macmillan, London.

Willmott, H.C. (1993) Strength is Ignorance; Slavery is Freedom: Managing Culture in Modern Organizations. *Journal of Management Studies*, **30**(4) pp. 515–52.

Willmott, H.C. (1994) Theorising Agency: Power and Subjectivity in Organization Studies in *Towards a New Theory of Organizations*, (eds M. Parker and J. Hassard), Routledge, London.

Willmott, H.C. (1995) Managing the Academics: Commodification and Control in the Development of University Education in the UK. *Human Relations*, **48**(9), pp. 993–1028.

3 From discipline to dialogue: individualizing and socializing forms of accountability

John Roberts

> Man's will to profit and to be powerful have their natural and proper effect so
> long as they are linked with, and upheld by, his will to enter into relation.
> There is no evil impulse till the impulse has been separated from the being,
> the impulse which is bound up with, and defined by, the being is the living
> stuff of communal life, that which is detached is its disintegration.
>
> (Martin Buber, *I and Thou*. 1937: 68)

Introduction

Accountability involves varied social practices by means of which we seek to remind
each other of our reciprocal dependence; of the ways our actions unavoidably make a
difference to each other. Such reciprocal dependence can be thought about in both
instrumental and moral terms; we are bound up with each other not simply in the
narrow, calculable ways that at work the realization of my plans necessarily depends
upon the effectiveness of others, but also more broadly in the intended and unintended
ways that my action or inaction always has myriad consequences for others, both near
and far. In my view it is simply impossible to separate out the strategic and moral
consequences of action. Yet the argument that I develop in this chapter is that
contemporary forms of organizational accountability currently embody and reproduce
precisely such a separation. Formal, hierarchical accountability, in which accounting
information plays a central role, is exclusively preoccupied with the strategic or
instrumental consequences of action. Broader ethical concerns are thereby priva-
tized, or live out a precarious existence in the informal spaces of the organization.
From a critical perspective the effect of this separation is to release instrumental or
strategic action from any possible ethical constraint or restraint. But it can also be
argued that such unrestrained instrumentalism is paradoxically damaging to itself in the
ways that it weakens the capacity for collective action. Both within and beyond
organizations there is an urgent need to bring the instrumental and moral dimensions
of accountability back into relation with each other.

From accounting to accountability

The shift of attention from accounting to accountability, which forms one theme of this book, is perhaps not obvious but several chapters represent various attempts to see through or get behind accounting's own preferred self-image of being a 'mirror' to action; a set of neutral techniques that do no more than objectively record and reveal the 'results' of organized activity. If one cannot argue with the figures one is seemingly forced to acknowledge their authority, and with this the authority of the accounting profession in its capacity to produce the 'true and fair' view of organizational events. Thus one remains caught in the 'mirror' image. The imagination is only able to conceive of accounting for more or something different; to apply these techniques to neglected areas – e.g. social or environmental costs – or to sharpen the resolution of the image through more sophisticated accounting techniques.

In an attempt to break the spell of the mirror image, in earlier work (Roberts and Scapens, 1985) we have sought to explore the uses made of accounting in the processes of organizing; in particular the ways that accounting information is used to make possible and perpetuate particular systems of accountability in and around organizations. From within this perspective accounting can be seen as a particular structure of meanings in terms of which the significance of organizational events is negotiated and defined, as the basis upon which expectations and demands upon staff are communicated and legitimized, and as the vehicle for the enactment and re-enactment of particular relations of power. The shift in attention from accounting to accountability is thus a shift from a preoccupation with technique and its refinement, to social practices and their consequences.

By viewing accounting in terms of its part in producing and reproducing systems of accountability in organizations, new avenues are also opened up for critique. Rather than seeking to improve the quality of the mirror image one can instead look to the conditions and consequences of accounting's use within organizations. In other words it becomes possible to challenge what is currently taken for granted in existing forms of organizational accountability. In part this involves observing how organizational events are themselves changed in the very process of measurement; how the use of accounting organizes as it claims only to report (Hines, 1988). In this regard the techniques of accounting are clearly not neutral in the effects that they produce. Beyond this however the way is opened for asking questions about both the instrumental and moral adequacy of existing forms of organizational accountability. It is this latter theme that will be explored in the chapter that follows.

In an earlier exposition of these ideas (Roberts, 1991), entitled, 'The Possibilities of Accountability', I argued that although accountability is central to social and organizational life, it is currently practised and embodied in and around organizations in a peculiarly split and destructive form. In this chapter I will restate much of this earlier analysis but then move to explore the potential of dialogue, as a process of accountability, to reconcile this split and with it some of the destructive moral and strategic consequences that flow from it.

The chapter begins by exploring ways in which accountability is central to the constitution and reproduction of an individual's sense of self and the nature of self's relatedness to others. It then considers the currently divided forms of accountability practised within organizations by drawing a distinction between what are described as the 'individualizing' effects of hierarchical forms of accountability and the 'socializing' effects of informal accountability. Having sketched the characteristics and effects of current forms of accountability, along with their subtle and unacknowledged interdependencies, the chapter then considers the emergent critiques of organizational accountability that can be found in both the managerial and critical literatures. Finally the potential for dialogue as a process of accountability within organizations is explored.

Accountability and the constitution of the self

In this section I explore the general relationship between accountability and the constitution of an individual sense of self. I will do this initially by focusing upon the genesis of 'self' consciousness in early childhood. I want to argue that accountability has a key role in making the self visible, both to self and others.

Merleau-Ponty suggests that the recognition of one's own image in the mirror marks a key moment in the emergence of our sense of 'self'.

> For the child understanding the specular image consists in recognising as his own his visual appearance in the mirror. Until the moment when the specular image arises, the child's body is a strongly felt but confused reality. To recognize his image in the mirror is for him to learn that there can be a viewpoint taken on him. Hitherto he has never seen himself, or he has only caught a glimpse of himself in looking at the parts of his body he can see. By means of the image in the mirror he becomes capable of being a spectator of himself. Through the acquisition of the specular image the child notices that he is visible for himself and for others.
>
> (Merleau-Ponty, 1964: 136)

The idea of a 'strongly felt but confused reality' is suggestive of a lived experience without the stable reference point of an image of self. A stable sense of self, Merleau-Ponty suggests, is only made possible by the visual image, which offers the first clear differentiation of inside and outside as self and other.

By way of an analogy, it can be suggested that to be held accountable holds a mirror up to an action and its consequences in a way that creates focus within the stream of lived experience; the focus of being an individual. Self is reflected and confirmed by being called to account by others.

The role of others is even more significant in Mead's related account of the emergence of the self. For Mead, the self is actually constituted through the child 'taking over' the attitudes of 'significant others'. Mead describes a two stage process whereby the sense of self is stabilized initially through the internalization of the attitudes of particular 'significant' others, and then more completely through the synthesis of a more generalized conception of 'other' in relation to which the self image can be fixed.

> At the first of these stages, the individual's self is constituted simply by an organization of the particular attitudes of others towards himself and towards one another in the specific social acts in which he participates with them. But at the second stage in the full development of the individual's self, that self is

constituted not only by an organization of these particular individual attitudes, but also by an organization of the social attitudes of the generalized other, or the group as a whole to which he belongs.

(Mead, 1934: 158)

As with Merleau-Ponty, visibility again plays a central role in the constitution of the self, but for Mead it is the attitudes of others that makes the self visible; that act as the mirror in which the self is discovered.

In support of his views Mead notes how children initially refer to self in the third person – as a 'me', an object of others' perception. Only later do children begin to use the first person 'I'; that is to take the position of active subject. Thus an individual's initial sense of self emerges through an internalization first of the attitudes of particular others, which is then stabilized against a generalized sense of others' expectations. In childhood the very survival of this nascent sense of self is felt to depend upon securing and preserving the good regard of parents (Becker, 1972). But of course the mirror of parental regard also contains a refraction of the normative order of the wider society; the self is constituted in large part in relation to others' expectations as to what a self must be to be included. For writers on moral development such as Kohlberg (1986) moral rules are initially felt to be external and are followed out of fear of punishment. At later 'conventional' stages of development, however, the concerns of the social group become internalized as standards of self-judgement.

Both Mead's and Merleau-Ponty's accounts of the emergence of the self suggest that at least symbolically the self is thoroughly social in origin; to define self is to mark the boundary between self and other, to differentiate self from not-self. But with the idea of the 'generalized other' and the notion of 'taking over' the attitudes of others, it is possible to see how the acquisition of a sense of self opens up the possibility of a kind of alienation both by and from others. The mirror image contains the danger of a total identification with the image it offers in a way that alienates the individual from lived experience and at the same time fosters an illusory belief in the autonomy and independence of the self. Two possibilities that flow from this are particularly pertinent to the later discussion of the distortions of different forms of organizational accountability. First, it is possible that the self is, as it were, captured and held by the images of self that others offer, so that their attitudes come to wholly define and confine an individual's own sense of self. Second, it is possible that individuals become narcissistically preoccupied with their own self-image and its elaboration in a way that denies the relational character of selfhood; others come to be recognized only as means or obstacles to the progress of the self. In both cases the *relational tension* that is implicit in self-identity is broken; in the former as alienation by others, in the latter as alienation from others.

So far, in order to explore the relationship between accountability and the constitution of the self, I have focused on the genesis of self consciousness in childhood. But of course this initial sense of self, although foundational, has then to be produced and reproduced throughout life in the rituals of daily interaction. I will argue that it is in this regard that forms of organizational accountability come to play a central role in the constitution of the self. Before going on to make this argument, some additional comments may be helpful.

In everyday life we tend to think of the relationship between the self and accountability as an exterior one; accountability involves an encounter with others' expectations and demands. Viewed more closely, however, the relationship between the self and accountability can be seen to be an interior one, since the self is discovered only in the process of being called to account by others. Accountability in confronting self with the attitudes of others comes thereby both to address, confirm and shape the self. To be held to account by others has the effect of sharpening and clarifying our sense of self, convincing us that our actions make a difference, and providing focus within the stream of day to day experiencing. Nor do others need to be present for accountability to be effective, for in taking over their attitudes, others realize a perpetual presence and become internal to processes of self-reflection. In this way being held to account by others can be seen to constitute the self since we come to recognize ourselves precisely in the ways in which we are made visible to others. The form of accountability, the way in which it is practised, thereby becomes key in shaping an individual's sense of self and sense of relatedness to others.

In the sections that follow I will explore the conditions and consequences in this regard of two very different forms of organizational accountability. In exploring what I call 'individualizing' forms of accountability I have in mind forms of hierarchical accountability which tend to generate a sense of self as essentially independent and solitary, with only an instrumental sense of connection or relation to others. Against this I will then go on to describe what I term 'socializing' forms of accountability in which the self is confirmed in a way that enacts and reinforces a sense of the interdependence of self and other.

The individualizing effects of hierarchical forms of accountability

The preceding section of this chapter attempted to describe the genesis of the individual's sense of self out of a dialectic of seeing and being seen. I also noted the potential for alienation in this process, either through being captured wholly by the image of self that others offer, or through coming to believe in the essential autonomy or independence of the self. Foucault's account of the effects of disciplinary power seems to involve a combination of these forms of alienation, and significantly these effects are themselves generated through the dislocation of this dialectic of seeing and being seen.

> Disciplinary power is exercised through its invisibility; at the same time it imposes on those it subjects a compulsory visibility. In discipline, it is the subjects who have to be seen. It is the fact of being constantly seen that maintains the disciplined individual in his subjection.
>
> (Foucault, 1979: 187)

What is distinctive about Foucault is his treatment of the individual. A number of writers have made use of Foucault's ideas on discipline to explore the impact of accounting techniques (Miller and O'Leary, 1986; Roberts and Scapens, 1990).

> The individual is no doubt the fictitious atom of an ideological representation of society, but he is also a reality fabricated by the specific technology of power that I have called discipline.
>
> (Foucault, 1979: 194)

The focus of what follows will be on the manner in which accounting helps to make a reality of the fiction of the individual.

Forms of disciplinary power are ubiquitous and diverse and are in no way restricted to accounting and the world of work. For example, education obviously plays a key role in socializing us into the routinized mentality of disciplined subjectivity. In the experience of work, however, discipline on the individual as individual first makes its effects felt in the form of the labour market. Although the employment contract is legally constituted as an exchange between equals, in practice choice is usually weighted heavily on the side of the employer, or their representative. Potential employees are encountered serially as 'applicants', and are screened and assessed in terms of some ideal image of what is required. For those subject to this process, power is typically judged to be so weighted in favour of the employer that any possibility of negotiation as to what is required is seemingly foreclosed. Instead, the force of action is turned by applicants back upon themselves in an attempt to create or at least present self in a manner that corresponds to the ideal. In the light of this ideal other applicants become competitors from whom one must distinguish self if one is to be successful in this process.

Failure, for some, is an inevitable concomitant of such a competition and confronts the individual with the task of explaining away or enduring the experience of rejection that the self has suffered. Whilst success carries with it the transient experience of acceptance of self, it has been realized in terms of meeting the employer's expectations; an individual is accepted not for their unique qualities but because they approximated most closely to what was required. An individual thereby gains a location in a hierarchy which is itself redolent with the symbolism of relative individual worth and value. Moreover, the continued occupation of this space is itself dependent upon subsequent performance, such that recognition and acceptance of self is constantly at risk in the routines of hierarchical accountability to which the individual is then subject.

Within such routines, in Anglo-American organizations at least, accounting has established itself as the most powerful and legitimate instrument for realizing the visibility of action. This raises two further questions. How does accounting realize its own invisibility, and relatedly what are the effects upon those it 'subjects', of the visibility accounting helps to create in the rituals of accountability that it makes possible? Part of accounting's invisibility arises from its ability to present facts and figures as objective; one can perhaps contest the detail of the figures but not the capacity of accounting to disclose the 'bottom line'. The quasi-scientific methods of analysis that accounting adopts allow it to claim to present a truth that is somehow independent of the individuals and groups whose interests it both reflects and serves. Although its language and categories of relevance infuse and shape our daily relationships with others, it is nevertheless used in the name of some poorly comprehended imperative, or remote interest – competitiveness or the City or Head Office – figures who can never be addressed directly or identified with any precision. It is in these ways that accounting imposes its ways of seeing, whilst itself remaining invisible. It realizes a pervasive presence in organizational life whilst its own origins remain ambiguous and uncertain.

Accounting is effective through generating an apparently inescapable and indisputable image of the results of organized activity. In this regard one of the most unsettling aspects of management or company accounts is the complete absence of individuals from them; at best the self appears in peculiar agglomerations of selves, for example, in terms of sales per employee or unit costs. Thus in the mirror of accounting information, the self is encountered only through the distorting prism of accounting's central values of cost, profit, cash flow or return on capital. However, despite this absence of an individual self in anything like recognizable form within accounting information, this information is nevertheless used in a way that shapes our own sense of self and the character of our relatedness to others.

I want to turn now to consider more closely the effects generated in those who are subject to the visibility that accounting creates. In exploring the effects of disciplinary power, Foucault draws attention to the ways in which it 'compares, differentiates, hierarchizes, homogenizes, excludes'. It is the sum of these effects that he describes as 'individualizing'. In the context of this chapter I can only offer a few illustrations of how such effects are generated in the routines of hierarchical accountability.

Removal from an organization is an unusual outcome of routine accountability. Nevertheless I would suggest that the spectre of this possibility haunts almost everyone in an organization such that the power of this possible sanction lies principally in its effects upon those who remain. The occasional enactment of a sacking or redundancy is enough to remind everyone of the conditional status of their employment, and to thereby reinforce the importance of the performance standards in terms of which they themselves are evaluated. Seeing others dismissed from the organization reminds everyone that personal security depends upon being able to demonstrate one's own continuing utility.

The spectre of dismissal leads to a permanent state of self-absorption; one is permanently preoccupied with concerns about one's own job security, which in turn depends upon fulfilling performance requirements established and monitored in routine accountability. The security of self comes to depend upon one's capacity to prejudge and correct action in the light of these expectations; the demands of others have become the lens through which one views oneself. Foucault describes this process in the following way:

> He who is subjected to a field of visibility, and who knows it, assumes responsibility for the constraints of power, he makes them play upon himself. He inscribes in himself the power relation in which he simultaneously plays both roles.
>
> (Foucault, 1979: 202–3)

This is the mentality generated by the disciplinary practices of accountability; the process whereby accountability serves to 'individualize'. Individuals are held (or hold themselves) in a constant state of preoccupation with how the self and its activities will be seen and judged by others. In an effort to anticipate the expectations of others the individuals stand as it were on guard over themselves. In this way the central values of accounting become incorporated within the self; they become the mirror in which one searches for one's own sense of value. At the same time within this mirror the self is discovered as solitary and singular; as an individual.

The preoccupation with how the self will be seen and judged by others can have a wholly defensive character, or can be embraced more actively in the form of career plans and goals. Thus, along with the fear of dismissal stimulated in routine accountability, are the more positive potentials of immediate praise and the future promise of the differentiation of self from others through progress up the hierarchy. The hierarchy here is taken as an index of relative personal worth, with each step up the ladder offering the individualized self the prospect of a more complete expression and realization of individual autonomy. Of course in practice such 'progress' is only achieved through a deeper embrace of the values of utility upon which this 'success' rests. Moreover, such concerns for utility are not confined to the individuals, for although they aspire to autonomy, managerial success depends critically upon being able to secure the conformity of others. In this way the individualized selves also come to view others in terms of the standards of utility which have become the measure of their own value.

Foucault suggests that such 'individualizing' effects are the very means whereby discipline realizes its power.

> It (discipline) must also master all the forces that are formed from the very constitution of an organized multiplicity; it must neutralize the effects of counter power that spring from them and which form a resistance to the power that wishes to dominate it; agitations, revolts, spontaneous organizations, coalitions – anything that may establish horizontal conjunctions. Hence the fact that the disciplines use procedures of partitioning and verticality, that they introduce between the different elements at the same level, as solid separations as possible, that they define compact hierarchical networks, in short that they oppose to the intrinsic adverse force of multiplicity the techniques of a continuous, individualizing pyramid. They must also increase the particular utility of each element.
>
> (Foucault, 1979: 219–20)

This quote can be taken as an almost literal account of the effects of routine hierarchical accountability, made possible and enacted through the techniques of accounting. In the peculiar mirror of activity that accounting provides, the self, others, and productive activity itself, are discovered merely as instruments to the monetary values it advertises. To secure self within the terms of such values individuals must maintain a state of constant vigilance over their own activity and incessantly compare and differentiate self from others in these terms. It is within this self-disciplining that the individualized self is constituted; anxiously absorbed with superiors' views of their utility, indifferent to subordinates except in so far as their actions will reflect on the individual, and aware of colleagues only as potential competitors for recognition. The atomized individual may indeed be the fictional creation of economics, but the workings of hierarchical accountability are such as to make an organizational reality of this fiction.

Foucault, however, also suggests that there are counter forces to such individualizing tendencies in the form of resistance that discipline itself calls out, and in the form of horizontal ties and the 'adverse force of multiplicity'. The section that follows will explore such adverse forces which I suggest can constitute an alternative form of accountability which in turn generates a very different sense of self and self's relation to others.

Socializing forms of informal accountability

In exploring the nature of socializing forms of accountability and distinguishing these from individualizing forms, I want to draw upon the work of Habermas, and in particular the distinction he makes between 'work' and 'interaction'. 'Work' he defined as follows:

> . . . by work or purposive rational action I understand either instrumental action or rational choice or their conjunction. Instrumental action is governed by technical rules based on empirical knowledge.
>
> (Habermas, 1971: 91–2)

By 'interaction' he understands:

> Communicative action, symbolic interaction. It is governed by binding consensual norms which define reciprocal expectations about behaviour, and which must be understood and recognized by at least two acting subjects.
>
> (Habermas, 1971: 92)

In his more recent work (Habermas, 1989) this distinction has been reformulated as a contrast between 'action oriented to success' and 'action oriented to achieving understanding'. In contrast to Habermas, my interest here is in the co-presence of these two orientations to action within the context of work organizations.

I would argue that accounting information and the systems of accountability that it makes possible embody and create an instrumental 'work' orientation. Thus in describing the individualizing effects of hierarchical accountability in the preceding section, I suggested how accounting embodies an instrumental orientation to both production and producers. That the 'facts and figures' that it generates, and the visibility that it imposes, serve to generate in those that it subjects a parallel instrumentality in relation not only to behaviour but also more completely to the self and to other selves.

Such a system of 'work' is maintained in a number of ways. Whilst accounting information could be seen to be concerned with generating a form of understanding, typically this is imposed rather than achieved. Of course details can be contested, and their precise significance negotiated, but in the overall process individuals come to take over its instrumental concerns. Moreover, accounting information is usually produced by methods and by individuals somewhat distanced from the activities that they claim to report on.

In an earlier paper (Roberts and Scapens, 1985) we argued that in enacting power relations within an organization, accounting information had the peculiar merit of being able to 'control at a distance'. Distance and the possibility of divergent interests both raise problems of trust within an organization (Fox, 1974; Luhman, 1979). The mobility of accounting information and the remote visibility created by management accounts both express, and to a degree resolve, such problems.

Paradoxically, however, the dominance and distrust of distant interests then comes to inhabit and shape local contexts of interaction. Most importantly communication within and between contexts of face-to-face interaction tends to be plagued by what Argyris (1990) calls 'defensive routines' in which the individualized self seeks to protect itself, often at the expense of the effective co-ordination of action. Thus in face-to-face accountability the potential for reciprocity is displaced by hierarchy; it is the subordinate who must account to the superior in the terms dictated by the categories supplied by accounting information. An individual's own understanding is in principle irrelevant in such accountability. Instead, the fear of possible sanctions, or the lure of individual incentives or career prospects is typically enough to secure an instrumental individual conformity. Success in the presentation of self, and for managers the presentation of their department's results to remote superiors, comes to take the place of a concern for the creation of a genuine reciprocal understanding of the conditions and consequences of work relationships.

Such outcomes of 'work' relations are the exact opposite of what Habermas has in mind when he talks of 'interaction'. With his concept of 'universal pragmatics' Habermas has explored the potential of non-distorted communication to form the basis of a rationally grounded consensus which might then serve as a *normative* institutional framework within which instrumental action could be contained and directed. In what follows I will suggest that alongside formal hierarchical accountability, there are other forms of informal accountability present in organizations that contain the potential for generating such a normative consensus.[1]

In highly defensive contexts, individuals' attempts to make sense of what is going on around them are possibly kept private, or shared only with spouse or friends remote from the work situation. Even here, the capacity to see through or into the presented reality has the effect of preserving some individual sense of personhood and integrity. More usually, however, the process of understanding is a social and collective product of work relationships. Those whom an individual works alongside or encounters elsewhere in the organization become the network through which an individual shares and builds a common understanding of organizational experience. The unsurveilled spaces of organizational life – corridors and toilets, chats before and after meetings, lunch-breaks and outings – all become the contexts for an alternative form of accountability in which the sense of events is negotiated. By means of such conversations not only can official versions of organizational life be challenged and reinterpreted, but they also form the basis of a diverse network of bonds and obligations, friendships and animosities, that humanize and socialize work experience.

Such talk is encouraged by certain conditions. I have already mentioned the inhibitions on communication that are part of the power effects of hierarchical accountability. In contrast, socializing forms of accountability are easiest where relationships are unmediated by hierarchy; between individuals of equal status or with no direct functional relationship. In such lateral relationships power cannot be used to impose a point of view or hierarchize individual difference, but thereby the understanding that is excluded from the formal hierarchy can be more safely and openly communicated.

Communication oriented to achieving understanding is also fostered when there is frequent face-to-face contact between individuals. Earlier I described how in search of recognition from within the formal hierarchy individuals come to view self and others in terms of the instrumental values of utility through which they themselves are judged. But of course the lived experience of self typically extends beyond these instrumental concerns, and hence the recognition offered through the hierarchy, although materially consequential, is often rather impoverished. By contrast the less guarded flow of communication made possible in lateral face-to-face relationships has the potential to draw individuals deeper into relationship with one another and thereby offers a fuller sense of individual recognition and identity. Indeed the absence of hierarchy, and the presence of others, means that individual differences and identities can only be mediated by such conversation. Rarely is consensus the explicit goal of such communciation, but undoubtedly it is the generative source of understanding, and of felt reciprocal obligation and solidarity, and at times it may unintentionally produce a fluid and transient consensus.

In contrast to hierarchical forms of accountability that generate a sense of self as singular and solitary, with only an instrumental sense of relation to others, what I have here termed socializing forms of accountability have the potential to confirm self in a way that immediately acknowledges the interdependence of self and other, both instrumentally and morally.

Tensions and hidden interdependencies between individualizing and socializing forms of accountability

By arguing above that both an individualized and socialized sense of self are only produced and reproduced in interaction, I am implicitly committing myself to a relational view of selfhood; to again quote Merleau-Ponty it is a view of the individual as 'compounded through and through of relationship'. In this respect it is the signal triumph of disciplinary mechanisms to be realized through social interaction but to thereby constitute a subjectivity that conceives of self as essentially autonomous, with only an instrumental or serial relation to others. But I have also suggested that informal networks of organizational accountability offer alternative images of self and self's relation to others. I want now to explore how these two forms of accountability coexist with one another.

Superficially they appear as wholly competing organizational orders. Both serve as sources of individual identity and yet these do not combine easily with one another; an identity rooted in the networks of the informal does not blend easily with an identification with the relative status of hierarchy. I have in mind here the active discouragement of too close a relationship with subordinates for fear that it will compromise an individual's ability to make 'difficult decisions'. The sense that promotion will represent a sell-out or betrayal of colleagues, or alternatively the distancing of self from former workmates on being promoted, or the difficulty and embarrassment on both sides of inadvertent social contact between disparate levels of the hierarchy. In such circumstances it is as if the individual feels that they are confronted with a choice between solidarity with workmates and the pursuit of their individual self-interest through the hierachy, and along with this a conflict between differently grounded identities.

However despite the individual conflicts generated in the ambiguous spaces between the senses of self sustained through individualizing and socializing forms of accountability, I suggest that the two orders subtly depend upon each other in a number of ways.

I earlier argued that the personal lateral networks of the informal serve to humanize and socialize the experience of work. In this way they make more tolerable the impersonal order of hierarchy. But the informal does far more than maintain the conditions for individual consent. So much of routine organizational work depends upon the effectiveness of lateral relationships within and between departments, and the ties and loyalties generated in the informal therefore do much to facilitate this work. In this sense the hierarchy relies upon the sense of interdependence generated in the informal, even if this reliance is ignored or denied. However the dependence between the two forms of accountability can also be seen to work in the other direction. There is a clear danger of idealizing the potentials of community that the informal contains; it is also often the source of its own schisms and conflicts. I have in mind here the possibilities of deep personal animosity that can infect relationships between colleagues, or the local abuse of power in the form of favouritism, or victimization. The possibility of racial or sexual abuse or other forms of 'scapegoating' in which a group can engage, or of group collusion or corruption that can threaten its responsibilities to the wider organization. In all these respects, as Weber (1979) noted, an impersonal order of hierarchical rules offers various forms of protection both for the individual and the wider organization. Such rules to a degree insulate collective action from the intrusion of personal likes and dislikes, and their procedures provide some recourse for individuals in the event of local abuse. Whatever the potential within the informal for a rational consensus grounded in communication, in practice bureaucracy at least restrains or contains some of the more destructive forces that can also emerge within localized communities. In some respects therefore the impersonal order of hierarchical accountability can be seen to compensate for the ways in which the informal fails to effectively manage the individual differences that it contains within itself.

There is one further interrelationship between the two forms of accountability to explore here. Habermas has argued that instrumental reason has increasingly come to 'colonize' or 'technicize' the life-world. But I think that in one respect the argument can be reversed. There is frequently a 'transference' relationship between the patriarchal structure of the family that is still dominant in the life-world and the hierarchical order of work. The seeming impersonality of the hierarchy masks the extent to which it is unconsciously imbued with the symbols and emotions of childhood dependence and counterdependence (Diamond, 1986; Hirschorn, 1988; Menzies Lyth, 1988). Such unacknowledged and unresolved transference relationships mark a psychological obstacle to the realization of a rational consensus grounded in communicative interaction. They mark a desire for dependence even if this is consciously denied, a desire for the comfort of an order that is, apparently, decided and provided for the individual. A desire for release from responsibility both for self and others, and the demands of reflection, thought and speech that this might imply.

Despite the seeming contradictions between individualizing and socializing forms of accountability, contradictions that are felt by the individual in the tension between solidarity with colleagues and individual self interest, I have suggested above that these two forms of accountability are practically interwoven and mutually dependent upon each other. Such unrecognized interdependence between these two forms of organizational accountability does much to explain the institutional resilience of hierarchical forms of accountability, and accounting's role within this. Nevertheless, within both the critical and managerial literature one can currently discern strong pressures for the reform of accountability. It is to these developmental tendencies that I will now turn my attention.

The reform of organizational accountability – critical and managerial prescriptions

In the introduction I stated that informing this exploration of accountability in organizations was a concern to explore how instrumental and moral aspects of accountability might be brought back into closer relation within organizations. As a set of social practices, accountability must be central to both social and in particular organizational life; through such practices and processes individuals are made aware both of themselves and the impact of their actions on others. Yet the preceding analysis of organizational accountability has described practices that, despite their subtle mutual dependence, seem to be split and contradictory. What I have called individualizing forms of accountability are exclusively preoccupied with instrumental or strategic action. The individualized sense of self that is the condition and consequence of hierarchical accountability comes to believe in the independence and autonomy of self; there is at best only an instrumental relation to others. By contrast, what I have called socializing forms of accountability through reproducing a relational sense of selfhood arguably restore an ethical dimension to work relationships. Yet whilst this does much to secure the routine interdependencies of work relationships, such ethical concerns are nevertheless excluded from formal hierarchical accountability.

Habermas explores this split or divide in terms of two different forms of integration; what he calls system integration which is realized through the media of power and money and social integration which is oriented by reference to norms realized through communicative interaction. For him the consequence of this divide is that strategic action within organizations, both individual and collective, has escaped from the confines of any normative regulation. As he puts it:

> Publicly administered definitions extend to *what* we want for our lives, but not to *how* we would like to live if we could find out, with regard to attainable potentials, how we *could* live.
>
> (Habermas, 1971: 120)

For Habermas, what is required is 'unrestricted communication' about the goals of life activity and, superficially, what I have described above as socializing forms of accountability describe the conditions under which such unrestricted communication can take place. In practice, however, such forms of accountability seem to be confined to local contexts of action, to settings where there is frequent face-to-face contact and a relative equity of power. Only very rarely is sufficient momentum and solidarity generated in such contexts to confront the formal organizational order; and even then such expressions of resistance are often themselves instrumentally defined. The more usual outcome is for any normative order realized through socializing forms of accountability in local contexts, to be subordinate to, and at times itself undermined by, the intrusion of instrumental interests promoted and reinforced by wider hierarchical systems of accountability.

The conclusion that Habermas draws is that an emancipatory interest can place little hope in the communicative potentials of organizaional relationships:

> *Communicative action forfeits its validity in the interior of organizations.* Members of organizations act communicatively only *with reservation*. They know that they *can* have recourse to formal regulations, not only in the exceptional but also in routine cases, there is no *necessity* for achieving consensus by communicative means . . .
>
> (Habermas, 1989: 310–11).

But just as this avenue for the reform of accountability seems to have closed, so one can discern a growing concern within the managerial literature for the strategic and organizational problems that are created by the individualized mentality that is the product of hierarchical forms of accountability.

This managerial critique of individualizing effects seems to have been stimulated by changes in the structure and intensity of international competition and, in particular, the competitive strengths of the Japanese. This strength has been traced to very different production and personnel practices within Japanese organizations, as well as very different inter-firm and state-industry relations in the Japenese economy (Pascale and Athos, 1982; Oliver and Wilkinson, 1992; Ouchi, 1981). Out of this comparison a whole range of new organizational technologies have emerged – culture management, employee commitment, transformational leadership, organizational learning, empowerment – each designed to reproduce in western organizations the staff commitment and product quality that are the supposed sources of strength for the Japanese. In the terms of my earlier analysis these new technologies can be seen as attempts to harness some of the socializing effects of commitment and loyalty to the organization's instrumental ends; what Willmott (1993) has termed the extension of technical rationality into the domain of the 'affective'. In this context I want to look very briefly at the recent work of Chris Argyris, since in his concern for the organizational consequences of distorted communication his work seems to relate most strongly to the theme of accountability that I am exploring here.

Building upon his earlier work on organizational learning (Argyris and Schon, 1974), and in particular the distinction between 'espoused theory' and 'theory-in-use', Argyris (1990) has recently developed a set of ideas about what he calls 'Organizational Defensive Routines'. Such routines for him mark the primary practical obstacle to implementing the newly espoused values of employee commitment, learning, and empowerment. His argument is that these newly espoused values and programmes can only be effective if there is a corresponding change in the organization's 'theory-in-use'. More typically, however, he argues that whilst what is espoused has changed, the underlying theory-in-use, the understanding that informs practice, has remained the same. In describing the traditional theory-in-use – what he calls 'model I' – Argyris talks of a model which is taught early in life about 'how to act in ways to be in control', particularly in relation to issues that can be 'embarrassing or threatening'. The values implicit in this model include a desire 'to be in unilateral control, to win and not lose, to suppress negative feelings'. This results in individual behaviour that is preoccupied with defending self in a way that projects blame onto others whilst ignoring the inconsistencies in one's own behaviour.

Whilst rational from an individual perspective, when viewed interactively such behaviour can be seen to generate very distorted patterns of communication – 'defensive routines' – in which the overt content of communication masks a very different but essentially private set of assumptions and understandings. These understandings are acted upon but never tested for fear of the possible negative consequences of hurt or punishment that might ensue. The organizational consequences of such defensive routines involve a sort of 'malaise' in which the learning that is necessary for the effective realization of the organization's collective goals and objectives is prevented because so much has become 'undiscussable' within the organization.

To counter such defensive tendencies, Argyris suggests the need for an alternative theory-in-use that values valid information, informed choice and responsibility for monitoring implementation processes. Open advocacy of one's position, attempting to minimize face saving, reflection in action and openness to constructive confrontation, he argues, offer the best route out of such defensive routines. Without such new values and behaviours the new organizational technologies will never be more than passing fads that falter in the distortions of communication that are skilfully reproduced by organizational participants.

The validity of this solution is not at issue here. For our current purposes it is enough to note how this work can be read as an implicit critique of what I have described above as the individualizing effects of hierarchical accountability. There are a variety of connections that can be made here. In emphasizing an instrumental relation to self and others, it is not surprising that attention should be placed on what is got out of relationships rather than on the actual dynamic of these relationships. The attempt within such accountability to locate praise and blame unequivocally, inevitably distracts attention away from the dynamic interaction of such behaviour over time. In using both the fear of exclusion and the promise of praise and future career reward, it is hardly surprising that the openness of communication should be repeatedly sacrificed to the cause of self-defence and self-advancement. Finally, and perhaps most importantly, it is not surprising that in reproducing a sense of self as singular and solitary, with only an instrumental relation to the organization and others within it, control comes to be thought of unilaterally rather than relationally.

And yet Argyris is of course right to point to the fallacy implicit in such individualized behaviour and thought. Effectively he is arguing that individual action is the consequence of the context and processes through which it is made possible. That the achievement of organizational objectives is the product of the quality of *relationships between* individuals, the interactive outcome of how individual actions are combined, rather than merely the sum of individualized performances that accounting seems to make it.

What is significant about Argyris's ideas in this context is that he is mounting a critique of individualizing effects from within instrumental reason itself. The paradox of unilateral control is that in pursuit of self-defence, conditions are created which undermine the collective capacity for effective organized action upon which individual security ultimately depends. The individualized sense of self that hierarchical accountability generates, blinds individuals to their practical interdependence with others; to how their actions contribute to the problems they define as external, to how rational self-defence becomes self-defeating.

Accounting for interdependence

I began this chapter by suggesting that accounting should be understood not in its own terms as an objective and neutral mirror held up to organizational events, but in terms of the part it plays in producing and reproducing systems of accountability within organizations. I then went on to argue that practices of accountability are central to social life in the way that they come to shape our sense of self and relation to others. The subsequent analysis sought to describe the peculiarly split nature of current accountability within and around organizations. Formal hierarchical accountability is exclusively preoccupied with the realization of the instrumental goals that are embodied and expressed in accounting. Drawing upon Foucault's analysis of the workings of disciplinary power, I suggested that this form of accountability, although grounded in social practices, realizes an individualized sense of self; a sense of self as singular and solitary, nervously preoccupied with how the self is seen, and in this way coming to see self and others in purely instrumental terms. Such formal systems of accountability, however, do not wholly define or confine the sense of self within organizational life. Drawing upon the work on Habermas, I then went on to describe what I called socializing forms of accountability that flourish in the informal networks of organized life; networks which potentially offer alternative sources of identity and most importantly confirm self in a manner that emphasizes the interdependence of self and other.

The following two sections of the chapter then reflected upon the conditions and consequences of these divided forms of organizational accountability. Although the two forms of accountability seemingly confront the individual with a choice between ties of loyalty and solidarity with colleagues and the pursuit of individual self-interest in the hierarchy, formal and informal practices of accountability nevertheless can be seen to depend upon one another. Socializing forms of accountability, I argued, not only humanize the experience of work but also do much to realize the routine interdependence of action in work relations. On the other hand, formal hierarchical accountability can be seen both to protect the individual and insulate collective action from the more destructive potentials of the informal. Moreover, the superficially impersonal order of hierarchy can itself become the source of a comforting dependence. Thus the two forms of accountability, despite the very different sense of self and relation to others that they generate, nevertheless seem to rest upon one another.

These divided forms of accountability are not without their consequences. From a critical perspective the split marks the way in which instrumental, strategic action, both individual and collective, has been released from any necessary ethical restraint or judgement. At the same time within managerial thought there is a growing recognition of the negative strategic consequences of a highly individualized mentality; defensive patterns of hierarchical communication and the lack of wholehearted commitment are now seen to threaten commercial success.

One way to summarize all this would be to suggest that although organizational accountability is currently split and divided within itself – a divide which is also part of the individual's experience of self – this split has begun to be recognized as both morally and strategically destructive. One of the dangers of accounting information is that it offers a fragmented, atomized image of activity; an image of organization as no more than the sum of individual efforts and results. Caught in this image we then fail to recognize that accounting's productive potential is only realized through how it is used in accountability. In contrast, the merit of viewing accounting in the context of accountability is that the interdependence of action comes into sight. What we need to account for is not our individual actions but how these interact with one another; the consequences, intended and otherwise, of our actions for others both near and far, and the way that these consequences, often in unrecognized form inevitably become part of the conditions of our own future action (Giddens, 1984). By its very nature this highly complex interdependence of action does not segment conveniently into instrumental and moral aspects; and yet it is precisely such a split, along with its negative consequences, that is embodied in contemporary forms of organizational accountability.

In this respect it is *the process of accountability* that is all important. Accountability involves no more than the institutionalized social practices through which we reflect upon the conditions and consequences of our actions and relationships. As I put it in an earlier presentation of these ideas:

> Accountability is a form of social relation which reflects symbolically upon the practical interdependence of action; an interdependence that always has both moral and strategic dimensions.

> (1991: 367)

Against the backdrop of an intense, pervasive and highly complex interdependence of action both within organizations, and between organizations and the communities within which they operate, the individualized mentality that is the condition and consequence of hierarchical forms of accountability seems simply inadequate and inappropriate. The question remains as to what form accountability could take in order to more adequately embrace and articulate the moral and strategic interdependencies in which we are all inextricably bound. By way of a conclusion I want to look at dialogue as a potential model for such a form of accountability.

The possibilities for dialogue

There is a very long history to the concept of dialogue but the following quote from Merleau-Ponty suggests that dialogue has the potential to disclose the relational character of selfhood:

> In the experience of dialogue, there is constituted between the other person and myself a common ground: my thought and his are interwoven in a single fabric, my words and those of my interlocutor are called forth by the state of the discussion, and they are inserted into a shared operation of which neither of us is the creator. We have here a dual being, where the other is for me no longer a mere bit of behaviour in my transcendental field nor I in his; we are collaborators with each other in a consummate reciprocity. Our perspectives merge into each other, and we coexist through a common world.
> (Merleau-Ponty, 1962: 354).

The individualized self is preoccupied with the boundaries of self, with how self is seen by powerful others, with hierarchy as an objective validation of self, and the status of self relative to others. All these are reflected senses of self-identity. Similarly, distortions within the realm of the informal can be seen to arise from a concern to secure or fix a certain sense of self (Knights and Willmott, 1989). Merleau-Ponty's suggestion in the above is that dialogue has the potential to dissolve this concern with objective boundaries. One is drawn into conversation and also out of oneself. Thought emerges from the process rather than being the product of a prepared individual agenda; no one can claim thought as quite their own, but rather it is the product of the relationship. And as the anxious or arrogant preoccupation with objective image fades, an alternative sense of self is generated, confirmed in the immediacy of relationship. Other is encountered here not as an object of threat or use in one's own overarching project for self, but instead as a fellow subject, different yet, like the process of dialogue itself, inextricably interwoven with the fabric of self.

Perhaps the experience of dialogue is rare, although suggestions of a similar process are to be found in the work of both Gadamer (1975) and Buber (1937). Nevertheless, what I want to explore here are some of the conditions that might allow such a form of conversation.

In the organizational literature, dialogue has recently been advocated by Senge (1990) as the necessary condition of 'team learning'. Building upon Argyris's analysis of defensive routines, and drawing very extensively upon the writings of Bohm (1989), Senge makes a distinction between two forms of discourse – discussion and dialogue. Discussion, he argues, has the same roots as percussion or concussion. Like a competitive game, points of view struggle against each other. The aim of the game is to win, which in conversational terms means for an individual's views to prevail and be accepted by the group. By contrast, the purpose of dialogue is 'to go beyond any one individual's understanding'. There is a free-flow of meaning between individuals; meaning emerges out of the process such that thought is seen to be a participative process. What Senge is describing is a form of conversation in which the individual is confirmed only in and through their wider relationship with others. As he puts it: 'the result is a free exploration that brings to the surface the full depth of people's experience, and yet can move beyond their individual views' (1990: 241).

Senge, following Bohm, suggests three basic conditions for dialogue. Participants must 'suspend their assumptions'; that is, make explicit and therefore open to the reflection of self and others the tacit assumptions that inform their points of view. At the same time everyone must regard one another as 'colleagues', whose views must be attended to with the same open attention; such an attitude is necessary to support the vulnerability that is part of making tacit ideas explicit. Finally, some form of facilitator is required to help the process and prevent a collapse back into discussion, although the necessity for such a role diminishes over time.

Notwithstanding the difficulty of meeting and sustaining even these conditions, I want to discuss two further conditions, or more precisely obstacles to such dialogue that are somewhat glossed over by Senge. The first obstacle concerns the effects of power. Whilst Senge draws extensively on Bohm's ideas he also notes his disagreement with him over the question of hierarchy. For Bohm, hierarchy is simply incompatible with dialogue. Bohm's own work on dialogue in fact itself draws very heavily on the work of a group psychoanalyst, Patrick de Maré (1991). De Maré's experience of large group dialogues leads him to suggest that they have the potential to include and hold individual differences in productive tension. The frustration and hatred that is the primitive response to different others, generates energy that, if held in relation through dialogue, then promotes thinking, reciprocal understanding, information and what he calls 'koinonia' or impersonal friendship. For de Maré such a process of dialogue is explicitly opposed to hierarchy:

> Dialogue is affiliative (a term derived from the word meaning the abnegation of the father), on the level, levelling, multi-personal, multipolar, and egalitarian, and therefore multidimensional. Arguments, on the other hand, binary oppositions, rhetoric, polemic performances, duologue, the true and the false, are all basically hierarchical.
>
> (1991: 43)

I would suggest that in refusing to confront the reality of hierarchical power, Senge's advocacy of dialogue falls victim to his own unquestioned belief in the legitimacy of instrumental reason; a criticism that can also be levelled against Argyris's analysis of defensive routines. Dialogue becomes just another tool for realizing commitment and learning in the service of unquestioned 'organizational' objectives. Dialogue may indeed be the means whereby shared meaning can be created, defensive routines may indeed be self-defeating in the context of organizational action. However, hierarchy is the means whereby individual and group interests come to be extracted out of the questioning process that dialogue establishes and then imposed on others. Whatever common interests a hierarchy contains, it also expresses and generates real divisions of interest within the firm. If dialogue is taken seriously then as de Maré states it may well be a 'levelling' social process that challenges the interests and assumptions of those in 'power'; a challenge that is likely to be resisted. Indeed the potential of dialogue as a form of accountability may lie precisely in its capacity to reveal the 'incoherence of thought' embodied in the unquestioned pursuit of growth and profit, without regard for the social and environmental consequences that flow from this.

Whilst the asymmetry of hierarchical power relates primarily to what I earlier described as individualizing forms of accountability, the second obstacle to dialogue can be discerned in the distortions of both individualizing and socializing forms of accountability. It concerns individuals' attachment to self-identity. For Bohm it is this preoccupation with self that lies behind the competitive character of discussion:

> . . . usually people play to win . . . People are frightened; they feel they've got
> to win, if only for their self esteem. If you lose, you feel that your self-esteem
> is wounded, therefore you identify with winning.
>
> (Bohm and Edwards, 1991: 171)

The combative nature of discussion arises from a felt threat to one's own and others sense of self. Throughout this chapter I have sought to emphasize the relationship between accountability and the constitution of the self. In discussing the constitution of self in childhood I noted not only the social and processual character of the self, but also the potential for alienation in the ways in which we can become trapped in and preoccupied with securing a particular conception of self. In this respect, others' difference is experienced as a threat to, and attack upon our own sense of self/ world. Part of the attraction of hierarchy lies not only in the way that it offers a means of securing material advantage, but also as a means of securing seemingly objective confirmation of the relative value of self, a value that is less easily fixed in the more fluid and lateral relationships of the informal organization. In the way that dialogue has the potential to carry thought in unexpected directions, to carry self beyond its known limits, and to reveal our dependence upon others, it thus threatens not only material interests, but also our symbolic investment in particular identities. Deetz expresses this potential in the following way:

> . . . communication is not for self-expression but for self-destruction. The
> point of communication as a social act is to overcome one's fixed subjectivity,
> one's conceptions, one's strategies, to be opened to the indeterminacy of
> people and the external environment. Communication in its democratic form
> is productive rather than reproductive. It produces what self and other can
> experience, rather than reproduces what either has.
>
> (Deetz, 1992: 343)

Such self destruction is no more than a realization of the transitory, processual, and relational nature of selfhood. Nevertheless whilst dialogue may have the potential to establish a social process through which change can be managed participatively, such change may itself be resisted precisely because it is experienced as a threat to the illusory solidity of self identity.

However it is also possible that dialogue offers the only possible route out of such a dilemma. It can be argued that the currently split and divided forms of accountability have already made the maintenance of a stable identity highly problematic. The defences of the individualized self only compound these difficulties in the ways that they seek to insulate self from, rather than re-establish and renew relation with others (Lasch, 1985; Frosh, 1991). Dialogue may offer a productive way out of such defence precisely because within it the self is confirmed in and through the immediacy of relationship with others. As Rorty puts it:

> . . . the person who has doubts about his own final vocabulary, his own moral identity, and perhaps his own sanity – desperately needs to talk to people, needs to do this with the same urgency as people need to make love. He needs to do so because only conversation enables him to handle these doubts and these needs. (Rorty, 1989: 186)

As the certainties of a reified sense of self begin to disintegrate so the self must find again its full place in the relational world that was ever its point of origin. But the need for talk extends beyond matters of self-doubt, although such modesty is appropriate once the incompleteness of thought is recognized. It is, I have argued, the reification of self that convinces us (wrongly) of the absolute character of autonomy, that makes the differentiation of self from other into a seemingly absolute separation. As the reification dissolves or collapses so the inescapable, unavoidable character of our practical interdependence with others comes into sight. The need to talk arises also from the necessity to collectively manage this interdependence; to discover and articulate the difference we each inevitably make for each other.

Conclusion

I began this chapter with a quote from Martin Buber, where he argues that the instrumental pursuit of power and profit only becomes a source of evil when this is elevated above and detached from the relatedness of being. In analyzing individualizing forms of hierarchical accountability, I have sought to describe the conditions and consequenes of the currently 'detached' form of organizational accountability. In this, the mystification of accounting information helps to fix, elevate and then impose upon others its own particular instrumental interests, without regard to the wider social or environmental consequences of the pursuit of such interests. Accounting thus serves as a vehicle whereby others are called to account, whilst the interests it embodies escape such accountability. To restore the balance it is not enough to confront managerial instrumentalism with critical moralizing; it can never be a matter of either/or. Instead the instrumental and the moral need to be brought back into relation. By confirming self in a way that simultaneously expresses and articulates the interdependence of self and others, dialogue as a process and practice of accountability has just this potential.

Notes

1. The contrast between 'work' and 'interaction' is at times evident in research work when conversation shifts from a functional perspective to the perspective of the individual who happens to have functional responsibilities. Sometimes remarks are prefaced by comments such as 'well, if you want my personal opinion'. However at this point new levels of understanding are offered that are typically more reflexive and more critical of the individual's experience of working in a particular organization. Such shifts of tone and content in communication reveal an active process of understanding within individuals, which is somewhat distanced from the instrumental rationality that pervades hierarchical accountability. It seems to demonstrate a capacity for reflection and the empathetic understanding of the experience of others that has escaped the confines of the individualized self-interest. Such shifts in the content of communication are made possible by the fact that, as researcher, one has no direct part in the disciplinary apparatus that surrounds the individual employee; the promise of confidentiality is usually enough to surface such reflexive and critical understandings. Nevertheless it would be naïve to imagine that such individual understandings do not also have an active presence within the actual processes of organizing, even though they are typically neglected and discouraged in formal systems of accountability.

References

Argyris, C. (1990) *Overcoming Organizational Defenses*, Allyn and Bacon, Needham Heights, MA.

Argyris, C. and Schon, D. (1974) *Theory in Practice*, Prentice-Hall, Englewood Cliffs, N.J.

Becker, E. (1972) *The Birth and Death of Meaning*, Penguin, Harmondsworth.

Bohm, D. and Peat, D. (1989) *Science, Order and Creativity*, Routledge, London.

Bohm, D. and Edwards, M. (1991) *Changing Consciousness*, Harper, San Francisco.

Buber, M. (1937) *I and Thou*, T&T Clark, Edinburgh.

Daudi, P. (1986) *Power in the Organisation: the discourse of power in managerial practice*, Blackwell, Oxford.

Deetz, S. (1992) *Democracy in an Age of Corporate Colonization*, State University of New York Press, Albany, N.Y.

de Maré, P., Piper, R. and Thompson, S. (1991) *Koinonia: From Hate, through Dialogue, to Culture in the Large Group*, Karnac, London.

Diamond, M.A. (1986) Resistance to Change: A Psychoanalytic Critique of Argyris and Schon's contribution to organisation theory and intervention. *Journal of Management Studies*, **23**(5) pp. 543–62.

Foucault, M. (1979) *Discipline and Punish*, Penguin, Harmondsworth.

Fox, A. (1974) *Beyond Contract*. Faber and Faber, London.

Frosh, S. (1991) *Identity Crisis: Modernity, Psychoanalysis and the Self*, Macmillan, London.

Gadamer, H.G. (1975) *Truth and Method*, New York.

Giddens, A. (1984) *The Constitution of Society*, Polity, Cambridge.

Goffman, E. (1971) *The Presentation of Self in Everyday Life*, Penguin, Harmondsworth.

Habermas, J. (1971) *Towards a Rational Society*, Heinemann, London.

Habermas, J. (1989) *The Theory of Communicative Action*, Vol. 2, Polity, Cambridge.

Hines, R. (1988) Financial Accounting: In Communicating Reality, We Construct Reality. *Accounting, Organizations and Society*, **13**(3) pp. 251–61.

Hirschorn, L. (1988) *The Workplace Within: the Psychodynamics of Organizational Life*, MIT Press, Cambridge, MA.

Knights, D. and Willmott, H. (1989) Power and Subjectivity at work: From degradation to subjugation in work relations. *Sociology* **23**(4) pp. 535–58.

Kohlberg, L. (1986) *Child Psychology and Childhood Education*, Longman, London.

Lasch, C. (1985) *The Minimal Self: Psychic Survival in Troubled Times*, Pan Books, London.

Luhman, N. (1979) *Trust and Power*, John Wiley, London.

Menzies Lyth, I. (1988) *Containing Anxiety in Institutions*, Volume I, Free Associations Books, London.

Mead, G.H. (1934) *Mind Self and Society*, University of Chicago Press, Chicago.

Merleau-Ponty, M. (1962) *The Phenomenology of Perception*, Routledge and Kegan Paul, London.

Miller, P. and O'Leary, T. (1986) Accounting and the Construction of the Governable Person. *Accounting, Organizations and Society*, **12**(3) pp. 235–65.

Oliver, N. and Wilkinson, B. (1992) *The Japanisation of British Industry*, Blackwell, Oxford.

Ouchi, W. (1981) *Theory Z: How American Business can meet the Japanese challenge*, Addison-Wesley, Reading, MA.

Pascale, R. and Athos, A. (1982) *The Art of Japanese Management*, Penguin, Harmondsworth.

Roberts, J. (1991) The possibilities of accountability. *Accounting, Organizations and Society*, **16**(4) pp. 355–68.

Roberts, J. and Scapens, R. (1985) Accounting Systems and Systems of Accountability: understanding accounting practices in their organisational contexts. *Accounting, Organizations and Society*, **10**(4) pp. 443–56.

Roberts, J. and Scapens, R. (1990) Accounting as Discipline, in *Critical Accounts: Reorienting Accounting Research* (eds D. Cooper and T. Hopper) Macmillan, London.

Rorty, R. (1989) *Contingency, Irony and Solidarity*, Cambridge University Press, Cambridge.

Senge, P. (1990) *The Fifth Discipline: The Art and Practice of the Learning Organization*, Doubleday, New York.

Weber, M. (1979) *Economy and Society: an outline of interpretative sociology*, University of California Press, Berkley.

Willmott, H. (1993) Strength is Ignorance: Slavery is Freedom: Managing Culture in Modern Organisations. *Journal of Management Studies*, **30**(4) pp. 515–52.

4 Narrating accountability: cognition and the production of the accountable self

Richard J. Boland, Jr and Ulrike Schultze

Abstract

Producing accountability requires both narration and calculation. We argue that Bruner's characterization of narrating and calculating as two distinctive modes of cognition is helpful for understanding the construction of accountability in persons and societies. Examining the modes of cognition assumed and reinforced by the principal technologies of organizing suggests that the narrative mode is consistently undervalued and often suppressed. As a result, accountability is understood in ways that limit inquiry, interpretation, argument and reasoning about it to a narrow subset of possibilities. Building on Roberts' description of hierarchical and socializing forms of accountability, we propose that group information technologies make it possible to re-establish the narrative mode of cognition on a more equal institutional basis with the calculative. We argue that this provides an opportunity for recovering accounting from the isolation of bureaucratic accountability and locating it within the sense making narrative of social process. We see this as an opportunity for more openly recognizing in the technology of organizing how the self and the moral order are constructed through the narratives of accountability.

Introduction

Accountability is the capacity and willingness to give explanations for conduct, stating how one has discharged one's responsibilities. Accountability therefore involves both an explaining of conduct with a credible story of what happened, and a calculation and balancing of competing obligations, including moral ones. These two faces of accountability are also seen in the etymology of the word 'account' and are crucial for understanding the social construction of accountability. In the Oxford English Dictionary, we see that *account* comes from both the Old French *a conter*, meaning *to tell a story* and from the late Latin *accomputare*, meaning to *compute*. Accountability thus entails the giving of an account as in a narration of what transpired (a recounting of events in a story form) and the giving of an account as in a reckoning of money (a calculation of net balances of events in a transaction form).

In this paper we relate the computational and story-telling roots of *account* to the hierarchical and social sources of accountability discussed by Roberts (1991). We argue that the computational and story-telling forms of accountability are not borne out of the formal structure and informal social interaction of organizations as Roberts suggests, but are instead made possible by the two modes of human cognition characterized by Bruner (1986, 1990) as the paradigmatic and narrative modes. Information technologies and formal organization structures of the last century have emphasized the paradigmatic mode of cognition at the expense of the narrative mode, leading Roberts and others to associate the formal organization with calculative practices and forms of accountability. We have come to think of the modern person primarily as a calculating self in calculable spaces (Miller, 1992), but that image is challenged by our exploration of the narrative mode of cognition and the powerful role it plays in constructing the accountable self.

The recent adoption of group information technologies and systems of computer supported co-operative work reveal how the narrative face of accountability is inherent in the formal as well as the informal organization. Accountability in both its computational and story telling faces is generated through the interplay of paradigmatic and narrative modes of cognition in settings ranging from the most formal to the most informal. We hold that the narrative and the calculative faces of being accountable are interdependent, each supplying the conditions for, and being enabled by, the other. Nevertheless, we see the narrative mode as the primary vehicle for making our experience meaningful (Polkinghorne, 1988: 16; Ong, 1982; Kerby, 1991; Shotter, 1984; Ricoeur, 1984).

It is through narrativizing a situation that the self and the basic categories for naming and knowing events are constructed. In a narration, the person as a self and the events which comprise a life situation are isolated and brought forth out of the seamless process of unfolding action. These events, the 'facts' of the matter, are first established through narrative and only then available for calculation and reckoning. Efforts at calculation, in turn, refine and elaborate upon narrativized categories which then become available in modified form for future narrativization of experience. To the extent that organizations and accountability are social constructions, the narrative mode of cognition is the engine of that construction process.

As an example of how calculation is taken to be the determining feature in constructing accountability, consider Miller's (1992) insightful analysis of the computational face of accounting. He begins his essay with Nietzsche's (1987) argument that 'man was actually *made* calculable'. Miller argues that accounting provides forms of visibility and techniques of measurement and comparison that create a calculable space within which the 'free' responsible human is increasingly governed through self-regulation. Information processing technologies document the individual as an objectified case. The individual is constructed as a calculable self by techniques of recording, classifying, combining, and comparing data, especially accounting data. This powerful Foucauldian argument of calculable self puts only one face of accounting and accountability into relief. We hold, however, that it presupposes a narrative capacity – an ability to narrate their experience and that of others in making sense of the world.

Drawing on Nietzsche to describe the requirements for a responsible, sovereign individual to emerge, Miller (1992) argued 'The individual capable of anticipating distant eventualities, of deciding what is to be the goal and what the means to achieve it, requires the capacity to calculate and compute' (p. 62). Notice that there is a particular cognitive style which serves as a precondition for the application of information processing techniques within calculable spaces. It is a means-ends cognitive style in which actors create or experience events that occur in a sequence, and make causal attributions about how they or others are responsible for creating outcomes of a particular sort. This narrative cognitive style is a precondition for the emergence of calculating selves and calculable spaces because it provides the background for a predictive chain of causal events upon which calculation of probability, efficiency or responsibility can be applied (Bruner, 1986; 1990).

The information technologies presumed in the arguments of Roberts (1991), Roberts and Scapens (1985) and Miller (1992) are the classical accounting and management information system technologies which collect and summarize transaction data, distributing standardized reports through an informational pipeline to an overseeing manager (Boland, 1979). It is not surprising, then, that they emphasize the calculative face of accountability in their discussion of formal organizational practices. Yet, the deployment of distributed and co-operative information technologies such as groupware makes narrative an equally visible element in the formal information system, and opens new opportunities for observing and theorizing the two faces of accountability as an irreducible whole.

Roberts' formal and informal systems of accountability

Even though accountability has taken on discipline-specific meaning in theoretical research (Sinclair, 1995), accountability is generally understood as the giving and demanding of reasons for conduct (Garfinkel, 1967). Roberts and Scapens (1985) explored the relationship between accountability and accounting, and proposed that accounting information systems reflect the 'abstract potential' of an organization's system of accountability. Using Structuration Theory (Giddens, 1979), they refer to the accounting system as the body of rules and resources that accounting practices produce and reproduce over time. In contrast, systems of accountability represent the accounting systems in use, i.e. the accounting system embedded in practice (Roberts and Scapens, 1985: 447).

Roberts and Scapens (1985) focused on the interplay between the two systems of accountability, the formal and informal, thereby extending accounting into the local context of face-to-face relationships in which people possess a shared knowledge and understanding. In this face-to-face setting, interpreting accounting numbers implies going beyond them. Actors with motivations, interests and personalities are added to the scene and the accounting numbers are thus brought to life in a narrative that makes sense with them (Boland and Pondy, 1986; Boland, 1993).

Roberts (1991) expanded on the interdependence between the formal and the informal systems of accountability, which he referred to as the hierarchical and socializing forms of accountability, respectively. The hierarchical form of accountability focuses on accounting as a reckoning function. Regarding the individual as the economic unit, it leads to the construction of the calculating, isolated and compartmentalized self. By commodifying and enumerating an individual's talent and skill according to a mechanistic scheme of categorization, he argued, people are homogenized and brought into hierarchical relationships with one another based on their relative worth. This sets up an environment of continuous comparison, contrast and competition. Individuals internalize norms and notions of perfection, turning accountability into a system of one-way visibility: one that sees without being seen. Hierarchical forms of accountability thus reflect Foucault's concept of disciplinary power which is deeply embedded in accounting practices (Miller and O'Leary, 1987).

In contrast, the socializing form of accountability serves a narrative sense-making rather than a calculative accounting function. It is situated in the interactions between people who share a common context and have the ability to talk face-to-face to one another. According to Roberts' (1991) definition of socializing accountability, spatial proximity is a necessary condition for the giving of an account. This is because the construction of the self in dialogue with others ensures that the self is embedded in relationship with others.

In this paper, we address what we consider to be shortcomings in Robert's two forms of accountability. The first concerns the positioning of the hierarchical and socializing forms of accountability in the realm of the formal and informal organization. We argue that these two forms of accountability are not borne out of the formal structure and informal social interaction of organizations, but are instead the result of interplay between two different modes of cognition. Information technologies and formal organization structures of the last century have emphasized the paradigmatic mode of cognition at the expense of the narrative mode, leading Roberts and others to associate the formal organization with the dominant calculative practices of accountability, and the informal social interaction with the less officially visible, narrative practices.

Roberts (1991: 365) also maintains that 'socializing forms of accountability will always be limited to local contexts where there is a relative absence of asymmetries of power and the possibility of face-to-face interaction'. This point of view is called into question by innovations in information technology. Network and communication tools, such as groupware, represent a new class of information technology in that they reveal a social rather than hierarchical perspective on the formal processes and systems of organizations. Unlike Management Information Systems that automated vertical, bottom-to-top flows of abstracted data, network technology enables horizontal flows of conversations. Electronic communication systems give voice, albeit a written and virtual one, to a multitude of organizational members untethered by traditional boundaries of space and time (McGrath and Hollingshead, 1994).

By ideal-typing the settings in which the two forms of accounting take place, Roberts' portrayal of socializing as a source of accountability is limited to face-to-face interaction, especially tacit behaviours, gossip and talk. We emphasize that narration as a mode of cognition is the principle occasion for socially constructing an accountable self and a world in which accountability is expected. We argue that the narrative mode of cognition is inherent in both the formal and informal organization.

By considering the importance of narrative as a mode of cognition we highlight the difference between 'talking' in Roberts' depiction of socializing and 'telling' in our understanding of it. If socializing were just talk, it would not, in our opinion, be a source of accountability. In its best sense, to talk is to put ideas into words and express them to others. But in its full sense, to talk is merely to speak, often trivially in chatter. Talking can have a haphazard quality. It is the expression of the speaker – the making of noise while putting a statement out into the world – irrespective of content or context. 'Talk is the medium through which a mindless routine is expressed and unfolds' (Weick, 1983: 25).

'To tell' through narration includes the noiseful act of talking, but adds to it an awareness that the speaker is relating things in an order that is meaningful. 'To tell' is to make a report on a situation, past or future, that implies a *teller* who is responsible for revealing or making known a particular explanation of events. 'To tell' also implies another (who could be the teller as a self) who is being instructed or informed through the telling. As MacIntyre (1984) reminds us, we cannot 'tell about' the present. When we narrativize we are telling about a sequence of events, along with the characters, intentions, and context that make them plausible, believable and meaningful. 'Telling', then, is a bringing of the past or the future into the present. 'Talk', if it is not also a narration, is only located in the present.

If a responsible self is to be possible at all, it will of necessity be a narrating self. A responsible self requires a meaningful ordering of experience into events which follow one another and a recognition of agents who are intentional and capable of creating and recounting such experience. A central point for us is that narrative is not only a form of expression but is also a mode of cognition. We argue that it is not the act of telling *per se* that makes socializing forms of accountability possible, rather it is the narrative mode of cognition. This mode of cognition has consistently been undervalued and even ignored in cognitive psychology in comparison to the paradigmatic mode (Bruner, 1986; 1990). The paradigmatic mode of cognition which is synonymous with an abstract, theoretical view of the world, is taken to be *the* mode of cognition not only in science and technology, but in all forms of human reasoning.

Narrative and paradigmatic modes of cognition

Jerome Bruner (1986, 1990) argues that the discipline of cognitive psychology has adopted a paradigmatic model of cognition to the virtual exclusion of all others. The success of this image of cognition is overwhelming, saturating not only the cognitive sciences, but extending through other social sciences and our everyday understanding of cognition as well. This dominant model views cognition as an information processing phenomenon in which concepts are coded in memory and manipulated by cognitive operators. Situations are represented as concepts in a problem space and thinking about them is depicted as movement within the problem space by means of heuristics or rational analytic procedures, making computations, comparisons and substitutions in a form of scientific reasoning.

Bruner's own early research helped to establish the dominance of the paradigmatic mode of cognition. Now, having contributed to the creation of this dominant and successful view of cognition, Bruner argues that its dominance has suppressed recognition and study of another, perhaps even more powerful and universal mode of cognition, the narrative mode. In the narrative mode of cognition, we selectively isolate events in our experience, populate the events with actors who have particular histories, motivations and intentions, and tell stories by setting the events and actors in a meaningful sequence. Narrating our experience in order to make sense of ourselves and the world we live in, is a ubiquitous but consistently ignored mode of cognition.

Carol Gilligan (1982) provides an insightful example of how the calculative, paradigmatic mode of cognition establishes itself as the only officially recognized one, even in such 'unscientific' issues as morality. She presents a beautiful analysis of how one 11 year old boy (Jake) and one 11 year old girl (Amy) answer questions from Kohlberg's highly paradigmatic instrument for measuring moral development. In one moral dilemma they are asked to consider Heinz who cannot afford to buy the drugs required to save his wife's life. They are asked, 'should Heinz steal the drug?'

Jake is clear from the outset that the man, Heinz, should steal the drug because the value of a human life is greater than that of property. As Kohlberg intended, Jake brings the dilemma into a hierarchical constellation of rights and responsibilities, which allows him to resolve it with deductive logic. The moral dilemma is thus reduced to a mathematical equation, and Jake scores well on Kohlberg's six-stage model of moral development: he is rated between stage 3 and 4.

Unlike Jake, Amy is unsure of what Heinz should do. Her replies seem evasive:

> 'I think there might be another way besides stealing it, like if he could borrow the money or make a loan or something, but he really should not steal the drug – but his wife should not die either' (p. 28).

When asked why he should not steal the drug, it becomes evident that Amy does not frame the dilemma as a hierarchy of values subject to calculation the way Jake did. Instead she reasons by narrating the possibilities for the unfolding relationship between Heinz and his wife:

> 'If he stole the drug, he might save his wife then, but if he did he might have to go to jail, and then his wife might get sicker again, and he couldn't get more of the drug, and it might not be good. So, they should really just talk it out and find some other way to make the money' (p. 28).

Gilligan highlights that Amy sees 'in the dilemma not a math problem with humans but a *narrative* of relationships that extends over time' (p. 28, emphasis added). She contructs a world populated with a network of connected people rather than a hierarchy of people standing alone. This precludes her from setting up the dilemma according to Kohlberg's paradigmatically inspired theory. Instead she tries to reconstruct the world by writing new scenes into the scenario. The interviewer, in an attempt to assess Amy's moral maturity, repeats the questions. Amy is just not giving an acceptable answer. The stories she uses to explain her reasoning are not codable within Kohlberg's measurement instrument. Eventually Amy loses her confidence and when asked yet again why Heinz should not steal the drug, she simply says 'Because it is not right'. The response finally fits one of Kohlberg's categories and she falls between stage two and three, clearly below Jake's superior 'moral reasoning'.

Modes of cognition and the construction of accountability and self

The main difference between the narrative and the paradigmatic mode of cognition can be traced to their organizing principles. Whereas the paradigmatic mode uses space as the primary dimension for organizing human experience, the narrative mode relies on time as an organizing principle. Even though time and space are metaphorically entangled with one another, there are marked differences in the way each can be used to guide our thinking in the world.

Accountability in its calculative form exemplifies the paradigmatic mode of cognition, representing situations as abstract constructs in a problem space. The paradigmatic mode reduces a problem space into an established set of factors or variables (Abbott, 1992; Abell, 1987). A chart of accounts is an example of the paradigmatic mode of organizing experience, with a hierarchical categorization scheme used to classify and record officially recognized events. Accounting periods are a further example of the paradigmatic roots of accounting: metering time into standardized variables represents a spatialization of time.

The treatment of time in narrative is vastly different. First, narrative does not adhere to artificial boundaries such as accounting periods. Instead it imposes its own boundaries of beginning, middle and end on a set of events. These time markers are specific to and contingent on the situation in which the narrativized events occurred. The beginning and ending are important elements in constructing a bracketed unit of time in which events can be composed into a coherent whole. Significance of individual actions and events are attributed based on their contribution to the plot. It is within this whole that accountability can be assessed. Second, narrative time varies in duration. A one second 'moment' in reality may be so central to the story that it is drawn out in a narrative, whereas a long period in which nothing interesting happens is glossed over. Third, the sequence of events as they are presented in the story does not have to correspond to the order in which they occurred in reality. It is up to the listener to assemble the events into a sensible sequence.

The different ways that paradigmatic and narrative modes of cognition use time and space is significant to the construction of self through accountability. The paradigmatic self is characterized by separation from others, segmentation and calculation. It is the calculating and strategizing self (Boland, 1994; Miller and O'Leary, 1987) that compares and contrasts itself against the norm. It is the self that is compartmentalized into established, commodified categories such as skills and traits which are used to assess net worth. Paradigmatic modes of accountability thus 'spatialize' and disperse the self. They provide an atemporal snapshot through which the self presents its face (Roberts, 1991).

The image that is reflected in the narrative mode of accountability, in contrast, is that of a self on a stage, acting out a scene. The self is cast as a character that rehearses possible courses of actions and reacts to other characters in the scene. As a character moving through time and space, the self makes its identity known. Besides having many paths which the self can follow, there are also multiple characters into which the self can cast itself. The 'Now Self' is thus the convergence of a host of possible past and future selves. These include desirable possible selves such as the rich self and the hero, or dreaded possible selves such as the bag lady and alcoholic self (Markus & Nurius, 1986: 954). In the narrative mode of cognition we can play with these possible selves, try them out by stepping into their shoes. The image of the self that emerges from the narrative mode of accountability is that of a complex of dialectically integrated possible selves.

Both narrative and paradigmatic modes of cognition 'falsify' the world by portraying it in very particular ways. Both modes, in their own way, punctuate experience as separate events in the world which are discrete and without compelling or required order (MacIntyre, 1984: 214). The beginning-middle-end structure which story-telling imposes on events, gives them a sense of wholeness, completeness and closure. Lyotard (1984) thus criticizes narratives, particularly meta-narratives, for conveying a teleological ideology of everything having its time and place. Also, the story's beginning and end indicates a moral choice (White, 1981). Seemingly unrelated incidences are given significance with respect to one another and the plot when they are brought into a chrono-logical relationship. Narrative chronology implies causality for a subsequent event and turns the prior one into a cause (Polkinghorne, 1988: 50). Narrative causal structure thus takes the form of 'first x, then y' (Bruner, 1986), where y is the consequence of x. Thus even 'true stories' are fictitious, not only because they highlight only those experiences that contribute to the plot, but also because of the implied causal nature of the relationship between events.

Paradigmatic representations, on the other hand, make a strong pretence that they correspond to reality and represent truth. Only one paradigmatic representation can exist at a point in time (Kuhn, 1970). This implies that a paradigmatic representation uniquely defines reality, and that the veracity of events as represented in the paradigmatic scheme of categorization cannot be called into question without challenging its entire apparatus of paradigmatic framing. Representations of events are deemed a mere translation of reality. The paradigmatic mode justifies its claims to truth by appeals to laws of nature or law-like regularities reflected in its representational space. It applies the principle of accumulation by using the rules of formal logic to prove a statement, linking it cumulatively to other statements (Polkinghorne, 1988).

Stories, in contrast, are on their face understood as meaningful reconstructions of the world. As such they are not provable by standards of analytic and cumulative logic and they demonstrate 'the type of reasoning that understands synoptically the meaning of a whole, seeing it as a dialectic integration of its parts' (Polkinghorne, 1988: 35). Their verisimilitude is thus judged on the coherence of the plot and the believability of the characters. The narrator's appeal to 'coherence systems' (Linde, 1993) such as common sense and other belief systems shared by the listeners or readers, indicates that stories are anchored in a culture. The only 'law' that can be considered outside the situatedness of the narrative, is the moral of the story. However, the moral can only be understood in the context of a culture. And even there, it is the narrative which in a sense 'proves' the moral of the story. Plausibility and believability in a possible world constructed in part by the story itself, are the basis for truth in the narrative mode. Unlike the paradigmatic mode, narrative cannot step outside of itself to corroborate its truth claims (Lyotard, 1984).

The function of narrative is to forge a link between the ordinary and the exceptional, i.e. the canonical and non-canonical. In the absence of an unexpected element or an odd event to induce a sense of trouble, people see no need to narrativize and repair the meaning of their world. To illustrate this point, Bruner (1990) uses the example of children who cannot narrativize when asked to explain why a girl is happy at her birthday party. However, they construct elaborate stories to explain why the same girl was sad at her party. In giving reasons for the girl's sadness, one child suggests that she had forgotten her birthday and did not have a dress to wear. People thus rely on the narrative mode of cognition in order to deal with anomalous events that violate the canons of normal behaviour. They use it to construct an imaginary or 'possible' world in which such behaviour is canonical (Bruner, 1986).

By making the exceptional accessible through the creation of a scenario in which it makes sense, narrative not only maintains the canonical world but also delineates the boundary between the canonical and non-canonical. It thus serves as the vehicle for establishing and repairing culture and the moral order. Because telling a story inevitably involves the isolation of significant events, the recognition of trouble, the restoration of the canonical, and the construction of plausible worlds and selves, telling a story invariably means taking a moral stance (White, 1981). Narrativizing our experience is the vehicle for constructing and maintaining the self: the narrator's as well as the listener's. The distinction between narrator and listener is blurred in the telling of a story because the narrator listens to himself and the listener reads meaning into the story, i.e. subjunctivizes the events.

An important characteristic of narrative as a literary genre is that narrators voice their perspective on the actions and intentions of the characters in the story, while calling upon actors to speak in their own voice (Abrams, 1988: 72). Narrative is therefore not distant and voiceless like the paradigmatic mode of thought. In a narrative mode of accountability, narrators make themselves visible, whereas paradigmatic accountability relies on remaining invisible, i.e. it sees without being seen.

Having dichotomized the two modes of cognition, we now need to pay some attention to their interrelationship. Derrida's (1981) concept of *différance* highlights for us that in an orthogonal pair of bipolar opposites, difference also implies deference. Until now we have made the point that the narrative mode of cognition defers to the paradigmatic mode. In its role as a *supplement* to the paradigmatic mode of cognition narrative is seen as having value to the extent that it serves the primary, paradigmatic mode. Lyotard (1984) illustrates this relationship between the two modes of cognition by highlighting that scientific practice does not recognize narrative knowledge as valid, even though it relies on narrative to justify and legitimate its truth claims. According to the rules of science, 'narratives are fables, myths, legends, fit only for women and children' (Lyotard, 1984: 27).

The narrative and the paradigmatic mode of explaining phenomena are therefore intertwined and inseparable (Lyotard, 1984). McCloskey (1990b) presents examples of how scientists use stories to explain their theories and theories to explain their stories. Similarly, Chatman (1990) argues that stories are used in service of arguments, and arguments in service of stories. A fable, for instance, is a narrative, but its narration is at the service of a moral. A moral is an argument, that applies an atemporal if-then logic.

These examples are an important reminder that we should not be unnecessarily dualistic in our conceptualization of narrative and paradigmatic modes of account-ability. Rather than focusing on the difference between narrative and paradigmatic ways of knowing, we will investigate how the two are necessarily used together both in the formal and informal organization in constructing accounts and accountable selves.

New technologies of organizing make different sources of accountability visible

Technology plays a significant role in enabling and constraining cognitive function. Writing technology marked the beginning of analytic and abstract thinking (Ong, 1982) thereby facilitating the paradigmatic mode of thought. The printing press was another revolutionary technology. It served as the vehicle for 'Enlightenment Thought' and was thus central to the development of modern science (Eisenstein, 1986). Our proposition that group technology has the capacity to re-establish the narrative basis of accountability in organizations seems paradoxical in light of Ong's (1982) and Eisenstein's (1986) findings. Would we not expect groupware which replaces face-to-face talking with remote writing, to further reduce the narrative content in communication? We believe this is not the case because, unlike accounting information systems, group technologies do not act as conduits that collect, process and distribute data. Instead they provide a medium for conducting group processes in which group members create and distribute information among themselves. Group information technologies are not so much computational as communicational, providing formal channels for information sharing.

Groupware is a new class of information technology that includes applications ranging from group decision support systems to workflow automation systems (Briggs and Nunamaker, 1994: 61). In order to focus this discussion, we will use Lotus Notes, a groupware product generally considered to define this class of information technology (Holtham, 1994), as an exemplar. This is expedient also because the empirical examples we will use to illustrate how narrative manifests itself as a mode of accountability in a groupware-mediated discussion, are taken from a Lotus Notes document database.

Notes claims to support group work by enhancing the communication between the members of a team, and by improving information accessibility (Briggs and Nunamaker, 1994: 71). To achieve this, Lotus Notes provides both electronic mail and advanced bulletin boards referred to as document databases. These document databases include features and search capabilities typical of databases, and are used to store documents related to the group's tasks, e.g. meeting agendas, minutes and work assignments, but they can also serve as a place for discussing ideas. For this reason, they are also referred to as discussion databases.

There are two features of groupware that are central to our argument that groupware elevates the narrative mode of accountability. The first is that groupware supports unstructured textual communication that permits authors to express themselves in their own voice. Information is considered to be contained in a document rather than in a structured record. This is an improvement over the technologies typically used in accounting and management information systems which only deal with structured information: data, records and files. The second is that groupware can overcome both temporal and spatial barriers. This is an improvement over face-to-face communication because people do not have to be in the same place at the same time in order to socialize. Social barriers are removed too, as social presence is reduced (Sproull and

Kiesler, 1991). Furthermore, an electronic conversation is not as ephemeral as its face-to-face counterpart. It is made immutable and mobile (Latour, 1990) and therefore more accessible and visible across spatial, temporal and social barriers. Groupware thus appears to be a hybrid technology that bridges the gap between the formal and informal systems of accountability. It is a formal communicaton channel that has the capability of transmitting and storing informal conversations.

The interplay of narrative and paradigmatic modes of cognition in a groupware database

We will now use the example of an electronic discussion in a Lotus Notes groupware system to explore the themes of narrative forms of accountability, visibility and the construction of self in a concrete setting. In 1993, a large American insurance company specializing in automobile insurance, made the decision to implement Lotus Notes company-wide. The company operates throughout the United States and Canada. Since every state has different laws concerning auto insurance, each division offered slightly different products and operated in individualistic ways. The organization was several years into a re-engineering effort to standardize both its processes and products across the divisions, when Lotus Notes was purchased to support such company-wide projects. The company's re-engineering effort was called the Product Alignment project. It required product managers from all divisions to agree on a common set of rules for the organization's insurance products. These rules would then be coded into software for policy quoting and writing to be distributed to the company's sales agents. We will use examples from this database to demonstrate how narrative accountability manifests itself in this network technology, and how the two modes of accountability are intertwined.

Below we analyse six messages from the Product Alignment database. We pick up this set of exchanges quite far into the Product Alignment process. Messages recounting the confusion resulting from different practices in different states, and of the visions for an orderly process and its attendant benefits have already been presented. Common rules have already been proposed and discussed. We enter the conversation as the team is summarizing a final statement of the driver assignment rule which states how multiple drivers and multiple cars are to be paired for an insurance cost quotation. There is a key person responsible for preparing the final statement of each rule, and S.A. has just entered the proposed final rule for driver assignment.

> *Message 1:*
> **Rule Number: 4**
> **Key Person: S.A.**
> **Rule Description: Driver assignment/FINAL**
>
> Policy premium is determined by assigning the highest rated driver to the highest rated vehicle, second highest driver to the second highest vehicle and so on. The highest rated driver refers to the operator whose age, sex, marital status and surcharges develop the highest premium. If there are more vehicles than drivers, rate each additional vehicle using a default class 'XX',

where rates are based on the lowest rated liability driver class available on the policy with zero points.

In this first message, S.A. states the rule in a way she believes accurately represents prior discussion. Befitting of a rule, it is an almost pure paradigmatic statement that conforms quite closely to the image of cognition as a movement through a problem space. Drivers and vehicles, with their official category descriptors are arranged in the problem space and the assignment of drivers to vehicles in order to calculate premium due is a programming logic for moving through the space: if x, then y, else z. The wording and form of the message is also paradigmatic, with formal sentence structures, an assertive tone and an abstract, impersonal voice.

Message 2:
Author: E.C.
Date: 09/08/93 09:44 AM

Comments at Sept 8–9 Evaluation

clarify rule to indicate that the lowest rated driver class on the policy (for liability) will be the one used for the default driver class. group agrees to use default driver class code 'XX'.

In the second message, we see the paradigmatic mode in evidence again, with an attempt to sharpen the categories and gain definitional precision as to what is meant by default driver class. Uncertainty in the rule statement of message one is thus reduced, which is highly valued in this information processing approach to problem solving. The message reveals how informality is evident in even this paradigmatic mode of group-ware usage, with no upper case letter denoting the first word of each sentence. The tone, however, remains distinctly paradigmatic with a strong voice of hierarchical oversight. E.C. is, in fact, the leader of the Product Alignment project and acts as the narrator of this database. His 'Sept 8–9 Evaluation' touched all the rules that were defined during the Product Alignment effort. His is the official voice, giving sanction to each rule. This message signifies closure of the group's effort to define the driver assignment rule. The discussion is now officially over; at least that is how it would appear from within a paradigmatic mode of cognition. But in the next message, we see the narrative mode of cognition employed to reopen a search for meaning in this rule.

Message 3:
Author: R.C.
Date: 09/13/93 01:15 PM

Highest to highest, Not

Our rules say highest driver to highest vehicle, but what we calculate is highest total premium for the policy. These two can be different, here's an example:

2 cars, 2 drivers.
1 young driver with a bad record.
1 mid-aged driver (say a widowed woman) with a good record.
One car with liability only, symbol 80.

One car with full coverage, symbol 60.
Assume symbol 80 has slightly higher factors (for liability).

In this case 'highest to highest' would probably put the kid on the symbol 80 vehicle. We all know the highest policy premium occurs when the kid is on the full coverage vehicle, which is the way we do it.

Over the years we've come to understand highest-to-highest as meaning the 'highest total premium for a policy by aligning drivers and vehicles'.

In message three, the supposedly closed issue of driver assignment is reopened with a story. The narrative mode of cognition easily disturbs the pristine, rule-based logic that had been asserted through the paradigmatic mode in messages one and two. This message presents a story in scenario form in which the rule breaks down. Its mockingly humorous title acts as a signpost announcing a challenge to and imminent change in the direction of the discussion: 'Highest to highest, Not'. Message three uses narrative to open up a part of the rule that had been black boxed. Hierarchical authority in the process of rule formulation is therefore undermined, and the paradigmatically-formulated claims in messages one and two are undone.

Message three employs numerous narrative strategies. The scenario is presented in a staccato, point by point style, but clearly operates as a story with characters, expected future behaviours, and a moral. It is through our subjunctivizing into the story fragments that the scenario becomes a narrative. The message presents a scene with two characters on stage: the kid with a bad driving record and the middle-aged widow with a good driving record. We can see them in front of us. Even though the author makes no reference to the gender of 'the kid', we all know that he is male. He is wearing torn jeans and his baseball cap back-to-front. He drives recklessly at high speed while his car is vibrating to the beat of heavy metal playing full blast. He is the epitome of a high insurance risk. The female character, on the other hand, represents reason. She is wearing sensible shoes and her hair is efficiently arranged in a neat bun. We feel sympathy for her, not only because she has lost her husband but also because she is overwhelmed by her hooligan son.

'We all know' these characters; 'we all can tell' who is good and who is bad; 'we all know' whose side we are on. This scenario draws on a shared culture, common sense and an understanding of canonicality to make its point. Message three is a concise example of how narrative draws its authority from culture and at the same time repairs and constructs that culture. The rule as stated in message one and two represents theory. The story as stated in message three is the organization's culture. When rule and culture clash, culture wins. Culture, with its basic questions of identity and morality, is the dominant order and rule must yield to it. If the rule is non-canonical, a repair of culture means a change in the rule.

The story is used to highlight two instances of non-canonical behaviour. The first relates to how the proposed rule for driver assignment contradicts the firm's current practices. The second relates to how organization practice has consistently (and knowingly) reinterpreted rules containing 'highest-to-highest' clauses to mean 'highest premium'. What 'we all know' are the practices. The practices of 'what we do' constitutes 'who we are' and in that sense transform an abstract rule making exercise into a visceral question of identity and self. Although the narrative in this message hints at a moral dilemma, it does not draw a conclusion. This invites readers to reach their own resolution of the story. As we will see in subsequent messages, the narrative succeeds in drawing other voices out. Narrative keeps the conversation going and therefore differs substantially from the paradigmatic mode of cognition which tries to close discussions down and seal the black box.

Message 4:
Author: C.C.
Date: 09/16/93 12:08 PM

Consistency

How we can have a 'final' rule that does not conform to our practice? Are we affirming the rule and planning to change our alignment algorithm; or have we decided to file the rule and await a market conduct audit to demonstrate that we are not conforming to our filed rules?

Message four is a direct response to the invitation of the previous message, and extends the use of a narrative mode of cognition. The author is obviously moved by the story of message three and his intention is to move others. As part of the author's effort to raise the consciousness of other participants, he extends the moral dilemma that lies compressed in the open-ended and staccato-like narrative of message three. Yet he does this without making explicit the moral of the story. Using the narrative style of a serial, the author poses alternative paths or story lines that the initial scenario could follow: the organization could continue along its immoral path of non-compliance with its own rules and not take the Product Alignment effort seriously, or they could follow the intent of the re-engineering effort and change either the rules or the organization's operations. Which of these possibilities will the story follow?

Instead of taking a lecturing, overtly moralizing stance by speaking in an 'I think you should . . . ' tone, the author adopts the role of an impartial narrator who stands outside the scenario and tries to point out the contradictions that he observes. Even though he uses 'we', a pronoun that includes him, the author of this message engages the 'we' to distance himself from the people he is actually addressing. The author is thus hiding the agentic 'I' in the message, as well as the 'you' towards whom it is addressed. The 'we' in this case, is a narrative convention which 'draws the reader into complicity, to participate as something more than an audience' (Harré, 1990: 95).

By hiding himself this way, the author brings the readers centre stage and challenges them to take a moral stand in the narrative that is their life. The story of messages three and four is at a crisis point, raising fundamental questions of self and accountability. Rules do not conform to practice – how do we live this story in a way that repairs our culture and identity? This is a crisis of accountability – how will they make an account of these events and how will they be able to be held accountable in future?

Message 5:
Author: J.D.
Date: 10/03/93 01:11 PM

Highest to Highest

I concur with some of the discussion on this point, and would suggest we address this with some sense of urgency.

This is a problem on several fronts.

1. The major issue in my viewpoint is that we don't operate as we describe ourselves: to regulators, agents, and consumers. Although there is not practical regulatory exposure (because of the impossibility in defining a priori the highest rated operator), it could cause some embarrassment, and lead to higher costs where agents receive quotes in manners other than through our automated methods.

2. The second issue is looming. Research has indicated that consumers would like to receive 'menu quotes', or the ability to choose limits and deductibles based upon the associated costs. Our agent research into a better system has indicated exactly the same thing (in fact, this was the most popular enhancement), and last our National Account standard and preferred partners all operate this way. Given our current assignment methodology, it is impossible for us to do this on paper, because changing limits or deductibles possibly effects assignment. It is even difficult from a practical standpoint in an automated environment; an agent cannot describe a fixed savings based upon a menu option, because the act of selecting options will influence subsequent driver assignment.
   I would suggest we define practically, and simply, the concept highest rated driver, and not vary it based upon coverage selections. We are therefore in sync with our external communication on this issue, and it allows us the ability to provide menu option quoting. Recognizing the downside is some erosion in rate for sure, but I would guess also less bias away from multi-vehicle full coverage risks, and lower operational expenses.

Message five is a response to the call to take a stand on the moral dilemma identified by the narratives of three and four. However, the author of this message is experiencing difficulty in speaking in his own voice. Even though the author boldly starts the message with 'I', the I-character's actions are tentative and submissive, e.g. 'I concur' and 'I would suggest'. There is a sense that the small 'I' cannot stand its ground in the face of the big 'we', resulting in the 'I' deferring itself to the hierarchical nature of the Product Alignment effort.

This message has both narrative and paradigmatic qualities, again illustrating the author's difficulty in positioning himself. In the opening statement, the author is able to declare this issue to be one deserving 'some sense of urgency'. This kind of declaration is not open to individual team members within a strictly paradigmatic mode. Yet, with group information technologies and the narrative modes of cognition they include, we have seen issues of morality, identity and now urgency all being explored through formal organizational channels.

In the first part of this message, the author poses a paradigmatic answer to the question of meaning posed in messages three and four. Recognizing the absence of significant regulatory exposure, he weighs the cost of 'embarrassment' of not operating 'as we describe ourselves' and declares the cost too great. Then, by animating the consumer and the sales agents, he lets them have a voice in this discussion. By posing an alternative practice of policy sales through menu selection, the author is employing a narrative strategy which raises a question of self. He goes beyond the 'we all know' references to culture writ large, and narrates the face-to-face interaction of an agent with a customer – how the agent as a self wants to live that interaction. We also catch a glimpse of the author's self when he takes a stand on the moral issue at hand: he prefers to operate in a way that the organization is not 'misrepresenting' its operations, even if this might mean 'some erosion in rate'.

In the second part of the message, the author blends narrative and paradigmatic modes. He declares the 'menu quotes' issue to be 'looming', framing it as a possible world he is about to explore. The author then employs a paradigmatic process of logical deduction to argue the impossibility of matching highest rated driver to highest premium car in the kind of menu selection world those consumers and agents desire. He relies on allies like 'research' and the customer-agent relationship to accumulate support for his claims. The conclusion that results from the paradigmatic analysis of the problem, results in a new, 'simplified', general rule.

Message 6:
Author C.O.
Date: 10/05/93 02:24 PM

Response to J.D.

Just wanted to share a little C[ommercial] V[ehicles] experience on this same issue. We, too, had wavered back and forth on the 'best' way to assign drivers. Despite some strong opinions that 'highest premium' was the way to go, we originally decided to go with 'highest driver to highest liability vehicle' logic, thinking it was easier to explain, programme, etc.

However, we ended up changing our logic on this a couple of months ago, back to highest total premium. In our case, we found that it was a common scenario for two vehicles to have identical liability rates, so that the quoting system then just assigned the first listed driver to the first listed vehicle in this 'tie' situation. However, when the app[lication] was sent in and processed we had no guarantee that the order of the vehicles/drivers was the same and often ended up with different driver assignments. This unforeseen problem, when added to the lost premium costs (which for C[ommercial] V[ehicles] can be significant with high-valued trucks with phys[ical] dam[age]), swung our thinking back to 'highest total premium'. Incidentally, I'm unaware of any problems we've ever experienced from a regulatory standpoint when filling a highest total premium rule.

This message is another example of how the narrative mode of cognition can keep an issue open and alive in conversation. As in message three, this message is used to challenge the closure that the paradigmatic mode of cognition just tried to impose. In it, C.O. responds directly to the paradigmatic logic employed by J.D. in message five. Notice the narrative mode throughout this message, beginning with his opening rhetorical move. C.O., in a sort of down-home neighbour-over-the-fence fashion says 'Just wanted to share a little C[ommercial] V[ehicles] experience . . .' He then puts himself and his group into the same situation J.D. is in. They, too, 'had wavered back and forth' and came to just the same conclusion as J.D. This is as if to say, 'we have lived your story and know exactly what you are thinking,' which should make his counter narrative all the more compelling and persuasive.

This message contains the three event features of a 'minimal story' (McCloskey, 1990a: 25) which includes a beginning stative event, an active event and an ending stative event that is the inverse of the first. The second event is regarded as the cause of the third. The story expressed in message six is one of transformation from a state in which the 'highest-to-highest' rule was adopted to a state in which the inverse of that rule, i.e. the 'highest-premium' rule, was attained.

This message, of course, is not the end of the exchange and we can expect the mix of narrative and paradigmatic cognition to continue through discussion of this and other rules. The important point for us is the way this mixture of cognitive modes which we take to parallel Roberts (1991) hierarchic and social forms of accountability are thoroughly intertwined and being displayed within the formal organization's information system. Similarly, the calculative practices and calculable spaces of the firm's accounting system that reflects these rules, will importantly have been constructed through the narratives they make within this same formal information system.

Concluding remarks

In this paper we have built upon Roberts' (1991) distinction between hierarchical and socializing forms of accountability, and have argued that the story-telling and calculating roots of *account* are the generative basis of these two forms of accountability. The two faces of giving an *account* parallel cognitive functioning generally, as seen in Bruner's (1986; 1990) discussion of the two basic modes of human cognition, the narrative and the paradigmatic. We propose that it is these cognitive modes that are the source of hierarchical and socializing forms of accountability, and not the formal accounting systems and the informal face-to-face talk of an organization as Roberts suggests. It is the ability to tell, i.e. to narrate events in a meaningful order, rather than the ability to talk, i.e. to express (maybe trivially) in spoken words, that makes a responsible self and socializing forms of accountability possible. The paradigmatic and narrative modes of cognition are evident in both the formal and the informal aspects of an organization.

To illustrate the narrative and paradigmatic sources of accountability we analysed six messages posted on a groupware system's discussion database. By using a groupware mediated discussion for our example, we move beyond Roberts' discussion of ideal types and present an empirical example of how network technology brings the ephemeral realm of informal face-to-face interactions into the formal channels of organizational communication. Narrative accounts are thus made more visible, immutable and mobile. This gives us reason to believe that networked group technologies which facilitate co-operative work and distributed cognition, hold the potential of elevating the much undervalued and frequently ignored narrative mode of accountability to a more equitable status with its paradigmatic counterpart. Our analysis of the electronic messages provides support for this contention.

These messages demonstrate a complex mix of both the narrative and paradigmatic mode of thought, indicating that the two are deeply intertwined and interdependent. A dynamic tension between the two modes of cognition is evident. The paradigmatic mode is employed for closing and black-boxing issues, and the narrative mode serves to reopen the same issues, keeping the conversation and the controversy alive. Our study looked only at written messages in a group technology, but Solli and Jönsson (*forthcoming*) made a similar observation in their studies of face-to-face management meetings. They found that in these meetings, participants recounted concrete case examples indicative of the narrative mode of thought to test how paradigmatically constructed rules would work. The narrative quality of those concrete examples presupposed an intricate understanding of the current practices and culture, and created a possible world in which the newly-formulated rules would operate. The test cases were used to highlight inconsistencies in the paradigmatic model of the world and to explore conflicting interpretations of the model.

In our examples we too observed that the narrative mode of cognition was used to explore exceptions and anomalies in order to introduce issues of morality into decision making. Narrative was thus used to delineate and restore canonicality in an organizational culture. We also saw how the narrative mode presents individuals with the opportunity to speak in the I-voice and thereby take a stand on moral matters. Through the narrative mode of cognition, participants in a discussion become accountable selves. Employing both the narrative and the paradigmatic modes of cognition, organizational members construct their system of accountability and also operate within it. Hierarchical and socializing forms of accountability are therefore not generated by the formal and informal aspects of the organization, but by the different modes of cognition that are employed in both of those aspects.

Acknowledgements

The authors gratefully acknowledge helpful comments by Rolland Munro in developing this manuscript.

References

Abbott, A. (1992) From Causes to Events. *Sociological Methods & Research*, **20**(4), pp. 428–55.

Abell, P. (1987) *The Syntax of Social Life: The Theory and Method of Comparative Narratives*, Clarendon Press, Oxford.

Abrams, M.H. (1988) *A Glossary of Literary Terms*, 5th edn, Holt, Rinehart & Winston, Orlando

Boland, R.J. (1979) Control, Causality and Information Systems Requirements. *Accounting, Organizations and Society*, **4**(4), pp. 259–72.

Boland, R.J. and Pondy, L.R. (1986) The Micro Dynamics of a Budget-Cutting Process: Modes, Models and Structure. *Accounting, Organizations and Society*, **11**(4/5) pp. 403–22.

Boland, R.J. (1993) Accounting and the Interpretive Act. *Accounting, Organizations and Society*, **18**(2/3), pp. 125–46.

Boland, R.J. (1994) Identity, Economy and Morality in The Rise of Silas Lapham, in *Good Novels, Better Management: Reading Organizational Realities*, (eds B. Czarniawska-Joerges and P. Guillet de Monthoux) Harwood Academic Publishers, Switzerland, pp. 115–37.

Briggs, R.O. and Nunamaker, J.F. (1994) Getting a Grip on Groupware, in *Groupware in the 21st Century: Computer Supported Cooperative Working toward the Millennium*, (ed P. Lloyd) Praeger, Westport, CT pp. 61–72.

Bruner, J. (1986) *Actual Minds, Possible Worlds*, Harvard University Press, Cambridge MA.

Bruner, J. (1990) *Acts of Meaning*, Harvard University Press, Cambridge, MA.

Derrida, J. (1981) *Positions*, Athlone Press, London.

Eisenstein, E. (1986) *Print Culture and Enlightenment Thought*, Rare Book Collection/University Library, University of North Carolina, Chapel Hill.

Giddens, A. (1979) *Central Problems in Social Theory*, Macmillan, London.

Gilligan, C. (1982) *In a Different Voice: Psychological Theory and Women's Development*, Harvard University Press, Cambridge, MA.

Garfinkel, H. (1967) *Studies in Ethnomethodology*, Prentice-Hall, Englewood Cliffs, NJ.

Harré, R. (1990) Some Narrative Conventions of Scientific Discourse, in *Narrative in Culture: The Uses of Storytelling in the Sciences, Philosophy, and Literature*, (ed C. Nash) Routledge, London pp. 81–101.

Holtman, C. (1994) Groupware: Its Past and Future, in *Groupware in the 21st Century: Computer Supported Cooperative Working toward the Millennium*, (ed P. Lloyd) Praeger, Westport, CT pp. 3–14.

Kerby, A.P. (1991) *Narrative and the Self*. Indiana University Press, Bloomington, IN.

Kuhn, T.S. (1970) *The Structure of Scientific Revolutions*, 2nd edn, University of Chicago Press, Chicago IL.

Latour, B. (1990) Drawing Things Together, in *Representation in Scientific Practice*, (eds M. Lynch and S. Woolgar) MIT Press, Cambridge, MA pp. 19–68.

Linde, C. (1993) *Life Stories: The Creation of Coherence*, Oxford University Press, New York.

Lyotard, J.F. (1984) *The Postmodern Condition: A Report on Knowledge*, University of Minnesota Press, Minneapolis.

Markus, H. and Nurius, P. (1986) Possible Selves. *American Psychologist*, **41**(9) pp. 954–69.

McCloskey, D. (1990a) *If You're so Smart: The Narrative of Economic Expertise*, University of Chicago Press, Chicago.

McCloskey, D. (1990b) Storytelling in Economics, in *Narrative in Culture: The Uses of Storytelling in the Sciences, Philosophy, and Literature*, (ed C. Nash) Routledge, London pp. 5–22.

MacIntyre, A. (1984) *After Virtue*, 2nd edn, Notre Dame, Indiana.

McGrath, J.E. and Hollingshead, A.B. (1994) *Groups Interacting with Technology: Ideas, Evidence, Issues and an Agenda*, Sage, Thousand Oaks, CA.

Miller, P. and O'Leary, T. (1987) Accounting and the Construction of the Governable Person. *Accounting, Organizations and Society*, **12** pp. 235–65.

Miller, P. (1992) Accounting and Objectivity: The Invention of Calculating Selves and Calculable Space. *Annals of Scholarship*, **9**(1/2) pp. 61–86.

Ong, W. (1982) *Orality and Literacy: The Technologizing of the Word*, Routledge, New York.

Polkinghorne, D.E. (1988) *Narrative Knowing and the Human Sciences*, State University of New York Press, Albany.

Ricoeur, P. (1984) *Time and Narrative*, University of Chicago Press, Chicago.

Roberts, J. and Scapens, R. (1985) Accounting Systems and Systems of Accountability – Understanding Accounting Practices in their Organizational Contexts. *Accounting, Organizations and Society*, **10**(4), pp. 443–56.

Roberts, J. (1991) The Possibilities of Accountability. *Accounting, Organizations and Society*, **16**(4) pp. 355–68.

Shotter, J. (1984) *Social Accountability and Selfhood*, Basil Blackwell, Oxford.

Sinclair, A. (1995) The Chameleon of Accountability: Forms and Discourses. *Accounting, Organizations and Society*, **20**(2/3) pp. 219–37.

Solli, R. and Jönsson, S. (1995) Housekeeping? Yes, but which House? *Scandinavian Journal of Management*, forthcoming.

Sproull, L. and Kiesler, S. (1991) *Connections: New Ways of Working in the Networked Organization*, MIT Press, Cambridge, MA.

Weick, K.E. (1983) Organizational Communication: Toward a Research Agenda, in *Communication and Organizations: An Interpretive Approach*, (eds L.L. Putnam and M.E. Pacanowsky) Sage, Beverly Hills pp. 13–29.

White, H. (1981) The Value of Narrativity in the Representation of Reality, in *On Narrative*, (ed W.J.T. Mitchell) University of Chicago Press, Chicago pp. 1–23.

Yates, J. and Orlikowski, W.J. (1992) Genres of Organizational Communication: A Structurational Approach to Studying Communication and Media. *Academy of Management Review*, **17**(2) pp. 299–326.

Part Two

Encounters in networks

The chapters in this section introduce a different unit of account, that of encounters in networks. The focus is on identity work in networks of membership. The authors acknowledge an indexicality that can take in the self, but only as one possible network among many. Instead, they foreground encounters, the moments in which participants are exchanging accounts.

In that this form of giving accounts often takes place in the mode of conversation, this arena is perhaps most familiar to readers. However, the focus of the chapters is not on accounts as a lens for studying interactions between 'individuals'. In ways already explained in Chapter 1, intertextuality offers possibilities for giving accounts that can be read in multiple ways. Multiple readings, far from seeming equivocal, create the opportunity to preserve multiple memberships, sometimes with unknown audiences. The analysis therefore foregrounds participants accounting to others, as putative members.

In Chapter 5, Kristian Kreiner is concerned to examine in what sense accountability may serve as a link between a participant and the group. He is also concerned to understand how the 'local scene of action relates to the wider organizational context' in ways that are provisional and partial. However, in setting out to reveal a central weakness of accountability models in cognitive psychology, he follows a quite different line. Against a literature that unproblematically asserts 'a focal actor whose action, decision, or judgement is being evaluated by others', Kreiner offers us an account of a critical incident in the formation of a European-wide project. In a surprising twist to the tale, one that vividly brings out the importance of recognizing a provisionality of membership that follows from the intertextuality to accounts, Kreiner demonstrates how notions of 'who is accounting to whom' can easily become turned upside down.

As with all the chapters in the book, the authors in this section are concerned with a possible domination of hierarchical forms of accountability over more lateral forms. In Chapter 6, Sten Jönsson openly contests the productiveness of the North American form of managerial capitalism. This, as recycled theoretically by Chandler in the US and by Channon in the UK, aligns accounts of organizational structure with a multi-divisional form. Drawing on his longitudinal study of experiments in a Swedish car manufacturer, Jönsson provides detailed examples of his thesis that identity is built by members keeping their accounts in line with the expectations of others. Of particular interest is the way in which Jönsson depicts 'trust' being extended: competence in one grouping of membership has an intertextuality that enables local participants to become spokespersons for 'external' contracting.

The final chapter in the section is provided by Simon Lilley. This analysis of the 'success' of information systems in a large European oil refinery again develops the section theme of accountability being mobilized in ways that link participants into groups, but provides a more machiavellian reading of the ways in which these links are literally created through a double translation process. First, managers at the refinery are translated into 'users' for the future systems that they have never requested. Second, as 'users', they are then translated into producers of the system, since they must specify the system they want. Lilley offers a meticulously detailed description of this process of a passing of the buck, one which also captures the cynicism, not only of the system designers, but also of the managers who are trapped into having to declare the systems a 'success'.

Running through all of these chapters is the theme of an alignment of accounts. This feature of accounts allows the authors to cover ground that is sometimes depicted as strategic conduct. As discussed earlier, participants can line up their accounts to bid for different forms of membership simultaneously. However, as Kreiner and Lilley show, such competencies can unexpectedly be turned against them. Further, any alignment of accounts may be entirely local and temporary, as both Jönsson and Kreiner show. Or become durable, as Jönsson and Lilley show.

5 Accountability on the move: the undecidable context of project formation

Kristian Kreiner

Abstract

The formation of European R&D projects provides us with an empirical scene for studying lateral (socializing) forms of accountability. The study reveals to us that acts and actors are only provisionally defined and that the assumed context of accountability changes dynamically. The conception of one focal actor being constrained by accountability in striving for the approval of some significant other leads to the realization that those significant others are themselves accountable and constrained in their evaluative response. Thus, accountability is not a unilateral exercise of power and authority, but rather a *mutual, dynamic relationship*, fuelled by actors' attempts to realign the various interests and redefine their bill of options. As in other strategic interactions, *timing* proves in this case to be crucial for the overall consequences of action.

Introduction

'Accountability', say Simonson and Nye (1992: 417), 'refers to the need to justify one's views and preferences to others . . . and to concerns about the evaluation of one's views and preferences by others.' Assuming that such concerns are in fact acted upon,

> accountability is a critical rule and norm enforcement mechanism: the social psychological link between individual decision-makers on the one hand and the social systems to which they belong on the other. The fact that people are accountable for their decisions is an implicit or explicit constraint upon all consequential acts they undertake'.
>
> (Tetlock, 1985: 307)

In this essay I will examine these ideas about accountability in an analysis of the formation of a cross-national R&D venture under the EUREKA programme.[1] My aim is, by means of this field study, to understand in what sense accountability may serve as a link between individual actors and their group, and thus, in what sense accountability constrains social action.

Generally accountability is conceptualized along the above-mentioned lines, but two distinct streams of accountability research can be identified in the literature. One stream has its roots in experimental cognitive psychology and is born on an interest in understanding how humans make choices and form judgements. The other stream of research has its roots in critical accounting and is concerned to widen understandings of economic reporting and surveillance systems.

The cognitive psychology research on accountability (here represented by Tetlock, 1985) aims to establish the significance of social settings for otherwise well-known cognitive processes. It portrays human actors as 'cognitive misers' who respond to the scene of action with a certain amount of mental laziness and inaptitude. When the awareness arises that judgements and choices are made in a social context, the actor turns into a politician and a strategist, fuelled by a desire to achieve approval and status (Tetlock, 1985, pp. 308–309). In controlled experiments it has been shown that the characteristics of such social contexts determine the complexity and quality of the cognitive processes preceding action. Thus, for example 'accountability to others of unknown views has been found in a number of studies to 'motivate' people to become more vigilant, complex, and self-critical information processors' (Tetlock, 1985: 314).

The other stream of research (here represented by Roberts, 1991) I refer to as 'critical accounting'. It has its roots in management accounting, but is highly critical of these roots. If there is a programme behind this research it appears to be to offer managers an alternative to traditional tools of economic surveillance and hierarchical control: 'The practical task is to recover accountability from the exclusive and apparently mesmeric grip of Accounting' (Roberts, 1991: 367). Thus, there is more to accountability than reporting systems, and there are other forms of accountability than the hierarchical one. The search for socializing (and lateral) forms of accountability is fuelled not only by ethical considerations, but also by concerns for the emerging 'new commercial agenda' that entails increased interdependence, new forms of belonging and affiliation, and the shift in focus from 'accountable for something' to 'accountable to somebody' (Munro and Hatherly, 1993). The visions for an alternative to hierarchical forms of accountability have been described in the following way:

> 'The routines of hierarchical accountability individualize, for they produce a nervous preoccupation with the image of the self as an object of use, which is either indifferent to others, or conceives of others only as competitors from whom one must differentiate oneself . . . The discussion of socializing forms of accountability suggest[s] that there exists a different experience of self and one's relation to others . . . A relative symmetry of power and face-to-face contact offer the possibility of a more complete recognition of self, the engagement of personal understanding and the challenging of others' views and expectations. Out of such relationships is built mutual understanding and ties of friendship, loyalty and reciprocal obligations; a sense both of individual difference and mutual dependence.
>
> (Roberts, 1991: 363)

The celebration of an 'emancipatory potential within lateral accountability' (Munro and Hatherly, 1993) is profound in this literature, but little trust in the realization of this emancipatory potential can be found. If Roberts' preconditions, in terms of a relative symmetry of power and face-to-face contact, cannot be established empirically, indeed the danger is real that 'lateral accountability will simply become subverted into an additional buttressing of hierarchy' (Munro and Hatherly, 1993: 387).

After discussing some of the special features of EUREKA projects as a 'decision-making environment', I will try to understand the socializing forms of accountability that present themselves in that particular local context. However, we need constantly to be aware that such local scenes of action relate to a wider organizational context. As Roberts (1991: 365) advises us,

> 'Socializing forms of accountability will always be limited to local contexts where there is a relative absence of asymmetries of power and the possibility of face-to-face interaction. These local contexts, however, are repeatedly subordinated to systems of hierarchical accountability sustained through the sanctions of power and money . . . '

Acknowledging the importance of the wider social context is not to accept that lateral accountability will necessarily be subordinated to surrounding systems of hierarchical accountability. Clearly, most of the understandings, obligations and resources that are mobilized in the local context will originate elsewhere. Often, I will claim, these sources are themselves 'local contexts' with more or less power asymmetry and face-to-face interaction. The aim is not to understand the local context by reducing it to some other, presumably already understood, logic. Rather, the aim is to see the present context as interwoven with other contexts, extending and exploiting previous relationships and, in the process of doing so, redefining the scene of action: for the focal, local context as well as for surrounding contexts governed by hierarchical and/or lateral accountability.

Specifically, I will develop two themes here on the applicability of accountability. Gradually, a first theme develops that it is difficult to establish what exactly is the object of accountability. The literature states (implicitly or explicitly) that there is a focal actor whose action, decision, or judgement is being evaluated by others. In practice, it is not so easy to determine who the actor is, what the conduct is, and whom are doing the evaluation. It seems that, in part, the action is 'constructed', evaluators mobilized and actors identified in the very process of accountability.

A second theme that evolves relates to the timing of accountability. The obvious time constraints of experimental laboratory research, and the highly institutionalized time structure of accounting, are not features of natural decision making environments, at least not in the form of EUREKA projects. The implications of the opportunity to negotiate *when* one is called to account for one's action, are manifold and somewhat surprising.

In drawing on my field study, the way in which the scene of action is structured and arranged will serve as an important indicator of the kinds of cognitive processes that we may ascribe to the actors involved. However, let me clarify from the outset that focusing on accountability as a constraint upon action should not make us forget all other types of constraints experienced in a practical setting. My interest is not to isolate the effect of accountability, but to see it in context with, and in interplay with, other types of concerns in the particular situation. The particular picture that emerges is that accountability is editing, formatting, organizing and re-aligning other types of concerns that actors bring to the situation. By being so edited and re-aligned these other concerns change in content and significance. As will become obvious later in our discussion, some such editing and re-aligning efforts are consciously designed and bring about strategically intended consequences, while other efforts seem to result in unintended and unanticipated consequences of sorts. The difference is not one of power and hierarchical position, but one of ability and luck in a strategic game in which each of the actors tries to enrol the others in his own plot. Enrolment is done willingly, if not always completely knowingly. A fitting way to label the dynamics is 'contribution pull' rather than 'power push'.[2]

The constant and strategic (re-)construction of the scene of action that adds dynamic and emergent features to the accountability phenomenon may prove to be specific to EUREKA as a scene of action. Eventually, we need to consider the general validity of the findings to other, less labile contexts.

EUREKA projects as context

As may already be known, EUREKA is a pan-European programme dedicated to the facilitation of cross-national and cross-organizational collaboration on market-near R&D. In the present context, we are less concerned with EUREKA as a programme, than with the individual EUREKA project. For a project to be notified as a EUREKA project, certain conditions must be met. Most important amongst these conditions are the following:

- the project must include partners from at least two different EUREKA countries.[3]
- the project task must be directed towards the development of some commercializable commodity or service.
- the project task must involve a considerable amount of original R&D effort.

The EUREKA project is, almost by definition, riddled with uncertainty: uncertainty stemming from cultural diversity, from unknown and unstable markets, and from the turbulence of technological development. EMRI[4], a longitudinal study of the progression and fate of a large number of EUREKA projects, further established that these projects come from extremely tumultuous parts of the economy. Thus, for example, close to 80% of the projects studied in EMRI were directly implicated in a merger or acquisition during the period of our study.

While also EUREKA projects come in great variety, it is generally true that the dominant managerial and organizational strategy in the face of such uncertainty was one of ensuring *resilience* (Kreiner, 1994). This was achieved by means of surprisingly loose project structures. Organizationally, the EUREKA projects were designed to entail as little mutual dependence between the partners as possible. The EMRI empirical findings can be summarized in this way (see Kreiner, 1994 for further details):

- planned exchange of personnel and equipment between the partners was almost non-existent.
- the total project work was broken down into *self-contained tasks*, so that each partner might perform and benefit from the EUREKA ventures even if partners should fail.

- in no case was there a delegation of authority over resources and staffing to the project.
- only in a few cases technical goals were defined jointly, and even then performance targets were very loose indeed.

Thus EUREKA projects provide an almost ideal opportunity for studying lateral accountability as it emerges between the loosely coupled participants. While participants remain formally within the structure of the host-organization and will be held accountable by their boss in the line-organization, within the project little emphasis on hierarchical accountability seemed to prevail. The absence of hierarchical accountability does not indicate that the EUREKA project would develop socializing forms of accountability. But according to our findings, they often do. No collaborative venture could succeed on the sole basis of the above-mentioned loose formal structure which is designed to maximize resilience rather than collaboration. In our study, the successful EUREKA projects were characterized by an unplanned, emerging and non-hierarchical structure with strong inter-personal commitments in the project group. It is not difficult to grasp the underlying logic of this combination of a loose formal structure with the development of strong inter-personal ties:

> 'Projects should be loosely structured in order to *survive [environmental turbulence] long enough* for *informal relationships and personal commitments* to develop as a foundation for *effective collaboration and interaction.*'
> (Kreiner, 1994: 12 – emphasis in the original)

The particular field study to be reported below was somewhat atypical, in the sense that social ties preceded the formation of the EUREKA project. However, that allows us to study accountability also at the stage of project formation. If the accountability literature tries to explain decisions, judgements and preferences, it is hard to imagine a more clear-cut decision than the one to form or join a project. We need to ascertain the existence of social ties amongst the actors and determine in what sense the decision is shaped by the concerns of approval and status within the group of actors. Success of a venture such as the EUREKA project depends on a form of collaboration that entails a mutual dependence far beyond the one regulated in formal contracts and agreements. The numerous contingencies and the immense uncertainty render hierarchy and formal structures relatively ineffective. These conditions seem to provide ideal opportunities for studying socializing forms of accountability. However, what do these forms look like, and how do they function?

Constituting the object of accountability

The concept of accountability grows out of the tradition of seeing individual judgement and behaviour determined by some underlying and preceding cognitive processes. In such cognitive processes a large part of the disciplinary power of accountancy resides. Relative to the critical accounting stream of research, the cognitive psychology studies are generally much more explicit about their assumptions regarding these processes and the ways in which they are influenced by the social setting. I will use the cognitive psychology account below to frame my discussion of an empirical case. However, I see no conflict between this account and the critical accounting research. In the latter case, these issues are simply not specified.

Human actor: information processor or politician?

Tetlock (1985) classifies the 'cognitive research programme' into two: one part which builds on an image of the human actor as an 'information processor', the other part building on an image of the human actor as a 'politician' or 'strategist'. The 'information processor' part is characterized by laboratory experiments that still (according to Tetlock, 1985) take a 'mentalist perspective' on the world, i.e. subscribe to the notion of the 'primacy of the cognitive structures and processes' (p. 300). In other words, it is assumed that people's knowledge about the world is 'mediated through these cognitive structures and processes' (p. 300). The 'information processor' part is further characterized by an 'individualist perspective', in the sense that the cognitive structures and processes are assumed to be independent of the context in which actual judgement and choice are exercised. The multitude of experimental results in this research programme add up to an image of people as 'cognitive misers', i.e.

> '[people] avoid mental procedures that require sustained attention, comprehension, or computing power . . . In brief, far from being maximizers – relentlessly searching for the best possible solutions to the problems confronting them – people seem to be chronic satisficers, frequently unwilling or unable to perform the demanding cognitive tasks that normative models specify as essential to good decision-making.'
>
> (Tetlock, 1985: 302)

The mentalist and individualist assumptions of the 'information processor' programme have been criticized and have been modified in subsequent research with the introduction of an actor with more strategic intentions. In Tetlock's words,

> 'the politician research programme begins where the cognitive research programme leaves off . . . the central objective of the politician research programme is to identify the behavioural strategies that people have developed for coping with fundamental or invariant features of natural decision environments (features likely to be present at least to some degree in all social and organizational settings).'
>
> (Tetlock 1985: 306)

One such 'fundamental or invariant' feature is the fact that judgement and choice are exercised in front of a real or imagined audience: an audience that may have expectations and beliefs concerning what judgements and choice should be made, and an audience that may react with sanctions (positive or negative) to the perceived virtues of the judgements and choices. Thus, the 'politician research programme' assumes that actors will reflect on who the audience is, what expectations the audience holds, and what sanctions the audience might level against the actor. In short, *'the accountability of conduct* is a universal problem of social life with which people must deal' (Tetlock, 1985: 309).

How accountability affects conduct is not immediately given. Actors' own aspirations need to be known before their response can be calculated. However, in the 'politician' research programme it is assumed that 'people are generally motivated to maintain the approval and respect of those to whom they are accountable' (Tetlock, 1985: 309).

I will bring these two hard core assumptions to bear on an empirical case study. The assumptions have, I believe, high immediate plausibility. However, the difficulties in applying them meaningfully to an empirical reality make them more functional in raising issues and questions than guiding the answers.

Empirical illustration[5]

Tom was said to have spilled his sherry when Eric told him about his new project. Tom was the uncrowned king of wastewater treatment and was in charge of the largest, most successful, and pace-setting firm in the industry. Even internationally, the firm was very well reputed. Why would the news about Eric's project so upset Tom?

It would immediately seem of little significance that Eric had agreed to do a project with Hans. After all, Eric was a university professor with a strong professional reputation and a huge international network of contacts and colleagues. His most celebrated scientific contributions fell within the area of biological wastewater treatment. Creating new projects was almost part of the daily order in these environments.

Tom and Eric had since many years enjoyed a quite symbiotic and close relationship. Eric had not only developed the technology that was used in the wastewater treatment plants designed and managed by Tom's firm. Eric had also educated well qualified engineers that had subsequently been hired by Tom. On the other hand, Tom provided Eric with access to the wastewater treatment plants which constituted a critical experimental facility for the continuous development of the technology of biological treatment. Thus, their collaboration had been highly successful for a long time and a conflict of interests was nowhere in sight: Tom pursued business opportunities and sought recognition amongst decision makers; Eric pursued academic interests and sought recognition in the local and international research community. Both of them were instrumental in the other's pursuit of success.

Hans was not personally known to either Tom or Eric. He came from a different country and represented a foreign, but well-known chemical company. Thus, while Tom and Eric owed each other 'everything', none of them owed Hans anything at all. Specifically, Eric was under no obligation to do a project with him.

We leave the case description for a moment to make a few observations. First of all, *if* Eric was seeking to achieve approval and status, surely it is not apparent that he got it. The spilled sherry is supposedly an unambiguous sign of disapproval – and there is no doubt that Eric knew disapproval was coming. Thus, in interpreting the motives of Eric we need to consider the following possibilities:

1 Eric was in fact motivated to seek approval and status, only Tom was not the significant other.
2 Eric was motivated by other things than approval and status, and chose to accept the costs of disapproval and conflict with Tom to pursue this.

It would indeed be unreasonable to claim that Tom was not a significant other to Eric. However, that does not rule out the possibility that Eric was in fact seeking the approval of some other significant other. If there are many alternative significant others that evaluate the conduct, then in each particular situation a choice needs to be made as to who are the *appropriate* significant others with whom one seeks approval and status. In that case, the question becomes what determines the alternatives and what motivates the choice amongst them.

The most obvious alternatives in the present case would be Tom and Hans. It would seem paradoxical if Eric were to seek the approval of the latter over and above Tom's. After all, Hans was a stranger to Eric and supposedly not a significant other in the first place. However, we may salvage the accountability perspective if we accept, with Mead, accountability also as a process internal to the self: 'Accountability does not . . . depend upon the perpetual presence of others for we can take over the attitudes of others towards us, so that accountability also becomes a process internal to the 'self' in the surveillance of the 'me' by 'I' (Roberts, 1991: 358). The interpretation that could be entertained is the one that Eric was in fact accountable to himself: that his identity[6] as a researcher forced him to accept Hans' invitation in spite of Tom's disapproval.

However, we may immediately observe that if we accept that Eric is simply enacting his identity as a researcher, then Tom's strong disapproval becomes the paradox. We would assume that such an identity is highly vested in, and was partly developed in the course of, their prior relationship, and not, as in this case, a cause of discontinuity. Alternatively, Eric could be instrumentally motivated by other things that were in conflict with the seeking of approval and status. We will return to this possibility when we know somewhat more about the case.

> The world of wastewater treatment is a quite divided one. There are two highly distinct ways of treating wastewater, one biological and the other one chemical. Differences in the composition of wastewater (in terms of pollutants and thus in definition of treatment objectives) provided a rationale for local specialization in one or the other type of treatment. However, as the pollution has increased everywhere and new stringent wastewater discharge standards are being introduced in many places, specialization must increasingly be understood as institutionalized patterns and the result of path-dependent competency development. Since a rigid reliance on only one of the techniques is no longer appropriate, these institutionalized patterns cover choices of primary versus supplementary treatment. One pattern is that wastewater treatment plants are designed to treat the water biologically, with a subsequent and supplementary chemical treatment. The alternative pattern is that the plants are designed to treat the water chemically, with a subsequent and supplementary biological treatment.
>
> Since both patterns may equally well reduce the pollutant residuals to acceptable standards, the choice between the two patterns is supposedly based on economic criteria. The biological-chemical pattern is expensive in terms of fixed capital, because the construction of huge tanks is necessary for the biological part. However, it is relatively inexpensive in terms of costs of operation because only small amounts of chemicals are required for the supplementary treatment. Conversely, the chemical-biological pattern is expensive in terms of chemicals, but since only a supplementary biological treatment is required, much smaller tanks and other facilities need to be constructed.

In natural environments where most parameters in the investment calculation are hard to assess and may change dynamically, it is only to be expected
that decisions are heavily influenced on the expert advice that can be
obtained. To the extent that such expertise is institutionalized locally, the
specialization in treatment patterns may be understandable.

The wastewater treatment on the home markets of Eric and Tom was
indeed very institutionalized. Local authorities would go to Tom for a design
of a new treatment plant because of his expertise in such matters. If in need
of an independent assessment of a plant design and its efficiency, these local
authorities would turn to Eric. In both cases, they would necessarily operate
within their field of experience and expertise, i.e. biological treatment. No
wonder that the market was dominated by the biological treatment technology.

This is not to say that there were no conflicting voices. Especially foreign
chemical producers were active in promoting a changing balance between the
biological and the chemical treatments. The commercial interests of these
companies were only too obvious, and their attempts to capture the market
were considered somewhat dubious in the atmosphere of professional expertise
(even science[7]) that Tom and Eric had created around wastewater treatment. It
was one such chemical producer, represented by Hans, who had invited Eric to
do a project together.

Tom's strong disapproval becomes more readily understandable when Eric's conduct
is construed as a betrayal of an order in which Eric and Tom had established carefully
calibrated identities. It is certainly not the simple act of agreeing to do a new project
that is the object of the accountability issue. Most such projects would not attract
much attention in the first place, and in those cases Eric would not have felt called
upon to account for his decisions. Not doing projects with others as such, but doing it
with a certain foreign chemical producer was the issue because, in this particular
combination of actors, that allowed a particularly frightening rationalization of intent
and implications.

Let it suffice to say that Tom probably felt his own identity being threatened. Eric's
acceptance of the invitation to collaborate would seem to gain the chemical producer
some credibility in his marketing effort merely from being aligned with the highest
scientific authority in this new project. Clearly, Eric felt an obligation to explain to Tom
why he would help to bring this precarious situation about. His explanation was
technical, namely to explore a new concept for wastewater treatment that would
exploit the residuals from the chemical treatment to speed up the biological treatment. However, Tom did not react to the intentions, but to some projected consequence. The synergy between the two treatment processes was attractive in itself, but
more or less inadvertently it put the chemical treatment prior to the biological one.
The 'natural order' would then effectively be undermined, and some well-established
identities be challenged.

Tom saw these consequences immediately, but not everybody, even in his own
company, construed the situation in such terms at first. Many different types of
consequences might have been ascribed to Eric's conduct, including consequences
that would have produced approval of, or inattention to, Eric's acceptance to do the
project with Hans.

Let me sum up a few points from the above discussion:

- it seems uncertain (and, in this case, a subject of constant contention and negotiation) whether the object of evaluation is the conduct in itself, some ascribed intentions and motives, or some projected consequence of the conduct. In practice, we could not conceive of conduct without imputation of intentions and consequences. Such imputations are social and negotiable. Accountability may not reliably constrain consequential acts when meaning is not taken for granted.
- while Tom's disapproval was rather manifest, it was far from effective in constraining action. Its ineffectiveness could be explained by the fact that it came too late: that the spilled sherry was Tom's emotional reaction to an already established fact. In Tetlock's framework, expected disapproval would still function as a deterrent, as a constraint on, in this case Eric's, conduct. Tom's reaction did nothing of that sort. Eric elicited this disapproval knowingly, if with hesitation, as I shall show below.

However, Eric's motives may still seem rather obscure.

Eric did not accept the chemical producer's invitation without serious considerations of the ways in which such a project would be received. In fact, he did not even take the proposal seriously at first. When Hans sketched his ideas for the new concept in a letter to Eric, he received a rather arrogant letter back telling him that he would have to read a whole library of books before he knew what he was talking about.

Two coincidences changed Eric's perception. One was that new government programmes had targeted phosphorus pollution, an area where Eric had relatively less expertise than on nitrogen pollution. The other coincidence was that Eric happened to hear a conference paper in which one of the world's leading experts on chemical wastewater treatment outlined ideas very similar to the ones in Hans' letter. After further consultations with that expert Eric was convinced that the ideas were worth pursuing. However, he was not at all convinced that they should be pursued together with Hans and his chemical firm. On the other hand, honesty prevented him from running away with the ideas, and therefore he wrote Hans a letter in which he set very stringent conditions on his participation in a project. Among the conditions were the following: that his own institute should conduct all experiments; that some additional experts should be included in the work, e.g. the leading expert on chemical treatment mentioned above; that he should be given full control over the project management and the technical committees; and that he should have an unconditional right to publish all results from the experiments. Eric later admitted that he was very surprised when the chemical company accepted these conditions. Unexpectedly, and not by his design, he found himself in a project which was controversial in respect to his relationships with Tom. That was when he decided to inform him personally.

It is indeed difficult to recognize the 'cognitive miser turned strategist' as he is depicted in the literature. Eric might have left the whole issue to its own fate after the first letter to Hans, and then he would have upset nobody, would not have shaken existing alliances and risked his personal reputation in the aftermath of having alienated the most important player in the field. He did all the things we would expect a 'vigilant, complex and self-critical information processor' (Tetlock, 1985: 314) to do, only he knew all along what views Tom would hold and how he would react.

Could the reason why he would go through all this simply be that somehow this new concept for wastewater treatment hit a cord in him? That is, that he considered it important, exciting, and rewarding to explore. Such genuine interest in the subject may be difficult to simulate in laboratory experiments, and cognitive misers may have found a completely rational strategy in the face of the ordinary trivial task environments in laboratories. Outside these artificial environments, people may have stronger or weaker feelings and opinions about the worth and excitement of various endeavours. When the feelings about a certain case are strong, the opinions of others may some-times be totally irrelevant, be considered wrong or discarded as mischievous. The descriptions of entrepreneurs we get in the literature may be relevant in this context. Nothing indicates that entrepreneurs 'avoid mental procedures that require sustained attention, comprehension, or computing power . . . ' and yet we are constantly told that their eventual success required them to withstand disdain and disbelief levelled at them from significant others like bosses, marketing departments, and common sense (Kanter, 1988; Peters, 1988; Beckman, 1979). It is possible, like in Eric's case, that disapproval is encountered not out of ignorance, but rather out of innocence (March, 1979).

It is possible that the identity of Eric as researcher may be used to explain why he felt 'obliged' to pursue the ideas with Hans. It is probably a better explanation than the alternative one, i.e. that he was exercising a rational choice amongst various alterna-tives. This latter explanation is made problematic by the amount of uncertainty surrounding the critical parameters of the decision, and by the fact that this explana-tion fits his initial choice not to participate better than his eventual change of opinion.

However, on this point we may have exhausted the accountability perspective, since apparently we are in need of identifying the spur to, rather than some social constraint on, Eric's conduct. The case illustrates that Eric could have legitimized inaction with reference to issues of accountability, but he chose to act and thus to travel outside his socially constructed 'home-base'.

It could possibly be claimed that accountability explains only a certain class of conduct, and that Eric's conduct in the case study belongs to a different class of innovative action. However, innovativeness could be argued to be less a quality about the action as such, than a rationalization of the action after the fact (Kreiner and Schultz, 1995b). Thus, any classification of conduct into separate categories is indeed highly problematic. That subsequent events redefine (or re-classify) action was demon-strated in the present case.

> Tom did more than just spill his sherry, which we take to be an initial sign of disapproval. He had no authority to forbid Eric to join the project; and certainly he could not too forcefully argue against the project without being seen as trying to prevent the technological development and the free academic research – and possibly even worse, to try to monopolize the industry. Had Tom done so he would have been met with general disap-proval and loss of status in the eyes of the public.

It seems that Tom, the significant other, who was supposed to do the evaluation (and thereby constraining the conduct of somebody else) was himself much more directly constrained in his reaction because he, in turn, is accountable for such reactions. Suddenly it appears that accountability, instead of being a constraint on behaviour, may act to protect innovative, hard-to-justify ventures in the face of a potentially self-serving audience.

> In fact Tom did something considerably more constructive. He happened at the time to be heavily involved in the creation of a country programme under EUREKA. Thus, the inspiration to turn Eric's project into a EUREKA project came readily to his mind. Within a short while, Tom returned with an offer neither Eric nor Hans could refuse: a much larger project, still dedicated to explore Hans' new concept but now with much more vigour, and with a substantial public funding component to compensate for the many times larger investment on the part of the companies. Needless to say, Tom's company was now amongst the participants. Everybody agreed to this new EUREKA project which was subsequently notified and implemented.
>
> In the process, Tom managed to put his own company into the driver's seat of the new project. While formally on equal terms with Hans, Tom represented a much larger proportion of the total investment and was the administrator of the EUREKA funds. In fact, Hans was pretty much placed on the periphery of the project process, the core of which now consisted of a well-established network of tightly knit actors. Hans was not a member of this network and never became one, being even further distanced by coming from another country. The feeling that 'somebody' stole his project would perhaps be understandable, only Hans never admitted to harbouring such a feeling. He did admit, however, that other persons in his company saw the situation in those terms.

We may sit back and appreciate the elegant strategic move taken by Tom in an otherwise precarious situation. He turned a threatening collaboration between Eric and a foreign chemical producer into a fairly contained part of a much bigger EUREKA project. In this new project there was ample room for Tom and his company. Acting in a constructive way, he could not be accused of putting a hindrance to technological development and Eric's freedom of research.

More relevant to our current discussion, there are two lessons to be taken from this last part of the case study. The first lesson is the fact that subsequent events may reconstruct the conduct that was the original object of accountability. The significance originally ascribed to Eric's acceptance of a project with Hans was one of betrayal: a betrayal of the commitment to biological wastewater treatment and the symbiotic relationship between Tom and Eric; a betrayal of some well-established identities. Such an interpretation would better explain the strong, immediate sign of disapproval. But with Tom's subsequent initiative, the consequence attributed to Eric's acceptance of the project was the formation of the EUREKA project which was a strong reaffirmation of the previous order and of the relationship between Tom and Eric. We repeat our contention that if the object of accountability can so dramatically change over a short period of time, the simple question 'accountable for what' becomes virtually impossible to answer. Then, almost by default, we are left with the issue of 'accountable to whom' which was one of the hallmarks of the new commercial agenda (Munro and Hatherly, 1993).

The second lesson relates to Hans' response to Tom's initiative. Even if the EUREKA project was a pursuit of his own ideas at a much bigger scale, and even if the EUREKA status relieved him of some of the investment burdens, Hans must have had doubts about letting Tom into the project. Tom and Eric had this kind of relationship that allowed Tom to invite himself. But not so in the relationship to Hans. He could have voiced his disapproval, however he didn't. We can speculate over the reason why he didn't.[8] One possible reason is that his disapproval would have been interpreted to signal an intention to monopolize scientific expertise for illegitimate commercial gains. With such a meaning attached to it, Eric would have been hard pressed to legitimize his decision to participate. But for Hans, who in this phase of the process was given the role of constraining conduct through communicating approval and disapproval, we come to realize the constraints, in turn, on his judgements. Once again we come away with an appreciation of the many constraints on the designated constrainer. Paradoxically as it sounds, these constraints may in fact facilitate 'new innovative' conduct.

The process of accountability

The case illustration above made one thing clear: the simple picture in the literature on accountability (in both streams of research) of one actor and one authority is not a valid one. Here accountability cannot explain the individual act because this act is intertwined with previous ones as well as subsequent ones. If we cannot isolate the acts, and if the constructed meaning of acts depends on the kind of reaction they receive from co-actors on the scene, then we should discontinue talking about accountability as a prior constraint on individual acts, judgements, or opinions. We might instead begin conceiving accountability as a process in which acts, judgements and accounts are produced interactively.

There are significant implications for our discussion of seeing accountability as a social process, extending in time, and with an interactional character. The most important one is the idea of *mutuality*. We operate in both modes, as actors as well as authority, always and all the time. We are aware that we are equally accountable for the way we respond to others' conduct, as they are for their response to our conduct. Interaction may occur within the same rungs of hierarchy or between subordinate and superior. In both cases, however, the critical point is mutuality: the fact that everybody is mutually accountable.

When we begin to analyse the interactive process as a whole, rather than the individual acts that constitute the process, we begin to appreciate accountability as an important, but non-specific undercurrent. Time and again we saw Tom, Eric and Hans being constrained by the explicit or implicit demand of the situation. To be required, in the process of interaction, to state the reasons for doing, saying or feeling something, constrained action less than it constrained accounts and evaluations of such action. In a double sense, however, the impact of accountability would better be described as creative than constraining. First of all, the inability of Tom to level negative sanctions against Eric forced him to completely redefine the scene of action, to adopt a pro-active strategy in order to circumvent his constraints in responding to the perceived threats of the situation. By realigning the various interests and redefine the bill of options, the burden of accountability was redistributed as well. Suddenly it was Hans who experienced the constraints on reacting and responding to a highly legitimate offer to form a much bigger and more ambitious EUREKA project. Secondly, the creative effect materialized in the need to provide rationalized accounts of action and evaluation. Tacit aspects of the situation need verbalization to be shared in social processes, and to force upon the participants to 'express the unexpressable' may prove to spur knowledge-creation (Nonaka and Takeuchi, 1995).

How different would the process have been, had none of the actors been accountable? If no one felt the obligation to give sense to their conduct in the face of the significant others? Then Eric would not have informed Tom; who would then not have had the chance to reconstruct the project; and had he proposed that, he might just have been rejected by Hans. The relationship between Tom and Eric would have been severed, as we saw in the case not from Eric's acceptance to do a project with Hans as such, but from leaving it to Tom's unfacilitated, emotional reading. When, at various points in the process, the actors ventured to give meaning to their initiatives and decisions, this became an invitation to sense-making of a more collective character.

In this discussion, I have tried to establish the interactional episode for a select group of actors as the object of accountability. It is not simply the individual act that receives social approval and reaction; the approval and reaction are in themselves social in nature. Thus, accountability is not a one-way relationship, but a mutual one; and it is not a static relationship, but a dynamic, constantly emerging one. The approval and status in the eyes of significant others may be less of a concern in the calculation and design of action at any particular point in time, as it is a supplementary goal for the interactional episode as a whole. It is very possible that disapproval will spur further interaction along the way that in retrospect proves to be significant and legitimate. Not only is it not apparent in our study that approval should be an overriding concern of, and constraint on, actors in a social context. It is a concern, but a concern that spurs and requires the actors to circumvent the current limits of the situation, and to redefine the situation so that some limits are removed. Accountability, in its more socializing forms considered here, is better described as an 'inspiring constraint' than as a limiting constraint.

The timing of accountability

However, these nuances to the functional effect of disapproval raise possibilities for managing the process with references to issues of timing. When should one be called upon to externalize intentions, consequences, and values, if we want to support and further the explorative, highly uncertain pursuits of innovations in R&D ventures?

Imagine, for example, that Eric had involved Tom at an earlier stage. Having not yet heard the expert on chemical treatment, Eric and Tom would easily have committed themselves not to work with Hans. After all, they did not consider him knowledgeable on wastewater treatment. Even with subsequent information, Eric might not have been able to reconsider his and Tom's shared commitments.

Imagine, as another example, that Eric had involved Tom at a later stage of development. Then it is likely that the commitments between Eric and Hans would have been formalized, into a project document etc. With such documents in hand, it would have been easy to prevent Tom from getting involved. In that case, the symbolic sign of disapproval would have been the only and final response, putting the future relationship between him and Eric in doubt.

Knowing that the process resulted in the formation of a fully-fledged EUREKA project, alternative histories appear very hypothetical. We don't know whether Eric was a shrewd strategist, or merely blessed with sufficient luck. But he seemed to postpone involving Tom as a 'significant other' until he had had a chance to explore the problems and possibilities a little further. In that way, his justification could be based on better information. But he didn't postpone it so long that there was no more room for action on the part of Tom. Striking this particular balance proved in this case to be highly important for the outcome of the process. Another balance between the two concerns would have produced a different outcome.[9]

It is fairly clear why Tetlock (1985) fails to take time into consideration. The experiments, on which that research bases its insights, are self-contained and finish with the test person making his or her judgement, decision or act. Accountability is reflected solely in this judgement, decision or act. In our case, accountability was reflected in the process following Eric's decision to form a project with Hans. Thus, studying accountability in experimental settings may miss an essential quality of social life, i.e., its continuity or intertextuality.[10]

Strategizing with respect to time is also not a conspicuous concern in Roberts' (1991) work. Lateral accountability *to somebody* is timeless, and timelags in accountability seem odd especially when, as quoted above, accountability is 'a process internal to the "self"'. But timelags may exactly be the way in which lateral accountability escapes the subversion into hierarchical forms. A suspension, but only temporarily, of the policing of the 'me' by 'I' (or by some other significant other) introduces play, experiments and 'technologies of foolishness' (March, 1988). Without such temporary suspension of accountability, other types of loose couplings would need to be fostered for the above-mentioned 'sense both of individual difference and mutual dependence' to emerge.

Conclusion

In this essay I have tried to understand a particular set of events in the light of the accountability literature. In the course of this attempt we have come to redefine the very object of accountability. The cognitive psychologists discovered the importance of the actors' social context for their cognitive processes. I came to discover the importance of the evaluators' social context for their ability to verbalize opinions and design reactions. If this picture is accepted, we come to see not individual acts, but strings of contingent acts as the object of accountability. In short, we come to see interactional episodes, more than the single acts of which they consist, as that which is governed by accountability.

In the interactional episode that was given as a case illustration above, mutuality was a pronounced feature of the process of accountability. This idea that accountability goes 'both ways' may be implicit in the socializing or lateral forms of accountability (Roberts,

1991). It is likely that mutuality is also a requirement of the new commercial agenda (Munro and Hatherly, 1993) that will not accept asymmetric power relations easily. The decision-making environment analysed above was characterized by mutuality and symmetry from the very beginning. That may certainly not always be the case, but it is more likely that it will be at the end of a project or venture, especially if it is a successful one. Otherwise, the venture will be consumed by surprises and uncertainties and conflicts. In fact, when Roberts (1991) warns us that the local contexts would be subordinated to a bigger context of hierarchical accountability, we come closer to suggest the opposite: the subordination of the hierarchical accountability to the dynamic building of mutuality and lateral forms of accountability. The special context of innovative ventures simply enforces a different social structure than the hierarchical one, because the latter is not instrumental in spurring the kind of action needed to cope with uncertainty and complexity.

I would not want to appear too naïve in asserting that such mutuality and lateral accountability characterizes all innovative ventures. Needless to say, much R&D is managed in a traditional surveillance and control mode. In our EMRI studies we found, however, that the likelihood of success was much greater among the projects operating in ways akin to socializing modes of accountability as compared to the more traditionally managed projects. Thus, the fact that bosses with a determination to manage their subordinates on the basis of arms-length surveillance and control still exist is a testimony to the inefficiency with which history and evolution selects the most adequate forms (March, 1992). A practical outcome of our study therefore has been to reveal limits to models of project management that (implicitly or explicitly) adopt hierarchical forms of accountability.

As a final thought, I want to return to the experimental finding that uncertainty generates better and more complex cognitive processes in actors. It is probably a finding that is corroborated both by empirical observations and by intuition. However, if social approval and status are the drivers of actors then the better strategy would be *not* to venture, *not* to explore, not to discard immediate feedback, etc. Accountability in its simple version would guide actors towards inaction, in which case they would really deserve to be labelled 'misers'. However, we may often observe actors who act inventively, with dedication as if they were motivated by what they are doing, not by others' opinion. There would be little emancipatory potential in lateral accountability if we could not recognize its relevance also in these cases where the constraining of action is not what needs to be explained. It would be a wrong conclusion to draw that creative people working under high uncertainty should not be kept accountable. However, they should be kept accountable for not attaining predefined outcomes and consequences. Yet, they should be required to explicate and externalize the rationales and visions on which they operate – not to control them and evaluate them, but to aid the knowledge creation in itself (Nonaka, 1994) and to invite others to engage and interact in the process. At some point in the process of innovation, the engagement and participation by significant others may be functional rather than inhibiting. Accountability, when free of attempts to manage it in a hierarchical mode, will become conducive for innovation rather than constraining consequent actions.

Notes

1. EUREKA is a pan-European programme with the aim of facilitating collaboration across national and institutional borders. The envisioned collaboration covers high-tech development projects that have participation of companies and universities from two or more member countries. Each member country supports participants of its own nationality, following their own policies and agreements. No central EUREKA funding is available, and there exists a central office in Brussels of only minimal size. Evaluated on the number of projects formed in the first ten years of the EUREKA programmes, the programme has been very successful (EUREKA, 1993).

2. I owe these labels to Jan Mouritsen.

3. The EUREKA countries are the western European countries, a growing number of eastern European countries, and lately also Russia. Thus, EUREKA projects bridge often large cultural differences.

4. EMRI is an acronym for EUREKA Management Research Initiative. EMRI was established in 1989 by the author and engaged a large number of researchers at the Copenhagen Business School and Aarhus School of Economics and Business Administration in longitudinal studies of individual EUREKA projects. EMRI was partly financed by the Danish EUREKA Secretariat.

5. My account of the events are based on several interviews with two of the actors mentioned and with many more persons participating in the project. The informants' accounts of the events were very similar, and they were reporting on events of much currency. However, we should not forget that our data are themselves accounts, and their similarities testify perhaps not so much to their truth-value as to the social cohesion of the project. For example, the account of the spilled sherry was given with strikingly similar wording by two separate informants, none of whom had actually been present.

   While my account of my informants' accounts is kept as close to the data as possible, my research questions have necessarily ordered the information into a coherent and directed picture of a historical process. While I claim that this picture is justifiable, I also realize that with a different research question the picture would have come out differently. Thus, there is good reason for the author to claim accountability for the data alongside the informants.

6. To avoid misunderstandings, let me assert that of course identity is socially constituted. That identity has a social origin does not prevent it from acting in the present situation as something definitely individual.

7. Eric praised his research institute for having turned wastewater treatment into a science, a claim that most people would consider fair.

8. In an interview Hans claimed that he welcomed Tom as partner in the project. He did not consider Tom a competitor the same way he himself was considered a competitor by Tom. Hans considered him a resource to the project on technological and financial dimensions. It is possible, however, that this attitude is the result of *post festum* rationalizations. I allow myself to speculate over alternative explanations.

9. In another EUREKA project, situated in an even more turbulent technological context, the importance of timing was confirmed (Kreiner and Schultz, 1995a). In that case, the number of exploratory connections to people outside the project was very large, but the likelihood that any such connection would produce usable results was very low. Thus, every exploration would be difficult to justify up front, and the only way exploration could be undertaken would be by requiring no justification until after the fact. Then, and only then, would the explorer be called upon to define what was the relation to the EUREKA venture.

   This issue is recurring in the early stages of innovation processes, when opportunity-driven persons (Kreiner and Schultz, 1993) perform what has been named as 'skunk works' (Peters, 1988) or 'bootleg research' (Burgelman and Sayles, 1986). All this unauthorized and informal exploration serves the function of postponing the point in time when resources are officially committed to the task, because such commitment of resources invariably requires convincing and legitimate accounts.

10. See the introductory chapter of this book.

References

Beckman, Svante (1979) Immunization – in defence of status quo, in *Surviving Failures, Patterns and Cases of Project Mismanagement*, (ed. B. Person), Almqvist & Wiksell, Stockholm. pp. 244–57.

Burgelman, R.A. and Sayles, L.R. (1986) *Inside Corporate Innovation. Strategy, Structure, and Managerial Skills*. Free Press, N.Y.

EUREKA (1993) *Evaluation of EUREKA Industrial and Economic Effects.*

Kanter, Rosabeth Moss (1988) The middle manager as innovator, in *Managing Professionals in Innovative Organizations. A Collection of Readings* (ed. R. Katz), Ballinger, Cambridge, MA, pp. 183–98.

Kreiner, K. (forthcoming) *EUREKA projects and contextual turbulence: The impact on managerial and organizational strategy.* Paper based on plenary address delivered at The Oxford Conference of Collaborative European Programmes and Projects in Research and Training. April 10–13, 1994. Oxford University.

Kreiner, K. and Schultz, M. (1993) Informal collaboration in R&D. The formation of networks across organizations. *Organization Studies*, **14**(2) pp. 189–209.

Kreiner, K. and Schultz, M. (1995a) Soft cultures: The symbolism of cross-border organizing. *Studies in Cultures, Organizations and Societies* **1**(1), pp. 63–81.

Kreiner, K. and Schultz, M. (1995b) Creative post-processing. On making turbulence valuable, in *Creative Action in Organizations. Ivory Tower Visions & Real World Voices.* (eds C.M. Ford and D.A. Gioia), Sage, Thousand Oaks: pp. 181–86.

March, J.G. (1992) The evolution of evolution, in *Evolutionary Dynamics of Organizations* (eds J. Baum and J. Singh) Oxford University Press, N.Y.

March, J.G. (1988) The technology of foolishness, in *Decisions in Organizations*, Blackwell, N.Y. pp. 253–65.

March, J.G. (1980) Science, politics and Mrs. Gruenberg. *National Research Council in 1979*, Washington, D.C.

Munro, R.J.B. and Hatherly, D.J. (1993) Accountability and the new commercial agenda. *Critical Perspectives on Accounting* **4**, pp. 369–95.

Murphy, Rodolfo, (1994) The effects of task characteristics on covariation assessment: The impact of accountability and judgment frame. *Organizational Behavior and Human Decision Processes*, **60**, pp. 139–55.

Nonaka, Ikujiro and Takeuchi, Hirotaka (1995) *The Knowledge-Creating Company. How Japanese Companies Create the Dynamics of Innovation*. Oxford University Press, Oxford.

Nonaka, Ikujiro (1994) A dynamic theory of knowledge creation. *Organization Science* **5**(1) pp. 14–37.

Peters, Thomas J. (1988) A skunkworks tale, in *Managing Professionals in Innovative Organizations. A Collection of Readings* (ed R. Katz), Ballinger, Cambridge, MA: pp. 433–41.

Roberts, John, (1991) The possibilities of accountability. *Accounting, Organizations and Society*, **16**(4), pp. 355–68.

Simonson, I. and Nye, P. (1992) The effect of accountability on susceptibility to decision errors. *Organizational Behavior and Human Decision Processes* **51**, pp. 416–46.

Tetlock, Philip E. (1985) Accountability: The neglected social context of judgment and choice. *Research in Organizational Behavior* **7**, pp. 297–332.

6 Decoupling hierarchy and accountability: an examination of trust and reputation

Sten Jönsson

Introduction

Trust is a *forceful* social phenomenon. This is the theme of this chapter, that trust requests a response in terms of accountability. This response is complex. It involves, I will argue, an accountability that is different in kind from one more typically associated with hierarchical forms of accountability. While both demand competence, trust demands an ability to manage a variety of contingencies within the area of entrustment. Equally, in leaving something of value in the hands of others, both imply risk-taking but trust also exposes relationships to the whim of those who rely on each other. So trust takes time to establish its modes of accountability.

The social force comes from the obligation to respond to *extended* trust. This response involves 'identity-building' in a social context. An identity is built by keeping one's conduct in line with the expectations of others. This emergence of 'identities', often loosely equated with the more functional notion of roles, has a constraining effect on members of a social group, known as 'bonding'. But there is more, in that the creation and reproduction of identity also has a productive effect. By conducting themselves in a visible way, what can be called identity work, the competent person strengthens expectations over their future conduct.

The extension of trust, created and reproduced through identity work, gives members of a group the energy to perform co-ordinated action without hierarchical control. We have all experienced how groups, where we have been members, have surpassed reasonable expectations or fallen through towards atypical, dismal performance. It seems as though organizational mobilization of these social forces could promote productivity as well as work satisfaction. Surely unproductive managerial labour can be avoided? Does work have to be drudgery that can only be kept going by artificial incentive systems?

Contrast this potential to the American form of managerial capitalism, the 'triumphant' combination of managerialism and hierarchy that has been chronicled in detail by Chandler (1962; 1977; 1990). The basic mechanism in the growth of the large corporation is shown to be a three-pronged investment in production capacity, market organization, and managerial structure.

If these three managerial resources are not maintained in harmony, so the thesis goes, an industrial nation will fall behind. For example, Chandler (1990) argues that British industry has suffered from not developing adequate managerial structures. On the other hand Goold and Campbell (1987) found that the most profitable companies in their sample of British corporations were using holding company structures and financial control instead of strategic planning, implying that strategic control of activities was decentralized while control over finances was centralized. Chandler (1991) countered by claiming that the conglomerates seem not to be able to uphold technological complexity and capital intensity, and thus, over time, have retreated to service and low technology industries.

The multidivisional form has come to be considered as the epitome of modernism; social engineering and managerial labour at the apex of its social significance. For Chandler, the successful large corporations have large headquarters that formulate strategies (the mind) and strictly control the corporate divisions (the body) to carry them out. In an implicit analogy with Decartes's mind-body split, strategy is thus formed at the centre and decentralized financial control is used to monitor performance. Financial indicators are objective measures of how well strategic intentions are being realized. The Cartesian corporation thinks first and acts later; and financial control provides the after-thought.

In a critique of the classical claim that the multidivisional form is superior in effectiveness, this chapter argues for neighbourly chats between teams in the organizational village as a viable alternative. Keeping each other accountable, giving accounts in the form of stories, and trusting, can reduce the use of accounting information to productive proportions. Examples from one important experiment will be described in detail in the second half of this chapter. But first, drawing partly on Meyer and Wittington's (1994) helpful survey of the debate over managerial structure, it is of some interest to attempt to map how the multi-divisional form was established as a superior governance structure.

Spreading the word

According to Mintzberg (1990), Chandler's key conclusions were that governance structure is a matter of design and that strategy formation is an analytic process carried out top-down, with strict separation between formulation and implementation of strategy. Thinking before acting, the corporation uses divisions, monitored through management control systems, to achieve effectiveness. Divisions are unrelated and resource allocation is carried out (objectively) on the basis of expected future return on investment given the strategy. The multi-divisional company was also portrayed as especially effective in responding to market demands. This image was useful as a counter argument to those who believed in stories told at the time about non-market relations inside the military-industrial complex (Galbraith, 1967) being the main explanation to the growth of the American corporation after the Second World War.

During the late 1960s a number of scholarships for studies at Harvard were awarded to young European researchers. Among them was Channon (1973) who published a prize-winning thesis on the strategy and structure of the British enterprise. Over the period under study, Channon expected to find an increased proportion of diversified and multidivisional companies. The correlation would be stronger over time and the multidivisional company would be expected to develop corporate staff, together with systems of control and incentive systems, to become evermore similar to the American ideal. The message was taken to Europe via the European Harvard research fellows and their work in the Management Schools of the Harvard persuasion, and through the assistance of McKinsey & Co, from Boston, in the restructuration of European companies. In British industry 32 of the 100 largest companies were known to have called in consultants to help them revise their administrative structures. In 22 of these cases it was McKinsey & Co which provided the helping hand (Channon, 1973, p. 239). Similar observations could be made in other European countries: if European companies did not emulate the American governance structures, they would certainly be taken over or driven out of business by American effectiveness.

Channon (1973), to continue his example, finds British industry lagging; but the fact that the proportion of multidivisional firms had increased from 8% in 1950 to 70% in 1970 was seen as a sign of progress. The holding company structure was still the most common in large-scale British industry as late as 1960, but 'neither the functional nor the holding company structure proved adequate to the task of managing the diversified enterprise' (Channon, 1973: 238). The rate of growth of the multidivisional form, especially during the 1960s, is taken to be a self-evident proof of its desirability. Certainly Channon is not explicit about using actual measures of performance as a dependent variable. Survival alone is assumed to be an adequate indicator of efficiency, an analogy with Darwin's arguments over the survival of the fittest.

What was wrong with the traditional British way of organizing companies? Channon points to the low degree of academic education among British managers, and low pay, but the main thrust is assumed to be the lack of clearly defined executive hierarchies. Time and again he returns to this deficiency in British management.

> In general, collective responsibility was more common in British concerns, where committees including divisional executives were frequently involved in the policy-making process.
>
> (Channon, 1973: 216)

The clear demarcation of individual responsibilities usually experienced in American firms (p.160) was often missing in British firms. It follows, although Channon does not make the point, that accountability was not individuated, but remained joint and general. Furthermore there was active involvement of the division general managers in top management committees, which Channon saw as casting doubt as to what extent careful and objective performance appraisal was practised at the top level.

> The group executive function found in many American companies, appeared to be notably missing in most British concerns.
>
> (Channon, 1973: 209)

Against the American prototype, there simply was not enough separation between the levels of thought (where strategy is made) and the levels of implementation (the incorporation of action) to provide effective management in a competitive world. It is interesting to note that key references, in Channon's explanation to backwardness, are to a lack of individually specified responsibilities, and to undue interaction between policy generation and implementation. This was not so long ago!

The question is whether there is any reliable evidence that the hierarchical, multi-divisional firm is more efficient? Certainly, Cable and Dirrheimer (1983), Hill (1988), and Ezzamel and Watson (1993) cast doubt on the wisdom of taking a proliferation of the multidivisional form as proof of its superior performance. If the survival rate of a governance structure is proof of performance, then the holding company form, being the most common among large British companies in 1960, and still surviving in large numbers (Meyer and Wittington 1994), requires explanation. One could also point to the recent success of Japanese industry in competition with American multi-divisional firms as a reason to doubt the belief that structure is the solution. But there are a number of other reasons worth exploring and these are now discussed.

Is the divisional form of governance passé?

In formulating his hypotheses on the holding company structure, Channon (1973) comments that British colonial history is expected to have given rise to overseas activity concentrated on former colonial territories. This geographic diversity will affect structure. The holding company is described as representing 'extreme decentraliza-tion' (Channon, 1973: 87) and thus suitable when it is necessary to adapt strategy to local situations. It is interesting to note that, in a similar manner, the multidivisional form was portrayed as well suited to respond to changing market conditions. It seems, as the 'ecologists' have been arguing, that there are differences between environments!

The American multidivisional form was developed to exploit economies of scale in a fairly homogeneous, and large, home market, while the inferior holding company was designed to adapt strategy to local conditions in global business. Now, in the mid-1990s, business is global and trend setting companies are pursuing 'multi-domestic' strategies. The perceptions of markets and competition have changed, therefore, since the time when Channon analysed British industry, but still there is firm belief in the superiority of multidivisional structures and hierarchical control. In the following discussion it is claimed that precisely these newer perceptions of the environment of the company warrant a research focus on internal communication processes and their relations to organizational problem solving.

First, the ability to adapt strategies to local conditions has come to be recognized as an important precondition for success to companies with small home markets, or with strong external actors (like unions, state, banks). In particular, it may be an advantage to effective management of differentiated technologies (Granstrand and Sjölander, 1990) to have decentralized structures; for these allow local strategic discretion in problem identification, problem solving and strategic brokerage between these two kinds of 'learning' activities in large organizations. With a higher density of specialist groups related to different technologies, all having to be co-ordinated to achieve joint solutions to complex problems, the company with facilitated communication will have a competitive advantage.

Second, the knowledge intensification in companies has been paralleled by a litera-ture on the design of organizations for lateral flexibility (Galbraith 1994, Galbraith and Lawler 1993), where the organizational design relies on peer communication in problem solving towards organizational performance. Shortly, after the next section,

I will explore how peer communication in the operational part of organizations helps form lateral responsibility relations. The value of such communication will appear in conversation that is closely related to actual work situations. That is, where problems are solved by competent persons 'doing things with words' (Austin 1962).

The value of work

In contrast to the Channon thesis over structure, the competitiveness of nations is now assumed to lie in increased value through extended use of symbolic-analytic work (Reich 1991). Work can be classified into three categories; routine production service, in-person service, and symbolic-analytic service (Reich, 1991: 174). *Routine production* is repetitive, done in large groups, and controlled by standard programmes. The controllers are themselves controlled often by information technology applications. *In-person service* is repetitive and consists of simple tasks. Work is controlled by others, but usually done in small groups and face-to-face with the customer, who might complain. *Symbolic-analytic work* consists of problem identification, problem solving, and problem brokerage. This kind of service can be done and delivered all over the world with the use of information technology, and it is well paid. Deregulation extends the market for symbolic-analytic work. In a global economy with capital markets open around the clock and dominated by institutional investors the wealth of nations will depend on their ability to provide valuable work. Symbolic-analytic work is associated with increased value.

In that he sees a widening gap between the wealthy symbolic-analytic workers and those in the other categories, marked by separation in many dimensions of that which constitutes the good life, Reich's (1991) analysis is rather depressing. The solution according to Reich (p. 311ff.) to the resulting fragmentation of society is a kind of positive economic nationalism that does not view the world economy as a zero-sum game. Citizens should take a primary responsibility for improving their countrymen's possibilities to live a full and productive life, to learn, and to move from obsolete industries to more rewarding jobs. All of this should be achieved inside mutually agreed international rules of fair play achieved by strategic trade negotiations. The recipe bears striking similarities to the 'Swedish model' of wage negotiations practised with great success during the first three decades after the Second World War, but now considered to be a problem due to its reliance on centralized policy making. Both strategies suffer from the petrifying effects of centralized rituals where 'chosen' representatives of opposite camps appear, pale and red-eyed, before media flashlights announcing that at last an agreement has been signed. The new rules have been promulgated and are supposed to govern our working lives until another round of negotiation between chosen representatives replaces them at the end of the contract period. Extended to strategic trade negotiations this kind 'lawyerism' is not likely to promote international co-operation. On the contrary, a trade war between Japan and the USA seems ever imminent – or is that to show how hard the representatives are working?

The problem with Reich's solution (and the Swedish model of wage negotiations for that matter) is its reductionist reliance on work categorization. It is true that in global competition valuable work becomes the centre piece of the discussion, but in knowledge intensified work (it is claimed here that all work has the potential of knowledge intensification) it is not enough to discuss in terms of just three categories of work. Instead the value of each unit of work must be discussed – situatedly – among competent persons concerned. This brings us to the core of the efficiency concept.

Even if reviews of the literature on organizational effectiveness tend to report several dozens of efficiency concepts (Quinn and Rohrbaugh, 1983), efficiency is usually defined in terms of value of output divided by the value of input. Difficulties with the measurement of efficiency (or for that matter effectiveness) stem from allocating inputs and outputs in time, from valuation problems and from the fact that it is often difficult to determine what is input and what is output. Economists will claim that market prices provide true measures, but a little reflection will lead to the conclusion that markets never do meet the theoretical criteria of the perfect market. If transactions are few it is unreasonable to assume that a 'market' price is an objective measure. Both seller and buyer in a transaction are satisfied that they have struck a good bargain. The seller is of the opinion that the price is higher than the value of the product he has sold and the buyer believes that the value is higher than the price. The only thing we can know with certainty, therefore, is that the price does not reflect the value that the two participants in the transaction attach to the product. The efficiency of the transaction or the setting where it took place will seem different from different perspectives.

The firm as an actor in a market will certainly value assets differently than 'the market'. The aim is to conduct transactions in a way that accumulates resources under the firm's control. Actors in the capital market trade the shares of the firm between them and transactions take place as long as actors value shares differently. The efficiency judgement of the firm will be based on different premises than the efficiency judgement of 'the market'. The rhetorical trick in academic discourse seems to be to separate inner and outer efficiency by a saying 'Doing the thing right, or doing the right thing', and suddenly the students understand what efficiency is. The privilege of formulating the criterion against which all acts are judged is assumed to rest with top management and ultimately with 'the market'.

These assumptions are less justified the more knowledge is intensified in companies. In knowledge intensified work, it often happens that top management is not competent to judge what are appropriate immediate objectives. The hierarchical position does indeed privilege decisions on objectives, but the lack of appropriate knowledge might in time undermine the legitimacy of hierarchy if formulation and implementation of policy are not carried out in consultation with the appropriate sources of knowledge. Communication structures will have to be adapted accordingly. In the meantime it may be permitted to discuss alternative bases of control in the everyday work of doing things with words.

An alternative view of control

To be competent means to be able to deliver the goods, to be trusted to keep promises, and to be held accountable for deviations from contract. By handing over discretion, by giving the power of disposition over important matters to others, we give up a reliance on forms of direct control over activities. This, as discussed in the introduction to this chapter, raises questions of competence.

Skill at work can be described in terms of levels at which judgement is applied. At a low level skill the person 'goes by the manual' or reads a wiring diagram sequentially to detect, say, a defect. At a higher skill level a person 'goes by function', which means being able to judge an operation by its functions. At the highest skill level a person can judge an operation in terms of objectives – what the customer wants from it – and is able to modify the operation (its functions or 'wiring') to achieve a desired output.

At each level there seems to be a corresponding range of communication requirements. At the highest level of skill the person should be able to communicate with a 'customer orientation'; for example, to discuss how the desires of the customer could best be satisfied. At the second level the person should be able to communicate on the tuning and maintenance of the operation. While on the lowest level the person should communicate on what is wrong, but perhaps not much more.

In this way, skill level relates to questions of communication. But this is not all. Communication also generates trust. A person enters a communicative game by adhering to its rules. The game is constituted by its 'constituent expectancies' (Garfinkel, 1963) which indicate (a) what rules the player expects to follow, (b) expects others to expect him to follow, and (c) expects them to follow. A trusted person is considered competent to apply judgement on behalf of others and thus to represent others in sensitive matters. Furthermore, the trusted person is entrusted with secrets and things of value; such as the baby-sitter who takes care of our child. Trusting a person means to expose oneself to risk (that our child will come to harm), but also can reduce complexity by freeing oneself from worry about a large number of possible situations and thereby creating an opening for concentrating on other matters (Luhmann 1989). So, for example, by entrusting my (precious) child to a *competent* baby-sitter, I do not have to specify what action must be taken in every conceivable situation that might arise at home. Instead of worrying about what might happen, I can take my wife to the opera. Obviously, if I sit there worrying about whether the baby-sitter is competent, I cannot enjoy the finer points of Mozart's work. Trust reduces complexity and therefore is an organizing factor.

Trust results from applying a *particularistic* principle, while strict financial control presupposes an application of universal principles. A particularist orientation means that focus is on the exceptional nature of present circumstances. The person involved in the current interaction with me is not a person to be treated like 'anybody else' according to some universal rules, but is a friend or a person of special importance to me. I must therefore protect and support this person, even if it means breaking some of these abstract rules. Indeed, it is by breaking rules for this person that I demonstrate friendship as well as competence. Clearly, although we will not discuss the matter further here, there is a fine line to be balanced between sustaining a friendship and 'doing' membership. I do not like to break the rules and I realize that there is a cost, but the fostering of a relationship and a joint judgement on what is the best action in this particular situation can have a higher priority in this case.

In fact both my friend and I 'know' that this breaking of rules is justified: that is, it is for the good of the company because we solve a problem for the company. We can account for our actions. But only if we are able to include the particular problem to hand in our account. It is on this particularist orientation in interaction between trusted, competent, problem solving persons that lateral responsibility is built. To understand this stance we must go back a few steps.

First, responsibility is a social construction. In order for a work group to be an organizational actor, it must constitute itself as an entity that is granted the right, by its neighbours, to enter into contractual relations with other entities. The social bond, holding the group together as an entity to deal with, is manifested in its ethos which is a product of a learning process given the task structure and other regularities, and which putatively influences what is 'reasonable' conduct by all individuals subject to the structuration of that entity (Jönsson, 1992). Membership carries a 'price' in terms of the discipline that the rules of conduct introduce.

The discipline of the group is laid down in the practices it generates. These, in turn, are neither mechanistic (lawlike reaction to antecedent conditions) or finalist (realization of projects or plans) (Bourdieu, 1977). Instead a particular type of environment, given that the activities carried out are reasonably cyclical or repetitive, will produce a *habitus*, i.e., a socially constituted system of cognitive and motivating structures that are 'collectively orchestrated without being the product of the orchestrating action of a conductor' (Bourdieu, 1977: 72). This points to a need to think beyond the idea of persons governing other persons. In the habitus positions and dispositions are developed jointly and mutually. In this way the habitus structure practices, assumes patterns and becomes regular, natural as it were, without mechanism or finalism.

When such a disciplined group enters into contract with surrounding entities, and when contracts are successfully realized, it will accumulate honour and prestige – what Bourdieu calls symbolic capital and I am calling trust – which gives access to resource pools in the environment. However, so that the resource pools can be mobilized in the fulfilment of contracts, the maintenance of such access requires symbolic investment in terms of resources and time. If symbolic capital assumes a hostile attitude or is distrustful, accumulation of power will be a preoccupation, self-sufficiency will assume a central concern in the establishment of defences, and efficiency will decline.

Illustrations of learning episodes from empirical action research

Two production departments (one foreman) of a small components plant in the Volvo group were studied over a period of three years (Jönsson, 1992). The departments were given extended authority to manage their own production and were provided with a personal computer with facilities to build local databases on the production process. Automation and strict quality requirements characterized production.

In automated production the rate of production is pre-determined by the machines. Improvement will relate to that which is normally called overhead (indirect costs) such as set up time, cutting tools, quality, maintenance etc. Activities which link batches and have effects beyond the individual product. Costs generated by such activities were allocated to products through the cost accounting system, which was based on standards deduced from a 'vehicle cost model' and the forecast volumes. The cost reports would report on allocated costs and part of the improvement work was to find out the causal links between activities and costs.

The intervention from the researchers was modest in the sense that there were some 'lessons' introducing the costing system of the plant and the use of the computer for the group's own planning. From then on the researchers visited now and again and interviewed on what had happened since the last time. The idea of this modest intervention was to initiate a learning process with minimal disturbance of the group and then to help maintain attention to the project by visits which were also data collection opportunities. Over the study period, productivity and quality rose and personnel turnover fell to a greater extent than in comparable units. This could be dismissed as a mere 'Hawthorne effect', but in this case the focus is on the manner in which improvement work spread.

We found that improvement did not occur in smooth learning curves towards some ideal target, but in episodes. While we visited the plant we were told stories. When asked what had happened since we last met the natural way for the group to report was to tell stories about projects or events.

First, one might suspect that the stories we were told about how the team went about reducing cutting tool costs, or testing a new cutting tool, were a function of the way we were collecting our data. But over the years of observation we saw a pattern in the way improvement came about: a triggering event (a cost report, a drop in quality, a new cutting tool introduced, group discussion) would focus attention on some problem with the process. The team, or the foreman unilaterally, declared the phenomenon a 'problem'. A period of fact finding, during which data on the problem were collected and fed into the computer, would follow. Then there would be a meeting or a discussion between the foreman and the shift or the operator in charge of the relevant part of the machine group in which the collected data (presented in graphical form) were interpreted. The meeting usually resulted in initiation of some change in routine to remedy the problem decided. If the follow-up showed that adequate improvement had occurred the problem would be declared solved, the new routine adopted, and attention could be directed towards some other phenomenon. This last shift may be thought of as constituting 'closure'.

For extended periods little in terms of improvement projects happened, but when they happened they seemed to assume this schema of attention, fact-finding, action, follow-up, closure. It is important to see that this schema does not rely on prior assumptions over primary motivating factors, other than the fact that they were opportunities for team member involvement and participation in a cycle of experiential learning. For example, Kolb (1984: 42) depicts the experiential learning cycle as Concrete Experience, Reflective Observation, Abstract Conceptualization, Active Experimentation. There was also an incentive in terms of a monthly, negotiated salary with negotiations every six months based on facts about performance indicators during the previous period. The negotiations in themselves functioned as attention directing reminders.

From group cohesion to contracting the outside

After a number of successful improvement projects, the word started to spread that something interesting was going on in plant X. The company magazine had an article on the team featuring a picture of the foreman holding a money-box. Production planning would consult with the team on the testing of a new cutting tool. The components division head asked for an information system with features like the one the team had. The division head also asked the foreman to travel among the plants of the division explaining to other teams how they had worked to achieve these improvements.

While the foreman was away the team found that they could manage their own business. They could always discuss matters by phone with the foreman if they wanted.

This habit of team self-management developed further when the foreman was asked to develop a one-day course in improvement work. During that time he worked half-time at home with a personal computer and if there was any problem with production the team would make a phone call to discuss things. The occasional visit by the researchers also helped build the prestige of the group.

The prestige and trust accumulated served as responsibility reinforcement. For example, being considered a competent unit opened access to further information, such as when the materials department could not refuse having their deliveries of cooling liquid to the group checked against the cost accounts. It was found that an incoming delivery of 12 barrels had, mistakenly, been charged to the group's indirect materials account. No such mistake was discovered after this incident. One might claim that accounting quality improved.

As the team fostered its symbolic capital and gradually established itself as a competent player in the organization, it started to contract with the environment. This was not a conscious strategy, but happened as an integrated part of problem solving.

One illustrative episode was when the team discovered that a significant reason for wear on the cutting tools used in lathing the inside surface of brake drums was sloppy sandblasting in the foundry. If sandblasting is done improperly there will be grains of sand on the surface of the blanks delivered to the brake drum line. Sand will wear the tools and tool costs will be higher than they could be for the team. By grabbing the phone and telling his colleague in the foundry what he thought about sloppy sandblasting our foreman could (a) establish a customer relation and point to cost effects of low quality, and (b) initiate quality improvement within the realm of another part of the organization.

Another episode on the brake drum line was when a team member initiated development by pointing out the fact that the robots in the spray box at the end of the line wasted paint. Before the brake drums were shipped, they were covered by a protective coat of paint in this box. Two robots, or rather mechanical arms holding paint guns and moving in patterns controlled by a programme, did the painting. Once it was pointed out, even an outsider could see that an awful lot of paint ended up in other places than just on the brake drums. Paint is a cost item for the brake drum line. The result of the episode was that the vendor was called in to re-programme the paint robots to avoid waste. We usually see robots as symbols of modern efficiency, and merely discovering that there in fact is a lot of paint on the walls in the paint box presupposes focused attention and a causal map. By challenging the presumption of efficiency of the ultimate symbol of modern technology, the robot, observation and reflection on the part of the team led to a contract with an outside vendor.

Inner and outer dialogue

This case study illustrates how an inner dialogue in the team generated successful problem solving which in turn gave the group recognition and prestige. Being recognized as a competent player leads to an outer dialogue aiming at contracts.

This outer dialogue became part of the continued problem solving process as well as 'business deals': for example, to let the students from the local technical senior high school come to the plant and programme a layout for in-data registration instead of calling upon the computer department. For the computer department this was a minor, fairly boring, chore that would have to wait its time in the queue. For the students it was an opportunity to participate and get a feeling for industrial problem solving. Maybe a new recruit was won in the process.

Conversation between competent actors, who mutually recognize each other as competent, seems to be the crucial factor in the establishment of lateral responsibility relations in this case. One is reminded of Wittgenstein's (1953) and Winch's (1958) two criteria for meaningful behaviour:

1 the actor must be able to give a reason (account) for an action, and
2 the actor must be bound by the present act to behave consistently in future similar situations. The actor must be seen to be following a rule.

The first criterion means that the actor must be capable of providing a justification or account for the act. It will usually not be necessary to account for all the alternatives at hand, but it is obviously necessary to show that there was a choice and to give reason for the actual choice. (If there is no choice there is no initiating actor and no responsibility.) The reason does not have to be true but must be recognizable as a reason and not incompatible with other information about the situation.

The second criterion establishes the rule-following aspect of action. As actors provide a reason for the meaningful act, they also announce an intention to behave accordingly in the future. A principle is celebrated and elevated to be a rule in the repertoire of rules which generates a pattern for future conduct, a constraining of conduct which, in turn, helps constitute social identity or role. Hereby accountability is established. The actor declares a willingness to be held accountable for this and subsequent acts. The giving of reasons constitutes explanation.

As such, accountability may be geared to the conceptual framework (paradigmatic meaning) or constitute a self-contained story (narrative meaning). The environment will signal its acceptance of the explanation by holding the actor responsible for this and future acts. This gives rise to the 'constitutive expectancies' of the game (Garfinkel 1963) mentioned previously. If trust is broken by actor moves which violate the rules of the game, Garfinkel found that individuals engaged in vigorous steps to 'normalize' the situation by returning to the original constituent expectations. People who tried to retain the original rules of the game were more frustrated than those who played along and were willing to redefine the rules of the game. Indeed, many parents complained bitterly to Garfinkel as the students he had encouraged to take part in his 'breaching' experiments evoked fury when they lay down under the table at mealtimes, or refused to speak when spoken to.

Social identities, or roles, are constituted by the expectations others have, but they can be changed in the course of interaction, provided that accounts are given and accepted. Through identity work we make it possible for others to calculate, rationally, how to achieve efficiency in their action. Certainly, keeping to a 'role' puts limitations on a person's repertoire of behaviour, but it also reduces complexity by freeing others to concentrate on more important matters. By taking basic rule-following for granted, the whole group can concentrate on other important matters.

A critical difference between inner and outer dialogue is the understanding that 'contracts' are implicit within the group, but explicit when they concern the outside. The very point of intimate relations is that they are not explicit. If I were to write down the assets and liabilities in our relations and show them to my friend the friendship would in all likelihood suffer. The businesslike account of our relation would serve to distance us from each other and the sense of friendship will be gone.

In the same way, a work group develops internal relations which are taken for granted and which work through being implicit. In the *habitus* much is taken for granted and energies can be devoted to tasks that the group sets itself. In negotiations with other groups a spokesperson is selected who will have the power to commit other members of the group and 'sign' agreements on their behalf. If contracts are reasonable, and successfully fulfilled, implicit links may also extend to surrounding units, but likely they will remain more in the nature of mutually agreed signals and exchange of information. The qualities of inner and outer dialogue will be expected to differ, but in both cases responsibility will enhance a development of relations through conversation.

Responsible behaviour leads to further access to information, which in turn enhances problem solving capacity. There is a progression in such processes which may prove vulnerable to betrayal of trust.

Discussion-dialogue and Habermasian validity claims

In the introduction to this article it was pointed out how, in the early discussion of governance structures, overlaps between units and levels in organizations were seen as signs of irrationality. In this view, exemplified by Channon (1973), for rationality (and by implication efficiency) to be secured, resources must be allocated on an objective basis, such as return on investment measures. On this basis we arrive at a thin and attenuated idea of communication – in structures which allocate responsibilities *and* information in order to monitor implementation of instructions.

If, on the other hand, conversation – taking the opinion of the other into account – is a crucial moment in the establishment of lateral responsibility relations, then the above mentioned threat to rationality (betrayal of trust) will certainly be real. But rationality in dialogue is a problem only if responsibility is individualistically defined and if rational choice is assumed to be based on self-interest. Then caring about other people's problems will not be part of the responsibility. Sharing information will not be part of the job. A contradiction between hierarchical and lateral responsibilities appears because dialogue presupposes the taking into account of the other's opinion, which lays a bond on self-interest.

A solution to the problem may be sought in the qualities of communicative action. If, as illustrated in the case described above, responsibility is socially constructed between groups or teams, then we should distinguish between the implicit commitments, that which holds the group together, and the explicit contracting with the outside. Habermas's (1984) categories of validity claims may be used to cast some light on this.

First, it should be noted that Habermas (1984: 11 ff.) analyses rationality from the perspective of instrumental mastery as well as from that of communicative understanding, the first termed 'realist' and the other 'phenomenologist'. In this discussion Habermas criticizes that the two are separated and that rationality is defined as cognitive-instrumental ability to choose, successfully, goal-directed interventions in the world. Responsibility would then presuppose autonomy and a monologic goal-orientation. In a context of communicative action, on the other hand:

> . . . only those persons count as responsible who, as members of a communication-community, can orient their actions to intersubjectively recognized validity claims.
>
> (Habermas, 1984: 14)

Such validity claims are used in argumentation to produce good reasons for modes of conduct.

According to Habermas, theoretical arguments use cognitive-instrumental expressions to claim the truth of propositions. In contrast, practical arguments use moral-practical expressions to claim the rightness of norms. Further, aesthetic arguments use evaluative expressions to claim the adequacy of standards of value. Finally, therapeutic arguments use expressive expressions to demonstrate truthfulness and sincerity. All expressions may need explication for comprehensibility (Habermas, 1984: 23). The point is that these types of argumentation interact and give meaning and opportunities of learning. Only against the background of an 'objective' world, and measured against claims of truth, can beliefs appear as systematically false. Only against a background of normative reality can intentions, wishes, attitudes and feelings appear as illegitimate. Progress in one type of argumentation provides opportunities in others. Dialogue among responsible actors will move between the types of argumentation, which will influence how the message assumes meaning when confronted with context, and this will take time.

The fact that sincere interpreters can arrive at different understandings of the same message brings out the issue of truth. The sense of a message emerges when set in context. The repair work has to be done through discourse. The path forward may lay in a truth concept 'à la pragmatism' (James 1974; Mead 1934). The main philosophers of pragmatism (James, Peirce, Dewey, Mead, Rorty) differ in their arguments about truth, but there is a common denominator in their orientation towards action. If it works; if you, after having been frustrated, are willing to act on a particular piece of information, then that information has truth value in a pragmatic sense. Competent persons, even those who may well disagree about goals, are often able to agree on the next best step provided that there is conversational communication.

Conclusion

In this chapter I have attempted to show how lateral responsibility, based on ethos rather than hierarchical power, can be seen as emerging out of communication. Communication inside a problem solving group generates commitments to the team that are made more binding as the team accumulates recognition and symbolic capital. Recognition from the outside, manifests itself in contracting with the outside. The team is then seen as a competent actor that has deserved to be trusted and to have its knowledge and opinion taken into account.

The resulting structures will be driven by the need of providing a habitus conducive to improvement of the value of work, as well as mobilization of attention to problems in a differentiated environment. Norms and practices develop constituting rules of the game that can be relied upon to serve co-ordinating purposes 'without the orchestrating hand of a conductor'. A broader rationality conception, in which the instrumental perspective is upheld at the same time as communicative understanding is sought, is developed. This takes time.

This emphasis on ethos is in contrast to the American influenced design of divisional structures and also differs sharply from a Cartesian-like assumption that strategy is formulated centrally and then implemented and monitored through 'objective' control measures. In a differentiated and changing environment, the communicative approach is claimed to have greater promise, but admittedly carries the risk of breach of trust. The safeguard against breach of trust is communication, in conversational form, between competent people.

This is not to say that hierarchical power should be eliminated, even if it can get in the way of progress sometimes; or even, as Munro and Hatherly (1993) suggest, subvert lateral relations into an extension of hierarchical forms of surveillance. Instead, the lateral co-operative structures should be seen as the informal organization that facilitates learning from organizational experience. Allowing local parts of the organization more room for self-management can generate societal responsibility that maintains the informal organization and enhances adaptation to changing circumstances through dialogue across hierarchical boundaries. This kind of responsibility also fosters accountability in terms of being a competent participant in dialogue, which means demonstration of ability to uphold contracts and contribute to problem solving. The dialogue is locally situated and based in the specificity of the topic under discussion. The typical aim of problem solving in organizational work is to produce new rules of the game – norms of good practice. Top managers are, of course, welcome to participate provided that they are sincere and behave responsibly.

In summary, the monological character of the classical multidivisional structure turns out to be functional only in very moderately differentiated environments. In this respect, the lateral structures that develop in organizations through organizational learning are certainly complementary to the formal structures. They can be expected to grow in importance when a knowledge intensification of work in organizations increases. When they do so, then organizational capacity to deal with multiple logics and change will be enhanced.

References

Austin, J. (1962) *How to do things with words*, Oxford University Press, Oxford.

Bourdieu, P. (1977) *Outline of a Theory of Practice*, Cambridge University Press, Cambridge.

Cable, J., and Dirrheimer, M.J. (1983) Hierarchies and Markets: An Empirical Test of the Multidivisional Hypothesis in West Germany. *International Journal of Industrial Organization*. **1**(1), pp. 43–62.

Chandler, Jr., A.D. (1962) *Strategy and Structure*, Harvard University Press, Cambridge, MA.

Chandler, Jr., A.D. (1977) *The Visible Hand. The Managerial Revolution in American Business*, Harvard University Press, Cambridge, MA.

Chandler, Jr., A.D. (1990) *Scale and Scope. The Dynamics of Industrial Capitalism*, Harvard University Press, Cambridge, MA.

Chandler, Jr., A.D. (1991) The Functions of the HQ Unit in the Multibusiness Firm. *Strategic Management Journal*, **12**(Winter) pp. 31–50.

Channon, D.F. (1973) *The Strategy and Structure of British Enterprise*, Harvard Business School, Boston.

Ezzamel, M., and Watson, R. (1993) Organizational Form, Ownership Structure and Corporate

Performance: A Contextual Analysis of UK Companies. *British Journal of Management*, **4**(2) pp. 161–76.

Galbraith, J.K. (1967) *The New Industrial State*, Houghton Mifflin, Boston.

Galbraith, J.R. (1994) *Competing with Flexible Lateral Organizations*, Addison-Wesley, Reading, MA.

Galbraith, J.R., and Lawler, E.E. (1993) *Organizing for the Future*. Jossey-Bass, San Francisco.

Garfinkel, H. (1963) A Conception of and Experiment with Trust as a Condition of Stable Concerted Action, in *Motivation and Social Interaction*, (ed O.J. Harvey) Ronald Press, New York pp. 187–238.

Goold, M., and Campbell, A. (1987) *Strategies and Styles. The Role of the Centre in Managing Diversified Corporations*, Blackwell, Oxford.

Granstrand, O., and Sjölander, S. (1990) Managing innovation in multi-technology corporations. *Research Policy*, **19**(1) pp. 35–60.

Habermas, J. (1984) *The Theory of Communicative Action*, Vol. 1. Heinemann, London.

Hill, C. (1988) Corporate Control Type, Size and Financial Performance. *Journal of Management Studies*, **25**(5), pp. 403–17.

Jönsson, S. (1992) Accounting for Improvement: Action Research on Local Management Support. *Accounting, Management and Information Technologies*, **2**(2), pp. 99–115.

Jönsson, S., and Solli, R. (1993) 'Accounting talk' in a caring setting. *Management Accounting Research*, **4**(4), pp. 301–20.

Kolb, D.A. (1984) *Experiential Learning. Experience as a source of Learning and Development*, Prentice-Hall, Englewood Cliffs, N.J..

Luhmann, N. (1989) *Vertrauen. Ein Mechanismus der Reduktion sozialer Komplexität*. Enke, 3. durchgesehener Aufl. Stuttgart.

Meyer, M., and Wittington, R. (1994) *Managing the large diversified firm in contemporary Europe: Triumphant multidivisional or stubborn holding company?* Working paper presented at the EMOT workshop on the constitution of Economic Actors, April 1994. Berlin, Germany.

Mintzberg, H. (1990) The Design School: Reconsidering the basic Premises of Strategic Management. *Strategic Management Journal*, **11**(3) pp. 171–95.

Munro, R., and Hatherly, D. (1993) Accountability and the New Commercial Agenda, *Critical Perspectives on Accounting*, pp. 369–95.

Quinn, R.E., and Rohrbaugh, J. (1983) A Spatial Model of Effectiveness Criteria: Towards a Competing Values Approach to Organizational Analysis. *Management Science*, **29**(3) pp. 363–73.

Reich, R.B. (1991) *The Work of Nations. Preparing ourselves for 21st-century capitalism*, Simon & Schuster, London.

Winch, P. (1958) *The Idea of Social Science and its Relation to Philosophy*, Routledge, London.

Wittgenstein, L. (1953) *Philosophical Investigations*, Blackwell, Oxford.

7 Refining accountabilities: opening the black box of management systems success

Simon Lilley

Introduction

Explaining the success of 'technical' systems is far from straightforward. At least this is one inference from seemingly endless arguments over where faults for systems failures lie. But this is to join the performance in the final act, when everything has been 'black-boxed'; when attributions of success or failure to different groups of participants have solidified prior conceptions about different entities and their capabilities and interests. This chapter attempts to open up the black-box of management systems 'success' by exploring ways in which accountability is defined and realized in practice.

Accountability is a process, as much as it is an outcome. And a complex social process at that, involving continuous attributions of agency to different groups of participants. Indeed, when appraisers of information systems seek to ascertain where credit or blame is to lie for the accrual of, or lack of, 'benefits', the details of this attribution process are often forgotten. Instead, the inscribed accountabilities that result are frequently seen as somewhat uncontroversial resources that can serve as ideal-typical metrics in any *post-hoc* investigation. Such moves act to reinstate and further naturalize extant accountabilities in ways that serve to enhance the invisibility of attribution during the accountability process, allowing a rather tidy story of victories and villains to emerge.

The research material presented in this chapter is derived from an examination of the development and implementation of a major management system in the refining sector of the oil industry. The focus of the research is on relations between the 'builders' of the system and those who come to be inscribed as its 'users'. Central to this story are negotiations over where their respective responsibilities for development and use began and ended. Or to put it another way, over where 'the buck' started and stopped. Systems builders attempt to 'pass the buck' as they dramatize where their responsibility stops, whilst those managers designated as users attempt to suggest that they cannot be blamed for 'non-use', since the system fails to completely capture the problems that they face in their day-to-day engagement with refining reality.

During these negotiations, views concerning the 'nature' of the final system and its relations to various other refining entities are seen to change, emphasizing the active nature of the accountability 'attribution' process. For accountability is not merely ascribed on the basis of the shape of a final system, processes of accountability ascription themselves affect the shape of the final system. Accountability does more than just *reflect* the positioning of independently formed centres of calculation and action in aligned chains of people and resources. Processes of accountability ascription are active in both the shaping of the form of alignment achieved and in the selection and shaping of the peoples and resources that constitute that alignment.

It is to the consideration of this dual process of accountability attribution and system shaping that this chapter is primarily devoted. As Cooper (1993) notes: 'the modern interest in technology puts the stress on immediacy of use, constant availability and the easing of effort' (p. 279). Modern technology 're-presents actions in space and time according to an economics of mastery and control' (*ibid.*). Such a conception of technology is just the one required as a firm basis for accountability. For when a system is seen to present opportunities for 'mastery and control' and such mastery and control is not achieved, then, in line with this logic, it is the master of the system, the user, who should be held accountable.

The rest of this chapter is devoted to explicating how the processes of accountability enter into a realization of this logic. A key feature of the study is the process through which the builders of systems are able to (largely) absolve themselves of accountability for systems success and, in their place, deploy a number of techniques that inscribe, and prescribe, *user* accountability for the accrual of systems benefits. In order to render users accountable, system builders sought to 'configure the user' (Woolgar, 1991) in ways that rendered such a site of accountability as the 'natural' choice. The chapter suggests that by laying the commercial accountability for returns on systems investment at the door of prospective users, system builders may insulate themselves from a questioning of *their* worth. Given the seemingly endless litany of prior system failures, such insulation may be understood to be of paramount importance for continued systems deployment.

The system builders

This possibility of mastery and control therefore appears as the objective behind systems introduction, if anyone is to be held accountable for the success of the system. And thus we have two accountabilities: an accountability for establishing the *potential* for mastery and control; and an accountability for the *realization* of that potential. Conventional systems and managerial wisdom suggests that the former is the province of the system builder, whilst the latter is that of the system user.

In seeking to submit this distinction to a somewhat more critical scrutiny, the discussion which follows seeks to address two key questions. First, how is the 'potential' of the system inscribed as the system comes into being? Second, how is accountability for the actualization of this potential attached to those participants who come to be seen as 'users'? To help answer these questions, we turn now to an examination of the development of an Oil Management System (OMS) at a major European refinery owned and operated by one of the 'seven sisters'. Observation and interviews were conducted with a variety of refining personnel over an eighteen month period, during which time the system under question was brought into being.

The Oil Management system to be built at 'Oiltown' was designed and implemented by a team made up from employees from a specialist systems design company ('ITCo.') along with some 'Mexaco Oil' employees. The size and constitution of the team varied through the development and implementation process. From the small System Design Team of four people who undertook the Feasibility Study, the team was to grow to a peak of between 25 and 30 people.[1] At the start of the implementation 'proper', approximately half of the team were Mexaco employees, although as the implementation progressed more ITCo. staff were taken on to carry out programming work. Non-programming staff were primarily involved in systems analysis, specification and administration.[1]

> ITCo. come along with the technical skills, the actual information systems skills and also with the experience of what they've done with implementing OMSs in other refineries. And Oiltown is providing primarily the user expertise, the local expertise, but also the people to support the system in the longer term.[1]

Within Oiltown then, we have a number of different groups with differing relations to the system that was coming into being. We have the programmers, some of whom are 'inside' Mexaco and some of whom are 'outside' in ITCo. (which was owned by Mexaco up until just before the implementation). And we have the non-programmers, all of whom are 'inside' Mexaco. Individual members of this latter group, however, tended to have relations of varying distance and fondness with the emerging system.

General orientation

The Mexaco staff involved in the Oiltown OMS implementation adopted a general approach to building the system that sought to deliver a commercial advantage to the refinery. Mexaco was seeking to replace a centralized and directive commercialism with a more dispersed and dynamic form of the beast.

> Capital must be made to circulate, no longer around a fixed point, but as an endless chain of investments and reinvestments, just as value must be made to radiate in all directions.
>
> (Baudrillard, 1990: 153)

Most of the 'value adding' opportunities in refining were seen to be oil based[2] and so the core application of the developing OM system was seen to be 'Production Programming'.[3] OMS was seen as an integral element of a wider change that sought to render activities in commercial terms in order to engender a commercial orientation within the organization; an orientation that is explicitly linked with the desire for mastery and control to which we have already alluded. It is important to note however, that a large technological system such as a refinery demands, and always has demanded, such a desire (Kallinikos, 1995). It was primarily the objectives which this mastery was to serve that were coming under question, although, as we shall see, this in turn affected the nature of the mastery desired.

The objectives of the system are to take operational information and hold it centrally, and then to analyse that information in terms of commercial rather than operational criteria. It's part of a wider project to alter the focus of the plant to emphasize commercial, financial issues.[4]

Through an intriguing sleight of hand, the lack of this sort of information prior to OMS was seen to be one of the key reasons behind the lack of demand for OMS from the site and also one of the key benefits of the introduction of an OM system. Reflecting Scarry's (1985) insights concerning the 'counterfactual' nature of the relations between technology and the body, the 'need' for information to improve the refinery's performance could not be articulated without information on the refinery's performance. Technology's seductive exchange with the body goes something like this:

Technology: I have this power.
Body: That power represents my powerlessness. I never knew that I was powerless, but with your help I can be powerful again.
Technology: I will dissolve your powerlessness and give you my power if you use it in the way that I prescribe and alter the context (and content) of your action to accommodate me.
Body: Sounds like a good deal to me.

To retail a currently popular phrasing, this conclusion may be seen to leave the body 'in' government but not 'in' power. And the effect does not diminish with increases in scale:

The measures on refinery performance were a lot cruder than they really are today, and they're pretty crude today. The refinery had measures of value added type profitability, but they're rather imprecise and aren't given quite as much credence as they would be if it were a solely operated company . . . Since the refinery wasn't really operating in a plc mode and since it's bottom line wasn't all that visible with credibility, that's why I think it wasn't pulling this into being beforehand. In a sense it's the management environment which sets the expectations and the criteria of success, for what [the refinery] is actually a division within Manufacturing and Supplies. It's an organizational issue really.[2]

In the absence of this 'pull', issues of accountability become even more problematic: if no one 'asks' for the system it is difficult to see who should be accountable for the exploitation of the 'benefits' it supposedly provides. Indeed, managers at Oiltown were not even seen, by the implementers of OMS, to be keen on information systems in general. This was deemed to be partially a result of overselling in the past.[3]

However, the introduction of OMS seemed, for most of the individuals interviewed, to be virtually a foregone conclusion. Sceptical managers may have been able to ignore OMS or partially divert its developmental trajectory but they seemed to believe that they had little alternative but to accept the implementation of some sort of OM type system. This perceived inevitability, coupled with a lack of demand, brought issues of the management of accountability to the fore. We will explore these issues in more depth. First, to further contextualize the issues of interest, we focus upon the 'nature' of the system for which accountability was to be defined and the processes through which emerging accountability ascription affected that 'nature'.

The central database

A central database at the core of OMS to organize the production of commercially oriented information was the cornerstone of the system at Oiltown. The aim was to have 'common rather than distributed information'.[4] A central database was seen to provide a neat way of organizing the interfaces of a number of subsystems[6], whilst the sharing of information that such an organization encouraged was itself seen to enable a wider integration of the refinery system as a whole.

> Hopefully the sharing of information in a common database will result in a better understanding and working relationship between departments.[4]

The importance attributed to a central database in part reflected design choices previously taken at the first two OMS implementations. The first OM system, implemented at Mexaco's Rotterdam refinery, had emerged out of what was seen at the time to be a peculiar set of local contingencies. However, the system so developed was subsequently seen to have had a wider applicability (Lilley, forthcoming). The Mexaco group thus embarked upon a series of OMS implementations at its major world refineries.

The initial ideal was to maintain a common, centrally supportable core at each of these sites with more 'peripheral' aspects of the system being locally designed and implemented to meet local needs. However, at the second OMS implementation at the group's 'Cobber Creek' refinery in Australia, changes were made to this common core that were seen, at the time of the Oiltown implementation, to represent significant improvements on the Rotterdam model. There had consequently been some debate during the early stages of planning and implementing the Oiltown system as to whether the database starting point should be copied from Cobber Creek or whether staff should stick with the original Rotterdam database basis. The Oiltown team plumped for the 'improved' system as their precedential guide.

> Cobber tables [are used] as a starting point, but we don't implement any columns we don't require, and we've implemented columns of our own as needed. The basic philosophy is to use the Cobber model until we cannot.[4]

However, basing the new system on this pre-existing template was proving to be problematic:

> We've not been able to use as much of the Cobber model as we first expected. Cobber Creek is a much simpler refinery than Oiltown and so we had to diversify from the model they used.[4]

Indeed, one of the designers said that 'we've had to make more changes to the Cobber Creek model that I would've expected use of the Rotterdam model to involve'.[7]

During the Oiltown implementation performance problems were starting to emerge with the Cobber Creek system, and programming staff at the refinery were keen to ensure that they did not transfer these along with its central database. These 'systemic' errors were something for which they would have been held accountable and this may partially explain the degree of their deviation from this starting point. Other staff at the site reinforced this low 'systemic' risk orientation. Technological positioning was an important battle ground. Staff brought into Oiltown to produce the system tended to be keen technological innovators (as were the system staff at Cobber) whilst 'indigenous' staff were happier to adopt tried and tested solutions. 'Riskiness' and 'newness' were seen by indigenous staff to be largely synonymous:

> Our general policy has been not to take technical risks. Yesterday's blue sky is quite good enough I think and no nasty surprises has been a policy I've been very happy with. And I do have a say because although the OMS project is separately managed, separately funded, and separately staffed, I still end up with the responsibility of running it once it's been developed, which of course is its benefits stage.[2]

Staff at the refinery were seemingly well aware of a possible future in which they would be held accountable for the accrual of benefits from an unworkable system. And, as the quote suggests, they were keen to intervene to prevent such an outcome.

Their position here was gathering some support through the Mexaco organization. Within the wider group the adoption of a Cobber Creek starting point was losing some of its attractive gloss as the system's performance problems became apparent. As we noted above, Cobber, the second OMS implementation by the Mexaco group, had looked like improving upon the original. However, this 'MarkIIness' had not turned it into the basis of all future implementations which is what earlier visitors to Cobber from Oiltown had suggested would be the case. It was now coming to be seen as something of a technological blind alley, a mistake in systems design from which future designers could learn important lessons. The complete, or near complete, systematization of oil management that had been attempted with the Cobber system was no longer seen to be on the cards. Rather, a new conception of the support of refining activities was emerging in which appropriate solutions to business problems had to be congruent with the 'technological' capabilities of implementable systems.

> [At] the second OMS implementation in Cobber Creek . . . they overstretched themselves in terms of the production system design and because of that they basically failed to meet their goals and are still trying to implement the system. They were just trying to go too far with the technology available.[8]

The Cobber system had sought to make oil management an automatic process in which a number of simulations of refinery plant processes would be run in order to ascertain the most profitable operating characteristics, given current product and crude prices, and current supply and demand. An overall simulation of the site then sought to draw these suggestions together and each of these levels of simulation would be rerun in the light of the output of other simulations until the overall 'value-added' of the system was optimized.

However, as the previous quote suggests, practice did not replicate this theoretical utopia and the system was prone to continual breakdown. Oiltown's attempts to ameliorate these problems were not altogether successful and the choice of this 'technologically sophisticated' starting point was, on balance, seen, as a retardant on the development of a usable system at the refinery (and hence as a basis for account-ability for the site's performance).

> With hindsight I don't think Oiltown would've gone for a Cobber system. Quite honestly it's not lived up to their expectations.[8]

Building system applications: planning for accountability

The key application of OMS at Oiltown was to be the production planning and scheduling system. And in the light of the problems emerging with the system that embodied their central starting point, the system builders recognized that they could not automate all the decisions that staff were required to make: 'so instead we're aiming to provide the information to make those decisions and provide facilities for him (sic) to use that to allow 'What if?' analyses'.[4] For example . . .

> The LP [Linear Programme] will provide a first cut schedule based on the planning information. This will then be given to the scheduler so that he (sic) can fine tune it on the basis of his knowledge. We're aiming to get an approximately 70–80% correct solution from [the LP].[4]

The authors of the feasibility study for the Oiltown OMS had been keen on the potential of an advanced scheduling tool with expert system functionality that was promised in the near future by the LP's suppliers. However, in the atmosphere of technological backtracking that pervaded refining systems at the time of the Oiltown implementation this was seen to be an unworkable technicist solution.

> If we took [the scheduling tool] as it was there would be a lot of work involved taking the [current] LP as output and breaking down the schedule to tank level because our LP isn't defined to tank level. So what we're instead taking is the raw LP output and we are breaking that down ourselves to tanks with what we see as a relatively straightforward algorithm.[1]

The decision to reject this system was also dependent on earlier choices concerning the level of resolution to be used when recording and modelling the refinery within the OM system, choices predicated upon knowledge of the performance implications of the more complex refinery representation that had been employed at Cobber Creek.

> There was a compromise made as to the number of operational data collec-tion points out of that mass of ironwork out there on the refinery that would be collated for production planning purposes. The design is for relevance in the overview level of production control, not in terms of the technical control or operations control of the plant.[2]

OMS thus came to be seen as a tool for, not a replacement of, refinery personnel. Staff savings were expected in some areas but the increased computer support that OMS was seen to necessitate meant that there would be little or no net reduction of staff as a direct result of the implementation. The OMS development was to be kept distinctly separate from improvements to the process *control* systems and this in turn affected the type of accountabilities for system success envisaged for OMS.[5]

> The object is to give people as much information as they need to do their job, *without trying to do their job for them* (emphasis added).[1]

The choices over which data should be captured, and at what level of resolution they should be recorded, reflected wider concerns surrounding the overall purpose(s) of OMS and the perceived limitations of the technology employed. Improvements were primarily to be made in the representations of the plant, *not* in refinery staff's ability to intervene in the plant processes. That is, OMS was very much an *information* system.

> If there is to be increased automation then that added sophistication needs to be within the control system itself and anything that comes from OMS would be in the form of price data, or some constraints and targets which would feed into the process control system. There are too many safety implications of expanding OMS into the process area. It's got to come the other way, perhaps being driven by information coming from OMS. There are two different standards of reliability that you have to consider in the two systems.[5]

Both the indigenous systems staff, and the programmers brought in to build OMS (one of whom provided the prognosis quoted above), were adamant on this distinction between OMS and the systems that directly controlled the operations of the refinery. There was no attempt to automate the control of the refinery under the auspices of the OMS system. Moreover, even the possibility of future developments in this direction was largely dismissed by one member of the indigenous systems staff.

> I think the perception is that at a certain level of detail process plants like this are a little bit like weather systems. There is a degree of unpredictability built into them and to retain responsibility for that continuous operation you probably need to put some human being in charge of it. Somebody who, if you like, can put the umbrella up when it's actually raining rather than when the weather forecast says it should be. And I don't see full automation as being in the scope of plans or realism for refineries. It is a question of how clever one can be, how smart, how effective.[9]

These views on the relations between the emerging technology and refinery operatives may be seen to provide the system builders with a particularly seductive 'let out clause' in the face of future failures to actualize promised benefits. Such failures would be the users' fault since the system designers were explicitly not 'trying to do their job for them'.

Moreover, such moves enable the builders to appear as sensitive to the needs of users although crucially, this sensitivity may be seen to be predicated upon a view of users as *remainder*, as the human flexibility that would oil the wheels of a currently imperfectable system. In other words, users' needs and capabilities would be taken into account because they *had to be*. It would seem as if there would be no hesitation in trying to do the user's job for them *if such a solution was seen to lie in the realm of 'technical' possibility*. 'Real' technological control would have to be (temporarily) deferred, configuring the user as the crux of a successful implementation.

The simulational nature of the system is glaringly apparent here. It is seen to be a 'montage or simulacrum which [will] always be by-passed, confounded and exceeded by practical experience' (Baudrillard, 1990: 155). The system was 'predictable' but the plant it simulated was not seen to be amenable to such a description. Indeed, at an old site with built in 'unpredictability' and concerns about the consequences of the automation of control, the importance of accurate and timely management information was, somewhat ironically, seen to increase. Not only was an automated control loop for refinery processes rejected, simple automation to allow remote human control of valves was also 'impossible' for economic reasons. Benefits of such an automation were not seen to 'warrant' or 'justify' the investment required.[2]

As a result, 'better' information was seen to be required due to the lack of immediacy in process control mechanisms, and in turn, this lack of immediacy was seen to introduce a constraint on the benefits derivable from OMS information.

> I think it means that if you've got operators running round the off sites and tankage areas in order to make blends and line them up to ships . . . you actually have to be as certain as you possibly can that the plan to which they're operating is viable and good, because you haven't got the chance of changing things so robustly at the last minute. And that means that it should pay off, it should add to the overall value, but it would be even more error free I suppose if you could automate that final step as well, or increase the automation in it.[2]

More space and more accountability for users were consequently created.

There were, however, problems noted with this approach: fundamental questions needed to be asked about the functions of the refinery operators. For accountability to be established some *translation* of extant refinery roles was seen to be required. Given that the control and planning systems were not to converge, effort was to be devoted to improving the interface between them, that is, the operators role. The operator is thus seen to represent an appropriate site of accountability, a source of human glue that could exploit the opportunities and avoid the threats that multiple simulations provided.

> I think the challenge in the future and the interface that is going to be concentrated on is actually the human interface. What is the operators job? What are his (sic) tools? What information is he being given and what responsibilities has he got?[9]

Whilst it was . . .

> . . . quite conceivable that in years to come the process side will grow some degree of . . . control intelligence, IS [Intelligent System] characteristics, so long as it's in real time and deals with automated oil flows, I don't have a problem.[9]

It was, however, important to ensure that OMS was not viewed in the same way.

> I think we have to be careful . . . that we don't kid ourselves that an OMS project is in real time and is associated with activating control valves.[2]

Control was thus seen to lie at the level of the 'real', a place where actual valves could alter actual oil flows. And control, was therefore only possible through a system that represented, and could intervene in, 'reality' at this level of resolution. The process control system mentioned above had been in existence for some time and operators were seen to have developed the tacit knowledge required to challenge its representations about their 'truth'.

OMS had no such history and was therefore seen to require a different level of respect, a level that entailed a deeper scepticism with regard to its simulational output. This disjuncture made the systems 'seductive'. And we can see here . . .

> . . . the intrication of the procedure of seduction in the procedure of production and power, as well as the irruption of that minimum of reversibility which exists in every irreversible process, secretly ruining and dismantling it while simultaneously ensuring that a minimal continuity of pleasure traverses it, without which it would be nothing.
>
> (Baudrillard, 1990: 161)

> Seduction . . . doesn't belong to the order of the real. It never belongs to the order of force or to relations of force. This is precisely why seduction envelops the whole *real* process of power, as well as the whole real order of production, with endless reversibility and disaccumulation – *without which neither power nor production would exist.*
>
> (*ibid.*: 159)

This continual disintegration of order and manufactured form is the very ground that production and power require for their perpetuation. It is what makes *these* processes seductive.

These 'problems' (or opportunities) of the irruption of reversibility within representations and simulations were seen to be particularly acute for operators who were simultaneously receiving both information from OMS and directions and information from the process control system. Given that the systems did not look likely to converge in the near future, there was seen to be a 'need to adjust human resources to technical capabilities'.[2] Differences in the 'reality' of the system's outputs and their implications needed to be made crystal clear to the operators.

> Look at it from the process operator's perspective: at the moment he's going to see two different screens, very different things, and he's probably going to be slightly confused. He's getting some information out of his [process] control screen, which is real, and some of it's calculated. And he's got plans which are there and targets to meet.[2]

It was thus important for operators to be able to divine the 'real' from a variety of sources of differing ontological status and work out how to act upon it, but for them to do so, these differences in status had to be made immediately apparent. Only with this clarity in place could accountability be transferred from the builders of the system to its users. Both users and their systems have to be appropriately 'configured' if the former are to be accountable for the performance of the latter (Woolgar, 1991).

Simultaneous simulation, understanding and the translation of accountability

The new LP system [the planning and scheduling modules of OMS] was seen as a success by the system builders: 'The Production Department seem to be very happy with it'.[4] And some wider 'unintended' benefits were also seen to have accrued as a result of the introduction of a new simulation of refinery processes. Staff in the Production Department had 'had a lot of work in terms of understanding why they're getting particular results'[4] due to the fact that they 'had to go through and test [the new LP] against [the old]'.[4] As a result Production staff were seen to 'understand the results they're getting a lot better'.[4]

Other applications that were deemed to be 'more important perhaps in that they are the more commercially orientated, rather than the more technically orientated activities', such as performance monitoring, were however 'much less clearly defined'.[4] There was seen to be no problem with the availability of data for the support of these applications, rather, the problem was seen to be in terms of 'identify[ing] what you are actually monitoring, what does it mean, performance monitoring?'[4] In short, although enhanced accountability was seen to be an inevitable part of the drive behind the system, the specific *nature* of that accountability was severely problematized by the shift to new systems.

> Are you measuring against your LP targets? Are you measuring against your process model targets? Are you measuring against both I suppose? And what sort of sensitivities and how do you want to see it? How do you want it grouped?[4]

Some of these problems were seen to be soluble through the use of more flexible reporting formats. Standard reports may not reflect and accommodate particular concerns. But fixed formats were seen to be required for accountability to *others* and we go on to consider mechanisms that were designed to fulfil this need in the following section.

Before doing so however, we will briefly examine these flexible reporting tools as they illuminate some of the myriad ways in which users were configured by the builders. Configuration of users was envisaged to be the most successful when the users were themselves involved in the process. The 'parameters' within which users could produce their own reports were a key source of direction in the enrolment of the self in these configurational moves. The extent of potential self control provided over the nature of user reports is a key source of configuration here and, as we noted, this configuration itself plays a key role in the translation and transfer of accountability.

The existence of a central core database from which flexible reports could potentially be derived provided both opportunities and risks for self-enrolment on the part of users, and requirements for database reporting were defined relatively late in the implementation of OMS. Each of the Mexaco programmers working on the project and each of systems staff in the wider Mexaco Group with an interest in Oiltown's OMS, had their own 'intuitive' views of what should be provided. There was however little agreement between these views and the diversity of reporting tastes within the wider Mexaco group was reflected at different OMS implementations. For example . . .

> At Trust refinery in [the USA] they ended up putting in a data capture system which was very reliable and they gave people facilities using Mac PCs. So they used the power of the Mac to allow people to do things like trending process data [and] extracting data into spreadsheets.[5]
>
> Both Cobber Creek and Trust gave some users access to the system prompt [Access to the 'system prompt' entails the opportunity, but not

necessarily the ability, to partially 'write' the system as one's usage needs arise]. The intention is not to do that here.[10]

> At Rotterdam they drifted from the ideal of open access to the system prompt and instead used a number of pre-defined specific screens. Other refineries have started from Rotterdam's final model and moved back towards the ideal [For this programmer 'open access' was seen to be the ideal].[10]

> Cobber Creek used general parameterized forms for reporting. So there were less forms than at Rotterdam, but they were more general.[6]

> Eurofine took an extract from their main database to a mini database on which users could write their own inquiries using the 20:20 spreadsheet package.[10]

And not only was there no general agreement within the Mexaco group over how database reporting facilities should be provided, there was also little consensus on, or even consideration of, this matter by those more senior organizational participants employed to oversee the development as a whole. According to one of the system builders:

> The [Oiltown OMS] Management Steering Group either doesn't have a view on this, or if they have, I haven't found it yet.[11]

Given this fairly limited 'external' colonization of a key area of their endeavours, the system builders within the Oiltown refinery settled on a number of different approaches to satisfying users' reporting needs. The different approaches to reporting on the part of the system builders were accommodated through the provision of a number of different reporting routes. However, some views were not seen to be directly amenable to 'technological' accommodation:

> There's three groups: there's the standardized reporting screens; there are . . . ones which have more flexibility; and really if none of them will suit, people will resort to the computer department.[5]

These differences in approach reflected different conceptions and representations of the capabilities and requirements of refinery staff and managers – conceptions and representations that were crystallized and reified by the limited range of reporting routes that were finally instantiated. The 'potential' of the technology employed was seen to interact with the competencies and wider context of refinery management. For example, a member of the BDU Systems Group who had been intimately involved with the development of the Rotterdam system and the early stages of the Oiltown implementation, believed that whilst relational database technology provided a simpler and neater way of conveying information between subsystems than a conventional hierarchical structure would allow, complications re-arose when the database was to be queried.[6]

This individual felt that managers would be 'too busy' to learn the skills required for sophisticated interrogation of the database, but they nevertheless were seen to want access to the sort of information that such queries would provide. Whilst staff and some managers could, and did, use spreadsheets (for example at Eurofine and later at Oiltown) to manipulate data extracted from the database, they were not seen to be capable enough, or willing, to use fourth generation 'natural' language tools to manipulate, and indeed extract, the information they required. Hence there was a reluctance at Oiltown to give users access to OMS at the system prompt level. Moreover, there was seen to be little experience at Oiltown of natural language type interfaces, whereas Lotus spreadsheets were quite widely used.[7]

> End users cannot use fourth generation languages. They need professional support both for security reasons and in terms of data definitions. There's no problem with simple systems but with larger scale systems the complexity of table linkages precludes their use by the non-expert.[6]

Similar views were expressed by one of the system managers at Oiltown with responsibility for OMS and the view was solidified in the database reporting made available at the refinery. Although predicting future demands for non standardized information, he saw little evidence of current expression of these demands.

> I always expected that the computer department would have to provide a facility where they would respond very quickly to particular queries. Nevertheless, I don't see any evidence of that sort of thing happening. I still expect it to happen. Once we've got all our data in the database I think managers are going to have need for *ad hoc* queries and they're not going to set these things up themselves.[5]

Others noted the practical limitations of the tools provided.

> We have an *ad hoc* reporting facility with an interface to the Lotus spreadsheet package. In theory it should allow the user to write their own completely *ad hoc* query to download any available data into Lotus for spreadsheet analysis. In practice the download is being carried out either by OMS project staff or more recently, by the Computer Support Committee.[4]

Lower level staff with more experience of spreadsheet usage were seen to have been potentially capable of producing the information they wanted using these simple tools, but they were not seen to be users of non-standardized information.

> I'm sure there'll be some [queries] that [managers] can't deal with. These facilities are still geared pretty much at looking at the raw data. They're going to have requirements which require a certain amount of processing of that raw data and I think that's going to require computer services . . . I guess you can do virtually anything with a Lotus spreadsheet if you put the time into doing it, but a manager's not going to do that . . . but I think for the majority of users those tools that we've provided should actually meet their needs.[5]

Whilst the manager quoted above was 'keen on *ad hoc*' facilities[3], they were seen to be dangerous. He thought that they could be provided to 'more sophisticated users' but that such users would still require a user support team to set up appropriate access to the database for them.[3] Another system builder . . .

> . . . envisage[d] *ad hocs* actually being done by the users themselves, without recourse to applications support.[4]

Although . . .

> One problem with this approach [to *ad hoc* querying] is that the size of the
> reports that can be generated by novice users could actually kill the
> machine.[4]

Cross referenced information emanating from more than one OM subsystem and
from other systems communicating with OMS, was provided by some standard screens,
but this sort of information was not seen as 'important' for refinery managers, its
production was not seen to be 'justified'.[12] OMS was seen as 'just' an oil production
planning system, access to, and combination with, other sources of information was not
seen as important.[12]

Higher management were not seen to be aware of what cross referenced information they required.[12] The 'activity based' nature of the site meant that such information
was seen to be required only in certain circumstances, for example, comparing relative
performance against budgets, and standard reports were already available for such
purposes.[12] More general information to assist in understanding wider, more fundamental questions, was not seen by management as appropriate to their roles and was,
perhaps more importantly, explicitly outside the scope of the OM system.[12] And the
system builders were keen to retain this restricted scope: '. . . we've avoided looking
for expansion'.[5]

'Strategic' information for refinery management was seen to come from Head Office
staff viewing trends to examine wider issues. Indeed, there was seen to be a very clear
differentiation between the time frames of various activities, as opposed to other
businesses, where the divisions between operations, tactics, and strategy were seen
to be 'largely arbitrary'. This restricted view of on-site managerial responsibility meant
that aggregated, cross referenced information on wider issues was seen to be irrelevant
to managers at Oiltown.[12]

Another concern was that users at the refinery were generally of 'limited' computer
experience.

> The users we targeted . . . were the ones that worked with PC's normally . . .
> because they were the type of people who were likely to need that sort of
> flexible facility.[5]

There was little availability of PCs on the site until about five years before the
implementation of OMS, and hence computing knowledge was mainly in the hands of
people new to the site.[11] Reporting of the database in non-standardized form required
quite detailed knowledge of relatively complicated Standard Query Language (SQL)
programming. The example below, which displays a monthly salary bill for each
department of an organization, comes from the British Standards Institution's Specification for Database Language SQL (BS 6964: 1988):

```
SELECT DNAME, SUM (SAL) FROM EMP, DEPT
WHERE EMP.DEPTNO = DEPT.DEPTNO
GROUP BY DNAME;
```

Despite the seemingly arcane nature of this sort of user-computer interaction, the
possibility of allowing users to make such queries was not precluded by all. Unknown
'experts' were thought to exist in certain departments, their expertise having been
acquired through 'hobby usage'.[10] As a result, one of the system managers with

responsibility for OMS was, from his programming perspective, keen to allow such users access to the SQL system prompt to enable them to structure their own queries.

> It makes things easier and allows them to do possible little odds and sods not anticipated in the programmes.[10]

Hobby users were seen by this builder as a potential resource that should be exploited. Ironically, the limited scope of the OMS information was not seen by him as a reason for not providing flexible access. Instead, OMS was seen to offer the potential of more open access than 'most company information systems since it doesn't contain much sensitive information, particularly personnel files and payroll'.[10] He did however note that there were quite big differences between users' 'levels of imagination and realization of the potential of the system'.[10] In his opinion, user imagination was the limiting participant, users seemed to 'want to be told what the system would deliver'.[10]

The 'dangers' of such an open approach for the other system builders, coupled with a perceived lack of demand for such facilities at Oiltown meant that this was not allowed to happen. This may reflect 'protectionism' on the part of the designers, reflecting a very real fear that they could lose control of the system. And, as we hinted above, even the analysis of data downloaded by a support group was seen to be beyond the willingness and capabilities of management.[7] For example, 'trend analysis' and the manipulation of OMS data using Lotus were seen by one systems manager as 'a more sort of advanced thing'[1] and, initially at least, these facilities were only made available to, and used by, key individuals, particularly technical specialists who were deemed to have the appropriate skills.[10] At first the Lotus interface only allowed the download of data from a single file but a sandwich student working on the project 'introduced the ability to download from multiple files'[4], although whether such *direct* access was available in practice remains unclear.

Opinions on appropriate reporting also seemed to change throughout the implementation. One of the system builders had, at the feasibility stage, thought that . . . 'access to the SQL prompt was the best idea'[11] but as the implementation 'proceeded and we realized the size of the system and the potential complexity of reports' he decided to opt for the 'same approach as Rotterdam and not allow such access'.[11] Not only were there doubts about the 'overall business benefits', such complex inquiries were seen to require 'programmers' and the training required to get general users to this level of competency was deemed to be 'unjustified'.[11] Instead the refinery opted for a fast response (in the order of half an hour) to complex queries from the Computer Services Committee. Users had not previously approached the CSC with information requests 'because of the slowness of response'.[11] As part of the general aim to encourage a more commercial orientation within the refinery, the CSC charged user departments for the time involved in answering such queries.[11]

In summary, these concerns and pressures resulted in the provision of *ad hoc* reporting through the use of SQL forms, written by support personnel, that took the form of menus. In some cases these menus could be parameterized by users, allowing them to select a subset of a pre-defined inquiry, to bring about the download of the data they required.[1]

> We thought we could cover that [*ad hoc* reporting] by Lotus 'Trends' [a trending programme, written at Rotterdam and picked up by Oiltown] and

tabular reporting of time against qualities . . . , any tank data, and some movement data.[1]

We decided that we would package the three of them into a user defined reporting set or group of facilities and we would standardize the interface to them so that the users used the three of them in the same way.[5]

The facilities provided were seen to represent a balance between provision of pre-defined reporting formats to reflect and embody 'business needs' deduced and constructed by the system builders in their discussions with users, and predicted and current user demands for ease of access to novel information. The forward looking orientation of OMS at Oiltown was recognized to require some flexibility in the design of future reports. Lessons learnt from previous and ongoing OMS implementations were built into the system's reporting structures. And system builders were, on the whole, happy with their response to these demands.

You can't afford to go to either extreme. And I think we've got the right balance here (laughter).[5]

In the next section, we examine how the realization of the benefits that OMS was expected to provide was managed at Oiltown.

Managing the benefits of OMS: the buck stops here

The views of the system builders concerning reporting facilities are illustrative of the view that they held of the OM systems' potential users and the ways in which such users were thereby 'configured'. This configuration is an essential part of the translation procedures that seek to render users rather than builders accountable for the accrual of systems 'benefits'. The view of users as 'needing to be told', as 'lacking in imagination', as 'unaware of business needs' provides ideal grounds for the builders' specification of what the system would do. All they then had to do was to make the users, rather than themselves, accountable for doing it. The importance of these moves was heightened by an increase in the demands for systems' accountability coming from the wider group.

Obtaining ratification and funding for OM type systems within the Mexaco Group became more difficult in the period preceding and during the Oiltown implementation as a result of the emergent 'perception of failure' surrounding the first two implementations at Rotterdam and Cobber Creek.[8] Whilst these failures were primarily attributed to changes in environmental circumstances and technical difficulties respectively, the resulting increased reluctance on the part of *some* senior managers to support large scale IS projects at refineries led to increased demands for the provision of systematic benefits management procedures on concurrent and subsequent projects of a similar nature. The key to successful benefits management was seen to lie in an early, *systematic* enrolment of the system's prospective users. One of the senior managers involved in the Rotterdam project, who was also a member of the Oiltown Management Steering Committee, had this to say on the subject:

I think the key thing is having solved the technical problems with putting the systems in, you then have a secondary problem in that if you don't use the system and . . . the users, aren't committed to it, then you don't get the benefits. And that is one of the key problems that we're facing really . . . , bringing the users along with the implementation of the system and ensuring that they use it after the event.[8]

The benefits management procedures employed at the Oiltown implementation were seen to be exemplary in this respect. Although 'a bit bureaucratic . . . having seen the lack of enthusiasm, certainly in the Rotterdam refinery' it was seen as important that an attempt be made to boost enthusiasm early in the project.[8]

> [One of the system managers] at Oiltown has picked up on this point . . . and he's actually generated some ideas on management of the benefits. And the way he approaches that is he actually allocates responsibility for recovering benefits to people who claimed for individual components of the system. He's aiming to delegate the responsibility and what he proposed is that as bits of the system are implemented they will be audited and what I've recommended is that twelve months after the completion of the whole system we audit it again, just to make sure.[8]

Accountability for various aspects of the 'claimed' benefits here were thus formally inscribed against individuals and groups of claimants. Through this process an indelible record of 'user involvement' could also function as a basis for a formal segregation of builders from this accountability, once the system had been signed off to the satisfaction of both parties.

An ongoing process of auditing against these claims further ensures that it is to be the users rather than the builders who are to be held accountable. A seductive approach to user involvement and participation is translated into a set of accountabilities that are expected to function as 'real' demands upon a set of users in a future in which system builders are notable only by their absence. Not surprisingly, it was the systems builders rather than the users who were most enamoured with such an approach. For example, although coming late to such an orientation the system manager referred to in the above quote adopted the approach wholeheartedly. He saw future projects as insupportable in the absence of such procedures and spoke ruefully about the lateness of his conversion.

> In fact for any project coming along now I don't think it should be sanctioned unless they have a Benefits Management plan in place.[5]

> It would have worked an awful lot better . . . if I'd done benefits management procedures right at the beginning of the project when we were getting the thing authorized.[5]

Concerns were, however expressed by the senior manager on the Oiltown Management Steering Committee about the manageability of such an approach, perhaps reflecting some awareness that what was being created was merely a translation system between different sites of simulation:

> Now whether, at the end of the day, that's actually a manageable thing, I don't know . . . it's a step in the right direction.[8]

And these concerns were partially reflected by the system builder at the refinery who proposed the approach. Coping with these complexities resulted in a questioning of extant refinery role allocations and thus a further translation.

> If you take performance monitoring where one person is responsible for setting the targets and monitoring what's happened and another one is responsible for actually taking some action to improve things then it's a little bit difficult to see . . . who's responsible for making the whole thing generate dollars at the end of the day.[5]

Other organizational changes underway at the time of the implementation increased the visibility of these issues, and problems were exacerbated by the ephemeral nature of some of the benefits thought to accrue from the system and made particularly acute by the emerging commercial orientation that OMS was expected to play a role in delivering.

> Many of the benefits are cultural and although lots of them are measurable, they are very difficult to cost justify.[4]

Nevertheless, despite the potential problems with the approach's application, benefits management at the refinery was seen to have furthered its cause. The uncertainty and impreciseness of the procedures were not perceived to undermine their effectiveness. Certainty could be achieved within the simulational realm, but steps outside to a supposedly 'real' presented problems. Still, this did not effect the principle being enacted and systems managers are, after all professionals, so they could not go back on their principles.

> The principle of using Benefits Management in order to make people think ahead about how they're going to use the system and what the implications are for their department has been really useful. Clear accountability is one part of it and can help. If you can get to the point where a person is responsible for producing a million dollars worth of benefit then it certainly helps to concentrate their mind a bit! (laughter).[5]

We return to consider further the implications of these moves in our concluding remarks. Before doing so, we briefly examine users' attempts to resist and subvert some of the demands that the system and its associated accountability regime placed upon them.

Precedent, practice and practicalities

OMS was seen to be an information system, not an automation of refinery processes, and in such circumstances precedentially sanctioned understandings and methods of working could conspire to circumvent the use of OMS, at least to a certain extent. OMS data and information were recognized as being partially remote from refining 'reality', as it was defined by Oiltown staff, and human involvement[25] was deemed to be essential for the prevention of reification of the system's somewhat dubious representations.

Acting blinkeredly on the recommendations of reified computer based models of reality was seen to be potentially disastrous and contextualized user expertise provided some defence against these dangers. Obviously such moves played right into the builders' hands. These claims necessitated an accountability that resided with the system's users. The age of the site and its somewhat *ad hoc* construction made the perceived dangers that supported this orientation all the more apparent. As we noted previously:

> I think the perception is that at a certain level of detail process plants like this are a bit like weather systems. There is a degree of unpredictability built into them and to retain responsibility for that continuous operation you probably need to put some human being in charge of it. Somebody who, if you like, can put up the umbrella when it's actually raining rather than when the weather forecast says it should be.[9]

Staff in the production programming department still had 'a lot of faith in paper systems' since they were 'often simpler and quicker to use'.[22] And in many cases the largely informal, personal contacts, with operators, lab staff and Head Office personnel continued to be seen as the route through which novel problems and queries would be solved and answered.

> When you just want a small piece of information it's quicker to telephone the lab rather than exit the system you're using, enter OMS, get the information, exit OMS, and go back into your original system.[26]

> Most of the information to do the job comes from personal contact with the blenders. I frequently check with the blenders to try and trace the cause of problems I've noticed on the system, such as why a particular product has been downgraded.[25]

This continuing importance of social contacts throughout the refinery presented an interesting tension around the emerging OM system. On one level it served to further configure the users as the 'natural' site of accountability for the accrual of benefits, whilst at another it enabled those users to bypass the system in their fulfilment of the demands such accountability placed upon them. And given the characterization of production programming presented in the quotes above, it is easy to understand how the e-mail system (whose introduction was contemporaneous with OMS's) was seen to be the most important change in computer support for production programming activities. Users seemed to be keener on exploiting the opportunities provided by computer mediated communication than on the use of computer produced information.

> The e-mail system has provided some really big benefits. That's definitely the change that's helped the most.[22]

Moreover, the refinery's attempts to gain BS5750 Quality Assurance accreditation meant that e-mail gained some precedence over previously widely used telephone contacts. BS5750 accreditation necessitated some formalization of these previously 'informal' contacts.

> If we note problems with a unit's performance we 'phone the unit supervisor to find out what's wrong with it and then inform the blenders . . . When BS5750 comes in we'll have to contact them via e-mail as well so that the contact is documented.[28]

Other changes in working practices predicated upon the introduction of enhanced computerized support were seen to be less welcome. Previously developed successful applications of simple computer tools were partially displaced by OMS and concerns were raised about the consequences of such actions. One of the refinery's Oil Accountants who was a regular user of the COMA (Computerized Oil Management Accounting) system was particularly peeved by changes made to this tool in order to facilitate its integration with OMS. His concerns were not restricted to the OM system. OMS was merely the latest of a long line of disturbances to his working that provided him with few tangible benefits.

> The COMA system is perfectly OK for my needs. The only problem is that every time a new system is introduced COMA has to be changed even if it's running perfectly well. They never change the new system to suit the old.[18]

For users in the production programming department OMS was seen, by some, to be too much of a move towards automation. Existing practices interacted here with notions of the importance of contextualized expertise and knowledge. Prior to the introduction of OMS, production plans and schedules had been constructed by production programming staff on Lotus spreadsheets, using information from the ITCo LP models. As we noted, there was a relatively high level of expertise in the use of spreadsheets at Oiltown refinery.[7] Rather than being seen as a tedious re-keying of information and a waste of time, processing of information and plans using spreadsheets was seen to have distinct advantages. Not least of which was a (more) human 'check' on the reasonableness of the plans produced.

> The spreadsheet is very good at identifying where differences have occurred. All differences require explanation – if the spreadsheet can't explain it we have to investigate further.[29]

LP plans derived from the system were seen to require 'tidying up'[26] and they were tidied up using a Lotus spreadsheet. Although as the following quote makes clear, the process would seem to involve a little more than just tidying up:

> We use spreadsheets to make up the blending requirements. *We take the original qualities in the tanks, what we want to end up with, and then mess about with the components on the spreadsheet until we get what's required.* That's then printed out and goes down as instructions to the blenders (emphasis added).[29]

Analysis and checking of plans and reports using Lotus was seen to be particularly important for 'vetting' purposes.[22] Use of spreadsheets made information and plans 'checkable'[22] and this was seen to be 'the most important function of spreadsheet analysis'.[22] Attempts to increase the automation in the production of plans and schedules were seen to be inappropriate by production programmers as it required 'contextual knowledge not held on the information systems'.[26] Indeed, complaints were made about OMS's inability to accommodate and reconcile free style commentaries providing explanations of deviations from the routine operation of plans and pieces of plant with OMS information on the 'technical' status of those plans and pieces of plant.[25]

So again we see users wanting a computer based storage and communication system rather than a 'technical' information system. These characterizations of users' tasks, provided by users themselves, are perhaps the clearest indications of the seductive power of the accountabilities that had been established during their involvement with the development of the emerging OM system. For although they point out that the system did not resolve all the problematic issues surrounding the planning, programming and scheduling of refinery production, and indeed, that in some cases it exacerbated them, they also clearly articulate a belief on the part of the users that they would eventually be the ones held to account for both failure and success. 'Involvement' with the development had heightened accountability, but not for the developers. There were new tools for, and increased expectations of, users at the site. And whether those tools helped or not, expectations would have to be fulfilled or explained away by the users in the absence of the makers of those tools.

In large part, these increased expectations upon users at the site were reified by other users who sought to act at a distance upon refinery activities. Staff at Mexaco Oil's National Head Office wanted *certain* plans about future refinery production produced and distributed by the OM system. Their positioning in the refinery production network meant that this was the sort of information they required. They wanted to treat the refinery as something of a modularized 'black box'. Given inputs, they wanted to know outputs and vice versa. Only with such certain and deterministic information could they provide the traders with opportunities to 'generate value'.

> Oiltown produces their production plans with [the linear programmes] for the next week to two weeks, at the most. And we [want the system designers to] somehow get an interface that takes the production rates out of [the LP] into OMS and extrapolates forward, quantity and quality. I mean we're working to this plan and we believe this plan is right and it's the correct model. It's the best data we have on the future. We shouldn't be allowing people to say, 'No, I don't think it's quite like that, if I were you I'd allow for this'. In this day and age we shouldn't be doing that. Those things should already be accounted for and embodied in the model. If it isn't, if somebody does now and again say, 'Look!', which they're going to do, then the model should be improved.[30]

The Head Office users' relative distance from the practicalities of refining on an imperfect site are made clear. Traders needed to believe in the certainty of the information they were provided with internally in order to be able to manage and make money out of the external uncertainty with which they were confronted. Refinery production programming staff were no more able to provide a definitive plan with the system than traders were able to provide a definitive figure for the oil price in two weeks' time. Users recognized the importance of *their* expertise to do *their job*, but the tasks of others were seen to be relatively programmatic and routinized. And such processes of attribution may be seen to enable both heightened accountability and self acceptance of that accountability by system users.

Discussion

The paper began by elucidating a distinction between two types of accountability for the promised benefits of management systems. An accountability for producing a system that potentially enables a user to exercise mastery and control, an accountability that is traditionally seen to lie with the system developer. And an accountability for the realization of that potential that is traditionally seen to lie with the user. But what if the attempt to establish the potential for mastery and control can itself destabilize and hence recede the possibility of the realization of this potential?

What if the desire for mastery and control harbours a *reversible imminence* (Baudrillard, 1983; Cooper, 1993) at its core? That is, when the search for control eliminates the possibility of *real* control: when control of the 'denatured' is all that can be attained since the denatured has replaced the *real* during the struggle for control. Such a possibility is far more volatile and irruptive than mere subversion or inversion, for it belongs to a different order of transformation. It signals the subsumption of representation to simulation: an *implosion* of the structure upon which 'the real' depends.

> Every *positive* form can readily accommodate its *negative* form, but recognizes the mortal challenge of a *reversible* form. Every structure can accommodate inversion or subversion, but not the reversal of its terms. Seduction is this reversible form.
>
> (Baudrillard, 1990: 141)

And if the very possibility of the real, of 'truth', is seen to be in flight, the possibility of mastery and control is a chimera. But a seductive chimera nonetheless that energizes its pursuers all the more through its inevitable non-attainability. There is nothing that is as attractive as the thing we cannot have. Indeed, this is, for want of a better word, the 'essence' of seduction that both undermines and thus continually reinvigorates the realm of production and 'the real'.

> To produce is to force what belongs to another order (that of secrecy and seduction) to materialize. Seduction is that which is everywhere and always opposed to production. Seduction withdraws something from the order of the visible, whereas production brings everything into view, be it object, number, or concept.
>
> (Baudrillard, 1990: 151)

Some nascent awareness of the simulational potential of systems is perhaps reflected in the insistence that users are the ones to be held accountable for systems success (or its lack thereof). Users who will be left to 'carry the can' are almost inevitably seduced by the reversible linkages between the simulational and 'the real'. However, the activities involved on their part in creating, maintaining and *working* with this distinction tend to remain unspoken and invisible in 'official' descriptions and prescriptions of the system development process. Users have to move between the front and back stages of the development and deployment if 'use' and subsequent benefits are to be performed. Reversibility and implosion along and across the distinction between the two simulated realms are necessarily chronic in a non-deterministic world, necessitating continual travelling back and forth on the part of the users as they engage in *'refining reality'*.

If the 'technical' system was truly systemic, if it were 'closed', then it would need no enrolled users and its builders would be accountable for its functioning. But we 'know' the system cannot do this, because, as we have noted, accountability *in action* must live in the realm of the social, not the technical. 'Free' humans may be accountable because they can exercise *choice*, and systems cannot, or so the theory, supported and instantiated by humanist doctrine, goes. But other forces are at work here in this attribution. Reality is too 'hard', too recalcitrant to submit *directly* to mastery and control.

Symbols are 'softer' and so we seek to bring the real into the symbolic through *representation*. But as we deploy our systems of control, as tools to 'capture' the world, the world changes in the direction of representational convenience (Cooper, 1992). And despite the fragility of this transformation, the real consequently becomes just another symbol within a simulational system that is no longer anchored to anything outside. It represents nothing but itself.

Systems may be seen to oscillate, therefore, between 'faithful' representation of the real, in which case the representation is not of a 'predictable' world amenable to control (Kallinikos, 1994), and simulation of the real *as* predictable and manipulable, in which case the very category of the real is dissolved. In general, a desire to maintain and enhance the visibility of the 'systematicity' of systems entails the ascendency of the latter, at least in 'official' accounts, and the 'problem' of accountability becomes one of *translation* within the simulational realm, primarily between simulations of processes and acts of intervention upon those processes, and simulations of 'value added' (or removed!). Such are the costs of life in a culture obsessed 'with the instantiation and instrumentalization of all things' (Baudrillard, 1990: 152).

Conclusion

Users' resistance to the demands being placed upon them by the emergent system is revealed in this chapter as being largely pre-figured and organized around the notion of accountability. A recognition of the emerging system as simulational leads users to reject some of its injunctions to ensure that they retain contact with 'reality'. They come to see themselves as accountable for results and benefits. Indeed, perceiving themselves as users, their accounts of systems development glorify their own roles as entrepreneurial and skilled, as the source of added value. They are not, they suggest, the sort to be seduced by simulations.

Ironically, one may see this is precisely what happened. Actions by managers, acting as users, brought about ongoing and interminably unstable mergers and divisions between the simulational and the 'real'. This should not be a surprise. Those who are designated as users have to work with, and through, seduction; a seduction that leaves them caught in an accountability trap. This seduction, whereby creative work between the simulational and the 'real' is performed – to maintain the dissimulation of the separate identity of the latter – is perhaps most apparent in the attempts of users to resist complete compliance with the demands of an over-arching system.

Seduction continually 'undoes' the real, providing grounds for its re-instantiation and thus opportunities for action. It is the shadow of the uncertain return of uncertainty that energizes the drive for certainty. It is the knowledge that risk is unavoidable that impels action to remove risk, however self-defeating such action may be. In short, it is the simulation of a real forever unattainable, forever contingent, forever incomplete.

This impossibility of the real provides endless grounds for play that seduces us into following a search for a chimera. And in a 'commercial world', accountability is the vehicle we drive on the road to nowhere. This theme is perhaps most apparent in the comments of one of the system builders who pointed out that:

> If you can get to the point where a person is responsible for producing a million dollars worth of benefit then it certainly helps concentrate their mind a bit![5]

At the point where accountability and responsibility for a 'real' figure can be inscribed to an individual, it no longer matters whether that individual has been provided with the tools that can enable a meeting of this promise, for the promise is already made. It is seen to be made by that 'individual', by the prospective user of the tool and not its developer. Indeed, it is unlikely that the developer will even be present when the promise is to be called in. And the laughter on the part of the informant that accompanied this comment perhaps reflects some awareness of this situation.

The putative user, through 'involvement' with the system, is configured *as* accountable for the delivery of such benefits because of (and in spite of) the system's (lack of) potential to support such achievement. In many ways the developer's task is successfully accomplished once the accountability is in place, regardless of whether the tool developed provides any direct support for the user. For the developer has indeed delivered a 'commercial orientation' on the part of refinery users. It is for the configured user to realize that orientation through an actualization of a configured self in a newly 'commercial' future.

As I have been discussing it, accountability is about a distribution of the future. An allocation of credit and blame for making the future happen that is taking place in the here and now. Indeed, it is this distribution of the future *as* capital into parts – allocated to individuals – that may yet come to be seen as:

> . . . a fantastic extension of the jurisdiction governing private property, to assign each individual to the management of a specific capital . . . a capital for which each individual will be answerable to himself, and under the sign of his own liberation.
>
> (Baudrillard, 1990: 154)

Accountability has come to be regarded as that which is our prerogative, our right. This is, as we have seen, in part a story of seduction. What I have added is an illustration of how each of us works within these distributions to turn accountability into our millstone.

Acknowledgements

The author gratefully acknowledges the financial support of the Economic and Social Research Council who sponsored the research that provides the empirical basis of this chapter. In addition to all those who gave their time to help me in this study, I would like to thank Fenton Robb, Rolland Munro and Jan Mouritsen for their helpful comments upon earlier drafts of this chapter.

Notes

1. Interview: Systems Manager 1 (Oiltown Refinery) 2nd Interview, 17th July 1991.
2. Interview: Systems Manager 2 (Oiltown Refinery) 1st Interview, 14th October 1991.
3. Interview: Systems Manager 3 (Oiltown Refinery) 1st Interview, 29th November 1990.
4. Interview: Systems Manager 1 (Oiltown Refinery) 1st Interview, 18th April 1991.
5. Interview: Systems Manager 3 (Oiltown Refinery) 3rd Interview, 7th November 1991.

6. Interview: Senior Manager in Systems Group of Manufacturing and Supply Business Development Unit, Mexaco Oil International, Corporate Centre, 25th March 1991.
7. Interview: Systems Manager 3 (Oiltown Refinery) 2nd Interview, 9th April 1991.
8. Interview: European Refinery Analyst, Manufacturing Development Group, Mexaco Oil Europe, 7th June 1991.
9. Interview: Systems Manager 2 (Oiltown Refinery) 2nd Interview, 7th November 1991.
10. Interview: Systems Manager 4 (Oiltown Refinery) 1st Interview, 10th May 1991.
11. Brief Conversation with Systems Manager 3 (Oiltown Refinery) 10th May 1991.
12. Brief Conversation with Systems Manager 2 (Oiltown Refinery) 27th November 1991.
13. The overlapping responsibilities and distrust were addressed by an organizational review that was outside the scope of OMS.
14. Oiltown Oil Management System (OMS) Feasibility Study, Stage 4 Report: December 1988, Mexaco Oil, Oiltown Refinery Ltd.
15. Interview: Production Programmer 1 (Oiltown Refinery) 2nd Interview, 20th June 1991.
16. Interview: Production Programmer 2 (Oiltown Refinery) 1st Interview, 11th April 1991.
17. Interview: Offsites Operator (Oiltown Refinery) 1st Interview, 16th May 1991.
18. Interview: Oil Accountant (Oiltown Refinery) 1st Interview, 15th April 1991.
19. Interview: Senior Laboratory Technician (Oiltown Refinery) 1st Interview, 15th November 1990.
20. Interview: Member of Reliability and Loss Control Group (Oiltown Refinery) 1st Interview, 13th May 1991.
21. Interview: Senior Process Engineer (Oiltown Refinery) 1st Interview, 13th May 1991.
22. Interview: Production Programmer 1 (Oiltown Refinery) 1st Interview, 15th November 1990.
23. Interview: Commercial Manager (Oiltown Refinery) 1st Interview, 5th June 1991.
24. Interview: Systems Manager 5 (Oiltown Refinery) 1st Interview, 28th May 1991.
25. Interview: Production Programmer 4 (Oiltown Refinery) 1st Interview, 5th February 1991.
26. Interview: Production Programmer 5 (Oiltown Refinery) 1st Interview, 21st February 1991.
27. Interview: Production Programmer 6 (Oiltown Refinery) 1st Interview, 15th January 1991.
28. Interview: Production Programmer 7 (Oiltown Refinery) 1st Interview, 14th February 1991.
29. Interview: Production Programmer 8 (Oiltown Refinery) 1st Interview, 21st February 1991.
30. Interview: Refinery Programming Manager (Mexaco Oil National) 1st Interview, 7th June 1991.

References

Baudrillard, J. (1979) *De la Seduction*, Galilee.

Baudrillard, J. (1983) *Simulations*, Semiotext(e), New York.

Baudrillard, J. (1990) The Ecliptic of Sex, in *Revenge of the Crystal: Selected writings on the modern object and its destiny, 1968 – 1983*, (ed and trans P. Foss and J. Pefanis) Pluto Press, London.

Cooper, R. (1992) Formal Organization as Representation: Remote Control, Displacement and Abbreviation in *Rethinking Organization: New Directions in Organizational Theory and Analysis* (eds M. Reed and M. Hughes) Sage, London.

Cooper, R. (1993) Technologies of Representation in *Tracing the Semiotic Boundaries of Politics* (ed P. Ahonen) Mouton de Gruyter, Berlin.

Kallinikos, J. (1994) *Predictable Worlds: On Writing, Rationality and Organization*, paper presented at the Workshop on Writing, Rationality and Organization, EIASM, 21 – 22 March, Brussels.

Kallinikos, J. (1995) The Architecture of the Invisible: Technology is Representation. *Organization*, **2**(1) pp. 117–40.

Lilley, S. (forthcoming) Disintegrating Chronology, *Studies in Cultures, Organizations and Society*.

Munro, R. (1993) Just When You Thought it Safe to Enter the Water: Accountability, Language Games and Multiple Control Technologies. *Accounting, Management and Information Technologies*, **3**(4) pp. 249–71.

Munro, R. (forthcoming) Managing by ambiguity: An archaeology of the social in the absence of management accounting. *Critical Perspectives on Accounting*.

Scarry, E. (1985) *The body in pain: The making and unmaking of the world*, Oxford University Press, New York.

Woolgar, S. (1991) Configuring the user: the case of usability trials in *A Sociology of Monsters, Sociological Review, Monograph 38* (ed J. Law) pp. 58–99a.

Part Three

Manoeuvres in networks

This unit of account concerns manoeuvres in networks. The authors introduce materials and devices in the form of accounting numbers. However, instead of assuming these speak for themselves, the focus is on accounting numbers as intermediaries and the opportunities these create to manoeuvre as their spokespersons.

In contrast to the chapters in Part Two, the authors in this section see participants as entrapped in 'networks'. In that participants are animated by little more than being the bearers of the culture in which they are embedded, the chapters in this section are united by what is sometimes known as an 'institutional' view. Where accounting numbers can be aligned with other accounts, this provides room for manoeuvre within networks to whoever can act as their 'spokesperson'. The analysis in this section therefore foregrounds participants accounting to members, as spokespersons. The authors assume that participants are spokespersons whose accounts are representing, perhaps re-presenting, the accounts of other members of group(s). The focus lies not between a given set of 'external' interests, that have already been presumed to be in conflict, but remains in accounts. The relational tension for participants lies between being read as 'representing' (a spokesperson) and being read as 're-presenting' (a member who is out of line).

The first chapter in this section is a study by Thomas Ahrens of the accounts of British and German managers. Ahrens is concerned to weaken an alignment of management practices from the 'mesmeric' grip of the practices of management accountants. Accounts of practices that were presented as a 'natural' and 'responsible' alignment of managers and accountants in the UK brewing industry become exposed startlingly as 'irresponsible' and 'irrational' by managers and accountants in the German brewing industry. As Ahrens summarizes, before 'accounting can be mobilized in processes of accountability it needs to be rationalized as a relevant analytical tool'. What Ahrens brings out is that the numbers of management accounting are never left to speak for themselves. When managers act as their spokespersons, there is a wide discretion over whom, or what, they can speak on behalf of.

This notion of local discretion is picked up in Chapter 9 by Carla Carnaghan, Mike Gibbins and Seppo Ikäheimo who discuss the alignment of financial disclosure in an interplay of accountability pressures. For these authors accountability pressures are multiple and variable. An irruption in the interplay of accountability pressures, for example in the form of strikes, is always threatening to close down room for manoeuvres. In these circumstances, financial disclosure can be drawn on as a device for advertising other accountability pressures. However, as the authors stress, the effects of financial disclosure are uncertain. Intertextuality is part of the managers' lived awareness and the authors point out that financial disclosure is often dropped, in favour of other manoeuvres, once the pressure from other accountabilities is off. The research on which this chapter draws is also important as it exposes, as untenable, the assumption of much capital markets research that financial disclosure is only justified if it helps shareholders. As the authors note, the shareholders in their study had little interest in the financial material disclosed.

In Chapter 10 Fabrizio Panozzo presents us with a cautionary study of the use of financial accounting by Italian trade unions. Laughlin, in a later chapter, notes how money can serve as an 'enabler of freedom' rather than as a determinant of the accounts of actors, but Panozzo sets out to show how this manoeuvre can be accomplished. In order to ensure its continuation as an organization, and attract members, the union has to advertise itself as sufficiently independent. However, the puzzle for the Italian trade unions is how to account for themselves in ways that preserve their autonomy, but still celebrate 'solidarity', its principle rhetoric. By pursuing the latter course, the union's accounts could easily lose its identity as 'sovereign' and become trapped in the rhetoric of democracy as an institution. In this particular case, rather than enforcing a hierarchical dominance, financial accounting is drawn in as an intermediary for ensuring difference. In a curious inversion of the usual narrative, accounting numbers appear as a spokesperson for the union's autonomy.

Caught within producing and reproducing webs of relations, the participants in this section of the book are constrained within an institutional framework. This, however, is a different form of entrapment to the arena discussed in the chapters which follow in Part Four, for the latter assume a dominance by the technology of accounting numbers. In providing room for participant manoeuvres, management accounting is always being caught within larger narratives; accounts that talk the numbers up, or talk them down. In demonstrating their inability to travel across institutional contexts, Ahrens also reveals a rigidity in the alignment of managers' accounts when these act as 'spokespersons' for the 'needs of the City' – especially when the latter is also aligned with management accounting numbers. Taken together with Jönsson's study, Ahrens might also be interpreted as raising the question of whether German alignments with bankers are sufficiently robust to withstand an encroachment by the North American version of managerial capitalism.

8 Financial and operational modes of accountability: differing accounts of British and German managers

Thomas Ahrens

Introduction

Like many contributions on accountability to the British management accounting literature, this chapter points towards some limitations of management accounting as a technique for analysing and rationalizing organizational action.

Drawing on observations made in British and German organizations, the chapter illustrates how management accounting, in order to function as a tool for analysis and rationalization, needs to be rationalized itself. If, for whatever reasons, management accounting is not accepted as a useful language for analyses of organizational action and plans, organizational members will not hold themselves and each other accountable to management accounting measures of performance. This chapter adds to the accountability literature by drawing out this aspect of management accounting's failure to pervade organizational structures.

The chapter contrasts the financial reasons behind a British brewer's arguments over repairs to the leaking roof of a warehouse with the critical reactions from German brewing managers, who felt that that decision should have been based on operational rather than financial criteria. As the German managers appear to relate more strongly to a physical rather than a financial reality of their organizations, two different modes of accountability emerge.[1]

The 'mesmeric grip' of management accounting

Suggestions have been made to curb the dominance of management accounting and hierarchical control technologies over organizational structures of accountability (e.g. Munro and Hatherly, 1993; Roberts, 1991; Roberts and Scapens, 1985). Accounting is depicted as standing in the way of state-of-the-art manufacturing, as well as inhibiting emancipatory moves to democratize the workplace.

From a commercial as well as from an ethical standpoint, then, management accounting is seen to play too great a role in current processes of accountability, 'the giving and demanding of reasons for conduct' (Roberts and Scapens, 1985: 447). For instance, Roberts (1991) argues that management accounting has been:

> [. . .] institutionalized as the most important, authoritative and telling means whereby activity is made visible (p. 359)

Regarding the processes of accountability surrounding organizational members, he holds that:

> One can argue with its [management accounting's] accuracy but not its methods of production or its categories of relevance (p. 361).

For all practical purposes, managers are caught in management accounting's 'exclusive and apparently mesmeric grip' (p. 367).

Munro and Hatherly (1993) also depict management accounting as dominant. They argue that management accounting is deeply implicated in reproducing and sustaining hierarchical contexts of accountability. Indeed, so strong is the complicity here that practices, originally advanced in the name of lateral accountability, are likely to be turned into ways of further intensifying surveillance. In a similar vein, Munro (1995) discusses the tenacity of management accounting to dominate structures of account-ability. Its alignment with the discourse of total quality management is seen to fabricate a dominant, novel language game of pseudo markets. Budgets may be being rolled back to make room for the new 'province' of quality, but their coercive function of inducing financial discipline remains.

Common to these discussions of accountability is a presumption of powerful struc-tures of hierarchical accountability in which management accounting plays an impor-tant part. One could almost speak of a literature on management accounting and accountability whose main purpose it is to investigate and caution against the domina-tion of the latter by the former. Through its focus on accountability it conceptualizes management accounting as more than mere technology and highlights some of the ways in which management accounting can be implicated in organizational action. Overall, management accounting is seen as central to organizational sense-making, and the finance function is portrayed as closely interrelated with a story of managerial power. Presented as a Foucauldian discipline, management accounting is seen, in the eyes of organizational members, to be capable of producing obligatory forms of accounts of organizational action, truthful or not. It is through such accounts that organizational members are seen to give and demand reasons for conduct.

A contrast with some observations from Germany

In what follows, I would like to contrast this particular image of management account-ing as centrally implicated in organizational structures of accountability with a scenario in which organizational members are less prone to accord overwhelming importance to financial reasons for their conduct; where management accounting appears as just one out of a number of possible valid representations of organizational action. In that scenario, management accounting would appear somewhat more removed from the managerial imperative.

Interestingly, this different image of management accounting was not only grudgingly accepted by members of the finance department, but they actively promoted it. The reason for this support by finance can be seen in a different understanding of what responsible management is. Operational as well as financial managers acted upon different criteria for sensible organizational action. In this different context of account-ability, management accounting and financial analysis assumed a different role. Through an elaboration of some of the dynamics of this context it is hoped that further insights can be gained into the ways in which management accounting can be implicated in structures of hierarchical accountability.

The contrast between those two scenarios for management accounting and account-ability is developed through an analysis of interviews and field work conducted in very similar British and German firms, which formed part of a larger project aimed at investigating possible differences between British and German management account-ing practice.

I drew on the method of comparing matched pairs of firms (Maurice, 1979: 47f; Sorge *et al.*, 1983), which suggests that a comparison between organizations which are similar with regards to industry, size, technology, and markets, but located in different countries, might indicate national characteristics of organizational control contexts. Recognizing that perfect matches are impossible, the research focused on the brewing industry, which has the advantages of relatively standardized production processes, similar products, and similar distribution channels in Britain and Germany[2]. Moreover, both the British and the German brewing industry are widely seen to have been exposed to intensified competition in recent years[3]. Matching the overall economic situation is important because one might expect organizations to rethink their uses of management accounting if they perceive themselves to be under heightened economic pressure.

The main disadvantage of comparing brewing in Britain and Germany is the difference in market structures. Concentration of market share amongst the largest British brewers is high, whereas the German market has traditionally been very fragmented. This disadvantage could partly be remedied by focusing research on large brewers with comparable production volumes. In Britain, three of the six largest and two smaller brewers were studied. In Germany, I included seven of the eight largest groups and one smaller brewer in the study. Except for the smaller brewers in both countries, all firms employ at least 950 people within their beer divisions.[4]

The research strategy involved confronting interlocutors with examples of organiza-tional practice in the other country. Using those examples as critical incidents to polarize opinions, they served to elicit managers underlying, usually hidden assump-tions which guided their day-to-day action and were thus part of their organization's overall control context and structures of accountability.

In the following section, I will report on how a British maintenance manager and a senior management accountant explain their brewer's decision not to repair a leaking warehouse roof for financial reasons. After discussing the comments of a German manager on this decision, I will then attempt to locate the arguments around the leaking roof as part of fundamentally different, wider contexts of accountability.

The tale of a leaking roof

> We just cannot budget everything we would like to budget for. [. . .] If efficiency has gotten so bad that you can't carry on, you spend the money

> on repair and maintenance. [. . .] My biggest concern is dilapidation. Machinery is still looked after relatively well, but buildings aren't . . . For instance, I got a number of quotes to have the warehouse roof repaired. It was going to cost £25,000[5] but they said no. So we have to live with it for another year.

This maintenance manager of a large British brewery was concerned about his organization's maintenance policy and particularly the upkeep of buildings. In his view, this policy had undergone change.

> Three or four years ago we submitted a budget that we believed in. [. . .] Last time I gave my best estimate and the next day [the brewery director] called me in his office. He was fuming with anger, red face. He thought we were hiding something in there [. . .] [and] told me to cut the budget.

In this example responsibility for the physical upkeep of plant was accorded little urgency. The organizational structures of accountability were such that nobody was held accountable for a leaking roof in a busy warehouse where filled kegs and shrink-wrapped cases of canned beer were stored. Conversely, the maintenance manager's efforts to become accountable, to give reasons for repairing the roof remained without consequence.

The internalization of external pressures

The maintenace manager explains the situation with what he saw as an organizational response to external pressures.

> It's more market driven now [. . .] and of course [we do] statutory obligations, health and safety, pollution . . .

Mainly as a consequence of market pressures, he felt, his budgeting activities became part of new structures of accountability.

> When we budget, we know it's gonna be cut. First my boss cuts something out, then the brewery director. But he's under pressure from [the general manager production], and he's got tough targets, too. It successively translates down. [. . .] Because if we get higher budgets, beer is more expensive [i.e. the transfer price is higher.]

No longer did he see himself as only being held accountable for the efficient maintenance of the brewery, but also for his contribution to the task of keeping down the transfer price for beer, which the brewery charged to its internal customers, the sales divisions. Thereby he became implicated in a new structure of accountability, one that reduced his ability to support maintenance proposals with operational reasons. Instead, he saw himself required to answer to the demands of an abstraction of markets which was relayed to him and his superiors through management accounting information.

Under this structure of accountability his interpretation of the meaning of budgeting changed, too.

> Budgeting really is sharing the available maintenance money. We just hope we meet the budget as the year goes along.

Budgeting was more closely associated with financial discipline than with the representation of planned resource consumption. To 'meet the numbers' (Munro, 1995: 147) became a motive of action more powerful than the upkeep of buildings.

Mobilizing City pressures

This view was echoed by a senior management accountant of that brewer. When I told him that I had been surprised to find the brewery personnel by and large accepting the argument that the roof could not be repaired for financial reasons, he related this financial argument to the expected profits which the brewer had communicated to the financial markets in the City of London.

> So, come hell or high water we have to deliver [the financial target], and if it means that we can't repair a roof, we're not gonna repair a roof because I don't think the people at the very top of the company can afford to go back to the City again and say, sorry, we gave you some different information, we can no longer meet that aspiration. So, we will meet that figure, but some of the action we're gonna take are fairly . . . dramatic. I know what you're saying, but if it isn't health and safety and if it doesn't damage the quality of the product, forget it . . .

For this senior management accountant, the organizational members' acceptance of financial reasons not to repair the roof was unremarkable. He did not comment on it at all. Rather, he explained to me how insignificant he found any concern about the roof. He did that by describing this issue as part of a context which he considered to be much more significant: the structures of financial accountability which tied the brewer to the City.

Accounting as rhetoric

In this example we find the aforementioned concerns of much of the literature on management accounting and accountability confirmed. Accounting did play a dominant role in this organization's structures of accountability. The translation of seemingly objective market pressures into the organization marginalized appeals to operational reasons for conduct. They were not demanded and could not be given. Accounting's dominance in the organizational structures of accountability was recognized by the responsible operational manager as well as a senior management accountant. If with varying enthusiasm, both tried to explain to me why one currently really could not repair the roof.

It is important to note, however, that the above material indicates a purely rhetorical dominance of management accounting. The interlocutors rationalize the decision about the roof with reference to pressures from the financial markets, but they do not demonstrate how such pressures are conveyed into the organization and, specifically, to the decision at hand. Why was this particular roof not repaired? What difference would it make to spend an additional £25,000 out of a profit of tens of millions? Why could the brewer not communicate to the City that their profit expectations needed to be lowered, as they had been for the brewing industry as a whole?

Whilst there certainly was considerable economic pressure in the British brewing industry at the time of the research, and whilst this particular brewer had reported stagnating or falling profits for the previous two years, returns on investment were still in excess of 10%. Was it not possible to establish those earnings levels as satisfactory? Much has been made of the dependence of British industry on the City of London's profit expectations to 'explain' what has become known as 'British short-termism', but the processes through which the City's expectations are formed (and managed), and simultaneously mobilized in organizations to justify cost cutting, have not sufficiently been explored. All we seem to know is that management accounting dominated structures of accountability are implicated in the reproduction of that short-termism.

A German comment

A look at how experienced German managers commented upon the decision not to repair the roof would suggest that the processes through which short-termism is reproduced are highly context-dependent. The quality control manager of a large German brewer, who also acted as the entire production department's main point of contact with the management accounting department, failed to understand the situation as outlined above in two respects. Firstly, he found the operation of a warehouse with a leaking roof totally unacceptable.

> We have very clear limits of what is justifiable, what is reasonable, how far you can go. If there are any problems regarding product quality [. . .] if it rains into the finished goods warehouse, then our person responsible has a problem because he must not use this storage space any longer. Or, if he does store something there, I will ban those products. They are no longer suitable for sale. That's it. [. . .] They are to be protected from the weather [. . .] finished goods are on principle to be stored indoors. [. . .] We have clear regulations and . . . that is that. If we have certain problems in that area they will need to be solved. We are not going to drift in that direction, just because of a lack of responsibility and competence we somehow manage to push the problem into another year or a different department.

What the two British saw as a flexible response to apparent external financial pressure, this German perceived as a gross violation of operational rules due to irresponsibility and incompetence. He clearly saw operational management accountable for operational procedures. In his mind, there were good reasons why those procedures had been laid down in regulations. They were regarded as unambiguous and 'there can be no two opinions' on the issue.

But were operational managers at this German brewer not also responsible for meeting the financial targets of the organization as a whole? This brings us to the second respect in which the German manager failed to understand the British situation. He did point out during the interview that, on principle, budgets were to be met. However, in case of unforeseeable events, which would require additional unplanned expenses, one would seek permission to obtain unused funds from other operational budgets. In his experience such budgets always existed, and must exist, because over- and under-provided budgets will on average even out, following the law of large numbers. One would only ask budget holders to budget on an expense level which entailed planned dilapidation if one wished to discontinue their particular operation in the near future.

Administration of budget cuts

Then what about unexpected budget cuts, which senior management considers necessary to administer during the financial year? What happens if, for instance, the production department is given the task to find a lump sum saving? In his view, such cuts cannot be made in an unproblematic top down fashion. They would first need to be evaluated by operational management.

> And then we check, how much of that can be realized? And one really makes inroads into one's reserves, but everyone knows his limits: there you are, this is what I can do, and that is what I can't. In the end you depend on the robustness of judgement on the part of those who are responsible. And on the mentality that budgets are not spent simply because they exist . . .

Whilst acknowledging that some budget holders might

> [. . .] confuse budgeting with an enlargement of [their] responsibilities, [their] relative importance in the firm [. . .]

in his mind, senior management cannot draw on some *a priori* financial imperative to override the operational responsibilities of budget holders. His understanding of organizational structures of accountability, which was echoed by other operational managers and management accountants who worked for that brewer, revolved around ordered production flows.

This order emerged from practice, both regulated and unregulated, and from technical innovation. Whilst he found that management accounting could, largely, represent the financial consequences of organizational action, organizational changes which were based on manipulations of the organization's accounting representation were seen to be intrinsically problematic. This is because management accounting could not represent the 'limits' of production, which were only known to those responsible. Far from being the most authoritative source of visibility of organizational action, management accounting was rather seen as a useful model for the representation of resource flows for the organization as a whole. And like all useful models, the simplifications which make it powerful also determine its inherent limitations.

Towards a different notion of accountability

What we seem to be finding in this German brewery is a notion of accountability which cannot be discharged with exclusive reference to management accounting measures. From the German manager's point of view, the decision not to repair the leaking roof in the British brewery was flawed because it failed to account for operational concerns. Excessively emphasizing financial performance, that decision neglected the judgement of the responsible operational manager. It would appear that for this German manager accountability was informed by ideas of operational responsibility and competence to a much greater extent than for his British counterparts.

How far can the notion of accountability which emerges from this example be generalized? Do we witness an unusual coincidence between personal idiosyncrasies and a temporary cessation of management accounting domination over the organization? In the remainder of this chapter, I will attempt to demonstrate that underlying this contrast are two fundamentally different notions of hierarchical accountability. The difference between operational and financial regimes of accountability will be shown to be related to the esteem in which operational and financial representations of organizational action are held, as well as the extent to which structures of accountability can be seen to span functional boundaries. This difference will be illustrated with comments on the treatment of investment proposals into quality enhancements.

Operational accountability

An alternative concept of the relationship between management accounting and accountability, of which the comments of the German manager above were indicative, would emphasize a notion of ordered production flows. Managers are held accountable for the maintenance and development of this order. Whilst such an order could clearly not be maintained at any price, it may also not simply be upset by demands to attain financial targets. Against such demands operational management can argue in terms of their 'responsibility' for the operational order.

A question of proof

The importance which such operational responsibility is accorded, even from the finance side, can be illustrated by the following accounts which two senior German management accountants gave of the co-operation between management accounting and operations. The first one worked for the same brewer as the manager quoted above.

> [. . .] as a management accountant, at some stage of the budgeting process one has to surrender to the expertise of your interlocutor. If he stubbornly insists on his viewpoint for long enough, for instance, a budget for external distribution of 2 million, because we're just going to be showered with long distance freight charges, then that is that. If you realize at year end that he has only used 1.5 million, you know he was padding, but you cannot conclusively prove to him in time that he does. Somehow you end up drawing the short straw. [. . .] So the only thing left to do is threaten with the whip of his disciplinary superior.

If there is a difference of opinion the burden of producing proof was seen to be on the management accounting side.

> Now when a technical unit needs to be replaced, that is a remarkably difficult topic. [. . .] In my opinion one cannot calculate it. You can record repair costs per piece of equipment and set it into relation to the replacement cost values, and if a certain percentage is reached, it would mean that piece of equipment needs replacement. We do those things, too. But in the end it depends on the assessment of the one who is responsible from production. If he says it needs to be replaced, well, then we are the management accountants, *Kaufleute*[6], we

dig deeper and ask, has it really got to be done? Can't we replace just a part? The other parts seem fine. [. . .] So we go to the engineers and talk to them.

Whilst the first senior management accountant emphasized the conflict potential in the relationship between finance and operations ('surrender', 'drawing the short straw', 'threaten', 'whip'), it is clear that the power of operational expertise was a fact of life for both of them. Discussions in which the management accountant can, for instance, attempt to understand the reasoning behind a replacement proposal were seen to be desirable, but there was a recurring emphasis that the last decision must rest with those who are operationally responsible.

Responsible experts vs 'techies'

The contrast with one British senior management accountant's views on how technical investment projects ought to be handled is striking.

> The local finance people from the brewery need to get involved because it has to be a cross-functional team effort. We've seen it. Otherwise you find, one day there is a hole in the wall and a machine installed and the forklift truck can no longer move the pallets along that corridor. Or the techies just buy some machine because they like it or it's cheap, but they don't consider the bottom line implications, and suddenly you have to employ more people in production than before.

He emphasized the disadvantages of technical specialist knowledge in isolation. Responsible management was therefore seen to require early finance involvement. What was the competent, responsible engineer in Germany, was here portrayed as a mere 'techie', too narrowly specialized to grasp the complexity of both operational processes in the brewery and doing business in Britain.

In Germany, on the other hand, even though German senior management accountants also sometimes criticized the narrowness of the operational perspective, the concept of operational responsibility was adhered to. If that results in overall inefficiencies it cannot be helped.

> Every year our filling manager has half a million left in his maintenance budget. We show him what happened over the last years but he won't listen. No, no, this year he really has something extraordinary to budget for. And his production director just doesn't address the issue with him. It's beyond our reach, we can't help it . . .

Functional separation of expertise

Not surprisingly, given the high regard for operational expertise at the German brewers, structures of accountability remain closely entwined with the functional hierarchy. For instance, the feasibility of board requests to cut budgets tended to be evaluated and administered within the functional hierarchy. The idea that competence and therefore responsibility should be limited to a well-defined group of activities was relatively widespread.

Management accounting was not seen to be an exception from that. As operational departments were accountable for the order of operational flows, so the management accounting department was accountable for the clarity and accuracy of its economic representations of organizing. This could, for instance, be illustrated by the comments of a senior German management accountant on management accounting practice at a large British brewer's. Their practice involved not to authorize technical investment proposals marked 'essential replacement' before management accounting felt that they had evidence that the proposal had indeed 'realized its essential nature'. In the senior German management accountant's opinion:

> The truth is probably somewhere in the middle, I mean, this is an extreme example [. . .] But from my perspective, of course I must say it would be desirable, because it would make my work a lot easier. [. . .] Of course, it is linked with responsibility because, if the thing really breaks down, everyone will say, see? I told you so [. . .] but for me the structure of the process is desirable, that it introduces an order into it [the ranking of projects] and thereby the decision becomes easier. Even though the board as a whole may still make the final decision, I would be in a position to make that decision more plausible and clearer for them.

Apart from making the obligatory reference to the link between operational responsibility and decision-making, he explained that he saw himself accountable to the experts who decide. In his mind, his own functional expertise was concerned with the production of plausibility and clarity. Rather than promoting strictly financial accountability of operational management to their superiors, he saw his role as producing information based on which management can incorporate financial considerations into their decisions.

Quantifying quality?

At this point, a British reader may be unconvinced by the argument. If management accounting information is provided, surely it will be used? Ignoring it or even opposing its production has to be considered as irresponsible? This is precisely the point. Before management accounting can be mobilized in processes of accountability it needs to be rationalized as a relevant analytical tool. For those German brewers, however, accountability was conceptually different. The incorporation of financial considerations was not at all taken for granted in every case. Typically, whenever quality improvements are involved, management showed little interest in management accounting representations.

> [. . .] they say, you don't need to calculate it, it's for reasons of quality [. . .] Quality is always something which nobody else can comprehend. (A senior management accountant.)

Quality as a category appeared powerful enough on its own to argue against giving or demanding financial reasons for conduct. If quality is defined as that which only functional experts can understand, cross-functional accountability is less important. The particular kind of simplifications which management accounting representations could contribute to a decision comes to be seen as unhelpful. Another management accountant would even extent this argument from quality to technology in general.

> This brings us back to the issue of technology; whether we can comprehend it
> at all. I mean, we can look at the cost aspects, but we cannot, for instance,
> evaluate the quality of the product and say, because of that sales have
> improved.[7]

Here, the notion of quality itself was accorded compelling reality status. Knowing that quality can be improved was perceived as almost making it necessary to act. In a context in which an emphasis on operational responsibility was entwined with intra-functional structures of accountability, quality arguments could be regarded as a particularly effective way of excluding financial reasons for conduct.

Financial accountability

Several British senior management accountants found this unacceptable; slightly quaint and certainly unprofessional. Whilst acknowledging that quality was difficult to quantify financially,

> [. . .] everything has got to be objectively measured, I think. And we do try
> and measure even quality. And it might be product quality. It might be line
> quality. Somewhere you should get a benefit from your investment. Some of
> it may be intangible [. . .] we do try and be objective as opposed to subjective
> in most of our investment appraisal.

Far from being inappropriate, the involvement of management accounting was here portrayed as a pre-condition of objectivity.

This involvement needed not to be confined to financial information. In response to critiques of management accounting's inadequacy to represent the conditions of the modern manufacturing environment, some management accounting departments incorporated non-financial measures in their reporting. In contrast with what I found at German brewers, however, if British management accountants felt unable to obtain at least some rough indication of the financial benefits of an investment, this would generally make the operational proposal appear unprofessional and unconvincing. It would not tend to be approved.

The perceived objectivity of management accounting

The particular structures of accountability which I found at the British brewers privileged a certain financial visibility which was often portrayed to arise from the City's evaluation of the organization. As one British senior management accountant described her new position,

> And here you can see kind of how the City is viewing you and what's it
> expecting you to do. And we're trying to translate that back into the relevant
> businesses and kind of try to manage the two.

With the brief to

> [. . .] give the division an insight into the City's expectations [. . .] obviously in
> a way we are fortunate because we can see how we're operating and how
> healthy we are as a total business.

The organization was first and foremost seen as a business. Through the use of management accounting it must therefore be possible to make visible valid reasons for conduct. Why invest in quality if it cannot be shown to help the business, for example, through increased sales?

The perceived subjectivity of management accounting

But can management avoid investing in quality without relying on subjective judgement? Are not all management accounting evaluations of investment proposals qualitative judgements in numerical form? However, with the numerical format seems to go an assumption of objectivity. Numerical judgement seems somehow less problematic. Some interlocutors thought that the organization of accountability around financial visibility had very real consequences for operational investment proposals in so far as it served as a pretext to favour certain kinds of investments over others. Investments could be prevented without being rejected. As the production director of a large brewery put it,

> 'They'll never say, no. They'll say, give me a justification, demonstrate the benefits to me, do another study.

Whilst operational proposals were presented as having to compete for funds with proposals from all over the business, some suggested privately that they regarded production as being disadvantaged by the ways in which future estimates were incorporated into those calculations. Overall, however, management accounting representations of the healthiness of the business as a whole were considered to be much more important and, at the same time, less problematic than in Germany.

Where management accounting is deemed to objectively rank a great variety of proposals, further arguments become less of a possibility. Within the value chain discourse, different functions that used to compete for funds were now depicted as tied to that one chain, serving the business as a whole. Production departments became supply departments, sales was renamed as demand. Rhetorically, conflict was toned down with reference to measurable economic truths. Where organizational structures and action were known by their economic significance for customer service, quality ceased to be important on its own. To be justified, quality improvements needed to demonstrably improve projected sales figures, accounting representations of the future.

Conclusion

This paper has contrasted the relationship between management accounting and accountability as it is familiar from the British management accounting literature, with one that is based on observations made in German brewing organizations. The discussion of a decision regarding building maintenance attempted to elicit contrasting possibilities for accountability through the ways in which organizational members mobilize accounts of management accounting. The same technique was used to place the arguments from that example in the wider contexts of what was labelled operational and financial accountability.

At the British brewers analysed, management accounting was mobilized as part of a discourse which revolved around seemingly objective 'needs' of the City and the customer (Ahrens, 1994). In what was described as a response to those needs, the organization was conceived of as a 'business'. Action proposals were required to address 'business needs'. Since those could only be made visible through management accounting representations, reasons for conduct were required to address management accounting implications. Whilst the management accounting perspective of the firm as a whole was also regarded as important in Germany, it would have been considered irresponsible to neglect the reasons of conduct which were given by those who were operationally responsible. For instance, I found more pressure at British brewers to account for the monetary benefits that were expected to result from investments in quality. In Britain, quality seemed to be more exclusively conceptualized as part of the commercial relationship between brewer and customer. Where management accounting came to conceptually dominate operational criteria, the possibilities to hold and be held accountable for entities outside external and internal customer relationships became few.

At the German brewers analysed, on the other hand, accounts of management accounting appeared to be embedded in fundamentally different processes of hierarchical accountability. Production management, for instance, seemed to successfully claim more exclusive responsibility for the conduct of operations, because it was generally accepted that there existed particular operational knowledge which could not easily be represented by management accounting. Much more so than in the British organizations studied, operations could thus be known from within the production function. Claims to knowledge by management accountants, on the other hand, were seen to draw on an expertise which could not help in judging the 'limits' of operations. Whilst it was perceived as offering a valid perspective on the firm as whole, management accounting's limitations were seen to lie in the representation of operational processes. Responsible managers could not exclusively rely on management accounting to account for their conduct.

Analyses of how management accounting can be mobilized to satisfy and reproduce structures of accountability allow us to move beyond discussions of how management accounting can rationalize organizational action. Rather, accountability can be understood as a discussion of those organizational processes in which the uses of management accounting itself are rationalized. In the case of the German brewers it could be seen that their relatively greater emphasis on professional boundaries for the judgement of different operations held a different set of possibilities for accountability; one in which the style of management and resource allocation was less geared towards the apparent satisfaction of management accounting's seemingly ubiquitous quasi-markets.

Acknowledgements

Thanks to the editors for helping me to clarify the mobilization of Anglo-German difference, and to Anthony Hopwood and Chris Chapman for discussing the interpretation of the material and earlier drafts.

Notes

1. This chapter's main focus is on the organizational level and it does not explain why those different modes were observed in Britain and Germany. It merely seeks to mobilize the

Anglo-German contrast to contribute to a more complex understanding of the roles which accounting can play in organizational structures of accountability. Wider 'factors' which have been suggested to be implicated in the greater prominence of accounting and accountants in Britain relative to Germany include education and training, institutions of organizational governance, characteristics of capital markets, industry structures, colonial and economic history, psychological factors such as individualism versus collectivism, and so forth. It is difficult to imagine that there can be an analysis which convincingly argues how those 'factors' give rise to observable accounting practices. Not only are so-called socio-cultural factors and their interrelationships notoriously difficult to define, but accounting practice itself, once it becomes a powerful source of sense-making within a culture, begins to shape its own socio-cultural context. In that sense, accounting's past needs to be included in the analysis of its present. For an insightful elaboration of differences in organizational and managerial processes in Britain and Germany which cautiously refers to aspects of the socio-cultural context see, for example, Steward *et al.* (1994).

2. Sales to licensed premises, such as public houses, bars, restaurants, etc., are relatively more important in Britain, so that more beer is filled into barrels. Conversely, packaging in returnable bottles is much more widespread in Germany. Even though this has implications for the layout and operation of filling lines, management accounting practice seemed unaffected by it. The same holds for the different types of beers brewed in the two countries.

3. In Britain, this is due to the Beer Order which limited the maximum numbers of public houses which the large brewers may own, thus inducing greater competition for sales outlets. Brewers' margins have come under pressure from retail organizations which now control the beer purchases of large numbers of public houses that had to be sold under the Beer Order.

   In Germany two developments are noteworthy. Following German unification, additional production capacity was built up by West German brewers which has recently begun to become increasingly superfluous as East German demand started to concentrate on East German products again. Also, a market segmentation into premium national brands and cheap supermarket own label products puts formerly healthy regional brewers under increased economic pressure as they have to spend more on advertising or accept falling margins.

4. Data was gathered through interviews at all of those brewers and during field visits at two of the larger brewers in each country. Visits were repeated and lasted several days at a time. Interviews were taped and transcribed. The research focused on management accountants and management accounting departments, but operational managers were also interviewed, and interaction between both groups observed. Notes were taken in meetings to record as much direct speech as possible. During field visits, notes of informal conversations as they occurred, for instance, on the way between offices, over lunch, whilst making tea, or being shown around production areas, and notes of observations were written down as soon as possible. Throughout the research process documentary evidence was collected.

5. Throughout this paper numbers have been changed in a way which preserves ratios between them but disguises magnitudes.

6. Engl. commercial/administrative people, but can also denote graduates from *Betriebs-wirtschaftslehre*, the German science of business economics.

7. This is the only quotation in this chapter which was recorded at a brewer with less than 950 employees.

References

Ahrens, T. (1994) *Accounting for Which Outside? Contrasting Perspectives on Strategic Conceptions and Action in Britain and Germany*, paper presented to the 2nd EIASM Workshop on Accounting, Control and Strategy, Brussels. European Institute for Advanced Studies in Management.

Maurice, M. (1979) For a Study of 'The Societal Effect': Universality and Specificity in Organization Research, in *Organizations Alike and Unlike* (eds C.J. Lammers and D.J. Hickson) Routledge and Kegan Paul, London.

Munro, R.J.B. (1993) Just When You Thought it Safe to Enter the Water: Accountability, Language Games and Multiple Control Technologies. *Accounting, Management and Information Technology*, **3**(4) pp. 240–71.

Munro, R.J.B. (1995) Governing the New Province of Quality, in *Making Quality Critical* (eds A. Wilkinson and H. Willmott) Routledge, London.

Munro, R.J.B. and Hatherly, D.J. (1993) Accountability and the New Commercial Agenda in *Critical Perspectives on Accounting*, pp. 369–95.

Roberts, J. (1991) The Possibilities of Accountability, *Accounting, Organizations and Society*, **16** pp. 355–68.

Roberts, J. and Scapens, R. (1985) Accounting Systems and Systems of Accountability – Understanding Accounting Practices in Their Organizational Contexts, *Accounting, Organizations and Society*, **10** pp. 443–56.

Sorge, A., Hartmann, G., Warner, M. and Nicholas, I. (1983) *Microelectronics and Manpower in Manufacturing*, Gower, Aldershot, Hants.

Steward, R., Barsoux, J.-L., Kieser, A., Ganter, H.-D. and Walgenbach, P. (1994) *Managing in Britain and Germany*, Macmillan, London.

9 Managed financial disclosure: the interplay between accountability pressures

Carla Carnaghan, Michael Gibbins and Seppo Ikäheimo

> The controller of a petrochemical company, commenting on the value of providing more information to the public, said, 'The pros are, the public has more information so it can understand you better; the cons are, it has more information so it can understand you better.'
>
> (Gibbins, Richardson and Waterhouse, 1989: 33)

Introduction

This chapter presents an analysis of financial disclosure as one managerial device for satisfying accountability pressures. Accountability pressures from stakeholders, who may be either individuals or groups, drive company managers into manoeuvres that highlight features of the company and actions they have undertaken to meet at least the most important accountability pressures that they have experienced.

As used in this chapter, *financial disclosure* includes accounting and other financial performance related information. We particularly focus on that which is deliberately released outside the company by managers to inform and influence shareholders, creditors and other external stakeholders. The *management* of financial disclosure refers to the activities company management undertake to produce a particular portrayal of the company to external stakeholders. The central point in this chapter is that a disclosure does not just appear, unaided. Rather, disclosure, together with the procedures by which it is aimed at its targets, are products of an extensive set of managerial activities. Within the limits and opportunities provided by disclosure laws and regulations, these disclosures are highly suggestive about what management believe is appropriate about the company.

Bringing ideas about managerial accountability to stakeholders and financial disclosure management together has been a key point in our research programme. Considered together, our findings improve the understanding of both accountability and disclosure in several ways. First, financial disclosures are shown to be the result of managerial activities which create a particular depiction of the firm; through deliberate choices of content, wording, timing, media, and other disclosure dimensions. There-fore, stakeholders receive a portrayal of a firm's activities and performance coloured by management's perceptions about stakeholders' priorities and interests – albeit mediated by existing regulation, the managers' own attitudes and reputation and internal accountability relationships. This contrasts with much of the current research on the stock market impact of financial disclosure, which tends to focus only on the 'news content' of particular disclosures, or the impact of particular regulations, and neglects management's incentives and opportunities to influence disclosure.

Second, the socio-psychological perspective on accountability which is used in this chapter provides a new and fruitful approach to exploring managerial incentives and interests, and therefore to explaining financial disclosure management. This perspec-tive facilitates delving more deeply into disclosure from the managers' point of view and allows us to consider the processes managers use to produce disclosures. Typical studies of disclosure and earnings management, such as those using signalling theory, agency theory, financial markets theory and positive accounting theory have been constrained within such restrictive hypotheses as the rational expectations model.

Third, the chapter's broad stakeholder perspective on accountability expands the accountability analysis beyond the usual shareholder-manager dyad to the multiple networks of accountability relationships between management and various external stakeholders and the internal accountability relationships within the management group. Our analysis thus reveals many complexities and ambiguities in accountability pressures which company management encounter when they consider opportunities or requirements to release financial disclosures.

Throughout the chapter, several examples of financial disclosure will be used to illustrate the chapter's points. Here are some introductory examples to indicate how diverse disclosure is:

- a machine tool manufacturer announces its annual earnings through a press release and standard inserts in several financial newspapers
- after having a major increase in profits, an agricultural products manufacturer discloses the first preliminary earnings announcement in the company's history
- a meat products company, normally not a frequent disclosure of financial infor-mation, issues several financial analyses and warnings during a strike by its factory workers, then becomes quiet again after the strike ends.

Many specific questions may be asked about the connection between management's accountability to stakeholders and the company's financial disclosure activities. We have organized the chapter by addressing the more obvious questions first, such as: Why do managers feel accountability pressures? How do they choose among conflict-ing pressures? Who are the stakeholders from whom managers feel accountability pressures? It should be emphasized that the answers here are likely to vary among companies, because each company's set of managers, stakeholders and disclosure opportunities may differ significantly from any other company's set.

We then go on to discuss what is managed financial disclosure in an accountability context. Here the questions we address are: What are the responses to and conse-quences of disclosure? How do factors such as managerial attitudes and internal accountability relationships affect disclosure management? Much of the chapter uses examples to show the variety of possibilities managers and recipients of disclosures may encounter. Prior to concluding comments, an extensive financial disclosure example illustrates and summarizes the major issues of this chapter.

Why do managers feel accountability pressures?

Stakeholders include all individuals or groups with an actual or potential interest in the firm such as shareholders, managers, employees, customers, society, job applicants, and environmental activists. To indicate the breadth of the stakeholder perspective, Figure 1, developed from work by Freeman (1984), contains an illustrative list of some major stakeholders, the stakes they have in the company, some criteria by which company management discharge accountability to stakeholders and some consequent possibilities for disclosure management. As the table shows, management are stakeholders themselves and have their own interests to consider in addition to dealing with the interests of other stakeholders.

Two conditions must be fulfilled in order to talk about accountability pressures to stakeholders in the context of financial disclosure management. First, there must be a stakeholder relationship. It may be derived from the resources stakeholders provide to the company, or from the stakeholders' ability to otherwise influence the company's activities. Both of these relationships motivate management to attempt to comply with stakeholders' wishes and portray managerial actions accordingly.

Second, there must be an information asymmetry between management and a given stakeholder or group. This means that management has information relevant to the criteria stakeholders use to evaluate the impact of the company's performance on their interests, which the stakeholders lack. This creates an information advantage for management and an opportunity for financial disclosure *management*. By disclosing particular information, company management may be able to influence stakeholders' behaviour. If stakeholders are not satisfied with what they learn about company performance via financial disclosures, they can take action such as selling their shares, complaining to the news media or contacting management directly.

By doing such things, or even by the possibility that such things could be done, stakeholders exert pressure on management to act in accordance with the stakeholders' interests and to explain or defend managerial actions in terms of those interests. This accountability pressure is central to financial disclosure and to the incentives for managers to manage disclosure. Empirical support for the influence of stakeholder groups on disclosures is provided by such studies as Roberts (1992), and Cowen, Ferreri and Parker (1987), who found that proxies of social stakeholder power had significant correlation with levels of corporate social responsibility disclosure.

Management face different types of accountability pressures. There are legal responsibilities to owners and employees, economic pressures from capital and product markets, social pressures from politicians and environmentalists, peer pressures from relevant professions, and so on. For example, the management of the agricultural products manufacturer which had a major increase in profits knew two months prior to their usual earnings announcement date that exceptionally good earnings might be achieved. This knowledge gave company management the opportunity to reconsider the timing of the earnings announcement. The timing issue was important to management, since there were major public concerns about the profitability of the agricultural products industry, particularly from the company's creditors. Making the

Figure 1
Illustrative Relationships Between Stakeholders, Accountability Criteria and Financial Disclosure Management

A. Stakeholders	B. Stakes		C. Accountability Criteria	D. Financial Disclosure Management
Parties whose behaviour can affect, or whose interests are affected by, the company's actions.	Resources provided and other interests that are affected by the company's actions.		Criteria by which stakeholders may evaluate the impact of the company's actions on their interests.	Ways company management can create the company portrayal they prefer.
Examples	*Examples*		*Examples*	*Examples*
	Resources provided	*Other Interests*		
Owners (shareholders)	Equity capital	Future returns	Company earnings, stock price changes, dividends	Income smoothing, timing of earnings announcement, accounting policy choice
Lenders	Debt capital	Future interest	Adherence to repayment schedule, observance of terms of lending	Discussion of investment plans, estimation of future cash flows
Top managers	Labour, expertise	Reputation, future pay	Wages, bonuses, personal value in external labour markets	Emphasizing management teamwork and creation of company value
Employees	Labour, expertise	Health, future pay	Wages, working conditions, employment stability	Managing financial news during labour negotiations, social responsibility reporting
Corporate customers	Sales revenue	Security of supply	Product price, quality, delivery reliability	Emphasizing long term product development and quality strategy
Environmentalists	Product endorsements	Health, clean environment	Environmental impact of production process and products	Social responsibility reporting, choice of appropriate media to report results

announcement ahead of the usual date provided the information necessary to convince creditors of the company's ability to pay interest and principal payments. In addition to the influence of accountability pressures from capital markets, the management decided to disclose the preliminary earnings announcement because peer professionals (financial analysts and colleagues) exerted pressure to follow standards of financial disclosure set by other companies, including making a preliminary earnings announcement at an appropriate time.

Responding to accountability pressures

The responses to accountability pressures depend on management's capability or opportunity to meet stakeholders' pressures and on management's confidence about what is required to meet those pressures. To say that management try to do what stakeholders want (always remembering that managers are stakeholders too) is consistent with the view taken in information economics (see Verrecchia, 1983, 1990; Dye, 1985a, 1985b) and agency theory (Jensen and Meckling, 1976) of focusing on managerial action in the context of owners' interests (assuming appropriate incentives are present). The psychological view, also consistent, is that each manager does this in order to obtain rewards, avoid punishment or maintain a self-image of being a responsible person (see Tetlock, 1985a, 1985b; Schlenker and Weigold, 1992).

However, doing what is expected is not so simple. Managers may be unsure what stakeholders expect. Perhaps the manager has already acted, or been forced to act by regulations or other circumstances, contrary to what is expected. Perhaps there are several sources of accountability pressure (for example, the present shareholders, the manager's own self-interest, the bank and a potential major shareholder considering buying an interest), and the manager believes those sources do not agree on what the manager should do. Conflicts in interests among various parties such as current shareholders, potential shareholders and lenders, is rather central to much of our economic and market system. Perhaps the manager has strong personal, moral or ethical beliefs about what should be done. In these more complex, but also very common situations, managerial responses are also more complex. Defensiveness, justification, effort to determine what is expected, attempts to persuade sources of accountability pressure to change their expectations, avoidance of action and other responses are all possible. In cases where accountability relationships contain conflict or where the news is not good, managerial defensiveness is particularly likely.

Referring to the examples at the beginning of the chapter, the machine tool manufacturer's press release is likely to contain defensive narrative justifying the performance if managers believe some, or all, stakeholders will be displeased about the annual earnings. Another example is the preliminary earnings announcement case of the agricultural products manufacturer. Company management felt accountable both to the shareholders and creditors. This financial disclosure was made to please shareholders by informing them of the company's good performance and to persuade cautious creditors, who were suspicious of the company's future, that the company was in good financial condition (See Gibbins and Newton, 1994 for an elaboration of these ideas with respect to auditors; Evans, Heiman-Hoffman and Rau, 1994 for an application to accounting; and a working paper by Gibbins and Ikäheimo, 1995 for an application to managed financial disclosure.)

The complexities in the accountability relationships company management face create problems for them to behave as expected with all parties. There may be no way to satisfy all stakeholders equally. But even if there is such a way, how do company management choose when to go along with what is expected and when not to? The perceived strengths of the accountability pressures company management encounter are determined by the enacted importance of each stakeholder's interests. When stakeholders' interests are conflicting, or when management must decide whether to attempt to meet expectations, the relative importance of each group plays a pivotal role in management's attempts to resolve the accountability pressure problem (see Pfeffer and Salancik, 1978; Weick, 1979). Accountability pressures, as perceived by managers, are not static but evolve as stakeholders act and respond to others' actions. These evolving accountability pressures may conflict with current practices of disclosure management making the disclosure management a more ambiguous activity for company managers.

Some specific factors in a disclosure context that influence the enacted importance of each stakeholder group include the organizational, institutional and cultural context of the firm. For example, in Anglo-Saxon countries, stockholders are typically seen as the most important stakeholders, while in Germanic and Latin countries and in Japan the role of creditors and employees as stakeholders is more important (see Moerland, 1995). In the latter circumstances, management may wish to put more emphasis on providing information on the company's capital investments, its ability to make payment on its debts, and its long term strategy. Rapid release of information may be less important. Information may be presented so as to stress long term trends, and credibility may be emphasized so as to assure creditors and employees that the information is objective. Thus a plastics manufacturing company in the United States may expend considerable time releasing information on new contracts and sales backlogs, as well as management earnings forecasts for each quarter and for the year. As its operations have environmental impacts, the company also provides a lot of discussion in its annual report on technology it is acquiring to reduce pollution or use resources more efficiently. In contrast, a German bio-technology company may spend considerable time discussing its cash flows and coverage of interest payments, and its labour relations programme and worker safety initiatives. A utility company in Canada uses very conservative accounting choices so as to reduce earnings. Management believe that disclosure of these low earnings in regular press releases helps to convince government agencies, which regulate the rates the utility company can charge customers, to approve a rate increase and to convince the public that a rate increase is required.

The concept of satisfying all stakeholders 'equally' is in any case problematic. There is always a problem of fair distribution of output between stakeholders, and accordingly there is a risk of conflicts. This risk is exacerbated by the self-interested nature of company management as a stakeholder group which also manages the company's resources and is involved in reward allocations. Management may attempt to reduce this risk by presenting each stakeholder's rewards in a positive manner relative to the stakeholder's investment. Financial disclosure management plays a central role in the creation of such portrayals.

What is managed financial disclosure?

Financial disclosure includes such releases as earnings announcements, strategy discussions, investor relations meetings, and interviews to discuss the consequences of labour unrest on a company's future performance. Financial disclosure management means constructing a portrayal of the company that is consistent with other managerial strategies and actions. While managers can manage disclosure to suit their own interests, they always need to consider stakeholders' possible disbelief of what they say. A disclosure that is not credible does not succeed as a demonstration of managers' accountability to stakeholders.

The concept of 'managed' disclosure implies information is not typically released to the public in a haphazard way, but also that disclosure is not so heavily controlled by law and regulation that the manager has no discretion in deciding at least some aspects of when, where and what information is provided and how the company portrayal is constructed. For example, the preliminary earnings announcement of the agricultural products company had (at least) two target audiences: the shareholders, to let them know that the company's financial performance was good; and the company's creditors, to reassure them that the company was capable of meeting its financial obligations. The timing of the announcement was chosen carefully: it was released earlier than usual so as to increase its visibility, but also timed so as to not be over-shadowed by the preliminary earnings announcements of other companies who were experiencing major losses. All this was done to portray the company in a way which assisted the management to direct company operations without any interference by creditors or shareholders.

The annual earnings announcement by the machine tool manufacturer is also a managed disclosure. Management must decide in making this announcement whether they wish to provide an explanation for why calculated earnings went up or down, whether they should provide information on last year's earnings as a form of comparison, and whether to make any predictions about the coming year's expected financial performance. Management may want to provide a pie graph showing how much of their revenue came from different geographical segments, or just provide total earnings. Prior to determining the earnings number, management may have reviewed, or changed, some accounting policy decisions, such as on how to calculate cost of inventory or depreciation expense, to ensure that the reported earnings were consistent with management's beliefs about how the company has performed. The company's auditors may have been asked to assent to any accounting policy changes so that the resulting portrayal of the company was credible. In this case, disclosure management activities were conducted to improve the image of management in the eyes of all the stakeholders.

Dimensions of disclosure

As suggested by the examples above, management have more to consider in making disclosures than just what information will be released. They must consider several other dimensions of financial disclosures, beyond the content (Gibbins, Richardson and Waterhouse, 1992). Management have to also decide what meaning to attach to the information being released (interpretation), and what to do to increase the believability of the information provided to the stakeholders (credibility). They have to determine how information is disclosed (medium used), whether multiple media will be used to release information or whether several stakeholder groups will be informed at once (redundancy), and the format for the disclosed information (organization). In addition, management have to time the announcement, either by choosing a particular date in the year or a time relative to some other event for the disclosure. The right-most column of Figure 1 has a few examples of these dimensions.

Management's choices among these dimensions and combinations of dimensions reflect managers' concerns about effects of stakeholders' behaviour. Will stakeholders be pleased by the news, or not? What degree of justification is needed? Is persuasion of certain stakeholders required? Management may choose to use a line graph to show several years of earnings (organization) because this shows that the company's performance is on a steady upward trend (which interpretation management provides, just in case recipients do not notice) and include this in a letter to shareholders (medium) because management believe this feature of the company's performance is particularly important in demonstrating its accountability to shareholders and will please them, or at least persuade them that management have their interests at heart.

If a large mining company makes a preliminary earnings announcement (timing) via a press release (medium), it may be because the earnings are significantly down (content) and the company wants to reduce the risk of shareholder litigation by getting the bad news out fast before more shares trade in ignorance of the news. Management may also want to call a press conference (redundancy) and show that cash flow is still strong, to reassure creditors. These are only a few examples of ways to manage financial disclosure in an attempt to influence the impressions important stakeholders have of the company and its management.

Regulation and the impact of changes in relative stakeholder importance

When the enacted importance of the stakeholder groups changes and/or the information demands of specific stakeholder groups evolve, this can have an effect on the disclosure management process. Such changes can occur, for example, when the company lists its shares on a stock exchange, thereby increasing the importance of investors and security market legislation; when new laws are amended to protect consumers or employees; when the company enters a new industry; or when the shareholders' mix and their relative interest in dividends versus stock price increases change.

In such circumstances, management can adopt new routines to respond. However, the adoption of new routines may be hindered by strong forces such as the resources already expended to set up current practices (sunk costs), political coalitions, internal accountability relationships, precedents set by the company or others in the industry, disclosure regulations and accounting standards, and lack of imagination (see Hill and Jones, 1992). These hindrances may make it difficult for the company management to effectively manage financial disclosure and internal conflicts may occur due to this inertia (see the extended example at the end of this chapter). Whether or not the company's disclosure process changes may in the end reflect the attitude of senior managers to disclosure.

Disclosure regulation originates from political, legal and cultural forces of certain countries reflecting the institutionalized perception of accountability pressures management is supposed to encounter. Although regulation may be amended to guarantee information availability for stakeholders, thus limiting the possibilities for financial disclosure management, such regulation also offers new possibilities for such managerial activities.

For example, a change in how costs should be allocated to inventories (such as in oil and gas accounting) provides an opportunity to make the change at such a time and in such a way as to communicate a desired message to stakeholders. Similarly, a new rule requiring disclosure of revenues by major product lines means management has to say something about such revenues but also gives management the opportunity to adjust the way it accounts for revenues, or even to reorganize the company's divisional structure, to produce a desired picture. Companies may exercise creativity and imagination in how to present the information and what level of detail to provide. Graphs may be used to show relative performance of a company's subsidiaries, or a detailed discussion of proposed capital investment over the next five years may be given. Thus, while regulations may indicate that certain information must be disclosed at a certain time and utilize a particular medium, the quality of those disclosures is often at management's discretion. Some companies may choose to release as little as possible while still meeting regulatory requirements, while others may see such mandated disclosures as an opportunity to influence specific stakeholder groups by providing additional information or utilizing presentation formats which highlight particular results.

Regulation may also make financial disclosure management a burdensome and unnecessarily complicated activity which may even endanger the existence of the company. As an example of the effects of regulation, Tennyson, Ingram and Dugan (1990) who studied the information content of narrative disclosures of firms in financial distress, found some evidence to suggest that management analyses of the financial statements appeared to address fewer themes useful in explaining bankruptcy than did the president's letter to shareholders. The authors speculated that regulation restricted the ability of the management analyses to provide useful information about financial distress. Financial regulation may specify a representation of the company that not only is not what management may prefer, but also that impedes management's ability to carry on business. For example, under U.S. regulation as well as that of many other countries, management must disclose financial setbacks in a timely manner. Yet disclosure of such information may impede management's ability to address the setbacks and result in a financial crisis which might have been avoidable. Bagby and Ruhnka (1987) refer to this as a self-fulfilling prophecy effect which can result in bankruptcy, losses to shareholders, or adverse economic consequences. Many companies now operate in a multinational context, so regulation in one country might require disclosures that have stakeholder consequences in another country.

Responses to and consequences of disclosure

Responses to disclosure are varied, and can be difficult to measure. The most extensive research has been into the stock market reaction to various kinds of financial disclosures. The reaction of securities markets to earnings announcements by firms has been extensively studied, finding typically a positive stock price reaction to 'good news', and a negative stock price reaction to 'bad news'. Lev (1992) documents a number of other consequences of disclosure found by researchers, including:

- investors' reactions to a sample of 634 strategy announcements by firms were examined by Woolridge (1988) and found on average to be positive
- Management's discussion of future prospects was found to have additional information content to that provided by the quantitative financial data provided in the financial statements (Hoskins, Hughes, and Ricks, 1986)
- announcements of dividend decreases which included a discussion of reasons for the decrease resulted in a less negative stock market reaction than such announcements not having an accompanying rationale (Woolridge and Ghosh, 1985).

The above points suggest that investors apparently will respond (via stock price changes) to disclosures concerning company strategy, prospects and managerial rationales. However, Healy and Palepu (1995) suggest that disclosures are not always effective in immediately mediating accountability pressures and, as argued above, might require careful management to have the intended effect.

Disclosures may cause other stakeholder reactions. Suppliers and customers may wish to change, terminate, or extend contracts depending on their beliefs about the meaning of a particular disclosure with respect to a company's solvency or long term prospects. Financial institutions may wish to change interest rates or conditions of debt covenants. Environmental groups may become less (or more) concerned about a company's potential to damage the environment. Labour groups may be influenced in their negotiating position. As stakeholders react to disclosures, this will bring renewed accountability pressures to bear on managers, who may then provide additional interpretation for existing disclosures, or develop new disclosures. The company's ways of managing disclosure will also evolve as additional disclosure experience is gained and reputation is built.

Related to the need for subsequent disclosures is an article by Eisenberg (1993) on U.S. litigation and management forecasts. Eisenberg comments that predicting earnings can be dangerous in the U.S. because, if the predictions are not achieved and stock prices fall, lawsuits on behalf of the entire class of shareholders alleged to have been injured are very likely to be filed against the company. He also notes that once forecasts have been made, an obligation is likely to be created to disclose any subsequent adverse information that undermines the prediction. A disclosure might therefore create a precedent and increase accountability pressures, necessitating more disclosures. Clearly, financial disclosure is an important management activity that requires considerable judgement on the part of management to inform and influence various stakeholders. The next section will examine the activities of managers involved in making disclosures, and the types of compromise that might be necessary to meet multiple stakeholder interests.

Managers' attitudes to disclosure

The disclosure management framework developed in Gibbins, Richardson and Waterhouse (1990) is focused around a concept called a disclosure position, which is defined as a relatively stable preference for the way disclosure is managed. It incorporates such factors as the firm's history, position in capital markets, regulation, corporate politics, and industry norms, and can be viewed as summarizing managerial attitudes towards disclosure management.

Social psychology research indicates that attitudes play a major part in determining behaviour (Fishbein and Ajzen, 1975). For example, Ajzen's (1985) theory of planned behaviour links one's beliefs about the consequences of particular behaviours, perceptions of others' beliefs about those behaviours, and perceived individual control over the behaviour to the likelihood of behaving in a particular way. All of these relate to the problem of managing disclosure under accountability. For example, the chief financial officer (CFO) of the meat products company mentioned in the introduction might personally believe that disclosing the financial analyses will result in a loss of competitive advantage, and the CFO is powerful in the company so his attitude results in such information not being typically released. However, the strike causes the chief executive officer (CEO) to assert a different attitude, more strategic in nature, that such information be made public to deter the workers from making excessive wage demands. The company's shareholders may also be assuming that the results of the strike will be even worse than what management perceives. The CFO may weigh each of these factors, including the CFO's own accountability to the CEO, and decide to release some financial analyses and interpretation of the possible consequences of the strike. The CEO is pleased with this decision, and the disclosures are released. After the strike is over, the CFO returns to not disclosing such information given the reduction in pressure from the CEO now that the strike has ended, reasserting his long-standing belief that it harms the company's competitive position.

This example shows how various factors come together to influence how disclosures are made. If the CFO felt that release of financial analyses was beneficial to the company shareholders, such disclosures might have been made regularly, without needing the changed circumstances of the strike and the pressure from the CEO. Conversely, if the CEO's attitude was against such disclosures but the CFO favoured them, the CFO's preference to disclose would have been overruled by the CEO. But when the strike occurred, the CEO would in turn feel pressure from shareholders and analysts to explain the consequences of the strike, which would lead the CEO to give permission to the CFO to release the financial analyses. In both versions, senior managers have stable attitudes about disclosure that, even though they differ, account for the company's normal disclosure practice, and in both cases, the circumstances of the strike caused a temporary change in that practice.

It can be seen that managers facing the same set of circumstances may choose to act differently because their attitudes about disclosure, perceptions of the consequences, accountability pressures, or their own control over disclosure activities are different. On the other hand, there are also forces that tend to produce similar financial disclosure behaviour across companies. One such force is again managerial attitudes: managers with similar education, professional background and experience in disclosure are likely to share at least some attitudes about disclosure – for example, most professional accountants would think that following established accounting standards is appropriate. Another force is imitation of successful disclosure behaviours initiated by other firms, especially by leaders in the industry. Disclosure research often shows industry commonalties, because if companies have similar economic circumstances, disclosure solutions that work for one company are likely to work for others like it. A third force is the institutional structure surrounding disclosure: the regulatory bodies, political influences, market structures and other institutions tend to drive companies in the same directions, even if those companies are not inherently very similar (see for example Meyer and Rowan, 1977; and DiMaggio and Powell, 1983). A fourth force promoting similarity of behaviour comes from disclosure itself: as every company matures and gains experience in disclosure, its disclosure practices develop their own legitimacy and momentum. Internal structures for disclosure management are created to respond to regulations, monitor industry leaders and otherwise regularize the process.

All these forces reinforce disclosure as a socially constructed phenomenon, responsive to a variety of influences beyond the economic events that are the raw material of the disclosure process.

Internal accountability relationships in disclosure management

The meat products company example above illustrated that perceptions of external accountability are modified or even determined by the views of top management, especially the chief executive officer, who sets the incentives and rules under which other managers act. Gibbins, Richardson and Waterhouse (1990) reported that the CEO's attitude to disclosure tended to be well known in the firm and was a common thread in the behaviour of other managers involved in disclosure.

Firms also organize their disclosure functions in ways that create internal accountability relationships. Sometimes the functions are organized to mimic, and always at least to connect to, the previously mentioned institutional structures of disclosure, such as accounting standard-setters or government regulators. In such cases, internal accountability involves technical correctness, being up to date on current professional and regulatory issues and other such forces in the firm's institutional environment. The oil and gas producer mentioned at the beginning of the chapter has this sort of internal accountability structure.

But the firm instead could organize financial disclosure more strategically, for example by giving operating managers more say and externally-oriented professionals less say. For example, a large mining company has established a 'disclosure unit' that is responsible directly to the chief executive officer for managing disclosure in the best strategic interests of the company. The unit is composed of operating managers and accounting and law professionals and meets when a disclosure issue arises, as determined or perceived by members of the unit or the CEO. The unit's accountability is only to the CEO (except for some legal rules, such as regarding 'insider' trading of shares on private knowledge) because the CEO has taken full responsibility for financial disclosure and the firm's accountability to external stakeholders.

Internal accountability relationships are also affected by each manager's role in disclosure and other management activities and the significance of those roles to the firm's disclosure outputs. These factors reflect the centrality and significance of disclosure to the company and the strategic value top management give it. As noted by Gibbins, Richardson and Waterhouse (1992), managers involved in disclosure may be centrally involved in the activities of other units in the firm, as they are in the mining company, or more peripherally, as they are in the oil and gas producer. Sometimes disclosure functions are widely spread among the firm's managers; sometimes they are highly centralized. Managers' disclosure accountability will be diffuse or focused, as a consequence. The agricultural products manufacturer has both kinds of internal accountability relationships regarding disclosure: various divisional managers are likely to be involved to various degrees, depending on what is going on, but the firm's public relations manager is always involved and is explicitly accountable to both the CEO and some external stakeholders for the firm's disclosure. Internal relationships are illustrated further in the extended example below.

Extended example

The financial disclosure management process is as complex as the firm's set of stakeholders, managers and disclosure issues. The larger the set, the more room for conflict among stakeholders, diffuse disclosure roles and responsibilities, and frequent attention to disclosure. All of these are likely to lead to ambiguous accountability relationships and an unclear role for the firm's disclosures in meeting stakeholders' information needs and serving management's intentions such as to influence stakeholders. But whatever the firm's success in this, the disclosure management process will reflect the firm's strategy, its organization, its governance, the attitudes of the managers involved, internal inter-manager accountability and other factors described above. The portrayal of the firm achieved through financial disclosure may be plain and simple, but the forces and intentions behind it are neither plain nor simple.

Here is an extensive summary example of the financial disclosure management process for a recent press release disclosure, showing how the process connected to the accountability pressures from stakeholders and how the disclosure dimensions were used. The example, drawn from one particular company in our research, illustrates that financial disclosure management is a social process, producing a socially constructed portrayal of the company, and shows how various accountability pressures influence financial disclosures processes, how changes in stakeholder relationships have an effect on disclosure management and why the managerial response to the pressures may be lengthy and complex.

The disclosure

The agricultural products manufacturer, mentioned several times in this chapter, issued a press release to disclose interim corporate earnings, including performance by business segment. The press release was issued two weeks after a press conference announcing an equity offer and one week before the prospectus for that share offer was to be published.

- The *stakeholders* management was concerned about were present, as well as potential shareholders, financial analysts, securities regulators and others involved in the capital market.
- *Managerial accountability* was defined by legal, business and personal relationships with a number of major shareholders, analysts and others, and by the chief executive officer's particular *attitude* of accountability to the investing community.

- The press release *medium* indicated that the issue was important enough to require carefully controlled disclosure but not important enough to arrange a press conference which is the company's routine for major disclosures.
- *Timing* was defined by the earlier press conference and the later prospectus release, which in turn were a function of management's *strategy* for going to the market at the appropriate time (more about this below). Timing was an issue not only because of management's strategy but because *disclosure regulations* contained rules about the release of information relevant to such an equity offer, particularly in relation to the planned prospectus.
- *Content* was chosen *strategically* to cover nine months of operations. The company normally releases six-month interim figures, but because performance is usually better in the second half of the year due to seasonal factors, management wanted to include some of that second half performance and settled on the nine-month period. Content was also influenced by *disclosure regulations* pertaining to such equity offers.

Knowing the details of the company's performance gave management an *information advantage* over external stakeholders. Management wanted to use this advantage to both *please* current shareholders and *persuade* others to become shareholders through the equity offer.

A controversy about the details disclosed

Division-specific profits were included in the nine-month performance report that was the subject of the press release. This was the first time the company had released divisional results, and doing so was the result of extensive deliberation and a number of forces acting on management.

- The company's *financial disclosure position* has been consistently quite conservative. Not breaking results down by division was consistent with *industry norms* and reflected some inertia on the part of the senior managers, whose *attitudes* to disclosure had not changed much even though the company was becoming more active in accessing capital markets. Not disclosing divisional results also reflected managers' wish *not to please* one group of *stakeholders*: competitors who could use the information against the company.
- Whether *disclosure regulations* required such divisional disclosure was contentious. There were some new requirements regarding industry-specific reporting, and as the underwriter of the equity offer interpreted them and advised the company, the company's present industry-based divisional structure meant disclosing divisional profits. Managers involved in the preparations for the share issue took this argument at face value and agreed to prepare such information. However, the company's external auditor did not believe that industry-specific profits were explicitly required in the regulations, but he was not prepared to correct the opinion of the underwriter, since he wished to be the auditor of a progressive company in the eyes of other auditors and companies. The auditor also felt mild accountability pressure from investors, who he thought would benefit from the information. Thus the regulations provided an opportunity for the company to improve its disclosure, but also a danger in that the regulations

specified severe penalties for errors in equity offer information, and the more detailed data left more room for error.

- The company's circumstances have been changing in several ways relevant to the divisional disclosure issue. First, one and half years prior to the press release, a new CEO was selected. He started to pay more attention to investor relationships than had his predecessor (a different *attitude* to disclosure and perception of his *accountability* to that group of stakeholders), and took under his direct control the public relations unit (this changed the *internal accountability* for disclosure and increased the *status* of disclosure in the company.) Second, the company's economic circumstances were changing. The CEO wanted to *persuade* investors to rethink their expectations for the company because he saw it changing from being a stable agricultural producer toward a more high-technology orientation. Divisional data were part of this *message* because the data showed that the company's high-technology division was growing and profitable. Third, six months prior to the press release, several financial analysts had visited the company asking for division-specific profitability figures (the analysts represented investors and therefore increased the *accountability pressure* management felt from those stakeholders). *Managers' attitudes* to this disclosure varied. Though most senior managers had not been in favour of such disclosure, three were. The manager of the public relations unit (who was now responsible directly to the CEO for disclosure effectiveness), the CFO and the manager responsible for shareholder records felt a strong need to provide such information. (All three were professionals who saw their accountability as partly defined by professional norms.) *Regulations* prohibited telling the analysts privately anything not disclosed publicly. The visits by the financial analysts increased the *enacted importance* of the shareholders and with the *internal accountability* pressure represented by the new CEO, changed senior management's preference to favour the divisional disclosure.

- Although these extensive accountability pressures for disclosing division-specific information existed, other stakeholders were perceived as continuing to oppose the disclosure. First, the company's traditional shareholders were not perceived by management to be very interested in division-specific results, since this information would not change their decisions to own company shares. (They were largely suppliers who used the company to market their products.) It was even believed by some managers who felt accountable to the traditional shareholders, that disclosing division-specific results would be seen as an action against those shareholders by indicating a change in management's perceived importance of stakeholder groups (*conflict in accountability pressures*). A second argument against such division-specific disclosure was that the accounting routines the company had did not include how to prepare division-specific results according to current accounting norms (*inertia*). The company had the necessary data but preparing it for external disclosure would be a costly process. The decision to prepare such information required the chief accountant to do an extensive amount of innovative work to do the calculations and design new routines for future disclosures. This was an opportunity for disclosure management of *content* because there was more than one way to calculate the necessary figures.

To complete the example, it should be noted that hardly any shareholders appeared to notice the information in the press release, as far as management as well as some major shareholders could tell, but financial analysts did notice the division-specific performance figures and apparently did not find them surprising. Consistent with their lack of newsworthiness, there were no changes in the stock price immediately after the release and no pressure for further *interpretations* by management. Though some managers had feared the *consequences* of the disclosure, there turned out to be no cause for immediate concern, though responses by competitors may yet happen.

Conclusions

This chapter has presented managed financial disclosure as an illustration of a complex, accountability-related activity which portrays the company to its stakeholders. When managers choose the content, timing, target audience, narrative interpretation and other features of the firm's disclosures, they are influenced by accountability relationships that lead directly, or indirectly through other managers, to the firm's stakeholders. The chapter has explored:

- the circumstances under which accountability pressures are brought to bear upon management
- managerial responses when accountability pressures are conflicting
- the categories of stakeholder who may be interested in financial disclosures
- factors which affect the relative importance of stakeholders in a financial disclosure context
- the dimensions of financial disclosure which may be managed to respond to the pressures by creating a particular portrayal of the company
- potential responses by stakeholders to disclosures and consequences thereof
- factors such as regulation, managerial attitude, and internal accountability relationships which affect the relationship between accountability pressures and financial disclosure

Examples have been given of simple, elaborate, stable and dynamic stakeholder relationships and of the kinds of accountability pressures and responses such relationships can produce. For all companies, stakeholder accountability is real; for many, such as the agricultural products manufacturer changing its mix of shareholders and the food products company undergoing a strike by its factory workers, stakeholder accountability is complex and demanding.

The chapter's discussion does not contend that managed financial disclosure is the only way of meeting accountability pressure from stakeholders. Running the firm well, creating an appropriate governance structure and anticipating changes in market forces are other ways (all of which have disclosure implications themselves). Nor does the chapter contend that stakeholder accountability is the only reason for managed financial disclosure. Corporate reorganization, take-overs and acquisitions, and responses to changes in disclosure laws are other reasons (these in turn have stakeholder accountability implications themselves). But the combination of stakeholder accountability and managed financial disclosure provides a very rich and provocative field of research, knowledge about which is growing.

Future corporate managers should also find the ideas in this chapter useful. Whether they become professionals, such as accountants or lawyers, or operating managers, they will experience the accountability pressures described in this chapter and will be touched by the strategy, process and effectiveness of their firm's financial disclosure management.

References

Ajzen, I. (1985) From Intentions to Actions: A Theory of Planned Behavior, in *Action Control: From Cognition to Behavior* (eds J. Kuhl and J. Beckmann). Springer-Verlag, Berlin.

Bagby, J.W. and Ruhnka, J.C. (1987) The Obligation to Disclose Business Plans Under Extraordinary and Adverse Conditions. *Securities Regulation Law Journal* 15(1) pp. 69–104.

Cowen, S.C., Ferreri, L.B. and Parker, L.D. (1987) The Impact of Corporate Characteristics on Social Responsibility Disclosure: A Typology and Frequency-Based Analysis. *Accounting, Organizations and Society* 12(2) pp. 111–22.

DiMaggio, P.J. and Powell, W.W. (1983) The Iron Cage Revisited: Institutional Isomorphism and Collective Rationality in Organizational Fields. *American Sociological Review* 48 (April) pp. 147–60.

Dye, R.A. (1985a) Disclosure of Nonproprietary Information. *Journal of Accounting Research* 23(1) pp. 123–45.

Dye, R.A. (1985b) Strategic Accounting Choice and the Effects of Alternative Financial Reporting Requirements. *Journal of Accounting Research* 23, pp. 544–74.

Eisenberg, J. (1993) Enforcement Issues and Litigation. *Securities Regulation Law Journal* 21, pp. 202–13.

Evans, J.H. III, Heiman-Hoffman, V.B. and Rau, S.E. (1994) The Accountability Demand for Information. *Journal of Management Accounting Research* 6 (Fall) pp. 24–42.

Fishbein, M. and Ajzen, I. (1975) *Belief, Attitude, Intention and Behaviour: An Introduction to Theory and Research*. Addison-Wesley, Reading, MA.

Freeman, R.E. (1984) *Strategic Management: A Stakeholder Approach*, Pitman, Boston.

Gibbins, M. and Ikäheimo, S. (1995) Financial Disclosure Management: Managerial Accountability in an Evolving Stakeholder Setting. Working paper, April 1995.

Gibbins, M. and Newton, J. An Empirical Exploration of Complex Accountability in Public Accounting. *Journal of Accounting Research* 32(2) (Autumn) pp. 165–86.

Gibbins, M., Richardson, A. and Waterhouse, J. (1989) Managing Financial Disclosure. *CA Magazine* (November) pp. 33–39.

Gibbins, M., Richardson, A. and Waterhouse, J. (1990) The Management of Corporate Financial Disclosure: Opportunism, Ritualism, Policies and Processes. *Journal of Accounting Research* 28 (Spring) pp. 121–43.

Gibbins, M., Richardson, A. and Waterhouse, J. (1992) *The Management of Financial Disclosure: Theory and Perspectives*. Research Monograph No. 20, Vancouver: The Canadian Certified General Accountants Research Foundation, 1992.

Healy, P.M. and Palepu, K.G. (1995) The Challenge of Investor Communication: The Case of CUC International, Inc. *Journal of Financial Economics*, 22 (June) pp. 111–40.

Hill, C.W.L. and Jones, T.M. (1992) Stakeholder-Agency Theory. *Journal of Management Studies* 29(2) pp. 131–54.

Hoskins, R., Hughes, J. and Ricks, W. (1986) Evidence on the Incremental Information Content of Additional Firm Disclosure Made Concurrently with Earnings. *Journal of Accounting Research* 24 (Supplement) pp. 1–36.

Jensen, M. and Meckling, W. (1976) Theory of the Firm: Managerial Behaviour, Agency Costs and Capital Structure. *Journal of Financial Economics* 3 (October) pp. 305–60.

Lev, B. (1992) Information Disclosure Strategy. *California Management Review* (Summer) pp. 9–32.

Meyer, J.W. and Rowan, B. (1977) Institutionalized Organizations: Formal Structure as Myth and Ceremony. *American Journal of Sociology* **83**(2) pp. 340–63.

Moerland, P.W. (1995) Alternative Disciplinary Mechanisms in Different Corporate Systems. *Journal of Economic Behavior and Organization* **26** pp. 17–34.

Pfeffer, J. and Salancik, G. (1978) *The External Control of Organization: A Resource Dependence Perspective*, Harper and Row, New York.

Roberts, R.W. (1992) Determinants of Corporate Social Responsibility Disclosure: An Application of Stakeholder Theory. *Accounting, Organizations and Society* **17**(6) pp. 595–612.

Schlenker, B.R. and Weigold, M.F. (1992) Interpersonal Processes Involving Impression Regulation and Management. *Annual Review of Psychology*, pp. 133–68.

Tennyson, B.M., Ingram, R.W. and Dugan, M.T. (1990) Assessing the Information Content of Narrative Disclosures in Explaining Bankruptcy. *Journal of Business, Finance & Accounting* **17**(3) (Summer) pp. 391–410.

Tetlock, P.E. (1985a) Accountability: The Neglected Social Context of Judgment and Choice. *Research in Organizational Behaviour*, **1**, pp. 297–332.

Tetlock, P.E. (1985b) Accountability: A Social Check on the Fundamental Attribution Error. *Social Psychology Quarterly*, **48**, pp. 227–36.

Verrecchia, R.E. (1983) Discretionary Disclosure. *Journal of Accounting and Economics*, **5** (December) pp. 179–94.

Verrecchia, R.E. (1990) Information Quality and Discretionary Disclosure. *Journal of Accounting and Economics* **12** (1990) pp. 365–80.

Weick, K.E. (1979) *The Social Psychology of Organizing*, Addison-Wesley, Reading, MA.

Woolridge, R. (1988) Competitive Decline and Corporate Restructuring: Is a Myopic Stock Market to Blame? *Bell Journal of Economics*, **1**(1) (Spring) pp. 26–36.

Woolridge, R. and Ghosh, C. (1985) Dividend Cuts: Do They Always Signal Bad News? *Midland Corporate Finance Journal* (Summer) pp. 20–32.

10 Accountability and identity: accounting and the democratic organization

Fabrizio Panozzo

Abstract

The internal organization and economic nature of trade unions have traditionally attracted only scarce research interests. Accordingly, little is known about the way in which economic discourses are involved in unions' activity and the roles accounting plays in these organizational contexts. The very existence of accounting may be flawed and the assertion itself that the union has an economic dimension may be hard to defend within a tradition of antagonism with the values of a 'managerialist' system. More likely, to account for the economic consequences of their action, organizations such as trade unions are likely to rely on original 'vocabularies of motives' (Mills, 1963).

Nevertheless, the case of an Italian union indicates that accounting practices can flourish also in labour movements, albeit heavily influenced by principles of participation and democracy. The paper tries to explore these specificities by looking at accounting as an organizational practice which acquires meaning in the context in which it operates; this allows a tentative look at some of the different meanings of economic accountability. An interpretation of these roles seems to move accounting away from its functions of objective representation of economic reality. Instead, self-developed and 'socializing' forms of economic accountability are used as instruments that legitimate the existence of several autonomous identities within a complex organized system.

Introduction

Within the theory of formal organizations, economic accountability is traditionally viewed as a mechanism that allows for the control and performance evaluation of individual and collective action. By rendering behaviour in economic terms accounting numbers are supposed to produce a rigorous, internally consistent and potentially manageable picture of complex social systems. Because of these alleged properties a fostering of economic accountability is often called for to stimulate economic awareness within public and non-commercial organizations. The attempts to 'managerialize' these kinds of organization rests on views of accounting as a merely technical and neutral mechanism and are thus oblivious of the peculiar nature of the context in which accounting is asked to operate. The relevance of organizational context is particularly crucial in those cases in which organizational culture fosters values which are radically different from those of the business firm. In this kind of organization, accounting work may be linked to issues other than those of inspection, formal control and efficiency. In particular in a 'democratic' organization such as a trade union accounting representations can be used by organizational participants to account for their activities not as 'controllable objects' but as legitimate components of a wider organizational context (Panozzo, 1994b). Therefore, the use of accounting is not guided by a conventional calculative rationality in which participants are asked to account for their action in order to allow for its general visibility. In a loosely coupled, democratic organization, identities, rather than being attributed by an external agency that measures and co-ordinates multiple interests, can be autonomously created by organizational participants. Rather than being 'calculated' and expressed in monetary terms, accountability incorporates a notion of 'interest' much closer to the Latin etymology of *inter* (= within) and *esse* (= being). A primitive understanding of what 'inter-ests' are thus expresses the will of agents to 'be within' and to attribute meaning to individual actions by reference to wider organizational and social processes. In such a context the idea itself of accountability appears closely linked to issues of organizational identity and has therefore to be supplemented by meta-economic concerns. The use of accounting can thus be interpreted as a critical factor in the expression of substantive, non-indispensably economic, values and interests.

In this chapter the relationship between accountability and the autonomous construction of organizational identities is explored by making reference to the roles of accounting within an Italian trade union. The first section introduces the institutional arrangement and economic functioning of the largest Italian labour movements. In the second section accounting work within the trade union is analysed as a socially and institutionally embedded practice which gets reproduced and individualized, asking for interpretation other than the technical one. The following three sections look at accounting work as deeply rooted in organizational culture and thus involved in the construction of peculiar notions of accountability and organizational identity. Finally, an interpretation of mechanisms informing accounting work within a democratic organization is proposed. Accountability is seen as dependent on notions of organizational identity constructed on political and ideological grounds. Questions of membership and belongingness are therefore likely to generate 'socializing' forms of economic accountability rather than producing hierarchical views of organizational functioning.

The roles of accounting in a labour union

Several reasons could explain a lack, or the absence, of accounting work in labour unions. As with other non-profit organizations, unions are not expected to develop, actively use or rely on formal economic representations of their functioning. This presumption is due to a common, and often unchallenged, understanding of the economic logic of non-profit organizations in terms of effectiveness rather than efficiency. In labour unions efforts are supposedly directed towards the achievement of organizational goals with a negligible relevance of the ways in which resources are used in order to achieve those results (Zan, 1994). Second, perceptions of accounting in labour unions may be ideologically biased (and they often are) by an understanding of it as an instrument of power historically invented and developed as a consequence of the class struggle of production relations (Braverman, 1974).

But in the Italian case an additional, and more tying, justification is that the law sets almost no legal requirements in terms of accounting records for these kinds of organization. In general the legislation concerning accounting has been very advantageous for Italian unions, aiming at reducing the intensity of all kinds of formal controls by the state. Moreover, unions were granted with several facilitating measures such as a less expensive acquisition of human resources with related minor obligations in terms of accounting records.

The one considered here is 'The Confederation', one of the largest Italian labour unions, which represents more than 5 million workers and has about 10,000 employees (both technical and 'political' personnel). This paper is based on research conducted in the Emilia Romagna region where the union represents 330,000 workers, 476,000 retired personnel, 6,000 unemployed, and has a total of 1,300 employees (640 in professional units, 425 in the confederal structure, the 'Chamber of Labour', 235 in services).

The Confederation as such is a second level organization that associates autonomous occupational unions and operates through 11 confederal offices, located at a 'provincial' level. Each of these structures elects its own political leaders and hires professional staff. The Regional Secretary General describes the 15 professional unions that merge into the Confederation as '. . . those that do the traditional union activities such as bargaining for better salaries and work conditions and in general the safeguarding of basic workers' rights'; and the confederal structure as the one that '. . . deals with more general political issues such as social security policy, income redistribution and taxation policies, legislation concerning labour and immigration. Confederal structures play a more institutional role by keeping contacts with local authorities and governmental bodies in the attempt to influence the decision making processes. The degree of the Confederation's institutional involvement can be very high and is often extended well beyond issues of conventional union concern'. In addition to that the union controls a number of service firms that offer legal and fiscal assistance to both members and non-members.

The bulk of the union's financial inflows (85% on average) comes from membership fees (on average: 1% of net salary for workers; 0.5% for retired personnel) with the rest originating from fund raising campaigns, usually related to particular events such as a strike, a celebration or the signing of an important national contract. Unions' statutes sanction the primacy of professional unions in the allocation of financial resources; they are seen as the natural beneficiary of workers' subscriptions which are automatically checked off by the employer. Resources are then reallocated to the rest of the organization on the basis of internally agreed apportionments: for instance, 4% to the national board of the professional union, 2% to the regional, 25–28% to the Confederation at the local level, 1% to the Confederation at the national level, etc. Mechanisms of resource allocation are only loosely defined by common national norms and therefore processes of local adjustment become the crucial point in which economic representation are enacted and notions of accountability delineated. The large autonomy enjoyed by each organizational unit has led to an almost uncontrollled articulation of the organizational structure with a consequent proliferation of accounting work. The main organizational features of the Confederation are aptly captured by one of its leaders.

> It was at the turn of the 60s that the Confederation deeply changed its organizational nature. During this period, the union experienced a process of institutionalization, where the internal staff grew and the organization 'fattened', while still enjoying positive financial inflows. It is here that the primacy of the 'political' got established. In this view, a good unionist is the one who negotiates a good collective agreement with the employers, independently of its costs and of the resources diverted from possible alternative activities. The consequence was a lack of investment on professional administrative competencies when they were most needed, that is when both financial inflows and administrative complexity were growing. Instead, political officers started to play with administrative variables and procedure, imposing their professional schemes and values (as unionists) on the administrative professionalism. It is such a contradiction between the growing amount and complexity of resources to be managed, and the lack of development of professional culture in administration and accounting which explains the 'minor status' of accounting work in this organization.

In front of the possible homogenization deriving from the intervention of administrative rationality, a proliferation of accounting work and administrative practices emerged as the major organizational characteristic. Each organizational unit (professional unions at the local and regional territory level, local and regional Confederal boards, service firms, etc.) is said to be 'autonomous' and thus 'holder' of its budget and financial statement. This results in a collection of more than 200 financial documents produced in the entire region, each reflecting the peculiar equilibrium that has been reached in the specific organizational context. The kind of financial statement produced by each unit is vaguely inspired by a common system of accounts, that was developed in order to allow a national consolidation of results. The one that is suggested by the national accounting scheme, is a form of financial accounting which at the same time and within the same document, attempts to integrate and give visibility to relevant activities which are named 'cost centres' in the generic attempt to more precisely define where and how the union's political action generates cost and 'creates' value. Not being mandatory from a legal point of view and only for internal use, the accounts produced are relatively independent of generally accepted accounting principles. The construction of economic representation is therefore open to local interpretations and manipulations of accounting rules that will never be 'audited' in order to produce a uniform picture. Every organizational unit records single items, keeps track of its own revenues and expenses, allocates costs and determines annual results without any reference to common procedure or standards. The internal organization of subunits (involving choices such as the institution of an 'affirmative action office', or the number of activists belonging to the political board) is left to discretion and guided by political opportunity. New departments may be created to co-opt into the leading coalition a representative of the radical Marxist minority. 'Cost centres' are put in place to monitor expenses but they never bring together the entire amount of a given category of cost. Costs tend to be attributed on a basis other than the economic and thus reinforce the 'political' meaning of union activities (shop steward training on negotiation techniques is a 'political' cost, not a training one). Mergers with other professional unions at the local level, give rise to new organizational units that are almost unaccountable from the Confederation point of view. New organizational units emerge when more than one industrial district exists within a given territory and the union articulates accordingly. Virtually all additional expansions of the organizational structure has a political antecedent but rests on the availability of financial resources and, ultimately, on accounting sanctioning. Each federated union, regardless of its dimensions and relevance, is entitled with financial resources, the use of which is jealously protected from all kinds of intra-organizational intervention. In any case the final result of this process of 'private' record keeping is a plethora of financial documents that offer only very limited possibilities for comparability.

But as a sort of reinforcement of the democratic equilibrium of 'distributed sovereignty', another organizing principle, 'organizational solidarity', leads with equal strength in the opposite direction. This principle supports the view of the Confederation as a unitary system, with a clear political strategy and a strong sense of identity. A tightening of organizational linkages is especially needed when disequilibrium in the performances of different subunits emerge. In fact, though formally dependent upon the support of workers, several occupational unions experience, especially in these last years, serious financial restraints. A number of them are often 'subsidized' through a complex system of redistribution of common resources in which organizational participants strive for an equilibrium between the imperatives of 'distributed sovereignty' and 'organizational solidarity'. At the end of the process each unit may receive only a part of the actual income, while other subunits may be actually financed with resources that originate in other parts of the organizations.

The individualization of accounting practices

The case of the Confederation significantly challenges conventional claims that workers' organizations are 'accounting free' systems (cf. Panozzo, 1994). As a matter of fact, the production of financial reports seems to be one of the major activities in which the union's professional bureaucracy is involved. This happens at every organizational level regardless of the relevance and role of the subunits that are accounted for and of the practical utility of the information produced. In general, the characteristics of accounting practices in the Confederation confirm those described in recent studies of accounting in trade unions such as: scarce financial information, and absence of effective systems of financial control (Willmann *et al.*, 1993); unsatisfactory accounting procedure and non compliance by federally registered unions required to produce annual reports (Griffin and Rozario, 1993).

The principle of loose coupling that shapes the structuring of the organization, opens the possibility for a pragmatic application of the principle of 'distributed sovereignty'. Organizational equilibria of power and influence, together with considerations of political opportunism, shape the interpretation of economic events and the accounting representation that is made of them. Reasons for the 'individualization' of accounting originate in the first place from the organizational model and the internal relationship between the branches and the federal office. The state of accounting documents reflects the constant search by subunits for *ad hoc* adaptation to local contingencies and the attempt to give economic relevance to the principle of autonomous action. This involves calculations that are ultimately transformed into accounting reports: one relevant example is the collection and allocation of financial resources. Being the only institutional link with members, occupational unions collect the entire amount of membership fees and then remit a portion of their income to the federal office. The only formal provision concerning this distribution of resources is the application of the generic principle of 'solidarity' among all organizational subunits. Within these very loose boundaries there is room for the establishment of a complex bargaining process in every local branch of the Confederation. The result is the reproduction of idiosyncratic practices: several unions recognize this transfer as a 'cost', others show in their accounts only the net worth of their income. The majority fall somewhere in the middle between these two extremes. A number of professional unions (namely the 'strongest' in membership terms) *de facto* operate as autonomous branches controlling the bulk of union finances. In striking antithesis, other unions are very strictly controlled by the federal office that sets precise standards for resources distribution and verifies their economic conditions. Furthermore, the financial structure of a number of professional unions is conditioned by historical or technical circumstances such as, for example, the allocation of a part of the membership fees of workers in the building industry to the maintenance of a specific social security fund. These circumstances gave origin to a number of different agreements, requiring idiosyncratic accounting records, with external bodies such as the social security service, the ministry of labour, the association of employers and with the Confederation itself. The form that economic representations will take are thus determined by the balance of power between each single union and a number of different actors both within and without the organization.

When occupational unions' accounts are controlled by the federal office, differences are likely to develop on another basis, namely the geographical one. An extreme variability in economic results can be observed among subunits operating in a similar 'competitive environment' both in terms of economic conditions and social support. In this case, differences are less likely to be determined by a more or less efficient use of resources than by context-specific fabrications of accounting reports. Particularly relevant is the treatment of personnel costs given that it may absorb up to 90% of a unit's total expenses. Salaries and wages may appear in the union's accounts either in their actual value or, especially in small geographical areas with few unionized firms, as a sort of 'average' allowance resulting from the 'socialization' of personnel cost. In this case the total amount paid is divided by the number of activists regardless of their formal relationship with the union. They include full-time officers, part-time retired workers but also, in the case of public sector unions, personnel whose cost is paid by the ministry or by nationalized companies as a part of the national work contract. The average cost thus obtained can be used by the local federal board to 'mould' the shape of each subunit's account.

The nature of personnel costs underlines the fact that a considerable share of union resources, namely those that have been classified as 'political rents' (Rosa, 1984), may be hard to comprehend in economic accounts. That's the case for shop stewards' unpaid time, employer contribution through the provision of facilities to activists to conduct union assemblies in paid work time. Also public money is used to support unionism through the abatement of social security costs for unions' full time activists. This is ultimately reflected on accounting reports through the attempt to attribute economic value to these 'immaterial' resources. Far from searching for a common procedure every occupational union invariably uses self-developed methods of valuation.

Accountability in a democratic organization

The state of proliferation and individualization of accounting practices calls for an interpretative framework that is, to a great extent, alternative to the technical one. From a strictly functional point of view, the use of accounting techniques in the Confederation could indeed be labelled as 'irrational' and therefore useless for the construction of a meaningful picture of the economics of the union. But, beyond their technical 'failure', economic accounts seem to acquire new meanings for those who use them. This in turn calls for a view that looks beyond the technical one by investigating the conditions and consequences of actual practices.

The first thing to notice in an interpretative perspective, is that the loose organizational coupling within the Confederation legitimates different 'rationalities' to interpret the roles of accounting according to a number of non-technical interests. Accounting operates accordingly, with the provision of an ever changing set of meanings that allows for the enactment of the myth of independence and subunit autonomy. In this respect, the production of economic accounts is conceivable as a sense making activity concerned more with the attribution of an aura of legitimacy and rationality to organizational action, than with the objective representation of economic 'facts'.

A political bias is infused on economic calculation and on the perceived 'quality' of accounts. Deeply ingrained cultural values being at stake, what is politically adequate also becomes 'true', overwhelming the perceived need to give economically correct information. This bias plays a critical role in the construction of the 'official' version of annual reports in many federated unions, and is therefore critical in understanding the roles accounting is expected to play in the Confederation. In many cases annual accounts are 'fabricated' with the aim of showing a 'zero profit' situation, the reason for such a manipulation being that a union 'cannot' show a 'profit' on its account. This perceived need has a deeply ingrained cultural origin that tends to overwhelm all other dimensions of economic representation.

Having traditionally enjoyed good economic conditions (revenues higher than operating expenses), many subunits within the Confederation are used to undertake a yearly 'make-up' of their accounts. These interventions are made on both revenues and costs. the actual amount that the professional union receives from workers' contributions is often recorded at a lower value to reduce the subunit's proportional share of financial contribution to the Confederation. On the costs side the common practice used to lessen professional unions' accounts is the setting of contingency or emergency funds based on groundless estimations of future 'extraordinary' expenses.

What emerges quite clearly from this active fabrication of economic accounts in the Confederation, is that accounting work tends to be seen as independent from any generally accepted standard of significance. Therefore, the information that is made available, being embedded in the contingencies of culture and politics, prevents the construction of a general 'economic' vision of organizational functioning. This would indeed require the existence of a shared understanding of accounting role and significance, but in the Confederation the ways in which accounts are elaborated depends also on local bargaining and political equilibria. Rather than a mechanism producing a neutral reflection of the economics of the whole union, accounting is used as a linguistic instrument in the process of social construction of organizational reality (Neimark and Tinker, 1986).

The tacit attribution of this role to accounting representations constitutes a radical shift from the technical sphere and asks for the broadest interpretation of accounting as a discursive practice. Viewed in this perspective, the production of rationalized pictures with the use of techniques of economic representation is not an end in itself, rather it can be understood in the realm of the construction of a less formal 'system of accountability' (Roberts and Scapens, 1985). This notion contrasts with the conventional idea of an 'accounting system' by looking at its actual role in the organizational context in which it operates. From this point of view accounting can be seen as a 'system in use' as opposed to the abstract potential of a set of formal rules and techniques of which it represents the organizational embodiment. The focus is therefore on accountability as an unavoidable and ritual feature of organizational life that has a particularly critical function in 'political' organizations such as the Confederation, where strongly held cultural values represent one of the major binding forces.

Seen from this point of view, the actual meaning of the economic account changes radically. Being inextricably interrelated with the subjective interpretations of participants, accounting can be seen as independent of the question of objective meaning, interpretation and understanding (Arrigton and Francis, 1993). This finally produces a major consequence with the shifting of the attributes of significance from information to action. Being independent of substantive meaning and abstracted from the information's content, any kind of value can be exclusively attached to the 'communicative action' of giving economic accounts. This interpretation of the role accounting comes to play in the Confederation is supported by a peculiar oranizational practice that has been established to 'certify' financial documents. When accounting records are produced, a group of elected auditors are asked to check whether economic representation is 'transparent', i.e. reflects the reality of organizational functioning. The unusual feature of this auditing procedure is that the auditors are not independent experts, rather blue collars chosen among the members of the union with, obviously, no accounting background. It is by no means technical knowledge that is needed to express an informed judgement about accounting records. Indeed, what the auditors audit is the fact itself that an economic account has been produced. It is the undertaking of this action and not in the information's content that the value of producing economic accounts is to be found.

Accounting and organizational order

The flourishing of accounting 'dialects' doesn't seem to undermine the properties of accounting as a particular vision providing a unique set of categories that indicate what is worthy of attention and has to be seen as relevant. Accounting maintains a subtle and crucial influence on organizational life, even if constantly reinterpreted and 'customized'. As with any other language, accounting has a latent power to define a particular characterization of entities and events and to constrain the way in which reality is perceived (Dent, 1986). In the Confederation accounting provides 'mechanisms around which interests are negotiated, counter-claims articulated and political processes explicated' (Burchell *et al.*, 1980). Organizational participants seem to be fully aware of these other possibilities that are offered by the accounting craft. Again the consequences of this awareness are closely related to the underlying principles of organizational functioning and provide a further, and more substantial, reason for the reproduction of accounting work. For example, the crucial principle of voluntary association and autonomy of the individual unions (and its equilibrium with the principle of solidarity) is hardly operationalizable, given its eminently political and symbolic nature. Few technical or professional attributes would allow for an 'objective individualization' of confederated unions. From the point of view of the federal office, unions can roughly be seen as actors doing the same job with a homogeneous technology, so that attempts to build distinction on a technical basis are impracticable. Moreover, union leaders and officers like to see themselves as engaged in a political job rather than emphasizing the professional dimension of their activity. But despite these circumstances, organizational actors are aware that 'identity matters' and that for its construction only symbolic tools are likely to be available. The variety of accounting practices indicates the existence of different styles of accountability that mirror the individual specificity of each subunit which is sanctioned in unions' statutes. Accounting for organizational action through the mystique of 'rational' economic calculation is, as such, a mechanism that certifies the legitimacy – and ultimately the morality – of each organizational unit that is entitled with resources. Leaders of occupational unions perceive that what is accounted for in economic terms gets legitimation to an extent that is far greater than the one obtained on a purely political basis.

The loose organizational coupling threatens the identity of single subunits and asks for a somewhat more reliable frame of reference in order to substantiate notions of 'autonomy' and 'solidarity'. Accounting plays a critical role in providing this powerful instrument for putting things into order by sketching the contours of each unit out of an indistinct whole. Accounting representations become a key component of organizational identity because of their ability to substantiate what may otherwise remain, in the domain of the political, nothing more than a formal recognition of existence. Ultimately it is the conceptualization itself of the Confederation as a nexus of independent organizational systems that owes much of its meaning to accounting representations. The organizational unit that is finally accounted for in economic terms (or better, constructs its own account of its functioning) receives the blessing of legitimacy and acquires a new kind of dignity and visibility. The endless debate in which the Confederation is constantly involved on an eminently political ground is quite rapidly settled with the definition of accounting boundaries.

The indistinct functioning of the political organization is thus condensed into the language of the economic resource. What would otherwise be 'invisible' can be translated into economic terms and obtaining this visibility means, for every subunit, to acquire reality (Meyer, 1986). Organizational identities thus shaped by accounting representations, are not, however, a mere recording of something that, in any case, would have been seen as the 'objective' economic reality. Those that accounting depicts as 'facts', only partially reflect the economic 'reality' of the organization being not just collected but rather created by the way in which they are arranged and classified. This 'incomplete' vision of organizational functioning highlights the complex ways through which a pattern of visibility is given shape. Income statements are not produced to reflect the economic consequences of union activity and thus to allow for 'technical' control; accounting is rather used as a 'constitutive device' giving shape and weight to what the unit signifies within the organization (Hopwood, 1986). By confining accounting within the boundaries of this 'symbolic' functon each professional union is protected from evaluation on the basis of technical performance. In other words – and in line with the conclusions of Meyer and Rowan (1977) on institutionalized organizations – the fact of producing accounting documents allows each unit to 'decouple' its activities from their formal representation. By 'consuming' accounting techniques, each organizational actor acquires a legitimized formal role which does not entail evaluation, inspection or hierarchical control. In this way issues of co-ordination and interdependence are handled informally and day-to-day activities can vary in response to 'political' considerations (Meyer and Rowan, 1977).

Accountability and identity

The way in which accounting systems become embedded in the Confederation's organizational practices illustrates the mechanism that intermingles symbols of formal rationality into political logic. The inability to construct an economic representation which is able to suggest an autonomous rhetoric, distinct and separated from the political one, reflects the hegemony of a social model in the definition of a framework for oganizational functioning. The principles of this model are overlooked even when financial matters are at stake, due to the impossibility of managing the union as if it was an expendable system, strictly committed to the attainment of stated goals. This framework affects the everyday life of the union, concealing the nature of those technical aspects that could be definitely coped with in the sphere of administrative rationality. Those relevant aspects that may influence internal equilibria tend to go through lengthy processes of debate and political confrontations, whose main function is the one of reframing them in a way that is consistent with the semantic structure of representative rationality. When union leaders, activists and officers are engaged in processes of internal negotiation, even accounting issues can acquire a manageable form by being expressed as '. . . a political problem'. All sorts of issues are thus diverted from their original premises and placed where political, rather than technical, expertise makes the difference. Interactions and negotiations are thus based on institutional resources that comprise, for instance, the ability to build consensus by phrasing and passing motions and the capacity of muddling through formal provisions for union communication, government and democracy.

Under these circumstances the use of accounting gets involved in the attempt to protect the uniqueness of the group in the face of the organization as a whole. The unrestricted expression of different subjectivities, once crystallized in definite patterns, endows individual groups of organizational participants with a distinctive position in the overall social structure. Any kind of mechanism intended to establish discipline via compulsory visibility is ideologically avoided. Therefore the conventional accounting imperative which fosters uniformity and 'commensurability' is apparently reversed through the possibility of playing language games with the 'objective' rules of economic calculation. The more these identities will develop and be reinforced by participants' behaviours, the more will the unit be valued for itself, not as a functional element operating within a comprehensive whole, but as an institutional fulfilment of group integrity and aspirations (Selznick, 1957).

The reproduction and individualization of these systems of accountability give visibility to the construction of 'difference' between organizational identities. Actors will possibly frame in a variety of different ways the relevant environment in which they operate, and their presence within them, by producing an economic representation of it. Yet the reliance on accounting representations as mechanisms of distinction involves something more than a simple matter of positioning. Determining the sense and the specificity of a presence within a complex system ultimately entails the specification by every organizational participant of its distinct organizational identity. It is mainly in this view that accounting is used in the Confederation. A view of accounting as an interpretative mechanism can thus result in a process of identity construction. This opens the possibility for the establishing of a tautological relationship between accountability and identity. Accountability can be more than a technique to inspect others' behaviour when it becomes crucial for organizational actors to possess a distinct identity.

In a democratic organization, and in loosely coupled systems in general, accountability is likely to be used as a mechanism of distinction in order to determine the participant's role or even affect their right to exist within a given context (Panozzo, 1994b). The Confederation appears like a paradigmatic case in which 'identity matters'; it is the nature itself of the organization, as internalized in deeply ingrained values, that sets the conditions for the distinction of identities.

Interests and accountabilities

The very notion of accountability in a democratic organization is closely linked to issues of identity and has therefore to be supplemented by meta-economic concerns. The decision to become a part of the organization and the meaning itself of the membership, are likely to be associated with attempts to fill the subjectively perceived gap between membership costs and the benefits that are economically measurable, such as a raise in pay or better working conditions (Olson, 1965, Offe and Wiesenthal, 1980). Should calculative practices be involved, they are likely to be understandable only within specific settings in which participants come to an agreement about which benefits are to be taken into account. Members may try to 'deflate' the costs they incur but they may also be willing to look for other categories of benefit that the membership may grant. The latter alternative could reveal an elusive but crucial supplement to the meaning participants attribute to their membership. In other words, the rigorous evaluation of the exchange relationship between the union and its members, leaves room for the expression of autonomous action as a constitutive element of the relationship on which the union is based. The union can be seen as a potentially meaningful space in which participants can express their willingness to act. In these processes actors may be willing to construct their autonomous identities primarily as a symbolic expression of their right to be a part of a system and to be considered as a legitimate component of a wider organizational context. The 'ontological' use of different types of interpretative and communicative resources, such as accounting, can thus be interpreted as a critical factor in the expression of 'primitive' (i.e. not strictly economic) interest. In such a context the relationship between communicative devices, organizational identities and membership can be seen in a different space, one that requires the reworking of the concept of interest. The kind of interest that relevant actors express in the construction of their identity could more aptly be conceptualized by reference to the Latin etymology of the word *interesse*. This original notion of interest derives from the composition of *inter* (= within) and *esse* (= being). A primitive understanding of what 'inter-ests' are, thus expresses the will of agents to 'be within' and to attribute meaning to individual actions by reference to wider organizational and social processes. An interested use of interpretative mechanism defines organizational identities not as stakeholders striving for the distribution of pay-offs, but as affiliated entities that are legitimated by the fact of 'acting within'. To express their willingness to act, actors are allowed to transform technical procedures and standard operating instructions to mobilize the ethical and the moral dimension as part of their process of affiliation (Munro and Hatherley, 1993). The image of the organization displaces the stakeholder model and focuses on the processes through which a community of interests is constructed and sense of affiliation is expressed.

An emphasis on concepts of community and affiliation also entails a different balance between matters of membership and accountability. In the stakeholder view, the homogenization of competing interests allows for their satisfaction but also entails the possibility to exercise co-ordination and control on the activities of members. The logic through which interests are expressed can be seen as the reflection of internal functioning. Therefore participants that compete for the allocation of resources will also be asked to produce a formal account of the ways in which they use them; i.e. of their 'performance'. The use of accounting will be based on the conventional idea of hierarchical accountability for which the attainment of visibility and shared understanding is crucial. Hierarchical accountability creates conditions in which participants are asked to give external and general visibility to their action in order to account for themselves and allows for the visibility of others' behaviour across physical distance (Roberts, 1991, Munro and Hatherley, 1993). This allows for inspection and surveillance with a focus on the functional roles individuals perform within the organization. In this way identities, rather than being autonomously created, are attributed by an external agency that co-ordinates multiple interests via the definition of control mechanism. Accountability precedes individualization and ultimately produces it as '. . . an absorption with self, with how one will be seen, which leads constantly to attempts to stand as if outside oneself in order to anticipate the expectations of others' (Roberts, 1991: 360). In hierarchical accountability a univocal understanding of situations and actions is imposed by the system and formal relations of power can be established.

But when membership through affiliation is stressed, the intrusion of hierarchical accountability is recognized to be potentially destructive of those identities that have been constructed within a community of interests. These are undermined by attempts to establish mechanisms of surveillance and control, since defence of such judgement would stand in the scrutiny of hierarchical vision that erases the underlying meaning attributed to membership. A substantially different notion of accountability is likely to develop when affiliation and belongingness become crucial factors on which membership is to be legitimized. Roberts (1991) has argued persuasively that in the context in which social integration is granted by binding consensual and cultural norms and the expression of situated judgements is widely accepted, accountability can acquire a 'socializing' form. Because the meaning of organizational events is socially and locally negotiated, this form of accountability requires a constant interaction between organizational actors. It can emerge in every organizational context as an informal account (often without numerical expression) of common experiences of work and interaction. This social construction of organizational achievements is likely to restrict the possibilities for accountability to be established as a conventional control mechanism. The institutionalization of negotiation practices opposes the idea of a 'technical' rationality that autonomously defines organizational performance and identity. Against the threat of economic normalization, forms of socializing accountability are developed to preserve differences and specificities within the organization. A membership based on affiliation can engage in practices that subvert the normalizing individualization of the technical. Constructing individual identities drawing on social constructions and symbolic resource could be seen as one way to strip away 'the monetary veil of economics from the social processes of belonging' (Munro and Hatherley, 1993). Practices of 'socializing accountability' are based on the reframing of the traditional order of who calls who to account. The case of the trade union shows that identities supported by accounting constructions can reflect the existence and the dignity of situated judgements and forms of 'self audit'. That is why confederated unions are not asked to account for their activity and the pictures they produce cannot function as codified messages to be sent outside to comply with procedures of economic control. The meaning of the activities in which they are engaged is more likely to be found in the reproduction of the ritual of affiliation in which participants principally account to themselves.

This may be true in general for loosely coupled organizations – especially in the public and non-profit sector – in which competing structures of legitimation and control are a constitutive element of the system. What they have in common with reference to economic accounts is that several other binding principles regulate their functioning and that 'accounting for control' does not provide an effective organizational 'glue'. Loosely coupled organizations are likely to define particular 'categories of economic citizenship' (Arrigton and Francis, 1993); members of these organizations share a sense of social solidarity, which is both a consensus with respect to experience and values and a common social and political identity. They recognize themselves as members of an identifiable community and with that they anticipate particular substantive expectation and obligations that follow from their membership. What is interesting for accounting research is to explore the consequences of these expectations on the way in which the functioning of the organization is to be understood. The fact that competing accounts of the organizational terrain may exist should encourage the search for explanation of how practices of socializing accountability emerge, compete and interact with other systems of accountability. Exploring the patterns of economic accountability and understanding the relevance of economic accounts in these organizations is an important part of moving toward a more general understanding of accounting in the context in which it operates.

References

Arrigton, C. and Francis, J.R. (1993) Giving Economic accounts. Accounting as a cultural practice. *Accounting Organisation and Society*, **18**, (2/3).

Berger, P.L. and Luckmann, T. (1966) *The Social Construction of Reality*, Doubleday, New York.

Braverman, H. (1974) *Labour and Monopoly Capital*, Monthly Review Press, New York.

Burchell, S. *et al.* (1980) The roles of accounting in organisation and society. *Accounting Organisation and Society*, **5**, (1).

Dent, J. (1986) Organisational research in Accounting: perspectives issues and a commentary in *Research and current issues in management accounting* (ed. A. Hopwood), Pitman, London.

Meyer, J. (1986) Social Environments and Organisational Accounting. *Accounting Organisation and Society*, **11**, (4/5).

Neimark, M. and Tinker, T. (1986) The social construction of management control systems. *Accounting Organisation and Society*, **11**, (4/5).

Griffin, G. and de Rozario, S. (1993) Trade Union Finances in the 1970s and 1980s, *Journal of Industrial Relations* (September) pp. 424–35.

Hemingway, J. (1978) *Conflict and Democracy, Studies in Trade Union Government*, Clarendon Press, Oxford.

Hopwood, A.G. (1986) Management accounting and organisational action: An Introduction in *Research and Current Issues in Management Accounting* (ed. A. Hopwood), Pitman, London.

Hoskin, K. and Macve, R. (1986) Accounting and the examination. A genealogy of disciplinary power. *Accounting Organisation and Society*, **11**, (2).

Munro, R. and Hatherley, D. (1993) Accountability and the new commercial agenda. *Critical Perspectives on Accounting*, **4**, pp. 369–95.

Offe, C. and Wiesenthal, H. (1980) Two logics of collective action: Notes on social class and organisational form. *Political Power and Social Theory*, **1**, pp. 67–95.

Olson, M. (1965) *The logic of collective action: Public goods and the theory of groups*, Harvard University Press, Cambridge, M.A.

Meyer, J. and Rowan, B. (1977) Institutionalized organizations formal structure as myth and ceremony. *American Journal of Sociology*, (September) p. 340.

Mills, C.W. (1963) Situated action and vocabularies of motives in *Power, Politics and People*, (ed. Horowitz) Oxford University Press, Oxford, pp. 439–52.

Panozzo, F. (1994a) *On trying to understand accounting practices in a loosely coupled system. The case of a trade union.* Paper presented at the EIASM Doctoral Colloquium in Accounting, Venice.

Panozzo, F. (1994b) *When identity matters.* Paper presented at the EIASM Workshop Accounting strategy and control, Brussels, September.

Roberts, J. (1991) The possibilities of accountability. *Accounting Organisation and Society*, **16** (4).

Roberts, J, and Scapens, R. (1985) Accounting systems and systems of accountability – understanding organisational practices in their organisational contexts. *Accounting Organisation and Society*, **10** (4).

Rosa, J.J. (1984) (ed.) *The Economics of Trade Unions*, Kluver Academic.

Selznick, P. (1957) *Leadership in Administration. A sociological Perspective*, Harper and Row, New York.

Willman, P. *et al.* (1993) *Union business. Trade union Organisation and Financial Reform during the Thatcher years*, Cambridge University Press, Cambridge.

Zan, L. (1994) *Economia delio organizzazioni non profit. Alcune premesse e un'applicazione.* (The economics of non-profit organizations. Propositions and evidence) Working paper, Università di Venezia.

Part Four

Centres of calculation

The next unit of account concerns the creation of centres of calculation. The key idea is that of an obligatory passage. Explanations for the dominance of a particular technology do of course vary, but, as the chapters in the previous parts indicate, it is clearly not enough to argue that management accounting is dominant, simply because it has been prescribed in a general way. History is littered with examples of failed prescriptions.

The themes emerging in this section of the book, together with the next, offer a different explanation. This is that accounting numbers are imposed as 'intermediaries' between stages of account-giving in the hierarchy. This sets up a 'precession' in the giving of an account. So, instead of accepting the story of accounting numbers being representational of some 'out there' reality, they can be better understood as the 'obligatory passage' through which account-giving must pass. In this view, offering to act as an 'agent' entraps participants into aligning their accounts with accounting numbers. Thus analysis in this section foregrounds participants accounting to each other, through intermediaries. The formulation of accounting numbers as an obligatory passage is particularly well contrasted with Laughlin's analysis of administrative 'buffers'.

In the opening chapter, Brendan McSweeney analyses extant explanations over how 'management by accounting' was introduced into the UK civil services. As Laughlin also remarks in the next chapter, the Financial Management Initiative was 'fundamentally concerned with good management'. So the question McSweeney is asking is how a debate over good management was turned into the prescription of a particular form of management accounting, responsibility accounting. Ostensibly the government agenda was to transfer best management practice from the private sector into the public sector, but this was beset with difficulties in covering all the forms of work the government wanted to capture. Drawing on official accounts from the period, McSweeney argues that only management accounting, in the form of responsibility accounting, was ambiguous enough in its prescriptions to fit their agenda. The irony is that responsibility accounting, with its rigid alignment of hierarchy and management accounting numbers, is forced upon the public sector at the very moment when its limitations are starting to be seriously debated in the private sector.

In Chapter 12, Richard Laughlin covers the same debate, but he does so by juxtaposing 'contractual' and 'communal' forms of accountability. He confronts an implicit abnegation of rights in the theory of contracting, by contrasting other forms of (moral) reason, especially those more usually associated with 'ethos'. Drawing on traditional notions of the sacred and the secular, Laughlin points to ways in which the Church, as a paradigm case, has sought to limit forms of hierarchical accountability by having both administrative 'buffers' and by honouring the guiding power of 'higher principals' and 'higher principles'. The existence of these other forms of rights suggests to Laughlin occasions when mechanical compliance in a principal–agent relationship can, and should, be countered. Clearly this also raises issues pertinent to the vexed question of the autonomy of the 'professional' and 'personal' and Laughlin considers the caring professions' strong case for rights that subsist outside of economic reasons. From this perspective he analyses the recent market and managerial reforms in the public sector and raises critical questions about their justifiability.

In the final chapter of this section, Katrine Kirk and Jan Mouritsen examine deteriorating accounting relations of a Canadian subsidiary with its head office back in Denmark. These authors address the issue of centres of calculation most explicitly, arguing how the architecture of responsibility accounting renders very different operating units as 'the same'. At first those at head office seemed open to accounts being based on local knowledge of market conditions and production opportunities. Stories of difference, if not accepted, are, in the beginning, at least accommodated. However, in the continued event of the subsidiary's failure to align its accounting numbers with expectations of head office, those at the 'centre of calculation' become more and more reluctant to leave the ground of accounting numbers in which all entities appear the same. Kirk and Mouritsen's findings point to an impressive durability in the accounts generated through management accounting; these remain firmly in position while other sets of accounts come and go. In that the subsidiary's auxiliary accounts become excluded as auxiliary, even irrelevant, Kirk and Mouritsen's analysis demonstrates the powerful effect of interposing an intermediary between participants. Thus, although the managers in the subsidiary and head office never become aligned exactly as the theory of contracting prescribes for 'agents' and 'principals', a domination effect is (re)produced in which the 'durable' accounts, in the form of financial numbers, travel across contexts while others do not.

We should not rush to suppose from these analyses that there is something very special about management accounting in its modes of inscription. Figures alone, even when made stable and mobile, do not create a disciplining process. While the public and the private sector are being made 'the same', it is clear that some differences remain, particularly in the ability for those in the caring professions to mobilize what Laughlin calls 'higher principals'. This alone should suggest there is more to the story of domination of accounting numbers than a simple readiness to accept an account that 'he who pays the piper, plays the tune' exists in the private sector as a higher principle. Against such gross oversimplifications, it can be argued that at least one crucial effect comes from interposing intermediaries between participants. The obvious effect is to strengthen participants' accounts on occasions when they align with the numbers and weaken participants' accounts when they disregard the numbers. The decisive effect, though, surely comes from placing accountors in a position in which they too will have to account, in turn, over the same material? This 'precession' in accounts keeps participants in a hierarchy, exactly preventing them from getting together as 'members'.

11 The arrival of an accountability: explaining the imposition of management by accounting

Brendan McSweeney

> One never commences; one never has a tabula rasa; one slips in, enters in the
> middle; one takes up or lays down rhythms
>
> Gilles Deleuze (1992)

How can we explain an attempt to implant comprehensively a particular version of management into a specific organization? The policy change to be examined, usually called the 'Financial Management Initiative' (FMI), in which accounting was central, sought to radically alter the structure and management of the UK government's Civil Service departments.[1] The initiative was described by the Prime Minister's Special Adviser on Efficiency as 'at the heart of a change of management style in the public sector' (Ibbs 1984: 108). Beyond the Civil Service, the initiative has been mandated or chosen as a model for many of the changes in the management and evaluation of the UK's wider public sector (Butler 1993). This chapter is not a study of the extent to which the initiative has been implemented nor an examination of its consequences (OECD 1993a; Russell and Sherer 1994); rather it explores the circumstances which enabled the policy change.

Whilst some features of the FMI have been extensively considered in the literature, few studies have sought to explain its 'genesis' (Gray *et al.* 1991). Much of that analysis has explained its arrival as the result of a single cause: either the election of a new government; economic pressure; or modernization (see for example, Humphrey and Olson 1994; Butler 1993; Plowden 1985). Each of these explanations is examined below. It is argued that they give an inadequate account of the rise of the FMI, as a similar change either did not occur earlier when the same condition existed, or it occurred elsewhere where the condition did not exist. A richer explanation is outlined by opening up each of the three explanations to a historical and interpretative analysis which explores the wider construction over time of a definition of the reality of the Civil Service such that the FMI way of acting was taken as the 'right', if not the only, way to do things (Meyer 1994: 234; Scott 1994: 83). This analysis not only explores some of the preconditions of this particular policy, but in doing so it addresses a number of issues central to understanding policy-making more generally. Instead of suggesting an alternative single, or first, cause to the three dominant ones examined, it problematizes their common unilinear notion of causality. Explanations of the FMI's emergence must, it is argued, consider the historical and diversely constituted cognitive and normative conditions of its emergence. Properties attributed to accounting by key actors in the policy making arenas, especially accounting's alleged capability to reveal succinctly what is pertinent and to transcend differences between the public and private sectors, are shown to have been significant in constituting those conditions.

An outline of the Financial Management Initiative

On 17 May 1982, the UK government announced that there would be a radical change in the internal structure and running of Civil Service departments (Cmnd 8616: 1982). The new policy was called the *Financial Management Initiative* (FMI). Objectives would be assigned to 'responsibility centres' within which costs would be systematically identified 'to enable those who are responsible for particular activities and objectives to be aware of and, whenever possible, held responsible for the cost of the resources they are consuming'. An accounting said to be profoundly different from that then in use in the Civil Service was to be comprehensively introduced and would, it was stated, have a central role in the restructuring and the 'management of resources within that structure'. The 'existing government accounting' (Cmnd 8616 1982) was criticized for analysing inputs only and being cash-flow based. The new accounting, which was not labelled merely as accounting but *'management* accounting', would, it was said, calculate costs on an 'accrual basis' and relate not only direct but also indirect costs calculated in that way to outputs.[2] This, it was stated, would impose the:

> . . . discipline of breaking down a department's activity between managers whose responsibilities can thus be clearly distinguished and objectives more clearly defined; whose costs and outputs can be more clearly assessed; and to whom greater authority can then be delegated to choose the best way of using the resources allocated to them in pursuit of the defined objectives.
>
> (Cmnd 8616: 1982)

From the launch of the FMI, government departments immediately, or eventually, were to: 'develop a structure of organization in which identifiable functions and objectives can be assigned to responsibility centres'. These centres, also called 'discrete units' were to be subdivided further into 'detailed cost centres' so that individuals, it was said, could be held responsible for costs they 'consumed' and be monitored against 'objectives' (Cmnd 8616 1982: 34).

Accounting was conceived within the FMI not merely as a 'policy tool' (Lane 1993: 225), but as central in the policy change itself. Within the FMI's image of how the Civil Service ought to be organized, management and accounting were virtually conflated. The FMI was said by the National Audit Office[3] to 'lie at the heart of good management' (NAO 1986: 11).

Perhaps today this conflation of management with accounting in depictions of the UK Civil Service no longer seems so extraordinary but, at the time, it can hardly be said to have had much currency outside the private sector and, even there, this was not a mainstream view. It seems worth returning therefore to the debates at the time with a view to re-examining a number of possible explanations for the changes imposed on the Civil Service. As systems similar to the FMI have been advocated or applied earlier or elsewhere also, the generic label *management by accounting* (McSweeney 1994) is used below to describe such approaches.

Change of government explanation

It was a result of the election in May 1979 of the Conservative Party to government.

This explanation might seem to be self-evidently true. Decisions on specific dates, such as the Prime Minister's minute to ministers on the FMI in May 1982 (Wilding 1983: 39) and the issuing at the same time of the launching working document: *Financial Management* (in Cmnd 8618 1982: Appendix 3) were mechanisms through which the changes were imposed on Civil Service departments. Two ideas are co-extensive in this explanation: that the change was a complete discontinuity with what existed before and that it occurred as a result of the election of a particular political party to government.[4] The continuation of that party as the UK's central government since May 1979 during which commitment to the FMI has remained current might also seem to support this explanation. But it is problematic to argue that without that government such changes would not have occurred.

In the post-war period there had already been five other Conservative governments. Some had sought extensively to reform the Civil Service, and the wider public sector, yet none had tried to do so through FMI type processes. But in response, it could be argued that the new Conservative administration was distinct from previous Conservative governments because it had become dominated by the policies of the 'New Right' (Honderich 1990) and that, as a result, as Fry (1988: 5) states: 'The Financial Management Initiative is the economic liberal gospel as applied to the Civil Service' (see also Pollitt, 1993). The treatment of management by accounting as a necessary consequence of New Right ideas is questionable.

A necessary link?

Before its election in May 1979, and for some time after that, the Conservative Party was uninterested in management by accounting. As Hogwood (1992: 173) states: 'At first, Mrs Thatcher did not appear particularly interested in changing the machinery of government in central government departments'. It was not mentioned in the party's election manifesto nor did it feature in any of the policy documents of 'think-tanks' said to have influenced the acceptance of the New Right ideas within the Conservative Party (Marsh, 1991; Metcalf and Richards 1990; Redwood and Hatch 1982). An attempt to explain this delay and yet still attribute the policy change solely to the new Government is Geoffrey Fry's statement, echoed in Humphrey (1991) and Humphrey and Olson (1994), that: 'the Thatcher Government's blows continued to rain down on the civil service . . . and ***eventually*** came to be translated into something akin to a grand strategy' (1984: 323) (emphasis added).

The Conservative Government's commitment to cut the size and cost of the Civil Service, and the wider public sector, which it had pursued from May 1979 is certainly amongst the official explanations given for the FMI's introduction (Cmnd 8616: 1982). But this does not explain why the FMI approach rather than any other was chosen, nor does it demonstrate a necessary link between the policy change and a New Right ideology. And there are counter-indications.

First, efforts to reduce the cost of public expenditure, which included cut-backs in the size of the Civil Service, had already been begun by previous governments. As the current head of the Civil Service states:

> Economy and greater efficiency were pursued through cuts in both manpower and general expenditure: the latter was effectively 'capped' by the introduction of cash limits in 1976. Reductions in manpower were implemented from 1976 and by 1979 the civil service was already some 15,000 smaller . . . The advent of the Conservative administration of 1979 saw a continuation of these developments . . .
>
> (Butler, 1993: 397)

A causal link between a desire to curtail the cost and size of the Civil Service and management by accounting can thus not be established as earlier governments also committed to that goal had chosen different methods of achieving it.

Second, advocacy of management by accounting in the UK and elsewhere can be linked to political groups, parties, and governments not regarded as New Right. As McSweeney (1994) reports, the main advocates in the late 1960s and in the 1970s of management by accounting for the Civil Service were associated with, or were members of, the parliamentary (social democratic) Labour Party. The Labour Party appointed and dominated Fulton Committee recommended it, and called it 'accountable management', in 1968 (Cmnd 3638: 1968). And throughout the 1970s Labour members of parliament (MPs) John Garret and Michael English, were amongst the most active and persistent advocates of management by accounting, especially in the parliamentary committees in which they had positions of significance (HC 535-I 1977). During its post-May-1979 period in opposition the Labour Party, whilst opposing some government policies for the Civil Service, and the wider public sector, has supported, and continues to support, the FMI approach. According to Sir Robin Butler, currently the UK's most senior civil servant: 'what has been striking has been the measure of agreement [with the approach] (1993: 397).

Third, the Conservative government of 1970–74 was also initially committed to the 'economic liberal gospel' (Fry 1988) and sought to reduce the size of, and radically alter the structure and management of, the Civil Service. Yet although it was fully aware of a FMI type approach, not least through the extensive discussion of the Fulton Committee's report in which it had participated, it introduced changes different from management by accounting into the Civil Service.

Finally, outside the UK especially, some governments ostensibly opposed to New Right ideologies have given similar emphasis to implanting management by accounting into their civil services (Hood 1991, 1995). Management by accounting is therefore not a policy unique to the New Right. Nor is it necessarily associated with it as some governments with New Right policies did not include a FMI type method in reorganizing their 'civil services' or other public sector activities (Broadbent and Guthrie 1992; Gray *et al.* 1991; HC 236-II 1982).

The election of the Conservative government in the UK in May 1979 is therefore an inadequate explanation of the arrival of the FMI. Whilst the decision of a specific government to attempt to change the running of civil service departments, through the introduction of management by accounting, was an essential part of what occurred, the depiction above of wider and antecedent factors indicates that there was no necessary link between the change mechanism chosen and that government's New Right policies.

This de-emphasis on centrality of a political party and the rejection of the notion that the change was an absolute discontinuity with what had happened pre-1979, suggests that whilst actors were influential they were constituted, legitimatized, and channelled by a much wider and historically constituted environment. The specific point is that the arrival of management by accounting in a particular setting was heavily dependent on wider, potentially linked, and longer-standing environments. But what might such an environment, or environments, be composed of? So far we have seen them not merely as dominated political systems, but also as supplying storehouses of technique, meaning, and legitimacy. Their constitutive role in events, organizations, actors and not simply their influence on them has been suggested. These ideas are explored further by examining the remaining two of the three mono-causal explanations of the FMI: economic pressure and modernization. Unpacking them reveals further aspects of interpretative and interpreting environments within which the policy was fashioned.

The economic crisis explanation

Economic crisis inevitably led to the changes which would have occurred regardless of which political party controlled the government.

In this explanation the 'economic' is treated either deterministically as a stimulus with an inevitable outcome or as a readily recognized reality with only one rational response. Often, in either conception, the causal economic condition is described as a crisis. This has been characterized either as acute: a 'jolt' (Butler 1993: 397); or alternatively as chronic: 'hard times' (Metcalf and Richards 1990: 186). But the notion that management by accounting is a mere consequence of exogenous economic influence is confronted with problems of definition, chronology and linkage.

Definitional

The 'economic' *per se* cannot be recognized. It is not self-evident. Instead it is commonly represented through a variety of measurements, including those of 'inflation', 'gross national product', 'balance of payments'. These representations are widely treated as complete or partial signifiers, indicators, measurements, or manifestations of that which is perceived to underlie them: the 'economic'. Claims about the effects of the 'economic', if they seek to be more than generalized assertions, must choose particular and partial indicator(s). But not only is the economic, even if we assume such a force exists, never directly accessible or identifiable, but the surrogate definitions and their attendant measurements are themselves contestable (Porter 1995).

However, even if it is assumed that the issues of economic indicator selection, definition and measurement are not problematic and that one, or a number, of such representations can be taken to stand for the 'economic' (Thompson 1987) they do not fit sufficiently as explanations of civil service reorganizations so that the economic cannot empirically be shown as the exclusive, or the primary, determinant of the introduction of the FMI.

Chronology

If either chronic economic conditions or acute economic pressure were the cause of the FMI, why were different re-organization methods chosen by earlier governments when it could be argued that economic circumstances were the same as, or even worse than, in May 1982? For example, it is necessary to consider in this context why a FMI-type approach was not adopted by the UK government in 1965, 1966 and 1967 when there were very large balance of payments deficits; in 1968 when Sterling was devalued; in 1973 when oil prices rose dramatically; in 1976 there were further balance of payments difficulties and International Monetary Fund intervention (Bellini *et al.* 1974; Hogwood 1992). Yet, during none of these periods did the government decide to reform Civil Service departments through management by accounting type methods and throughout many of these crises no changes, of any variety, were introduced. Even changing the manner in which these departments are run, in whatever way, is not a necessary consequence of belief in the need to deal with an economic crisis. Sir Robin Butler's explanation for the non-implementation of much of the Fulton Committee's recommendations, including management by accounting, is that attention was 'diverted by the country's economic problems in the early and mid 1970s' (1991: 365–6).

A crisis – economic or other – is never a crisis in itself. It is defined as a particular type of crisis in relation to a specific set of beliefs about what characterizes the world (Cowen 1986; Nelson and Winter 1982). Although Inkenberry (1989) suggests that the imitation from elsewhere of a different approach is 'especially likely in the wake of a crisis or dramatic failure', it is not an inevitable response. An intensification of the familiar and the traditional has also been observed (Donnelon *et al.* 1986). Even the perception of failure of existing methods may be followed by an increase in, not a reduction or elimination of, that approach (Power 1994; Hood 1991).

Changes in civil service, or wider public sector, structure and management, of any type, cannot be correlated with periods of intense dissatisfaction with economic conditions. Thus economic crises have not necessarily been associated with such reforms in the dual sense that: (a) they have sometimes been proposed in the absence of such crises, and (b) a crisis cannot always be linked with such changes. There is no empirical confirmation of a fit. This finding is consistent with increasing criticism within the public administration literature of reliance on exogenous factors as an explanation of policy-making (Danziger 1978; Sharpe and Newton 1984). As Connolly states: 'Efforts to reduce politics to other forces such as [the] economic . . . are doomed to produce a serious misreading of the phenomenon under investigation' (Connolly 1983).

Changing interpretations of the economic

The concept of the 'economic' as an uninterpreted force was distinguished above from an interpretative belief about conditions and consequences and judged to fail as an explanation of the FMI. But it is suggested below that various changes in the interpretative notions of the 'economic' occurred in the policy making arenas. These shifts, it is argued, were part of the preconditions of the acceptance of a FMI approach.

At the time of the FMI's launch the government considered the Civil Service to be a problem and, more specifically, an economic problem. It argued that as part of the solution, the Civil Service should copy what the government lauded as the 'private sector's' management method, which it defined as the FMI approach. That praise of the private sector, treated as both nationally and globally uniform in its management, and denigration of the public sector (including the Civil Service) as an economic problem is not a view with a lengthy history in the UK, rather it emerged into prominence only within the past three decades (Sampson 1992).

In 1965, for example, the government's view was that central to economic improvement was reform of the management methods of the private sector, and manufacturing industry in particular.

> As the industrial structure becomes more rationalized the need and opportunities for specialized management expertise will become greater; and the Government are anxious to do what they can to increase numbers of professional trained managers in control of industry and commerce. British professional standards are respected throughout the world, but in the past industrial management as such has tended to remain somewhat outside the mainstream of professional life.
>
> (Cmnd 2764: 1965)

Even in the mid-1970s the eulogized homogenized notion of the private sector was not yet dominant (Young and Lowe 1974). The 1974 *Hudson Report* could, for example, still confidently assert that there was an increasing need to have in the private sector 'a distinguishable mandariante *with modern skills and a coherent sense of operation purpose* to replace, by degrees, the traditional (and unambitious and, in important respects, pre-modern) British business elite' (Bellini *et al.* 1974: 121) (emphasis in original).

The characterization of the public sector has also changed. In 1965 most of the public sector was described by government as 'productive' and 'playing an important indirect role . . . in helping economic growth' (Cmnd 2764: 1965: 177). By 1970, however, the new government justified its reorganization of the Civil Service on the grounds that 'government has been attempting to do too much' (Cmnd 4506 1970). Such questioning of the role and scope of government, which was also occurring elsewhere, grew, regardless of party, during the 1970s. Whilst the arguments made were not exclusively self-defined as 'economic' such a characterization was significant.

During the 1970s, the tone of parliamentary debates about public expenditure began to change noticeably. Whilst demands for spending to be increased on specific items had not entirely disappeared, they were less frequent and had become muted. There was more talk about 'value for money' (HC 535-II 1977; Flint 1978; Hopwood 1984; McSweeney 1988, 1994). As Robinson (1981: 164/5) has commented: 'Members of the Opposition parties [which was mainly the Conservative Party] were not the only ones demanding that public expenditure be controlled . . . MP's from the government side were also less insistent in their demands'. In 1977 public expenditure could be described by Sir Stanley Holmes, a leading local government representative, as 'the favourite area of attack inside society' (HC 535-III 1977: 736). By 1979, the public sector had been described by the government as 'at the heart of Britain's present economic difficulties' (Cmnd 7746: 1979: 1). In 1980, the Chairman of the Public Accounts Committee and Labour MP Joel Barnett exemplified the cross party attitude when he stated to the Secretary of State for the Environment 'I assume we have a common objective in terms of better control and cutting out waste in the public sector (HC 115-II 1980: 192). Whilst the public sector was being increasingly criticized, the private sector, treated as a homogeneous entity, was being increasingly praised. Former leading civil servant Sir Anthony Part described this condition as the 'deification of private enterprise coupled with denigration . . . of the Civil Service' (in Sampson 1992: 35). But the judgements went further than unfavourable comparisons. A method of management assumed to be uniformly used throughout the private sector began increasingly to be described as the model which the public sector should follow.

Why might a policy of imitation have gained support in the policy making arenas? Imitation had been suggested earlier, in the 1950s, (see for example Barnes *et al.* 1951), and probably earlier. Unlike influenza, diffusion of ideas does not spread merely through physical contact. Imitation is 'a socially meaningful act' (Strang and Meyer 1994: 101).[5]

The eulogization of the private sector and the increasing denigration of the public sector would not automatically have suggested that what were regarded as the management techniques of the former could, and should, be copied by the latter. It is suggested here that the growth in the arguments for the desirability of emulation of what was represented as *the* private sector management method, which the FMI was held out to be, required the development of the ideas of fundamental similarity of the two sectors. As Strang and Meyer argue, 'perceptions of similarity provide a rationale for diffusion' (1994: 103–5).

A constraint on the idea of similarity was the idea that public sector organizations were, and should be, run in a manner distinct from private sector entities. The first were 'administered', the latter 'managed' (Lane 1993; Alford and O'Neill 1994). In the late 1960s the Fulton Committee critically stated that 'few members of the class [senior civil servants – the administrative class] actually see themselves as managers' (Cmnd 3638 1968). Within the wider context of an increasingly praised private sector and the intensification of criticism of the public sector, the claim of administrative uniqueness of the Civil Service came under growing attack in the name of a universalized management (HC 535-III 1977: 662). Elsewhere also the 'ideal-type general public administration model' had come under increasing attack (Lane 1993). More generally, John Meyer has observed the rise of a standardized management theory:

> An older world in which schools were managed by educators, hospitals by doctors, railroads by railroad men [civil services by civil servants] now recedes into quaintness. All these things are now seen as organizations, and a world-wide discourse instructs on the conduct of organizations. This produces a great expansion, almost everywhere of management.
>
> (1994: 44–53)

Within the UK, a flavour of the growing criticism and promotion of a universal notion of management is as follows. The Fulton Committee's advisers stated that 'in our experience, management in the Civil Service has . . . much in common with management in industry', but complained that:

> Management control techniques in the Civil Service are mainly based on the requirements of public accountability and most of the emphasis has been on

control systems designed to prevent error. More positive concepts of management control – setting standards of performance for individuals or groups, expressing these in terms of budgets, ratios, indices of efficiency or jobs to be done by a certain time and monitoring achievement against them – has made very little headway in the Service.

(Cmnd 3638: 1968: Vol II)

The Committee stated that the Civil Service did not need 'generalists [but] . . . a new breed of managers . . .' (Cmnd 3638 1968: Vol II, 99). The idea that the Civil Service should adopt some 'business methods' was not new,[6] but earlier these were treated merely as techniques to be applied to some unusual or low-level (usually clerical) activities. In 1950, for example, Sir Edward Bridges, when Permanent Secretary at HM Treasury, stated that whilst:

Government Departments have . . . made great progress in adopting business and commercial techniques, where they are appropriate to their rather specialized tasks . . . the real difficulty is to devise methods of financial control which are appropriate to those fields of public administration where quantitative measurement has little application.

(Barnes *et al.* 1951: 2)

Throughout the 1970s, various individuals, professional bodies, academics, and firms of consultants argued in evidence to parliamentary committees and elsewhere that there was one best way of running ('managing') all entities and all their activities (Heclo and Wildavsky 1981; Cockburn 1977). For instance Professors Kempner and Ball stated in evidence to the Expenditure Committee in 1977, that: 'All managers are concerned with the allocation, and proper social use, of scarce resources. The Civil Service does not differ in this respect. All managers must develop a sense of commercial enterprise' (HC 535-III 1977: 935). This view was also expressed by other Committee witnesses including the Consultative Committee of Accountancy Bodies.

Not only was it being argued that the private sector should be copied. A uniform view of how it was managed was being presented in order to assert that there was only one way in which the public sector ought to be managed. The process was as Meyer (1994) describes it: 'isolate and define – often in a way at some remove from reality – properties of the model . . . theorize the particular elements to be copied as central to the virtues of the model' (1994: 36). Responsibility accounting was central in the characterization of what was alleged to be the management method uniformly used throughout the private sector and which should be adopted by the Civil Service so that it could, it was said, be managed and not merely ineffectually and wastefully administered. Whilst by the 1970s (and before) organization theory had become fragmented (Pugh 1985), the notion that such accounting was applicable to all types of organizations and that its centrality was a prerequisite to effective management remained dominant. Indeed, it was very rarely questioned in management accounting textbooks. Although there was a growing body of critique of that characterization of accounting (Miller 1994a), even the arguments based on contingency theory were given at most a peripheral mention in such texts (Gordon and Miller 1976; Waterhouse and Tiesson 1978; Otley 1980). Accounting was treated as breathtakingly general in application, and also readily applicable or replicable, because of its alleged capability to accurately identify the fundamental reality, whatever the particularities of a situation might be. As all states of affairs were considered to be unambiguously identifiable by accounting as they 'really' were, it was also regarded as the optimum means of monitoring and controlling all civil service activities.

The virtual conflation of accounting and management and the claim that this characterizes the private sector which should be copied by the Civil Service have been recurring themes of management by accounting's advocates. The Fulton Committee, for example, stated that: '. . . it is generally accepted that accounting is no longer a matter of book-keeping but of financial management in its widest sense . . . and it is recognized that the training and experience of an accountant can fit the right man (*sic*) for the highest managerial position' (Cmnd 3638: 1968). The Expenditure Committee in its 1977 report (and on other occasions) argued that: '. . . in business, accountants are commonly appointed to high level management posts and their role extends beyond management accounting and internal audit; in the Civil Service they are confined to executive work and excluded from policy making and their career prospects and pay compare unfavourably with the private sector and with other specialists in the government service' (HC 535-II July 1977: xlviii). The Committee recommended a management by accounting approach which it described as: 'analogous [to] systems in the private sector' (HC 236-III 1982: 156). The Secretary of State for the Environment stated in evidence to the Public Accounts Commitee that:

> What I do have every reason to suppose is that the quality of public sector accountancy is abysmal . . . I just do not believe that Parliament or Ministers generally have a degree of information about the financial systems that they administer which enables a standard of accounting to stand comparison with what is available to the private sector.
>
> (HC 115-II 1980: 203)

Many advocates of management by accounting have represented it as the exclusive private sector management method. Yet, there is no evidence, indeed there is counter-evidence, of inter- and intra-country managerial heterogeneity (see for example Goold and Cambell 1989). But as Strang and Meyer (1994: 105) state: 'perceived similarities may be constructed despite substantial differences'. It is a theoretical model that is mimicked (Jepperson 1991; Strang and Meyer 1994).

The 'economic' and specific notions of the 'economic'

The mono-causal explanation that the FMI was a consequence of economic determinism was rejected above as a match between economic conditions and changes in the UK Civil Service management was demonstrated to be false. This argument was based on a historical analysis of the UK experience. It is also consistent with Hood's cross-national analysis of what he calls 'new public sector management' (1991, 1995), which included the UK's FMI. His conclusion was that 'there appears to be no simple relationship between macro economic performance and the degree of emphasis laid on new public sector management' (1995). But the manner in which an economic crisis is conceived may influence the definition of the solution. The formulations of economic conditions, and the significance of the public sector within them, that emerged during more than a decade before 1979, were pertinent in creating a context within which management by accounting was more likely to be chosen. Thus a discourse about economic conditions and remedies can be regarded as part of the conditions of the emergence of the FMI. But the discourse was not static. It was not some general notion of economic crisis, or necessity, but more specific views about the cause and cure into which management by accounting was fitted. What is being argued here is that not only does the economic as something non-discursive not have effects (Ricoeur 1986), but even at the discursive level, it is not as a general notion that the idea of the 'economic' operates but through more specific characterizations.

The third mono-causal explanation in the literature on the FMI, modernization, is now considered. Its conception as an ontologically given determining force is, like its two predecessors above, also rejected. Discussion of it as an interpretative notion reveals some additional discursive characteristics of the policy-making arenas in which FMI ultimately emerged.

The modernization explanation

Management by accounting is the modern way of structuring and running an organization and it was therefore inevitable that it would be comprehensively adopted for the Civil Service.

Claims that the FMI was an inevitable consequence of modernization have relied on either of two explanations: design or natural selection. In both, the FMI is assumed undoubtedly to be the most modern (and the most desirable) approach available (Hoskin and Macve 1994: 18). In the first, organizational change is a rational choice – modern approaches are recognized as such and are adopted. In the second, such approaches are construed as having a momentum of their own. A variation has been to argue that the Civil Service had been managed in a way that somehow delayed its adoption of the most up-to-date management method. The new approach was said, for example, to be 'long overdue' (Plowden 1985: 394). But Plowden's statement is exasperation not explanation. It is an unreflective expression of universalism (there is one best way) and evolutionism (it is inevitably accepted).

It is difficult to reconcile either the 'natural selection' or the 'rational recognition' explanations of the implantation of the FMI in the UK Civil Service with either the timing of its launch, or its absence (or comparative insignificance), in the 'civil services' of some other countries such as Japan, Germany, and Switzerland (Hood 1995; Shand 1995). If management by accounting is the modern, and modernization has a momentum of its own, or is readily recognized, why was such an approach not comprehensively introduced into the Civil Service before 1982 and why have some countries at least as 'modern' as the UK not adopted it?

A counter-argument might be that management by accounting was only invented/ developed in the 1980s, or late 1970s, and accordingly it had only become the modern approach shortly before the launch of the FMI. Certainly management by accounting is treated in this reverential manner in some of the public administration/political science literature on the FMI which describes it with the naïve enthusiasm of the newly acquainted. But management by accounting was not new at the time of the adoption of the FMI. As the earlier discussion above of its prior advocacy demonstrated, it had been explicitly considered in the UK public policy-making arena since at least as early as the 1960s. Its elaboration and related practices have a much earlier history (Hoskin and Macve 1986; Miller and O'Leary 1987; Miller 1994b). Indeed, by the 1980s not only had the management by accounting approach been available and advocated for generations, but also, perhaps ironically for the modernization model, it had already become the object of growing criticism and scepticism in both academic and professional literature. These included claims that management by accounting can result in efficiency *dis*-improvements, as well as improvements; that the actual ability to predict, or to know, even in retrospect, what will be, is, or was, the consequence of any change in managerial practices is weak (Hopwood 1982); and that action often works obliquely to stated goals. Writing from within a modernization model, Humphrey (1991: 178) has described the FMI as 'outdated', and Metcalf and Richards (1990: 17) call it 'very dated'.

Modernization as an explanation of the adoption of management by accounting would suggest not only that acceptance would be rapid but that it would also be extensive (if not comprehensive). It would have been as Hoskin and Macve (1988: 68) claim 'irrevocably launched' – at least until it was superseded in a future time by an even more modern approach. But, as discussed above, localized instances of its application in the Civil Service during the 1970s remained highly restricted (HC 535-III 1977). There is also evidence not only of its advances, but also of its retreats from the Civil Service (see also Bougen *et al.* 1990). Hobson, for example, stated that he:

> remember[ed] that cost accountancy [a necessary component of management by accounting] was introduced into the War Office by Sir Charles Harris in the First World War, and promptly ejected at the end of it.
>
> (1951: 87)

Notions of the modern

It is difficult to see how modernization as a causal explanation can be reconciled with the absence of chronological synchronism between, on the one hand, the widescale knowledge of the ideas of management by accounting (well before the Second World War) and advocacy of its comprehensive introduction into the Civil Service, and on the other hand, the decision to comprehensively implant it only much later, in the 1980s.

Setting aside modernization as a deterministic idea, however, does not preclude its importance as an image framing much of the rhetoric in play. The aspiration, or claim to be, 'modern', to be 'forward looking' (HC 535-I 1977), defined in particular ways, was it seems influential in mobilizing support for management by accounting in the Civil Service. A eulogy of being modern according to Vattimo (1992: 1) 'characterizes the whole of modern culture'. Being modern continues to be regarded as a decisive value.

Calls for the reform of the UK Civil Service have often been made in the name of modernization. Thomas Balogh, for example, in a 1959 essay *The Apotheosis of the Dilettante: The Establishment of Mandarins*, described the Administrative Class as 'the smooth extrovert conformist with good connections and no knowledge of modern problems' (in Kellner and Crowther Hunt 1980: 24). The commissioning of the Fulton Committee was the culmination of over a decade of growing and increasingly vocal criticism of the Civil Service in general, and the Administrative Class in particular. The

Committee's Management Consultancy Group argued that the Administrative Class in the Civil Service, whose members overwhelmingly were Oxbridge arts graduates:

> generally lacked the qualifications or experience or interest in the skills of numerate management . . . and that their effectiveness suffered largely from an irrelevant educational background and relative isolation from developments in management outside the Service.
>
> (in Garrett 1976: 842)

The Institution of Professional Civil Servants, a trade union which represented many specialist classes in the Civil Service, stated that 'the structure, organization and management of the Civil Service is no longer appropriate to modern needs' (in Ridley 1968: 9). In 1970, the Conservative government pledged itself to 'improving the machinery' of the Civil Service and stated that such changes 'must be designed to remedy the major difficulty which faces government in a *modern* complex society' (emphasis added) (Cmnd 4506: 1970). The Labour Party's manifesto for the 1979 general election said that the Party would: 'Bring forward proposals to reform the machinery of government and the structure of public administration to bring them in line with *modern* conditions' (Labour Party 1979) (emphasis added).

But why might particular interpretations of what it is to be 'modern' have facilitated the FMI policy? Below are explored some changes and features of what 'to be modern' was widely taken, and came, to mean. Specifically, some of the capabilities attributed in the policy-making arenas to what were treated as the qualities of the modern are considered, namely, the adequacy and desirability of treating organizations as composed of measurable states rigorously connected to one another through predictable and controllable causal relations. This description does not purport to be a complete depiction – an unattainable condition – rather it serves to indicate yet further that policy is constructed within a wider context and to suggest some features of the FMI's conditions of emergence.

Unlimited calculability

Transparency through measurement has been the dream of all advocates of management by accounting. The FMI sought the quantification of outputs to the 'maximum practicable extent', 'accurate attribution and monitoring of costs', and 'full knowledge of all relevant financial information' (Cmnd 8616: 1982). Increased quantification of civil service activities had already begun in the early post-war period, and more especially during the 1960s, and throughout much of the 1970s, when there was a growing use of quantitatively based techniques (Williams 1967: 3).

But the scope of quantification was contested. The examination of witnesses during the 1970s by various parliamentary committees which were considering the running of the Civil Service often reports divisions between those who argued for extensive quantification (and monetarization) and those (frequently, but not exclusively, top Civil Servants)[7] who argued that there were areas of activity where quantification, especially of objectives and outcomes, could not, and should not, be attempted (Donnison *et al.* 1975: 28–9). Arguments for comprehensive quantification included the claims that it was the modern thing to do; that to manage properly was to do so numerically; that it would bring considerable benefits; that the private sector did it;

that it would replace, and expose, arbitrary judgements; and that the Oxbridge arts graduate – 'mandarins', 'generalists', 'amateurs' – accused of resisting the 'numerate manager' were doing so because of their own innummeracy (Cmnd 3638 1968; HC 535-I 1977; Kellner and Crowther-Hunt 1980; HC 236-I 1982). 'The dominant characteristics of the top of our Civil Service are against this kind of numeracy . . .' (John Garrett MP in HC 535-II: 1977).

Over time the emphasis on increased quantification in the Civil Service amongst many advocates of civil service reform seems to have changed from primarily seeking an expansion in the type and range of numerical based techniques used, to advancing the idea that everything the Civil Service did should be calculated and that everyone must become a calculator (McSweeney 1994), and be calculated (Miller 1994). The erosion of the distinction between administration of the Civil Service and a universal notion of management, and more specifically a numerical management discussed earlier, seems pertinent here. The efficacy of calculation was said to have already been proven elsewhere. The intensity of quantification in an idealized private sector was exaggerated, and the extent of unavoidable interpretative activity was ignored by most, if not all, of management by accounting's advocates: 'practically everything business does is numerical' (the Secretary of State for the Environment in oral evidence to the Committee of Public Accounts, HC 115-II 1980).

It is likely that the desirability of extensive quantification derived some of its appeal from the much wider prestige of numbers, what Vattimo calls 'fanaticism for quantification' (1992). The argument here is that the increasing dominance of a view that comprehensive quantification was possible and desirable drew support from a wider environment in which quantification was both extensive and growing (Davis and Hersh 1986). Numbers were treated by management by accounting's advocates in a correspondence/mirroring, rather than a pragmatic or other non-foundational, sense – that is they were considered to be capable of representing the 'full knowledge' (Cmnd 8616 1982) of a pre-given reality in a wholly non-judgemental manner. The unquantified was deemed arbitrary and inferior and the advocates were unaware of, or were silent about, the judgemental qualities of quantification processes and the interpretations of their numerical outcomes. Theodore Porter, referring to the use of calculation by bureaucratic agencies in the USA, argues that the acceptance of the 'objectivity' of quantitative policy studies has more to do with fairness and impartiality than with their truth (1994: 207). This, he states, situates quantification 'within a *modern* political and administrative culture' (1994: 227) (emphasis added). That appeal to the notion of the modern treats what might be the significance of quantification within such a culture in the USA as universally valid. But in the UK's public sector, for those advocates of management by accounting who primarily considered it to be the means of reducing or eliminating the arbitrariness of civil service decisions, truth and fairness were not separated to such an extent. It was management by accounting's assumed calculative identification of absolute truth, and the transparency of that truth for others, such as parliamentary committees, which they spoke of as the guarantor of impartiality.

Causality: inputs and outputs

But being modern (including attributing great significance to quantification) would not necessarily be interpreted as requiring the application of management by accounting.

Successive governments, both Labour and Conservative, since at least 1964, considered themselves to be modernizers (Havighurst 1979) yet until 1982 none had chosen management by accounting. But the programmatic reorganizations which, apart from gross methods such as cash-limits and employee number reductions, were the main type during the 1970s whilst differing in significant respects from the later FMI approach, also had similarities (Cmnd 4506: 1970; Cmnd 6440: 1976; Heclo and Wildavsky 1981; HC 54: 1981: 96; HC 236-I 1982: xxiv; Gray and Jenkins, 1986; Hennessey, 1989: 591).

Like the FMI, the stated goal of the programmatic reorganization was 'a comprehensive approach' (Cmnd 4506 1970: 5), albeit on a much more general level than had been, and would continue to be, suggested by management by accounting's advocates. Central to both also was input-output planning and analysis: making goals explicit and matching quantified outcomes and related costs to those goals.[8] But the principal difference was the level of analysis. The programmatic policies sought to modernize the Civil Service through newly created 'giant departments' (Cmnd 4506 1970), not the accountable individual as in management by accounting/functional costing/accountable management: 'Large was deemed to be beautiful and, most importantly, programmable' (McSweeney, 1994), not only in the UK, but elsewhere also (Lane 1993).

The programmatic approach also sought like the FMI to make responsibilities 'more sharply defined', but the level of analysis and accountability sought was not the individual as emphasized in the FMI, but the 'giant' department. During the programmatic period (mainly the 1970s)[9] management by accounting's advocates argued that a 'strategic' approach alone was insufficient as: 'it is necessary not only to specify and evaluate expenditure on a programme basis but to relate programmes to the internal management structure and its system of control' (Garrett 1972: 148) (see also for example HC 535-I 1978 and HC 236-I 1982). But this first required an acceptance in the policy-making arena of the idea that aims or goals could, and should, be explicit and preferably quantified. The formulation of the aspiration for the FMI to convert every level within the Civil Service into webs of accountable quantified (and often monetarized) input-output relationships could draw on the programmatic policy's same, albeit much less detailed, way of conceiving the Civil Service. Accounting was treated as the optimum mechanism for representing those relationships.

The programmatic scheme's attempt to formalize and implant an input-output approach at a broad level in the Civil Service, was part of a wider and growing characterization of organizational life in that manner. Cynthia Cockburn, for example, notes that:

> It was around 1969 or 1970 that the management movement [in local government] began to take on a new character . . . The second aspect now underlined was effectiveness, and idea that has two faces, one about inputs and one about outputs (1977: 18).

During much of the 1960s and into the 1970s, a management theory which focused on the notion of explicit, monitored, and optimized input-output relations known as *management by objectives* (Drucker 1954; Odiorne 1965; Batten 1966) was extensively promoted in the UK (Humble 1965; Garrett and Walker 1969; Reddin 1971;

Garrett 1972). Whilst apparently formulated first in the USA,[10] it had, according to Garrett: 'flourished more widely in Britain than anywhere else in the world' (1972: 198). The Fulton Committee regarded its 'accountable management' to be superior to, but an extension of, management by objectives. When measurement of performance was not possible, the Committee urged the use of management by objectives.

The FMI therefore emerged from within a context where the notion of input-output analysis had been discussed and actions taken to implement it for more than a decade. The most significant difference in the FMI policy compared with its predecessors was its aspiration to extend that analysis deep into the Civil Service, to the level of each individual civil servant. Linking inputs to outputs with that degree of detail requires the reduction of standardized activities and accomplishments to a common yardstick. Quantification, and more specifically monetarization, and thus accounting seemed ideal for that task (Meyer 1994).

Which modernization?

At the beginning of this section it was argued that 'modernization' conceived as a causal force which operated and succeeded outside specific interpretations, had been given too much inevitability and too little content in the literature. By the time management by accounting was comprehensively introduced into the Civil Service it had already been articulated and practised elsewhere for many generations. The time gap is so lengthy that a deterministic notion of modernization does not fit as an explanation for the imposition of management by accounting. Instead, it has been argued that the notion of being 'modern' has explanatory content. Various interpretations and applications of that aspiration have been shown to be part of the FMI's antecedent conditions. This discussion does not, of course, aspire to be complete in the sense of including everything about the constitutive effects of the criterion 'modern' within the policy making arenas in which the FMI was adopted. Rather, I have sought to outline just some of the motifs central to understanding the rich texture of interlinked social interpretations of modernizations, particularly those that have been part of the pre-conditions of the emergence of the FMI. The picture which emerges reinforces the argument of the preceding two sections, namely that seeking a single exogenous cause of the FMI is futile as it was cognitively and normatively fabricated out of much wider, complex, and historically constituted environments.

Some implications

The discussions in each of the sections was a response to the three mono-causal explanations of the genesis of the FMI which have dominated the literature. Attempts to name the precise moment when it emerged and to specify a single cause are shown to be inadequate. Linearity is a trap which forces an impoverished representation of events, their constitution, and their interrelationships. Instead, 'the causal complexity of political history' (March and Olson 1984: 741) has been elaborated by considering aspects of the interpretative environments governing the FMI's launch. When the three dominant explanations are examined in that manner, rather than as sole and determining causes, a richer history emerges.

Characteristics of the FMI's conditions of adoption discussed included: the changing evaluations of the private and public sectors; the dependence of the arguments for imitation of the private sector by the Civil Service on the definition of the latter as similar, but inferior to the former; the decline in the notion of public administration and the growth of the idea of universally valid management; the virtual conflation of management and accounting through appeals to myths of a private sector uniformly run in that manner; assumptions about accounting's privileged access to absolute truth; and the constitution of the preconditions of change within antecedent and extra-organizational contexts. These continuing and changing ideas of actors in the policy making arenas were distilled largely from archival material: principally governmental and parliamentary reports and records of oral and written views of diverse organizations and individuals. Throughout the chapter, quotations from this material are woven into the analysis. Whilst these extracts are attributed to individuals, committees, or whoever, there is a sense that it is not they who speak the ideas, but rather, to borrow from Gadamer (1975), it is the ideas that speak them.

Rather than suppressing the complexity of the policy change process by attempting an explanatory history governed by a single theme such as the 'the triumph of ideology', 'the demands of necessity', or the 'march of progress', the chapter challenged such a possibility by providing three 'microhistories' (Snyder 1991; Braudel 1990). There is no presupposition that these histories are exhaustive. Furthermore, additional microhistories, for instance of the concept of the accountable individual, the emerging roles of management consultancy firms, or the transfer of theories about US public sector management within the policy making arena are also possible.

A theme that unites each of the three microhistories is a belief by advocates of management by accounting in the capability of accounting calculations to identify the absolute truth. Information with this property they assert, could only have munificent effects. That faith in accounting's representational ability transcends political party distinctions; it is depicted as an essential means of economic improvement as it is said to be central to managerial success; and it is presented as that which is quintessentially 'modern'.

This depiction of the growing prestige of calculation, and accounting calculation in particular, in the policy making arenas runs counter to the literature which argues that we now live in a post-realist world in which the prefix 'post' is taken to mean that realism has been surpassed, taken leave of, and overcome. Appeals are made in that literature to a particular understanding of relativist, post-modern, post-structuralist, or linguistic turn notions of language and knowledge to claim that all that 'ways of seeing, knowing, and representing have irreversibly altered in recent times' (Snyder 1991) and that all that remains of foundational notions of truth are 'remnants' (Tsoukas, 1996). This would imply that rather than realist notions of quantification providing legitimacy for the strengthening of this precondition of the FMI, and for the initiative itself, its status would already have been low and indeed declining. But, ironically, such arguments are themselves made within a modernist notion of progress: the 'post-modern' (or whatever description) as a replacement of the 'modern'.[11] In contrast it is suggested here that, during the pre-FMI period, the status of realist notions of the possibility and desirability of organizational quantification grew, rather than declined at least within the UK public policy making arenas.

Policy-making does not take place within the confines of academic literature, but within a much wider space in which such literature may play a significant, but not an exclusive role. Furthermore, even the suggestion that realism no longer has credibility within the academy (see for example Hines 1991; Lavoie 1987) is incorrect. The basis of that erroneous claim has usually been to treat the characterization of reality as contingent and relative in the fractional 'anti-realist' literature (with whose views this author is sympathetic) as a general or predominant condition. Whilst there has indeed emerged within the academy growing criticisms of 'realism' – as that which asserts the capability of representations (quantified or otherwise) to re-present non-interpretively a wholly anterior and exterior reality – there is also strong support in the academy and elsewhere (Smith 1994; Ruccio 1991).[12] In the public policy-making arenas at least, the period in which the FMI developed was not characterized by a decline in the status of such realism. There was, as Porter (1995) describes it, 'the spectacular growth of quantification'. In the policy-making arenas 'common sense' or 'folk' notions of objectivity, not post-modernist sophistication, dominates. Accounting for the advocates of management by accounting was at the apex of objectivity in organizations.

The chapter's three 'microhistories' were largely restricted to one 'nation-state' and to the post-war period. As a result they may have underestimated the effects of some trans-national, global, and longer-term factors on the emergence of the FMI. Further analysis of those aspects would enhance our understanding of the arrival of the FMI. But such influences are not reducible to grand notions such as 'global diffusion' or 'long-term colonization by accounting'. The international variations in both the type, and timing, of changes in Civil Service management and evaluation policies means that the explanatory capability of such universal theories are at best limited. As the descriptions of the specific conditions of management by accounting's implantation into the UK Civil Service suggests, analysis of management-policy changes must consider the locally situated and historically constituted narrative environments within which each change is shaped.

Acknowledgements

This chapter extends the analysis of the FMI in McSweeney (1994) for whose development I am especially grateful to Anthony Hopwood and Peter Miller. The comments of Jane Broadbent, Francesca Coles, Sheila Duncan, Richard Laughlin, and Rolland Munro on this chapter are acknowledged.

Notes

1. In 1981–2 the Civil Service pay bill was estimated to be £5,000 million. This, and other staff costs, such as superannuation, accounted for about 7% of planned public expenditure (Cmnd 8293: 1981: 1).
2. Comprehensive introduction of accrual accounting remains incomplete in the UK Civil Service. Its application has been far more difficult than the advocates of management by [accrual] accounting anticipated (see Cm 2626 1994 and OECD 1993b).
3. A body with some similarity with the US General Accounting Office.
4. A variation of this explanation has been to attribute the policy change to one person: the Prime Minister Mrs Margaret Thatcher.

5. The eulogy of allegedly successful organizations as targets for imitation seems common as a theoretical gambit in the spread of management approaches within the private sector also. See for example Peters and Watermans' *In Search of Excellence* (1982); numerous books about what are described as the transferable techniques responsible for the success of Japanese firms; and tales of allegedly successful implementation of activity based costing (for example Cooper and Kaplan 1991).

6. Nor has it ceased being used:

> Only by taking a progressively more business-like approach can the Government continue to bear down on the cost to the taxpayer . . . The proposals are firmly based on improvements in accountancy practice and financial control that have taken place decades ago in most other large organizations . . . The development of resource accounting and budgeting will represent a significant improvement in public sector financial management techniques based on principles first laid down in the Financial Management Initiative in 1982.
>
> (Cm 2626: 1994: iii)

7. In clerical work that is done . . . but if you try to do it elsewhere you run into very big difficulties . . . It turns out to be a very, very complicated business' (Lord Armstrong of Sanderstead, formerly Head of the Civil Service in HC 535-III 1977: 650).

8. In January 1967 the Conservative Party, then not in government, put forward a five-point plan for the public sector including a 'total systems approach' which included: clear definition of objectives; a listing of the alternative methods of achieving each objective; choice of the most practicable and economical method with the aid of a computer (Young and Lowe 1974: 124).

9. The first UK application of 'programmatic analysis' was probably in the Ministry of Defence as early as the mid-1960s, having been used earlier in the USA Defence Department (Donnisson *et al.* 1975: 27; Townsend 1975: 59/60; Garrett 1972: 141). Later, the Labour Government established planning units in each Civil Service department, some of whom experimented with Programme Planning & Budgeting. Its use was endorsed in 1969 by the Select Committee on Procedure (HC 410 1969). It was formally abandoned in October 1979 having already been neglected for some time.

10. The term 'management by objectives' is usually attributed to Peter Drucker (1954) (Odiorne 1965: viii). Garrett (1972) says that Drucker's original description was 'management by objectives and self-control'.

11. For criticisms of the claim that the post-modern is a replacement of the modern see for example Lyotard (1984); Vattimo (1991); Ruccio (1991).

12. Growing criticism of correspondence in the academy is not incompatible with growth in explicit support for it there also. Whilst it is possible that in some disciplines in some countries post-modernism is dominant (Wood 1990), it is not so in accounting in any country. For a recent defence of realism in the 'strategy' literature see Ansoff (1991).

References

Alford, J. and O'Neill, D. (1994) *The Contract State – Public Management and the Kenneth Government*, Deakin University Press, Melbourne.

Ansoff, I. (1991) Critique of Henry Mintzberg's The Design School: Reconsidering the Basic Premises of Strategic Management. *Strategic Management Journal* **12**, pp. 449–61.

Armstrong, Lord (1977) Oral evidence, 24 January 1977, to the Expenditure Committee (General Sub-Committee) HC 535-II (1977) *op cit.*

Barnes, B., Marshall, A.H., Hawworth, T., Ryan, J. and Hobson, O. (1951) *Financial Control: Its Place in Management*. Institute of Public Administration, London.

Batten, J.D. (1966) *Beyond Management by Objectives*, American Management Association.

Bellini, J., Pfaff, W., Schloesing, L. with Barth, M. (1974) *The United Kingdom in 1980: The Hudson Report*. Associated Business Programmes, London.

Bougen, P.D., Ogden, S.G., and Outram, Q. (1990) The Appearance & Disappearance of Accounting: Wage Determination in the U.K. Coal Industry. *Accounting, Organizations & Society* **15** (3) pp. 149–70.

Broadbent, J. and Gutherie, J. (1992) Changes in the Public sector: A Review of Recent Alternative Accounting Research. *Accounting, Auditing and Accountability Journal* **5** (2), pp. 3–31.

Butler, R. (1991) New Challenges or Familiar Prescriptions. *Public Administration*, **69**, pp. 363–72.

Butler, R. (1993) The Evolution of the Civil Service – A Progress Report. *Public Administration* **71**, pp. 395–406.

Connolly, W.E. (1983) *The Terms of Political Discourse*, 2nd edn Martin Robertson, Oxford.

Cooper, R. and Kaplan, R.S. (1991) Measure Costs Right: Make the Right Decisions in *Getting Numbers You Can Trust: The New Accounting*, Harvard Business School Press, Harvard, pp. 41–8.

Choudhury, N. (1988) The Seeking of Accounting Where It Is Not: Towards a Theory of Non-Accounting in Organizational Settings. *Accounting, Organizations & Society*, **13**, pp. 549–57.

Cmnd 2626 (1994) *Better Accounting for the Taxpayer's Money: Resource Accounting and Budgeting in Government*, HMSO, London.

Cmnd 2764 (1965) *The National Plan*, HMSO, London.

Cmnd 3638 (1968) *The Civil Service* Vol. 1 Report of the Committee and Vol. 2 *Report of A Management Consultancy Group*, HMSO, London.

Cmnd 4506 (1970) *The Reorganisation of Central Government*, HMSO, London.

Cmnd 6440 (1976) *Cash Limits on Public Expenditure*, HMSO, London.

Cmnd 7746 (1979) *The Government's Expenditure Plans (1980–81)*, HMSO, London.

Cmnd 8293 (1981) *Efficiency in the Civil Service*, HMSO, London.

Cmnd 8616 (1982) *Efficiency & Effectiveness in the Civil Service*, HMSO, London.

Cockburn, C. (1977) *The Local State: Management of Cities and People*, Pluto Press, London.

Danziger, J.N. (1978) *Making Budgets: Public Resource Allocation*, Sage, London.

Davis, P.J. and Hersh, R. (1986) *Descartes Dream* Penguin, London.

Deleuze, G. (1992) Ethology: Spinoza and Us in *Incorporations* (eds J. Crary and S. Kwinter), Zone, New York.

Donnison, D., Chapman, V., Meacher, M., Sears, A. and Urwin, K. (1975) *Social Policy and Administration Revisited*, revised edn, George Allen & Unwin, London.

Donnellon, A., Gray, B. and Bougon, M.G. (1986) Communication, Meaning & Organized Action. *Administrative Science Quarterly*, **31**, pp. 43–5.

Drucker, P.F. (1955) *The Practice of Management*, Heinemann, London.

Flint, D. (1978) The 'Value-for-Money' Audit. *Accountant's Magazine* (June).

Fry, G.K. (1984) The Development of the Thatcher Government's 'Grand Strategy' for the Civil Service: A Public Policy Perspective *Public Administration*, **62**, (Autumn) pp. 322–35.

Fry, G.K. (1991) The Fulton Committee's Management Consultancy Group: An Assessment of Its Contribution *Public Administration*, **69**, 4, pp. 423–39.

Gadamar, H-G. (1975) *Truth and Method* 2nd edn (tr. and eds G. Burden and J. Cummings) Sheed and Ward, London.

Garrett, J. (1972) *The Management of Government*, Penguin, Harmondsworth.

Garrett, J. and Walker, S.D. (1969) *Management By Objectives in the Civil Service* CAS Occasional Paper, HMSO, London.

Gergen, K.J. (1994) The Mechanical Self and the Rhetoric of Objectivity in *Rethinking Objectivity* (ed. A. Megill) Duke University Press, Durham.

Goold, M. and Campbell, A. (1989) *Strategies and Styles*, Basil Blackwell, Oxford.

Gordon, L.A. and Miller, D. (1976) A Contingency Framework for the Design of Accounting Information Systems. *Accounting, Organizations & Society* **1** (1) pp. 59–70.

Gray, A. and Jenkins, W.I. (1986) Accountable Management in British Central Government: Some Reflections on the Financial Management Initiative. *Financial Accountability & Management* **2** (3) pp. 171–86.

Gray, A. and Jenkins, B. with Flynn, A. and Rutherford, B. (1991) The Management of Change in Whitehall: the Experience of the FMI *Public Administration,* **69** (1) pp. 41–59.

HC 535-I, HC 535-II, HC 535-III (1977) Eleventh Report from the Expenditure Committee Session 1976–77 *The Civil Service* Vols. 1, 2 and 3, HMSO, London.

HC 318 (1978) 3rd Special Report from the Expenditure Committee, Session 1977/78 *The Civil Service: Observations by the Comptroller and Auditor General on the 11th Report from the Expenditure Committee in Session 1976/77*, HMSO, London.

HC 115-I, HC 115-II (1980) First Special Report from the Committee of Public Accounts, Session 1980–81 *The Role of the Comptroller and Auditor General* Vol. 1 *Report* Vol. 2 *Minutes of Evidence*, HMSO, London.

HC 54 (1981) First Report from the Treasury and Civil Service Committee Session 1980–81 *The Future of the Civil Service Department*, HMSO, London.

HC 236-I; HC 236-II; HC 236-III (1982) Third Report from the Treasury and Civil Service Committee Session 1981–82 *Efficiency and Effectiveness in the Civil Service* Vol. 1: Report, Vol. 2: Minutes of Evidence, Vol. 3: Appendices, HMSO, London.

HC 61 (1987) Thirteenth Report from the Committee of Public Accounts, Session 1986–87 *The Financial Management Initiative*, HMSO, London.

Heclo, H. and Wildavsky, A. (1981) *The Private Government of Public Money*, 2nd edn, Macmillan, London.

Hennessey, P. (1989) *Whitehall*, Harper Collins, Glasgow.

Hobson, O. (1951) A Review of the Methods Described in the Foregoing Chapters in B. Barnes *et al. op cit.*

Hogwood, B.W. (1992) *Trends in British Public Policy*, Open University Press, Buckingham.

Honderich, T. (1990) *Conservatism*, Penguin, London.

Hood, C. (1991) A Public Management for All Seasons? *Public Administration* **69** (1) pp. 3–19.

Hood, C. (1995) The 'New Public Management' in the 1980s: Variations on a Theme. *Accounting, Organizations & Society,* **20** (2/3) pp. 93–109.

Hopwood, A.G. (1984) Accounting and the Pursuit of Efficiency in *Issues in Public Sector Accounting* (eds A.G. Hopwood and C. Tomkins) Phillip Allan, London.

Hopwood, A.G. and Miller, P. (eds) (1994) *Accounting as Social and Institutional Practice*, Cambridge University Press, Cambridge.

Hoskin, K. and Macve, R. (1986) Accounting and the Examination: A Genealogy of Disciplinary Power. *Accounting, Organizations & Society,* **11** (2) pp. 105, 136.

Hoskin, K. and Macve, R. (1988) The Genesis of Accountability: the West Point Connections. *Accounting, Organizations & Society,* **13** (1) pp. 37–73.

Hoskin, K. and Macve, R. (1994) Reappraising the Genesis of Managerialism: A Re-examination of the Role of Accounting at the Springfield Armory 1815–1845. *Accounting, Auditing & Accountability Journal,* **7** (2) pp. 4–29.

Humble, J.W. (1965) *Improving Management Performance*, British Management Institute, London.

Humphrey, C. (1991) Accountable Management in the Public Sector in *Issues in Management Accounting* (eds D. Ashton, T. Hopper and R.W. Scapens) Prentice-Hall, Hemel Hempstead.

Humphrey, C. and Olson, O. (1994) *Caught in the Act: Public Services Disappearing in the World of 'Accountable Management'*, Paper presented to EIASM Workshop, December 12–14, University of Edinburgh.

Ibbs, R. (1984) Better Services at Lower Cost, in *Papers Presented at the Annual Conference 1984*, The Chartered Institute of Public Finance and Accountancy, London.

Inkenberry, G.J. (1989) *Explaining the Diffusion of State Norms: Coercion, Competition and Learning in International Systems*, Paper presented at the annual meeting of the International Studies Association, London.

Jepperson, R.L. (1991) Institutions, Institutional Effects, and Institutionalization, in *The New Institutionalism in Organizational Analysis* (eds P. Powell and P.J. DiMaggio) University of Chicago Press, Chicago, pp. 143–63.

Kellner, P. and Crowther-Hunt, N. (1980) *The Civil Servants*, Macdonald Futura, London.

Labour Party (1979) *The Labour Party Manifesto 1979* Labour Party, London.

Lane, J. (1993) *The Public Sector: Concepts, Models and Approaches*, Sage, London.

Lavoie, D. (1987) The Accounting of Interpretations and the Interpretations of Accounts: The Communicative Function of the 'Language of Business'. *Accounting, Organizations & Society* **12** (6) pp. 579–604.

Lyotard, J.F. (1984) *The Postmodern Condition: A Report On Knowledge*, Manchester University Press, Manchester.

McSweeney, B. (1988) Accounting for the Audit Commission. *The Political Quarterly* **59** (1) pp. 28–43.

McSweeney, B. (1994) Management by Accounting in *Accounting as Social and Institutional Practice* (eds A.G. Hopwood and P. Miller) Cambridge University Press, Cambridge.

March, J.G. and Olson, J.P. (1983) Organizing Political Life: What Administrative Reorganization Tells Us About Government. *The American Political Science Review* **77**, pp. 281–96.

Metcalf, L. and Richards, S. (1990) *Improving Public Management*, 2nd edn, Sage, London.

Meyer, J.W. (1994) Social Environments & Organizational Accounting in *Institutional Environments and Organizations: Structural Complexity and Individualism* (W.R. Scott, J.W. Meyer and associates) Sage, London.

Miller, P. (1994a) Accounting As Social & Institutional Practice: An Introduction, in A.G. Hopwood and P. Miller (eds) *op cit*.

Miller, P. (1994b) Accounting & Objectivity: The Invention of Calculating Selves & Calculable Spaces in *Rethinking Objectivity* (ed. A. Megill) Duke University Press, London.

Miller, P. and O'Leary, T. (1987) Accounting and the Construction of the Governable Person. *Accounting, Organizations & Society,* **12** (3) pp. 235–65.

National Audit Office (1986) *The Financial Management Initiative*, HMSO, London.

Nelson, J.S. (1993) Account and Acknowledge, Or Represent and Control? On Post-Modern Politics and Economics of Collective Responsibility. *Accounting, Organizations & Society* **18** (2/3) pp. 207–99.

Nove, A. (1973) *Efficiency Criteria for Nationalised Industries*, George Allen & Unwin, London.

Odiorine, G.S. (1965) *Management by Objectives: A System of Managerial Leadership*, Pitman, New York.

Organization for Economic Cooperation & Development (1993a) *Public Management Developments: Survey 1993*, OECD, Paris.

Organization for Economic Cooperation & Development (1993b) *Accounting for What? The Value of Accrual Accounting to the Public Sector*, OECD, Paris.

Otley, D. (1980) The Contingency Theory of Management Accounting: Achievements & Prognosis. *Accounting, Organizations & Society,* **5** (4) pp. 194–208.

Peters, T.J. and Waterman, R.H. (1982) *In Search of Excellence: Lessons from America's Best-Run Companies*, Harper & Row, New York.

Plowden, W. (1985) What Prospects for the Civil Service? *Public Adminstration*, **63** pp. 393–414.

Pollitt, C. (1993) *Managerialism and the Public Services: The Anglo-American Experience*, 2nd edn, Blackwell, Oxford.

Porter, T. (1994) Objectivity As Standardization: The Rhetoric of Impersonality in Measurement, Statistics, and Cost-Benefit Analysis in *Rethinking Objectivity* (ed. A. Megill), Duke University Press, Durham.

Power, M. (1994) The Audit Society in *Accounting as Social and Institutional Practice*, (eds A.G. Hopwood and P. Miller) Cambridge University Press, Cambridge.

Reddin, W.J. (1971) *Effective MBO*, British Institute of Management, London.

Redwood, J. and Hatch, J. (1982) *Controlling Public Industries*, Basil Blackwell, Oxford.

Ridley, F.F. (ed.) (1968) *Specialists and Generalists; a Comparative Study of the Professional Civil Servant at Home and Abroad by a Group of University Teachers*, George Allen & Unwin, London.

Robinson, A. (1981) The House of Commons and Public Expenditure, in *The Commons Today* revised edn, (eds S. Walkand and M. Ryle) Fontana, Glasgow.

Rose, R. (1984) The Programme Approach to the Growth of Government. *British Journal of Political Science*, **15** (1), pp. 1–28.

Ruccio, D.F. (1991) Postmodernism and Economics. *Journal of Post Keynesian Economics*, **13** (4) pp. 495–510.

Russell, P. and Sherer, M. (1994) *Managerialism in the Public Sector: Recent Developments in Accounting and Management Control*, ICAEW, London.

Sampson, A. (1992) *The Essential Anatomy of Britain*, Hodder & Stoughton, London.

Scott, W.R. (1994) Institutional Analysis: Variance and Process Theory Approaches in *Institutional Environments and Organizations: Structural Complexity and Individualism* (W.R. Scott, J.W. Meyer and associates) Sage, London.

Scott, W.R., Meyer, J.W. and associates (1994) *Institutional Environments and Organizations: Structural Complexity and Individualism*, Sage, London.

Shand, D. (1995) Financial Management Reforms in Government: An International Perspective in *Making the Australian Public Sector Count in the 1990s* (ed. J. Gutherie) IIR, Sydney.

Sharpe, L.J. and Newton, K. (1984) *Does Politics Matter? The Determinants of Public Policy*, Clarendon Press, Oxford.

Smith, B. (1994) The Unquiet Judge: Activism Without Objectivism in Law and Politics, in *Rethinking Objectivity* (ed. A. Megill), Duke University Press, Durham.

Speight, H. (1967) *Economics & Industrial Efficiency*, 2nd edn, Macmillan, London.

Snyder, J.R. (1991) Translator's Introduction, in Vattimo (1991) *op cit*.

Strang, D. and Meyer, J.W. (1994) Institutional Conditions for Diffusion in *Institutional Environments and Organizations: Structural Complexity and Individualism* (W.R. Scott, J.W. Meyer and associates) Sage, London.

Thompson, G. (1987) Inflation Accounting in a Theory of Calculation. *Accounting, Organizations & Society*, **12** (5) pp. 523–43.

Tsoukas, H. (1996) The Word and the World: A Critique of Representationalism in Management Research. *International Journal of Public Administration* (forthcoming).

Vattimo, G. (1992) *The Transparent Society*, Polity Press, Cambridge.

Walker, D. (1982) How the Heseltine Formula Could Turn Ministers into Managers. *The Times* 7 September.

Waterhouse, J.H. and Tiesson, P.A. (1978) A Contingency Framework for Management Accounting Systems Research. *Accounting, Organizations & Society*, **3** (1) pp. 65–76.

Wilding, R. (1983) *Management Information and Control: the Role of the Centre Management Information and Control in Whitehall*, Royal Institute of Public Administration, London.

Williams, A. (1967) *Output Budgeting and the Contribution of Micro-Economics to Efficiency in Government* CAS, Occasional Paper, HMSO, London.

Wood, D. (1990) *Philosophy At The Limit*, Unwin Hyman, London.

Young, S. and Lowe, A.V. (1974) *Intervention in the Mixed Economy*, Croom Helm, London.

12 Principals and higher principals: accounting for accountability in the caring professions

Richard Laughlin

Introduction

Accountability can be seen as a relationship involving the 'giving and demanding of reasons for conduct' (Roberts and Scapens, 1985: 447). This view assumes that some individual, small group or organization has certain 'rights' to make demands over the conduct of another, as well as seek reasons for actions taken. This chapter will be exploring the nature of these 'rights', why they exist and the rationale for their legitimacy.

In particular, the chapter explores the possibility of 'alternative' rights: the conditions where the one who accounts and is held to account rejects or rebels against the seeming rightful authority of the 'one who holds to account' (Stewart, 1984: 16). The nature of these alternative 'rights', the grounds for their legitimacy and their ramifications for models of accountability, I suggest, are of critical importance.

The empirical cases I draw on to amplify these themes are all taken from what Gorz (1989) refers to as the 'caring professions' (i.e. those devoted to education, health and other social services). It is here where there is a potential clash with deep seated professional values, stemming from the inculcation of the 'rights' of 'higher principals' (e.g. God, the Church, professional bodies or personal conscience). Thus, as will become apparent, such rebellion, potential or actual, has far-reaching effects on the nature and design of the accountability relationship.

In pursuing this notion of alternative 'rights', this chapter challenges some of the taken for granted assumptions of the theory of contracting (and consequent accountability) which dominates both economic theory and law – for a more detailed critique see Broadbent, Dietrich and Laughlin (forthcoming). In both disciplines the 'principal' (the one who holds to account) is perceived to have a natural 'right', primarily because the 'principal' has ownership of resources. The assumption is that, if the use of these resources is transferred to the 'agent' (the one who accounts and is held to account), then, in return, the expectations of the 'principal' should be met by the 'agent'. That this cannot always be ensured is, of course, well recognized and, particularly in the economic theory of contracting, it is treated as the problem of 'moral hazard'. Nevertheless, no 'solution' to this problem ever questions the 'rights' of the 'principal' to try to ensure compliance.

This chapter problematizes this seemingly natural and fundamental 'right' for 'principals' to expect compliance. Instead, I portray the circumstances when the wishes of economic providing 'principals' can be overridden by the expectations and requirements of what, in this paper, will be referred to as 'higher principals'. By posing circumstances in which their general theoretical claims are inappropriate, this chapter creates an inevitable distance from the contracting models of law and economics in thinking about accountability processes.

The chapter has two major parts. The first substantive part summarizes a model of accountability as being concerned with the 'rights' of the 'one who holds to account' has over the 'one who accounts and is held to account'. For ease of expression I will continue to call these 'principals' and 'agents' respectively, but to avoid the unfortunate connotation with a narrow economic interpretation of these terms the following discussion will refer to them in quotation marks. In order to further demonstrate a distancing from the economic theory of contracting, I will critique this traditional principal/agent model in terms of its assumptions in relation to the unquestioning significance given to the 'principals' and their expectations for the conduct of 'agents'. This discussion will introduce the role of 'higher principals' into the modelling.

The second half of the chapter develops this theme by looking at examples from the public sector in the UK, as well as the Church of England, which highlight the dynamics of this model. A church is of course a paradigm case for considering the importance of 'higher principals' and I wish to contrast the rather less conflictual situation in the Church of England with the strident debates in the UK's public sector. This comparison is couched in terms of the expectations of 'principals' and their clashes with professional values. It also highlights the way public sector 'agents', through subtle absorption processes, have managed to deflect increasing demands by the 'principals', but at some considerable cost (using the term broadly) to individuals. The chapter concludes with reflections on the implications of this new dimension for the model of accountability presented in the first half of the chapter.

Reconsidering a model of accountability

A useful place to start the argument that concerns the first half of this chapter is to look again at the summarized picture of contracting and accountability relationships that I developed in the late 1980s (Laughlin, 1990). While the accountability literature has moved on since this paper was published, the ideas presented still provide a powerful foundation for understanding some key elements in the accountability process. The key elements involved are contained in diagrammatic form in Figure 1.

The central part of Figure 1 assumes that a 'principal' transfers resources to an 'agent' with expectations as to how these resources are to be used. A fundamental assumption of this model is that it is this transfer of resources that gives the 'principal' 'rights' to specify action expectations and demand reasons for conduct undertaken by the 'agent' (Gray, 1983). One way of clarifying and defining the nature of these expectations concerning the usage of these resources is through 'contracts' (Gray, 1983; Tricker, 1983; Stewart, 1984; Gray, Owen and Maunders, 1987). Such contracts

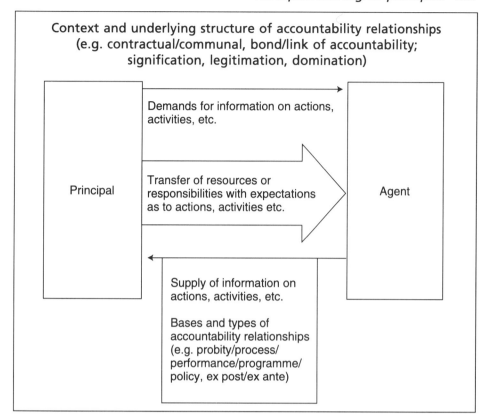

Figure 1
Accountability
Relationships: A
Summarized
Picture of
Theoretical
Insights

can be informal or formal and/or specific or imprecise but are assumed to be in existence in some form or other when resources are transferred.

With regard to the role of the 'principal', Figure 1 assumes that the 'principal' has an unquestioned right to have control over the behaviour of the 'agent'. For the first part of this section, I will continue with this assumption and then challenge its validity at the end. Of course, implicit within Figure 1, is an allowance for any 'deviancy' of the 'agent'. Yet this descriptor is carefully chosen: in all cases it is assumed that departure from the 'principal's' wishes *is* 'deviant' behaviour. It is always taken to be 'legitimate' to excercise control over the 'agent's' behaviour. Implicit in the model is a mundane and largely unquestioned bias towards the authority of the 'principal'. The rationale for this bias, as indicated in the introduction, is that resources, invariably of an economic nature, are being transferred from the 'principal' with legal expectations that something will be exchanged in return. 'He who pays the piper plays the tune' is the underlying and unquestioned logic of economic exchange.

The formality and specificity of these expectations help set up what is conceived of as an implicit contract. This has ramifications not only for the demands for information, but also on its supply from the 'agent' and the 'bases' and types of accountability relationships which may result. Stewart (1984: 17), for example, talks about these bases of accountability in terms of a 'ladder'. The rungs of his ladder start with 'accounting for probity and legality' which reports that funds have been used in an appropriate manner. Appropriate, in this sense, is usually loosely defined and related to legally acceptable pursuits rather than in terms of definable actions and activities. The next level is 'process accountability' which accounts for the details of the action processes followed by the 'agent'. The next two levels are 'performance accountability' and 'programme accountability' which together are intended to provide an account of the total work performance of the 'agent' in terms of the specific goals set by the 'principal'. Finally, 'policy accountability' complements the 'performance' and 'programme' levels presenting the account in broad policy terms in relation to the goals.

Each level is intended to supply an expanding and more detailed account of actions undertaken by the 'agent'. 'Probity and legality' information deals only with the legality of expenditure patterns and leaves considerable freedom to the 'agent' to pursue whatever actions seem appropriate. 'Process' information is only about the means adopted, rather than the ends of actions and activities. Again this leaves considerable freedom to the 'agent' to pursue whatever is deemed appropriate as long as the processes adopted are made visible to the 'principal' and, hence, open to some possible disciplinary reaction. Performance, programme, and policy information are intended to declare, in precise terms, the ends achieved by the 'agent' according to the ethos and specific goals set by the 'principal'. All this assumes, of course, that the behaviour of the 'agent' is largely open to being predetermined by the 'principal's' precise goal expectations; which can be specified in meaningful terms.

This summary brings us conveniently to the role that measurement (and accounting measurement in particular) plays at all levels of Stewart's 'ladder'. It is at the performance and programme levels that the significance of accounting technology is most apparent. It is here where the interpretation of goals into measurable outcomes are most prominent. And it is here where accounting measurement is not only most innovative, but is also most dangerous.

The dangers of spurious surrogate measures for complex goals are well recognized in the literature. Yet the significance or 'aura' (cf. Gallhofer and Haslam, 1991) given to the measurable (being visible and immediate) as distinct from the unmeasured and unmeasurable (being largely invisible and hence can be forgotten) remains a powerful 'reality' yet one which remains somewhat under-researched. Once accountability is set in the control context of a relationship between 'principals' and 'agents', the role of measures, spurious or otherwise, becomes significant and potentially highly influential on the actions and activities of 'agents'.

Coupled with each different 'accountability base' is an appreciation that, at each step of Stewart's ladder, the supply of information can be either *ex ante* (what the 'agent' is going to do) or *ex post* (what the 'agent' has done) (cf. Birkett, 1988; Johnson, 1974; Jackson, 1982; Heald, 1983). To know what the 'agent' is going to do prior to the actual action performed provides an opportunity for the 'principal' to exercise some control over anticipated behaviours that are not in accordance with the 'principal's' wishes. Ex post reporting, on the other hand, involves a reduced degree of direction over the behaviour of 'agents'. To undertake a 'correction' of the effects of previous conduct may be considerably harder than preventing forms of conduct in the first place. In this respect, ex ante performance, programme, policy, process and probity accountability bases (all five levels in Stewart's ladder), in terms of expectations and reports, can be considered to help form a significant set of 'control technologies' (Munro, 1993) which try to ensure the conduct of 'agents' meets the 'principal's' wishes. Whether any of these devices is sufficient to ensure a full compliance by the 'agents' is less certain.

This brings us to another element in the accountability relationship – namely the more implicit contexts which surround the relationships between 'principals' and 'agents' (i.e. the outer encompassing box in Figure 1). Some of the more contextual work on accountability (cf. Birkett, 1988; Laughlin, 1990; Roberts, 1991) has started to typecast these contexts into two major types which Laughlin (1990: 97) describes as 'communal' and 'contractual'. The 'communal' context encompasses a less formal set of accountability relationships where expectations over conduct, and information demand and supply, are less structured and defined. This is similar to Roberts' 'socializing' form of accountability or Birkett's 'gemeinschaft' model. The 'contractual' context, on the other hand, encompasses a much more formal set of accountability relationships where action expectations and information demand and supply are tightly defined and clearly specified. This is much the same as Roberts' 'hierarchical' form of accountability, or Birkett's 'gesellschaft' and 'bureaucracy' models.

Both 'contractual' and 'communal' forms of accountability can technically lead to expectations and reports which straddle Stewart's ladder and can be of an ex ante or ex post form. Unlike Stewart (1984), who attempts to distinguish between what he calls a 'bond of accountability' (which formally and contractually defines accountability relationships) and a 'link of account' (which is an informal 'recognition of responsiveness' (Stewart, 1984: 25)), no such distinctions are made when talking about 'contractual' and 'communal' forms of accountability – *both* are forms of accountability and *both* can be equally powerful in their reporting expectations and their control intentions. Invariably, in a 'contractual' form, the expectations of 'principals' may be more formalized and defined, involving greater use of written commands as well as financial or management accounting-type measures in the control technology, as well as in reports from the 'agent'. Written commands and reports are clearly significant control instruments, but the unwritten rules of conduct, and the informal 'reporting' requirements, in a 'communal' accountability relationship, can often be just as powerful in terms of control intentions, albeit deploying different technologies.

Finally, following Giddens' structuration theory, Roberts and Scapens (1985) and Macintosh and Scapens (1991) point out that each and every accountability relationship contains particular structures of signification (meaning), legitimation (morality) and domination (power). The important point being made here is that in each 'system of accountability' there is a moral relationship involved, whereby an individual or small group is exercising domination over another to ensure that something, meaningfully defined, is done by that person or persons. This draws attention to the essentially complex ideological nature permeating any and all accountability relationships.

Trust and the potential for value conflict

Raising the ideological, moral issue is important. However, even with this addition, Figure 1 remains very static. Nothing in the above suggests why, in certain cases, 'contractual', as distinct from 'communal', forms of accountability emerge. Equally little, if anything, is portrayed in Figure 1 as to why a particular type of accountability relationship (probity, process etc.) is brought into play. However, it may be possible to build on the contents of Figure 1, without having to reject the thinking in its entirety. If this is so, a dynamic can be provided as well as a critique concerning challenging the natural rights of 'principals'. The following will address two aspects of this expansion: first, in relation to the element of trust; and second, in respect of the potential for value conflict. In the following I will explore each of these in turn in the context of Figure 1.

The question of trust in the accountability relationship has been discussed, to a limited extent, in the literature (cf. Fox, 1974; Armstrong, 1991). The debate on trust works within an assumption of the rightful authority of the 'principal' (a point which still needs to be debated – see below). However, that notwithstanding, it highlights the important point that the type of accountability relationship is dependent upon the level of trust (from the perspective of the 'principal') concerning the likely obedience of the 'agent' in fulfilling the 'principal's' wishes.

Fox (1974) talks of 'high trust' and 'low trust' between parties. Where there is 'high trust' that the 'agent' will fulfil the expectations of the 'principal', then sophisticated and formal controls are invariably not seen as necessary. On the other hand, where there is 'low trust' the 'principal' will be at pains to try to exert greater control over the behaviour of the 'agent'. Invariably this may lead to the use of more formal control mechanisms by the 'principal'. Relating this to the contents of Figure 1, it is possible to conjecture that the presence of 'high trust' may lead to the use of 'communal' forms of accountability, where expectations are left ill-defined and ex post probity and legality forms of reporting are likely to be acceptable (if needed at all). In a 'low trust' situation it is possible that 'contractual' forms of accountability will be more apparent with expectations clearly spelt out and, where possible, expressed in measurable form, with all levels of Stewart's ladder operational, with ex ante reports probably being the norm.

The second and somewhat more important modification of Figure 1 relates to the potential for value conflict between the expectations of 'principals' and those of 'agents'. This brings us to the heart of the themes being developed in this chapter. The implicit economic authority of the 'principal' is unequivocal on how to deal with this potential value clash – as remarked earlier, 'who pays the piper plays the tune'. There is no room in this model for moral or value disagreements – the 'agent' must, despite anticipated self-seeking behaviour, in the final analysis, fall into line. Resistance is not justified and must be removed through more sophisticated control systems. Yet it is important to look more closely into any resistance and trace when, if at all, this is legitimate. Introducing these concerns provides some dynamism into the model in Figure 1. It also introduces some changes to the model itself. I will take this analysis in two stages.

Firstly, it is important to highlight under what conditions, using the unchanged model in Figure 1, that value conflict between 'principal' and 'agent' is most likely to occur. Whilst it is difficult to be precise, a reasonable assumption is that value conflict will be more apparent in conditions when low levels of trust exist between 'principals' and 'agents' and when more sophisticated control systems are in place. In a similar way, where high levels of trust, and when looser control systems are in operation, then the potential for value conflict becoming explicit is less. Figure 2 depicts these postulated relationships.

The roots behind the thinking of Figure 2 is the greater freedom given to the 'agent' in the latter case as compared with the former. 'Communal' accountability (with or without ex post probity and legality reports) allows the 'agent' freedom to define how best to proceed. This 'freedom' is not freedom to choose in an absolute sense. It is freedom to choose and adopt the thinking and intentions of the 'principal'. It is relative to the subtle controls exercised by the 'principal' to keep the 'agent' in line, without the latter necessarily being aware of the influence of the former – see Munro (1994) for more about these subtle forms of control and accompanying 'accounts'.

This espoused freedom can be purposefully encouraged in certain types of 'high trust' relationships. When this freedom is 'abused', according to the perception of the 'principal', this 'deviancy' is noted and then trust is dinted and it is likely that increased formal controls will be exercised. This shifts the modelling away from high to low trust and corresponding change in the accountability processes. These tighter rules create less absolute and relative freedoms for the 'agent', and, at the extreme, define what he or she should be doing in precise measurable terms. It is at these points that the potential for value conflict is most likely. At the far extreme the 'agent' becomes slave-like. Apart from the obvious abuse over individual freedom this causes – a reason for value conflict at this basic level – this form of control runs the most risk of conflicting

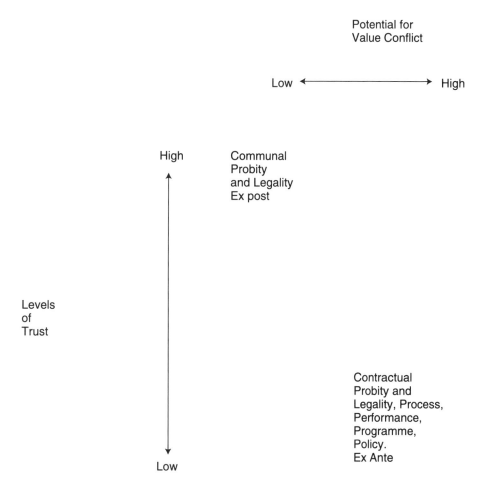

Figure 2
Accountability
Models, Trust &
Value Conflict:
Tracing Inter-
relationships

with other fundamental values. It still does not say why this should be so, however. This brings us to the second dimension of the argument.

One of the central reasons for this potential fundamental conflict of values is to do with professional and personal autonomy. The presence and call for autonomy is one of the central characteristics of the modern theory of the professions which marks out a profession from other occupational groups (Friedson, 1970a, 1970b). The attainment and retainment of autonomy (or 'the control over the content and terms of work' (Friedson, 1970a, p. 136) or 'monopoly of competence' (Larson, 1977) or 'occupational control' (Johnson 1972)) is something for which many occupational groups strive but few achieve. Once achieved, invariably these occupational groups will create their own professional societies which become the guiding authority for defining the values and practices of the professions. In such situations the introduction of an economic 'principal' who wishes to determine the behaviour of the 'agent' (the autonomous professional) in ways which are not conducive to professional norms will run the risk of potential fundamental value conflict.

Another way of looking at the same value conflict is via the rather more emotive language of the potential threat of 'economic reason'. The rationale of the economic 'principal' may well contain a rationality of cost and return which is described by Gorz (1989) as 'economic reason'. What Gorz shows through a careful and thorough analysis is that 'economic reason' is expanding its territorial domain yet is 'unaware of how narrow its proper limits are' (Gorz, 1989, p. 2). What Gorz shows is that there are many activities which are rightly susceptible to 'economic reason' whilst many are not. The real question Gorz is trying to determine is:

> . . . which activities can be subordinated to economic rationality without
> losing their meaning and for which activities economic rationalization would
> be a perversion or a negation of the meaning inherent in them.
>
> (Gorz, 1989: 132–3)

A clash of values between 'principal' and 'agent' could, therefore, be traceable to an attempt at using economic reason in areas where they undermine the central 'meanings' of the professional activities of the 'agent'.

Gorz's model can be developed and enriched using quasi-religious symbolism and the language of 'sacred' and 'secular' and the fear of a 'secularization process' (cf. Durkheim, 1976; Eliade, 1959; Laughlin, 1988, 1990; Laughlin and Broadbent, 1988, 1994). In this context it is assumed that certain individuals (for our purposes the 'agent') have a clear view about what is important and central in the way of values and activities (which can be typecast as 'sacred') as well as what is treated as unimportant and peripheral (the 'secular' or the 'profane'). Where what is deemed as 'secular' attempts to infiltrate, colonize or control the 'sacred', then this 'secularization process' must be resisted to prevent the 'sacred' being compromised and perhaps obliterated. The infiltration of 'economic reason' is an important example of a perceived 'secularization process', but it is only an example – albeit a significant one – of the general processes at work. The introduction of this language aims to highlight the more general concern that sometimes the expectations of 'principals' may be such that they clash with values of 'agents' which have been engendered with deep seated conviction similar to religious beliefs. In these circumstances 'agents' justify their rebellion through appeal to 'higher principals' which, if we were using the religious symbolism in a literal sense, would be God but could be just as easily, professional societies or even personal conscience.

In ending this section perhaps three further points could be made. Firstly, raising this whole point about legitimate resistance suggests a certain privileging of the 'sacred' values of 'agents'. Whilst this is undoubtedly the case, it at least introduces this dimension explicitly into the accountability relationship and, hence, opens up this as an important dimension for research on accountability relationships. The model in Figure 1 is not only biased in that it privileges the values of 'principals', it leaves this privileging implicit. Secondly, the above says nothing about the preferred accountability relationships of 'rebelling' 'agents'. We have already seen that the nature of the accountability relationship varies in a contractual (low trust?) and communal (high trust?) context. Both are, however, related to the economic 'principal's' wishes. The issue of how and in what form the 'rebelling' 'agent' accounts to 'higher principals' is, however, also recognized but must be left for future research to explore. Thirdly, it is important to note that the infiltration of 'economic reason' is, according to Gorz (1989), at its most inappropriate with regard to what he calls the 'caring professions' (i.e. those devoted to education, health and other social services). For, to Gorz (1989 p. 143), it is 'possible for the efficiency of carers to be in inverse proportion to their visible quantifiable output'. This is because the service 'depends on a person-to-person' relationship, not on the execution of predetermined quantifiable output' (Gorz, 1989 p. 143). To introduce 'economic reason' into these professions is a dangerous 'secularization process' which needs to be resisted. This is raised at this point since it provides an important introduction to the empirical examples, all drawn from what Gorz calls the 'caring professions', which are now discussed in the remainder of the chapter.

Exploring the role and workings of 'higher principals' in the caring professions

Whether occasionally, or often, the expectations of 'principals' can be expected to clash with the values of 'agents' who are guided by the requirements of 'higher principals'. The following discussion provides some appreciation of an underlying logic which may be at work in these cases. The empirical material is drawn from my studies of the 'caring professions', with a particular emphasis on the Church of England and the public sector in the UK.

Adapting the thinking of Figure 1 in relation to the Church of England is not easy. It is particularly difficult to decipher who are 'principals' and who are 'agents'. In a series of studies, I have traced the complex flow of financial resources in this ancient institution (Laughlin, 1984, 1988, 1990) and conclude that there are a number of key providers and users of financial resources. Hence, using the logic of Figure 1, there are a number of 'principals' and 'agents'. These are presented in diagrammatic form in Figure 3 and briefly described below.

At the parish level (of which there are approximately 11,000 separate units), congregations provide resources to the Parochial Church Councils. These, in turn, allocate resources to various actors and their activities within the parishes. They also provide resources for diocesan and central purposes, but this can be ignored at this stage and will be picked up later when exploring the diocesan level relationships. Being

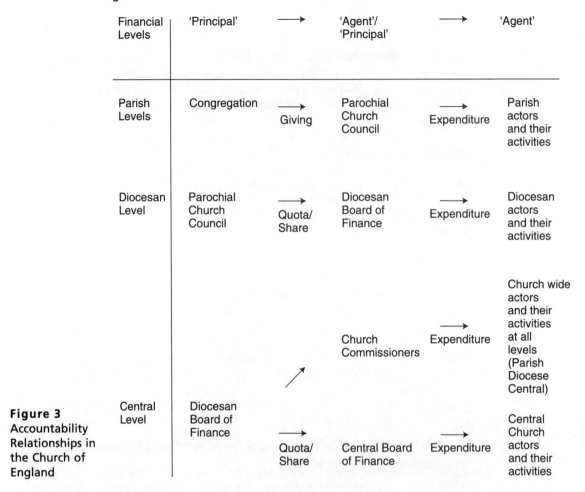

Figure 3
Accountability
Relationships in
the Church of
England

the suppliers of financial resources, the congregations are therefore the 'principals', with the Parochial Church Councils acting as 'agents'. However, because of their expenditure powers, the Parochial Church Councils, in effect, become 'principals' of such actors as the clergy, administrators, voluntary workers etc. It is this latter group, therefore, who become 'agents' in this second accountability relationship. So the Parochial Church Councils stand as either 'agents' or 'principals'.

At the diocesan level, of which there are 43 separate units – 44 including Europe! – Parochial Church Councils supply financial resources to Diocesan Boards of Finance. This transfer of resources follows the definable resource provision formula called a 'quota' or 'share' system and is to cover costs of a range of diocesan *and* central activities. Diocesan Boards of Finance, in turn, allocate part of their resources to such diocesan actors as bishops, diocesan officers etc. in order to fund their activities. Thus, Diocesan Boards of Finance are also to be considered 'agents' in one relationship and 'principals' in another.

The Diocesan Boards of Finance, in turn, transfer resources to the Central Board of Finance and the Church Commissioners. In consequence of their transferring resources to such actors as the Boards and Councils of the General Synod, the Church's central governing body, this Central Board of Finance becomes a 'principal'. Similarly, the Church Commissioners transfers resources to a range of actors and activities across all levels of the Church of England. So again, the Central Board of Finance and Church Commissioners, who are 'agents' in one relationship, become 'principals' in another. Like the Parochial Church Councils and Diocesan Boards of Finance, they are hybrids in being simultaneously both 'agents' and 'principals'.

One clear finding that has emerged from my various studies is that expectations that attach to the transfer of resources are very ill-defined for all 'principals'. Accountability is 'communal', and reporting is ex post and devoted only to issues concerning probity and legality. In all cases, the 'agents' highlighted in the far right column of Figure 3 (i.e. the parish, diocesan and central actors and their activities) are largely left to define their activities without explicit direction from the 'principals' highlighted in the far left column of Figure 3 (i.e. the congregations, Parochial Church Councils and Diocesan Boards of Finance). Most obviously, the Parochial Church Councils, Diocesan Boards of Finance, Central Board of Finance and Church Commissioners provide an administrative machinery for the unconditional provision of an adequate resource base for the work of the 'agents'.

This said, it is also possible to suggest that, in their hybrid form of 'agent/principals', these institutional arrangements act as if they were set as a type of *buffer* between the 'principals' and 'agents' to prevent the former from directly affecting the latter's conduct. If there are points of tension in the Church with regard to finance and accountability relationships, it is between the 'principals' (those on the far left of Figure 3) and the 'agent/principals' (those in the middle of the Figure) – the Parochial Church Councils, Diocesan Boards of Finance, Central Board of Finance and Church Commissioners. In all cases, however, any pressures are muted by a realization that these 'agent/principals' remain *intermediaries* – entities who are there to 'buffer' and serve the 'agents'. Whilst some short term pressures may be exerted by 'principals', in the final analysis they share the philosophy that the 'agents' should be protected from too much intrusion in the way of making them more accountable. In fact, as Figure 3 indicates, two of the 'principals' (Parochial Church Councils and Diocesan Boards of Finance) are also 'buffers' ('agent/principals') in other relationships. As a result, money passes between these bodies in the Church of England with little in the way of formal controls, or expectations. It is an organization where 'high trust' dominates and, despite much current murmuring coming from questionable financial investments by the Church Commissioners, is unlikely to change in substance in the foreseeable future.

The absence of formal controls is made possible by all participants in the Church of England being aware of the underlying values which guide its workings. The Church of England is founded on 'sacred and secular' principles. It has a clear hierarchical view about what is important and central and what is more secondary. It is the foundational example of Eliade's model of sacristy. God is the 'principal', to those who adhere to this value system, before whom all participants must look for guidance and direction. Institutionally this involves setting aside certain individuals (primarily the clergy) to be the mediators for understanding the wishes of God. They need to be free – 'autonomous' using professional jargon – to perform this function in the way they deem appropriate.

A further aspect of this fundamental value system is that it has a very clear philosophy concerning the role of finance. Put simply finance is not there to direct, determine and control, but to *enable* this independence. To move into a controlling mode assumes that the actions of paid 'agents' can be programmed and, by implication, that understanding the wishes of God can be determined. In contrast, finance is seen only as something that is needed to allow these individuals space and time to discover the 'will of God'. It is needed, therefore, for this enabling purpose and only for this.

The Church of England's financial arrangements seem designed to prevent any change in these arrangements. As 'agent/principals', the Parochial Church Councils, Diocesan Boards of Finance, Central Board of Finance and Church Commissioners act as built-in 'buffers'. Any attempt to introduce greater levels of control, even by the 'buffers' themselves, are prevented from having a marked effect on the actions of 'agents'. The 'buffers' are the initial forces to absorb such challenges. However, where they come from the 'buffers' themselves, they can be squashed by the clergy and their final authority – the desires and directions of 'higher principals' (no less than God!). Nobody, and certainly not the administrators who largely make up the 'buffers', has the courage or ability to pursue this challenge and generate the level of change required. The clergy are accountable to God and to the congregation under their charge in ways that they alone determine and no administrator could dare to impose any alternative 'account' which might conflict with this. As a result, money is seen as an enabler of freedom rather than a determiner of activities of actors.

In relation to the Church of England, therefore, and returning to the language of Figures 1 and 2, expectations surrounding the transfer of financial resources and formal accountability requirements are both minimal. 'Communal' accountability is the norm and ex post probity and legality reports are standard practice. 'High trust', in an absolute rather than relative sense, is at work; or at least there is an unwillingness, or institutional blockage, to think otherwise.

As a result, in the final analysis, 'agents' are encouraged to be free to determine their own way forward under the direction and guidance of 'higher principals'. Value conflicts with the 'principals' are minimized, even though, on occasion, some short term discomfort may be experienced. However, should the various 'principals' try to exert greater rationalizing over the conduct of 'agents', they have to exert this attempted influence through the 'agent/principals' – the 'buffers' – in the first place.

Removing the buffers from the 'caring professions'

Similar logic applied to the public sector in the UK prior to 1979. This was possibly for similar reasons, although historical links between the UK's public sector, or any types of 'caring professions', and the Church are complex and far from clear. However, it is interesting that there are marked similarities between underlying values in these professions and those in the Church and also in their collective attitude to the role of finance.

Some of the nuances of this philosophy which underlay, and arguably still underlies, thinking in the 'caring professions' is nicely captured in the following quote from Gorz (1989):

> These jobs are done well when they are performed out of a 'sense of vocation', that is, an *unconditional* desire to help other people. Receiving remuneration for the help she or he gives should not be the doctor's basic

motivation; such a motivation is in competition with a strictly professional motivation which could and must take precedence in case of need. In the occupations in question, the relationship between doctors and patients (or between teachers and pupils or between carers and those in their care) is *distinct from their commercial relationship and is presented as quite independent of it*: "I'm here to help you. Of course, I also intend to earn a living. But money is what enables me to do my job not vice versa. What I do and what I earn has no real relation to one another".

The patients (or pupils, and so on) recognize this incommensurability by the fact that they still feel indebted to their doctor (teacher etc.) even after they have paid for them. They have received from the latter something greater than, and different from, what money can buy: the service provided, even when it is well remunerated, *also* is of the nature of a *gift*, more precisely a giving of *him* or *herself* on the part of the doctor (or teacher etc.). She or he has been involved in the service he or she has provided in a manner that can be neither *produced* at will, nor bought, learned or codified. She or he has shown an interest in the other person as a human being and not just in their money; he or she has established a relationship with the other that cannot be expressed in terms of a predefined technical procedure or computer programme.'

(Gorz, 1989: 144–45 (emphasis in the original))

Rather than see it as a determiner of activities, Gorz makes finance an *enabler* of professional activities in the 'caring professions'.

This philosophy was institutionalized in the organizational arrangements of the public sector in the UK prior to 1979 (when the Conservative government came to power). Finance was decoupled from service. It was controlled centrally and allocated according to need, to enable the work of service to proceed unhindered by financial pressures or concerns. It is what Miller and Rose (1991) have called a societal model of 'welfarism' at work, whereby there is greater paternalistic support (through the provision of an enabling resource base) but also an encouragement for a more open and concerned debate about service quality independent of connections to resources consumed.

From the perspective of our model of accountability, 'communal' forms dominated with a sole concentration on a concern for probity and legality. The transfer of resources was not seen as a way to define the activities to be performed – this was located in a separate professional debate that was seen as independent of the resource transfer. Rather the transfer of resources was seen as a paternalistic support of the actors to allow them the freedom to define what they should be doing according to professional norms.

All this changed with the election of the Conservative government in 1979. Mrs Thatcher, the then Prime Minister, was determined to fundamentally change the workings of the public sector which she saw as wasteful and inefficient. She was not alone in this attitude, with fellow cabinet members of a similar persuasion. However, it was her personal initiative that encouraged the establishment of the Government's Efficiency Unit, headed up by Sir (now Lord) Derek Rayner, who was seconded from a highly successful retail shopping chain. In his first few years in office he conducted a number of investigations into the public sector. These 'Rayner Scrutinies' as they came to be known were to '(a) promote greater value for money (b) remove obstacles to good management (c) to encourage quick and effective implementation of feasible changes' (Jackson, 1988).

Out of these 'Scrutinies' a clear policy started to emerge which has come to be known as the 'financial management initiative' (FMI) (cf. Richards, 1987; Jackson, 1988). Richards, writing in 1987, made plain that FMI: 'symbolizes everything that has happened in the field of management change in the public sector in the last eight years' (Richards, 1987: 22). Whilst the emphasis has changed recently, with the emphasis on agencies coming from the 'Next Steps' initiative, the FMI roots are still clear to see (cf. Greer, 1994; Zifcak, 1994). FMI is fundamentally concerned with the design of 'good management' (Richards, 1987: 25). The first definitive summary of FMI came in September 1982 with the publication of the White Paper 'Efficiency and Effectiveness in the Civil Service' (Cmnd. 8616). 'Good management' became defined in this White Paper as follows:

> The main objective is to promote in each department an organization and a system in which managers at all levels have:
> i.   a clear view of their objectives; and assess and wherever possible measure outputs or performance in relation to these objectives;
> ii. well-defined responsibility for making the best use of their resources including a critical scrutiny of output and value for money;
> iii. the information (including particularly about costs), training and access to expert advice which they need to exercise their responsibility effectively.'
> (Efficiency and Effectiveness in the Civil Service, 1982: 23)

Hood (1991) sees FMI, or the 'new public management' as he describes it, having seven key operational characteristics. First, the importance of financial devolution to units directly offering the services. Second, the design of explicit standards and measures of performance. Third, the necessity to postulate clear relationships between inputs, outputs and performance measures for these units. Fourth, increased accountability for these units. Fifth, a stress on private sector styles of management. Sixth, a stress on competition and contracting between units. Seventh, and finally, a stress on efficiency and parsimony in resource usage.

Key to FMI is an apparent financial freedom. FMI is dressed up in terms of the greater freedoms given to the service provider in terms of financial devolution. Yet, in fact, there is a greater level of control and systematizing of activities. Previously, the coverage of costs through a centralized fund removed the responsibility for determining expenditure patterns, although to those who adhere to Gorz's depiction of the 'caring professions' such a denial of responsibility is no great loss. Yet what is implicitly behind FMI is not freedom but greater control. The allocation of funds to service units is given, *not* to spend as the units deem appropriate, but to perform certain definable activities which are specified in and through the expectations and accountability demands of 'principals'. It is, in theory, a redefinition of tasks to be performed using the financial and accountability vehicle for this purpose. As such, using the accountability language contained in Figures 1 and 2, relationships become more 'contractual' whereby process, performance, programme and policy become defined through the expectations and the resulting reports to 'principals'. In this situation the freedoms of the 'agent' are heavily curtailed, trust is dissipated and the potential for value conflict between 'agent' and 'principal' increases.

It is true to say, although there are clear signs that the pressures are increasing, that the full expression of FMI has not to date been at quite this extreme. It was also anticipated that FMI would find different expressions in different public sector areas (cf. Jackson, 1988). This is indeed the case. However, it is also the case that the full expression of this model in terms of definable, measurable, output expectations in relation to resource usage has yet to be fully worked through (see Broadbent, Laughlin and Read, 1991; Laughlin and Broadbent, 1991, 1993; Laughlin, Broadbent and Shearn, 1992, for more details). Devolution of financial responsibility is in place, yet the expectations concerning what outputs should be achieved through these resources are only starting to emerge. However, two things are already clear. First, the increasing ability of the 'principal' – the entity designated as supplying the resources – to define the nature of professional activities of the 'agent', is clearly in place. Prior to 1979 a similar institutional arrangement was in existence to the one described above for the Church of England. Institutional 'buffers', such as Local Education Authorities, or District Health Authorities, existed. These 'buffers' not only provided an administrative machinery to supply the requisite resources for the 'agents', the service units such as schools and hospitals, for them to perform their self-defined professional work, they kept the financial 'principal', interpreted as the government, from any potentially unnecessary intrusion. However, the 'principal' is no longer the provider of resource to *enable* professional work to occur as defined according to professional norms. Neither are the institutional 'buffers' allowed to perform their buffering role. Both are to work in concert to transfer resources *with expectations*. The 'principal' becomes the new definer of these professional activities and these definitions become passed down through the financial transfers being allocated through a redefined administrative machinery – e.g. the new 'funding councils' intended, in the longer term, to replace the Local Education Authorities and the making of District Health Authorities into clearly defined 'purchasing' bodies. Second, the definition of these expectations is being increasingly circumscribed by the nature of measurement. Particularly accounting-type output measures are being linked to input resources. To date, this process is far from completed, but the overall direction is clear.

To the 'agents' much of this change, with its 'commodification' of tasks, is a de-professionalization of activities which clashes with professional values. From the perspective of the 'agents', the introduction of FMI in the public sector brings what Gorz calls 'economic reason' into areas where it is deemed to be inappropriate. As indicated above, Gorz's analysis makes plain that the activities of the 'caring professions' cannot be programmed in the way that FMI sets out to do – these activities are not programmable in the way 'economic reason' requires. Gorz's analysis does not rule out the relevance of 'economic reason', but is at pains to point out that it has its limits. Yet, sadly, its proponents seem 'unaware of how narrow its proper limits are' (Gorz, 1989 p. 2). Instead, it is offered as a cure-all for all 'principal/agent' relationships. In some cases, this may be appropriate, or may not be significant enough to threaten the nature of the activities of the 'agent'. However, in others, it becomes a 'perversion or negation of the meaning' (Gorz, 1989: 132–33) of the activities themselves. The chances of this being the case with the 'caring professions' is high. The introduction of programmable, measurable expectations undermines the very nature of the gift-relationship that is the basis of many of the activities that cannot be so neatly packed.

The overall direction of change is seen by the professions as a dangerous 'secularization process', one which needs to be resisted because it inevitably clashes with the expectations of professional values and norms (see Laughlin, Broadbent, Shearn and Willig-Atherton, 1994; Laughlin, Broadbent and Willig-Atherton 1994b). As such, the overall direction of change sets inevitable clashes with the new breed of 'principals' which FMI changes have generated. Unlike the Church of England where these professional values are acknowledged, respected and protected, this situation no longer applies in the public sector. Despite the extensive disquiet from a wide spectrum of society, the Conservative government in the UK appears determined to fully implement FMI across all public sector programmes. It is busy creating a new breed of 'principals' who are determined to tightly programme and define the nature of professional activities. Of course such an agenda is not overtly declared. Rather, the 'reforms' are dressed as 'improving' education, or health, or whatever. However, any even-handed evaluation of whether this is actually occurring is not being undertaken and this alone tends to suggest some other agenda at work. A not unreasonable conclusion is that we are witnessing attempts to de-professionalize the 'caring professions'.

Resistance in the caring professions

Given that reforms are being currently implemented and that, for professional reasons, resentment is high about this imposition, it is not unreasonable to assume that professionals will not lightly accept the dictates of their new 'principals', or the new 'economic reason' inherent in them. Evidence to date suggests that this is indeed the case. Initial observations from a comprehensive study over time of a number of schools and GP practices imply a skilful and complex absorption process of the changes, minimizing their intrusion into the 'sacred' core of the institutions (Broadbent, Laughlin, Shearn and Dandy, 1993; Laughlin, Broadbent, Shearn and Willig-Atherton, 1994; Laughlin, Broadbent and Willig-Atherton, 1994). Head teachers and other senior staff in schools, together with practice managers and nurses in GP practices, are being set aside to soak up the changes. Thus, by varying forms of organizational arrangements, the perceived core values of teaching and health can continue unhindered by the intrusion of 'economic reason'. This is possible since, as yet, the expectations of the 'principals' are not yet refined enough to prevent this absorption process.

It is interesting to note, therefore, that new, if informal, 'buffering' or 'absorbing' mechanisms are emerging in the public sector. The idea of absorption is central to the roles of the 'agent/principals' in the Church of England, as was the case with the pre-1979 'buffers' (another set of 'agent/principals') in the public sector. However, in both cases these are and were, in the case of the public sector, institutionalized into definable and accepted roles. However, in the case of the public sector, this institutional support has been removed. The new informal 'buffers' are the organizational reaction to a problem which the professional 'agents' have solved through certain definable arrangements. Unlike the Church of England, however, pressures are continuing to be exerted and advertised as the 'need' for change. Eventually, it is possible that the informal public sector 'buffers' may well end up being a 'colonizing' force for change. Being part of the 'agent' institution, and with growing pressures on the services from the 'principals', they might cease their informal 'buffering' role, change 'sides' and assist the operationalization of, rather than absorb, the new expectations. This has not happened to date, but it is not impossible. A change of this magnitude has already been noted in other organizations (cf. Laughlin, 1991; Dent, 1992).

Conclusion

Rather than summarize all the arguments given above, it is important to highlight the central conclusions of this chapter. Quite simply, my intention has been to raise questions about the legitimacy of a 'principal' always having the right to define the nature of the activities of the 'agent'. The possibility for contesting this as a right, together with the ramifications for understanding the nature of the accountability relationship, have been the central themes of this chapter.

Perhaps, in ending, I could raise two points which not only summarize the argument in a little more detail, but also raise matters which must await further research and papers. First is a set of issues related to the dominant theme of the paper – that of rights. A key question is when, and in what circumstances, should the rights of 'higher principals' overrule the 'rights' of economic 'principals'? This chapter has only partially addressed this concern. The assumption behind current models of accountability, even those of a more contextual nature as depicted in Figures 1 and 2, is that this is not even an area for debate.

Ownership of financial resources is assumed to give the 'principal' rights to have certain 'things' either exchanged for, or done in lieu of, the transfer of resources. But the point of this chapter is to make plain that a 'rebellion' by certain 'agents' to these dictates – in some circumstances – is not without reason. Rebellion can ensue because they are following the demands of 'higher principals'. The assumption, in this chapter, is that the wishes of these 'higher principals' should predominate – at least on occasions where the demands of the economic 'principals' requires conduct that clashes with the values and concerns of these 'higher principals'. Whether this reason is justifiable, or whether the wishes of the economic 'principals' should begin to guide the conduct of 'agents', is of critical importance, but must wait for further analysis. At least what the chapter accomplishes is to put such a question on the research agenda, rather than simply assume that 'he or she who pays the piper plays the tune'.

Second, in this debate about 'rights', accountability processes appear as central. What I have raised in this chapter are not two, but three forms of accountability processes. First is where 'accounts' are designed to satisfy the formal requirements of economic 'principals', where contracts rather than trust predominate. Second is where 'accounts' are designed to satisfy the informal requirements of economic 'principals', where there is high trust in the 'agents' to act in interests of 'principals'. Both of these forms are more traditional appreciations of the accountability relationship. The form of these different 'accounts' have not been extensively discussed in this chapter. Inevitably, the former will constitute more formal 'accounts', similar to those with which accountants are familiar, with a tendency towards measurability of action and outcome. The latter, on the other hand, will be markedly different from this. They will invariably be much more informal but, to date, little insights on their design is available. Munro (1994) has, however, started the process of defining some of the parameters of these informal 'accounts'.

A third form of 'accounts', the less traditional accountability reports which have been discussed in this chapter, exists in relation to satisfying the needs of 'higher principals'. I have only addressed this aspect tangentially in this chapter. What remains unclear, therefore, is the actual nature and design of these 'accounts'. This, like so many themes in the paper, must await future research to answer. The important point to note is that to follow the dictates of 'higher principals' does not mean that the necessity for 'accounts', in an accountability framework, becomes unnecessary. This much is clear.

References

Armstrong, P. (1991) Contradiction and Social Dynamics in the Capitalist Agency Relationship. *Accounting, Organizations and Society*, **16** (5/6) pp. 1–25.

Birkett, W.P. (1988) Concepts of Accountability, Paper presented to the British Accounting Association Annual Conference, Trent Polytechnic, 1988.

Broadbent, J., Dietrich, M. and Laughlin, R. (forthcoming) The Development of Principal–Agent, Contracting and Accountability Relationships in the Public Sector: Conceptual and Cultural Problems. *Critical Perspectives on Accounting*.

Broadbent, J., Laughlin, R. and Read, S. (1991) Recent Financial and Administrative Changes in the NHS: A Critical Theory Analysis. *Critical Perspectives on Accounting*, **2** (1) pp. 1–29.

Broadbent, J., Laughlin, R., Shearn, D. and Dandy, N. (1993) Implementing Local Management of Schools: A Theoretical and Empirical Analysis. *Research Papers in Education*, **8**, pp. 149–76.

Dent, J.F. (1991) Accounting and Organizational Cultures: A Field Study of the Emergence of a New Organizational Reality. *Accounting, Organizations and Society*, **16** (8), pp. 705–32.

Eliade, M. (1959) *The Sacred and the Profane: The Nature of Religion*, Harcourt, Brace and World, New York.

Efficiency Unit (1982) *Efficiency and Effectiveness in the Civil Service*, Cmnd 8616, HMSO, London.

Fox, A. (1974) *Beyond Contract: Work, Power and Trust Relations*, Faber, London.

Friedson, E. (1970a) *Profession of Medicine*, Dodd, Mead and Co, New York.

Friedson, E. (1970b) *Professional Dominance: The Social Structure of Medical Care*, Aldine Publishing Co, Chicago.

Gallhofer, S. and Haslam, J. (1991) The Aura of Accounting in the Context of a Crisis: Germany and the First World War. *Accounting, Organizations and Society*, **16** (5/6), pp. 487–520.

Gorz, A. (1989) *Critique of Economic Reason*, (trans G. Handyside and C. Turner) Verso, London.

Gray, R.H. (1983) 'Accounting, Financial Reporting and Not-for-Profit Organisations'. *AUTA Review*, **15** pp. 3–23.

Gray, R.H., Owen, D.L. and Maunders, K.T. (1987) *Corporate Social Accounting: Accounting and Accountability*, Prentice Hall, Hemel Hempstead.

Greer, P. (1994) *Transforming Central Government: The Next Steps Initiative*, Open University Press, Buckingham.

Heald, D. (1983) *Public Expenditure: Its Defence and Reform*, Martin Robertson, London.

Hood, C. (1991) A Public Management for All Seasons?. *Public Administration,* **69** (Spring) pp. 3–19.

Jackson, P.M. (1982) *The Political Economy of Bureacracy*, Philip Allan, London.

Jackson, P. (1988) (ed.) *Financial Management Initiative*, CIPFA, London.

Johnson, N. (1974) Defining Accountability. *Public Administration Bulletin,* **17** (December) pp. 3–13.

Johnson, T.J. (1972) *Professions and Power*, Macmillan, London.

Larson, M.S. (1972) *The Rise of Professionalism: A Sociological Analysis*, University of California Press, Berkeley.

Laughlin, R. (1984) *The Design of Accounting Systems: A General Theory with an Empirical Study of the Church of England*, Unpublished Ph.D. Thesis, University of Sheffield.

Laughlin, R. (1988) Accounting in its Social Context: An Analysis of the Accounting Systems of the Church of England. *Accounting, Auditing and Accountability,* **1** (2) pp. 19–42.

Laughlin, R. (1990) A Model of Financial Accountability and the Church of England. *Financial Accountability and Management,* **6** (2) pp. 93–114.

Laughlin, R.C. (1991) Environmental Disturbances and Organisational Transitions and Transformations: Some Alternative Models. *Organization Studies,* **12** (2) pp. 209–32.

Laughlin, R. and Broadbent, J. (1991) *Accounting and Juridification: An Exploration with Specific Reference to the Public Sector in the United Kingdom.* Proceedings from the Third Interdisciplinary Perspectives on Accounting Conference, Manchester, pp. 1.10.1–1.10.16.

Laughlin, R. and Broadbent, J. (1993) Accounting and Law: Partners in the Juridification of the Public Sector in the UK?. *Critical Perspectives on Accounting,* **4** (4) pp. 337–68.

Laughlin, R., Broadbent, J. and Shearn, D. (1992) Recent Financial and Accountability Changes in General Practice: An Unhealthy Intrusion into Medical Autonomy?. *Financial Accountability and Management,* **8** (2) pp. 129–48.

Laughlin, R., Broadbent, J., Shearn, D. and Willig-Atherton, H. (1994) Absorbing LMS: The Coping Mechanism of a Small Group. *Accounting, Audition and Accountability Journal,* **7** (1) pp. 59–85.

Laughlin, R., Broadbent, J. and Willig-Atherton, H. (1994) Recent Financial and Administrative Changes in GP Practices: Initial Experiences and Effects. *Accounting, Auditing and Accountability Journal,* **7** (3) pp. 96–124.

Macintosh, N.B. and Scapens, R.W. (1990) Structuration Theory in Management Accounting, *Accounting, Organizations and Society,* **15** (5) pp. 455–77.

Miller, P. and Rose, N. (1991) Programming the Poor: Poverty Calculation and Expertise, in *Deprivation, Social Welfare and Expertise* (ed. J. Lehto) Report 7 National Agency for Welfare and Health Research, Helsinki, pp. 117–40.

Munro, R. (1993) *Just When You Thought it Safe to Enter the Water: Multiple Control Technologies and the Making of Members' Moves.* Paper Presented to the ESRC Interdisciplinary Perspectives on Accounting Workshop, January 1993, Manchester.

Munro, R. (1994) *Calling for 'Accounts', Monsters, Membership, Work and Management Accounting.* Proceedings from the Fourth Interdisciplinary Perspectives on Accounting Conference, Manchester, 1994, pp. 4.9.2.–4.9.11.

Richards, S. (1987) The Financial Management Initiative, in *Reshaping Central Government* (eds J. Grettan and A. Harrison) Policy Journals, London, pp. 22–41.

Roberts, J. (1991) The Possibilities of Accountability. *Accounting, Organizations and Society,* **16** (4) pp. 355–68.

Roberts J. and Scapens, R. (1985) Accounting Systems and Systems of Accountability – Understanding Accounting Practices in Their Organisational Contexts. *Accounting, Organizations and Society,* **10** (4) pp. 443–56.

Stewart, J.D. (1984) The Role of Information in Public Accountability, in *Issues in Public Sector Accounting,* (eds A.G. Hopwood, and C.R. Tomkins) Philip Allan, pp. 13–34.

Tricker, R.I. (1983) Corporate Responsibility, Institutional Governance and the Roles of Accounting Standards, in *Accounting Standard Setting: An International Perspective* (eds M. Bromwich, and A. Hopwood) Pitman, London pp. 27–41.

Zifcak, S. (1994) *New Managerialism: Administrative Reform in Whitehall and Canberra* Open University Press, Buckingham.

13 Spaces of accountability: systems of accountability in a multinational firm

Katrine Kirk and Jan Mouritsen

Introduction

With activities spread across the world the management of multinationals often rely heavily, if not exclusively, on accounting information. Direct supervision cannot be carried out across large distances. There are thus strong pressures to introduce means of communication and control in geographically dispersed firms that reduce the friction of space. The friction of space – it takes time, money and effort to travel – is often offset by an informational mode of management that creates and feeds on accounting information (Cray, 1990; Hedlund and Zander, 1985; Hulbert and Brandt, 1980; Mouritsen, 1995; Sheth and Eshgi, 1990).

An accounting system creates and presents certain financial and economic relations for a firm. It portrays headquarters and subsidiaries as a set of relationships that are produced to facilitate interaction and control. It is an *intermediary* (Law, 1994) which 'translates' between contexts, in order that headquarters can act on and intervene in the affairs of subsidiaries. Through accounting systems, the concerns of headquarters govern the translation of subsidiaries' activities in ways that present them as integral to headquarters' strategies.

So, accounting systems bring subsidiaries 'closer' to headquarters. Budgets, targets and accounting reports make subsidiaries visible and facilitate intervention with a distance. Geographical distance is translated into paper – or a computer screen – as deviancies from expected results. The informational mode of management produces a sense of subsidiaries being 'directly supervisable', even if in a form where their activities are translated – and decontextualized from the particular local complexities – to suit the language of accounting performance.

The translation between the context of subsidiary and context of headquarters is not automatic. Although an intermediary is required, it does not act on its own. An intermediary such as accounting may speak loudly but never does so without a set of actors that puts them in motion and responds to them (Roberts and Scapens, 1985). Accountability – the ongoing demand for and provision of explanations, justifications, and excuses (Giddens, 1984; Munro and Hatherly, 1993) – edits and gives importance to accounting performance. An accounting system is important only if mobilized; it is not inherently part of organizational systems of accountability but may be mobilized and used. Its importance depends on people taking it seriously and acting towards it and, in a sense, it exists only in being drawn upon.

However, as accounting often connects between organizational activities and their relevance to owners and financial markets, profitability measured in accounting terms is typically, not to say always, an integral part of modern organizational life. Therefore, accounting performance is often part of firms' systems of accountability. This is what makes accountability a particular accomplishment in most firms. It is often an *outcome* of the mobilization of accounting performance by and around which people are deemed (in)competent, (un)reliable, or (un)trustworthy. People have to convince others – typically on grounds that somehow incorporate accounting performance – that their decisions and actions are reasonable and sensible even in situations where accounting performance is prima facie unsatisfactory.

This raises two related questions. Where does the space for accounting come from – how is it *produced*? And how is it involved in situated interaction – how is it *mobilized*? A space for accounting is an effect formed between the contexts of production and mobilization of accounting performance. Accounting performance is produced as a structured, ongoing and recurrent practice of informing about the firm's affairs in a fixed format. It is mobilized in being laid out and in being drawn into explanations of its implications. The space for accounting thus involves a dialectical relationship where its production and mobilization relate institutional and local conduct to each other in reproduced systems of accountability.

Outline of the chapter

In this chapter the two questions of production and mobilization of accounting systems frame a discussion of accountability in a Danish multinational, Danco, which established a subsidiary in Canada, Cansub.[1] For Danco, the accounting system is considered a potent intermediary that guides the construction of Cansub as a profit centre. Danco's management control system relies on the profit centre principle. Each subsidiary is given the authority to decide costs and revenues to produce a profit to which it is accountable. In this way, Cansub's characteristics are defined by its membership of a class of subsidiaries rather than by its uniqueness. Cansub is produced by Danco as a repetition of the management control procedures that exist in all other subsidiaries. The production of Cansub as an organizational space is dependent on a corporate management control strategy based on the profit centre mind.

The mobilization of the accounting system is organized around the production of explanations that connect Cansub and Danco through accounting performance. In these explanations, carried out against what everybody saw as meagre accounting performance, sales and manufacturing activities are important significations involved in complex ways in the production of explanations. They do not receive attention from headquarters independently of the explanations and translations mobilized in systems of accountability. Particularly, the repair work in accountability (explanations, justifications, and excuses) involves debating the accounting performance – profits and productivity – which has pointed Cansub out as a loss-maker. This accounting performance is ambiguous, however, because it cannot account for all the conditions that make losses come about. It is not always bad management that leads to losses; it may be market conditions or inadequate production technology. Similarly, it may be loss-making 'only' in the short run while the long run may be profitable. The allocation of blame and credits for Cansub's accounting performance is a complex system of account-ability concerning the fragile project of pointing out competence, reliability, and trustworthiness.

These points will be elaborated in the following sections. The next section discusses the production of the space for accounting. It illuminates how the accounting system inscribes subsidiaries according to the headquarters' strategies rather than to their own uniqueness. The third section turns to the mobilization of accounting systems in systems of accountability. It illustrates how accounting performance is repaired through talk. The fourth section attempts to draw these two points together. It suggests that the space for accounting is simultaneously a condition for and an effect of accountability. Even if accounting performance can be argued to be 'wrong', it continuously re-creates agendas and concerns for managers to deal with.

The production of a space for accounting

In categorizing Cansub, accounting systems construct it as an organizational space amenable to intervention at a distance. Categorization is 'to render indiscriminately different things equivalent, to group the objects and events and people around us into classes, and to respond to them as to their class membership rather than to their uniqueness' (Bruner *et al.*, 1956: 1). Danco's interest in categorizing Cansub lies in the prospect of controlling it – or responding to it – based on criteria borrowed from outside rather than inside it. According to an outside view, the production of Cansub as organizational space is less a mirroring and representation of it than a construction of it for its potential inclusion in a different space. The distinction between headquarters and subsidiary echoes a distinction between centre and periphery and illustrates that all spaces do not count equally.

The work of centres is to mobilize peripheries. In this mobilization, centres categorize the affairs of a periphery so that it becomes an extension of the former's strategies. The periphery is not interesting to the centre for its uniqueness. On the contrary, peripheries are interesting when centres can produce, categorize, and inscribe them so that they are amenable to intervention (Miller and Rose, 1990). In producing spaces, centres re-create the remote places to be fitted into a set of concerns which belong to the centre.

In multinationals, headquarters often render subsidiaries visible via accounting systems measuring their activities and reporting their consequences as budget perfor-mance, profitability, and productivity. Through accounting systems a 'regime of truth' is formed about events (Loft, 1986: 140). The accounting shapes what 'counts' and produces an optic by which events produced at the subsidiary can be translated (into profits) and transported (via information systems) to headquarters. Headquar-ters, in this way, aligns the subsidiary with its own interests and concerns. This alignment is created by the accounting system's idea of responsibility manufactured for headquarters to be able to look to its interests and concerns. But, then, what is Danco's accounting system specifically?

Danco's accounting system

Danco has subsidiaries in several countries most of which are in Europe (Eurosubs) and only one outside Europe in Canada (Cansub). They sell the same product range, just as they use (or, at least will use) the same production technology. The products are known for their quality and they are sold at a premium price. Danco's subsidiaries are given the responsibility to produce and sell the products. In a profit centre this adds up to a profit responsibility, as the subsidiaries are given the task to manage costs and revenues in an integrated form.

In principle, Danco requires only a limited set of information about the subsidiaries' affairs. Danco is interested in the results of the subsidiaries' affairs rather than in the affairs themselves, and information on profits and profitability is, in principle, adequate for Danco to monitor the subsidiaries. They are given maximum freedom to manage their own business without interference from Danco. Danco is quite explicit about this, and it clearly pointed out that performance evaluation is based on subsidiaries' profitability, and they are given 'maximum freedom with responsibility . . . [as] Danco has decentralized decision-making authority that entails tight control . . . [so that subsidiaries are] challenged to choose the right way to go'.

This kind of independence also requires delivery. It is not only to do a good job in sales and production given the circumstances. It is also to accommodate the singularity in circumstances of the various markets so that whatever differences between subsidiaries, they will be levelled out before performance evaluation takes place. As Danco points out, subsidiaries are 'challenged to choose the right way to go' because of the management control system. They are not only compared, but they also have to look to the others to learn about the necessary profit targets. The differences in competition and knowledge of the production process, for example, are seen as less important than profitability itself.

Danco's insight is accounting performance. This accounting performance structures and underscores the firm's formal organization and allocation of responsibility that separate the subsidiaries and constructs them as able to determine, or at least influence, the consequences of their actions. Accounting performance is an individualizing activity that constructs subsidiaries as causal mechanisms between a budget and a set of outcomes (Miller, 1992; Roberts, 1991). It sets out a chain of command that guides managers in their search for explanations of surprising accounting performance, such as variance from budgets and targets. Such variances can

> direct attention to persons who should have answers. In looking at revenues, costs, or variances, we should determine whom we should talk to in that specific situation.
>
> (Horngren and Foster, 1991: 190)

In multinational firms, overseeing production and sales activities in different countries is hampered by distance. Accounting performance transforms the geographical place – with its topography, situated work, and organizational struggles – into a digit which exists in a computer system whose place as electronic panopticon is more in headquarters than in the profit centre (Sewell and Wilkinson, 1992). The digit is freed from the limiting physical ordering of work as it produces a language-form on numerals. Through abstraction, standardization, calculation, categorization, and quantification, numerals enable people who are not geographically present to understand and potentially intervene in the action of remote places (Latour, 1987; Miller and O'Leary, 1987; Miller and Rose, 1990). By letting accounting translate between peripheries and centres of calculation, accounting inscribes organizational life and provides a basis for overcoming absence (Robson, 1992). Accounting inscriptions decontextualize local action by being mobile, stable and combinable and thus provide a basis for translations between present and absent settings (Latour, 1988). The power accruing from such numerals is that they facilitate comparisons of various kinds: with budgets, with other organizational entities, with other organizations, and over time. Through these comparisons, centres attempt to evaluate relative efficiency and effectiveness of peripheries and to identify deviances to be explained.

To implement the power of comparison, the subsidiaries have to be constructed in similar ways; belonging to a class. This manoeuvre involves disregarding the uniqueness of each subsidiary and creates boundaries and contexts that separate the subsidiaries as a class from Danco. In effect, Danco may use the same means of control vis-à-vis all subsidiaries. Danco thus creates a technology of managing which idealizes and generalizes management problems of the different subsidiaries, and the complexities, subtleties, and uniqueness of the subsidiaries' work are marginalized. The similarities between subsidiaries are heralded.

Figure 1 illustrates the mechanisms that make Danco's subsidiaries similar and let them belong to a class. Their products are similar and their specifications are of high quality. Production people in Cansub are just as experienced as in the Eurosubs, as people from Europe are transferred to Canada. The management control systems are similar. The profit centre principle applies to all subsidiaries irrespective of geographical location, and the budgetary controls are similar. In all, the structuring of production, sales, and management control is largely similar. The subsidiaries belong to a class which is defined by its relation to the management control system.

From Figure 1, management control systems portray organizational spaces as similar (the first four rows of Figure 1). Of these, the issues of organization, financial control, and budgetary control show *how the subsidiaries are made similar*. Possible differences, for example, regarding the maturity of markets and the experience of the technology, are marginalized (the last four rows of Figure 1). This construction of organizational spaces as similar – i.e. they look alike – enables Danco to use its knowledge from and about Eurosubs to make its judgement about Cansub and make comparisons which Cansub's management have little to say about. The similarities between the subsidiaries are centred, while the differences are marginalized.

Similarity makes each subsidiary, such as Cansub, amenable to comparison and intervention on grounds that are more available to Danco than to any of the subsidiaries' managers. These grounds, for example, concern the history of productivity, performance and profitability of the other subsidiaries. Their histories, although all more than eight years old and probably partly forgotten or idealized, stand out as a benchmark for Cansub. At least, Danco says, 'competition between subsidiaries alerts them to improve'.

In this way, Cansub is inserted into the context of Danco's problems and strategies rather than mapped according to its own unique characteristics. It is more an *alignment of relations* between Cansub and Danco than a mapping of the affairs within Cansub since these are constructed primarily to help intervention. For Cansub, the

	Cansub	Eurosubs
Product specifications	Products are known and established in Europe. Specifications similar in Canada and Europe.	
Organization	Danco-people manage Cansub, particularly in production. Sales and marketing managers are locals.	
Financial control	Subsidiaries are profit centres. Budgets are approved by Danco, if they acknowledge its targets concerning growth and productivity.	
Budgetary control	Quarterly performance evaluation: budget performance, profits, and productivity.	
The market's knowledge of the product	Product has bad image, and the market is not accustomed to similar products.	The product is well-known and the market has a tradition for using it.
Position in the market	Danco is virtually unknown in the geographical region, and the market share is 0%.	Danco is well-known with market shares between 80–95%.
Process of becoming a subsidiary	Newly established production site without any previous sales.	Gradual involvement: export, sales agents, sales subsidiaries, added production.
Production technology	Most is old as it is acquired via an acquisition.	All new and internally developed.
Danco's expectations concerning the subsidiaries	Quick growth as evidenced in strategy plans.	Steady growth. Predictable sales figures, and plans and budgets are typically held.

Figure 1
Similarities and differences between Cansub and Eurosubs according to the debates.

production of an accounting profit is not dependent purely on its own decisions. Part of Cansub's set-up involves a transfer of a technology and a particular range of quality products. These strategic decisions are prior to Cansub's profitability problem, as local managers struggle with understanding the market and making the technology transfer work. Although Cansub is formally 'on its own', Danco exercises its influence on Cansub's profitability by stating a set of strategic parameters, borrowed from other subsidiaries beyond the control of Cansub. Also, although Cansub has no formal links with other subsidiaries in terms, for example, of internal transfers, the Eurosubs do present a context of performance against which Cansub is measured and evaluated. Cansub is thus hardly independent of the Eurosubs, irrespective of its set-up as profit centre.

Anticipation of accountability

Managerial decisions do not flow automatically from the visibility achieved through accounting performance. However, as accounting performance reappears regularly its anticipation influences people's conduct. If headquarters is known, or at least expected, to act upon subsidiaries in ways that are based on accounting performance, the latter may incorporate this expectation into their conduct. The anticipation of an accounting system emphasis in accountability disciplines managers and helps construct a vocabulary of agendas, motives, and concepts of performance. The awareness of headquarters' readiness to intervene makes subsidiaries exposed to an ongoing examination where possibly, or likely, they have to explain, justify, or excuse their accounting performance.

In the subsidiaries, the accounting numbers in quarterly performance reports are more than scorecards; they alert managers and orient their actions. They edit the accountability issues and preconstitute them in profits and productivity. The mentality to let accounting numbers count dramatizes their power. When Danco requires explanations and intervenes, Cansub gives way and accepts that 'they can do what they want. It is their money we are spending'. In comparing the subsidiaries, Danco wants them to be each other's environment, to 'challenge them to choose the right way to go'.

'Control' is often portrayed as a simple after-the-fact activity: checking whether past action meets requirements and standards. However, control is also an intervention into the activity being subjected to surveillance; to control is also to instil awareness of control (Deetz, 1992; Roberts, 1991). Defined in this way, accounting systems mediate a 'set of values and ideals about what is approved and what is disapproved' (Macintosh and Scapens, 1990: 460). People incorporate their knowledge of being controlled into their actions. When the subsidiary's action is aligned with headquarters' expectations, it produces an ex ante effect.

The knowledge that one will be subjected to control within the limitations of a specific accounting performance will condition people's conduct. Acceptance of the control relationship involves conforming with organizational or institutional norms. This is demonstrated through drawing on accounting systems in a way that signals compliance with standards of performance. However, this more structured form of accounting visibility is a potentiality rarely fully realized. Often, the anticipation of accountability will make people strategic. In a 'dialectic of control' they will try to evade its discipline through repairing (explaining, justifying, excusing) on accounting performance in its mobilization (Argyris, 1990; Dermer and Lucas, 1986; Goffman, 1959).

The mobilization of a space for accounting

To be consequential, accounting performance has to be laid out, put into context, and acted upon in specific organizational situations and episodes. Accounting performance is a medium mobilized by people to explore, learn about, demand, and provide explanations about others' affairs. A subordinate and a superior debate accounting performance and attempt to explain what is going on beyond the accounting figures. To provide an account is to produce an explanation that connects accounting results with a specific context often questioning, if not rejecting, the accounting performance as a reflection of the firm's conditions, problems and goals.

The mobilization of accounting performance in accountability is oriented towards seeking explanations for surprises. In doing this, superiors attempt to detect whether subordinate efforts have been sensible and, thus, learn whether a manager has 'really' been reliable, competent, and trustworthy. Accountability in this situation may be said to *repair* accounting and explain why the possible negative consequences of (unfavourable) accounting performance are to be implemented lightly, if at all. Excuses may be produced to argue that a particular outcome was not inflicted by the person held responsible, and justifications are produced to argue that a seemingly negative outcome is positive (Lyman and Scott, 1970: 114). Justifications and excuses are employed by the subordinate who responds to the superior's inquiry into accounting performance.

In the example at hand, Danco conducted quarterly accountability sessions with its subsidiaries based on profits, budget performance, and productivity. Cansub was new and had no history within Danco. Danco was aware that this created ambiguity for performance evaluation, and it accepted (for a while) Cansub's accounting performance in spite of its making losses. Cansub could excuse 'red figures' referring to its lack of knowledge of the market (because the product was new) and of the production technology (which was also new). Accounting performance was deemed imprecise, although not irrelevant, and additional explanations in terms of strategy beyond it were of relevance. However, this justification did not continue to be strong. After some quarters, Danco started to ask more forcefully into the affairs of Cansub, and Danco built its arguments more based on the overall management control system than on the uniqueness of Cansub. The demand for explanations from Danco changed in nature, and a new dynamic was created, some of which is illustrated in Figure 2.

Figure 2 shows that Cansub sees accounting performance differently than Danco. While Danco assumes that the management control system is in order since it works in other subsidiaries, Cansub suggests that Danco's insight be limited. Particularly, it is argued, market conditions are different from Danco's view of them, and the technology has special problems in Cansub. This creates a pattern of talk by which Danco maintains the importance of accounting performance while Cansub attempts to repair it, editing and adding elements to its explanation. It suggests that the management control system is not able to capture properly the causes of the variances observed in accounting reports.

The accounting performance portrays the subsidiary as red figures, as an unbroken line of losses. These were negotiated, debated and reconstructed – in short, repaired – through talk. The process of reparation involves questioning the validity of the accounting system's ability to accurately reflect the business concerns of the subsidiary. Mediating factors were such as the market and the production technology (see also Figure 1).

Subject	Danco quotations	Cansub quotations
Corporate reporting requirements	If new subsidiaries can't fulfil requirements, something is wrong with their control system.	The corporate planning and budget system has been developed for a mature organization. We have to make up the data . . . it's useless.
Accounting information relevance	We don't ask them for anything they wouldn't need anyway to manage the company well.	Management accounting replaces trust.
Intensifying control	We want to be sure that things are going in the right direction.	Who knows the market – managers who are 5,000 miles away or us who work in it every day?
Forecasting product costs	Even if they don't have accurate information, an intelligent guess is better than nothing. At least we know that they are being forced to think about costs.	They consider it more important to get the figures in the correct format than to get correct figures. We tell them something to make them happy, but it's a waste of time.
Subsidiary duties	It is a major concern that Cansub is losing so much money. We have to keep a close eye on what they are doing to reduce our risks. They can say what they like; the money they are losing is Danco's.	They can ask for anything they want, and we will do our best to give it to them. It's their money we are spending over here.
Local versus corporate tensions	Subsidiaries always complain that headquarters doesn't understand. It's nothing to worry about.	Danco has no experience in North America. We can't succeed before they realize it is a different kind of market. People don't care about specs. They care about price and stupid things like colour.
Intraorganizational relationships	The Group as a whole can save money in the long run by treating each other a little more professionally. . . . Competition between subsidiaries alerts them to improve.	We would like to trust other departments and make oral agreements, but the case of the packaging machine (: bad delivery from another Danco entity) forces us to make formal contracts. It takes time, and it really shouldn't be necessary.

Figure 2
Talk in
accountability.

The resistance to accounting performance introduces a dialectic of control by which its version of Cansub's problems is called into doubt. Cansub is not in disagreement with Danco's rights to require accounting performance. Cansub questions the basis on which Danco enforces the accounting version of its problems. All the issues raised question the relevance of the accounting performance. Cansub suggests that it is severely hampered by lack of real knowledge as they 'need to make up data'. The lack of 'knowledge of the market' makes Danco's requests meaningless for Cansub. Cansub starts telling 'them something to keep them happy', partly because systems have replaced the 'need to trust'. All these explanations are justifications which introduce Cansub's context and marginalize Danco's context. The latter is different. Danco's context is that subsidiaries always complain, that subsidiaries have to be pressured to develop normal managerial procedures based on calculations. Danco's perspective is that subsidiaries often evade formal plans and calculation and rely more on ad hoc processes.

Repair-work (explanations, justifications, excuses) is conducted against a hypothetical situation. Accounting performance is constantly challenged as poorly reflecting the situation of Cansub. It is debated against the hypothetical proposition that had the representation of the subsidiary's affairs and results been more 'appropriate', the grounds for accountability would have been quite different. The argument is that a 'correct accounting' would have minimized, if not effaced, the accountability problems. There is a *politics to explanation* partly because it is impossible firmly to know when an explanation is good enough. The ambiguity involved is that a situation designed to be certain through the production of a space for accounting is fragile. Accounting performance is loosely coupled to contextual intricacies in unique situations and episodes.

The warehouse affair

An example of situated repair-work is the story of the rented warehouse. Cansub was making a major sales effort in the fall of 1990 and the budgets were optimistic of its effects. In the beginning of 1991 sales suddenly increased dramatically, exceeding budgets by 30% for January, and the season was only just beginning. It seemed that the sales campaign had been more effective than management had dared to hope.

Estimates showed that, at this volume of sales, Cansub would be out of stock within six weeks with the current workforce (two shifts) and unable to fill incoming orders. Agreeing that it would be fatal for a small newcomer in the market to obtain a reputation for not delivering, Cansub management decided to take action. With the sudden increase in sales, it was decided to increase production and to rent an external warehouse immediately, because its own warehouse next to the plant would not be able to hold expected amounts of stock. The production line was increased from two to three shifts with the purpose of getting ahead before the expected big sales boom of the high season in April. A new warehouse would solve the current problem, and would come in use for long-term growth in volumes. A one-year contract was signed.

The chairman of Cansub's board, who is a Danco top manager, said in a later interview that he cautioned against making this decision, but the Cansub management was intent on doing it. According to him, three shifts represented 60–65% capacity utilization, and four shifts would have been possible. Thus Danco managers did not understand why Cansub managers felt so compelled to make a longer-term commitment on the warehouse just to handle a peak load.

In March, sales dropped to nearly zero. It was then discovered that a *change in tax legislation* had provided an incentive for potential customers to buy products quickly, draining expected future orders. Only a few of the regular customers had not placed orders in January, and few of the orders came from new customers.

Cansub management recognized the mistake (and identified it as a mistake) when it was brought up at a board meeting and explained what had happened. In the same breath, Cansub management explained that the effects of the sales campaign had not yet been realized but were expected very soon which justified keeping the three shifts in operation. The contract on the warehouse could not be helped.[2]

Top management in Danco were displeased. They felt that Cansub management could have avoided jumping to conclusions about the sudden growth in sales. One Danco manager's incredulous attitude was expressed in an interview: 'How could they think it was a result of their marketing campaign when they knew all the customers beforehand?'. Cansub's marketing manager answered: 'Many of our customers are large industrial contractors who purchase on behalf of their customers. Our strategy in the marketing campaign was to create an end-user demand for our quality, which would then create a pull demand from the industrial contractors'. Danco argued that the marketing department should be aware of the tax regulations of relevance to Cansub's products at all times: 'If they had been doing their job properly, this would not have happened'.

The 'warehouse affair' had occurred recently when we visited Cansub, and one board meeting had been held meanwhile. At this meeting, the Cansub managers agreed, the board members from Danco were patronizing. Danco accused Cansub of not having made a cost-benefit analysis before the two decisions, of not having listened to sound advice, and of not being attentive to the external factors influencing sales. The Danco board members spent much effort on trying to get Cansub managers to admit that they had been wrong (which Cansub insists they had already acknowledged before the meeting) and that the conclusion to be drawn from the affair was that they should make decisions based on rigorous calculations of future effects. Although Cansub acknowledged the mistake, they saw it as an unfortunate effect of an unanalysable environment, which could not have been foreseen at the time decisions were made.

Through such repair work Cansub and Danco try out their different *theories of causality* and attempt to clarify where responsibility lies and what it is. They debate which outcomes Cansub management should have been able to establish. Each tries to create a story by which performance gets located because of a series of events that Cansub management has or has not put in motion. Danco's point is that 'lack of proper management control systems', 'too little care about costs', the 'needs to reduce risk', and 'subsidiaries' normal complaints' lead to reduced profitability. Cansub, in contrast, suggests that 'lack of experience in the market', 'lack of trust' from Danco, and 'lack of insight into the technology' for the time being makes it a loss-maker.

Constructing causality

In episodes of accountability the debate concerns hypothetical issues that centre around the question of what would have happened if other decisions had been made. The chain of affairs that would have been set in motion had the decisions been different is difficult to unravel. Accounting performance is an ambiguous arbiter in this debate because the 'reasons' produced for variances from standards are rarely depicted in the accounting technique. The possibilities to rely solely on accounting performance to get final answers to intricate accountability problems are meagre.

The difficulty of knowing persuades Danco that it is not necessary to accept the theoretical principle of a profit centre management style. According to the profit centre principle, Cansub is to be controlled largely on its profits. Profits, their presence or absence, are seen to reflect most of, if not all, accountability issues, as the prospect that accounting performance can be read directly is emphasized. However, in accountability episodes, Danco does not allow this. In contrast, Danco probes the underlying activities in the cost and revenue segments of the firm separately. Danco disregards the profit centre principle and demands explanations about the details of decisions (such as the warehouse affair). In episodes of accountability, the boundaries of the intermediary are loosened up. The process of explaining, justifying and excusing involves a deferral of taking stock of whatever knowledge is available at a certain time. The probing is – in effect – a possible unending tour of exploration into the mechanisms that produce a certain accounting performance and the possible mechanisms that produce these mechanisms. In demanding and providing explanations, superior and subordinate engage in a spiral of talk that has no logical or clear-cut ending. To end talk is thus not innocent. Talk is a power-relationship where Danco defines when enough talk has been done. Danco may decide when explaining has gone far enough and can decide how much talk is necessary. Danco can also refuse to listen and close talk. This was the case when Danco chose to fire Cansub's CEO.

Talk does not guarantee that the parties involved come to an agreement where they are all satisfied. The resistance mobilized in talk is not easy to fend off honourably by Danco because Cansub's arguments do make sense. However, this resistance is not possible in the long run because Danco needs to justify Cansub according to a reasoning which is different from local explanations. Danco has to maintain that the management control system has the potential to challenge the subsidiaries 'to choose the right way to go'.[3] There is a limit to the possibilities of repair. Not only do subsidiaries need to be profitable, but they also need to be so within a decentralized management system that purports to play by rules that give all subsidiaries the same treatment. Danco, even if it wanted, cannot allow continuous losses because the other subsidiaries, the Eurosubs, would wonder.

Accountability and accounting performance

The space for accounting is an effect of the dialectic between its production and mobilization and is both the medium for and outcome of accountability. It is a durable medium because it is anticipated and acted upon. Its use reinforces its usefulness as it is only by being mobilized that it is shown to be taken seriously. The space for accounting is thus a medium as it recurs regularly in fixed format, and it is an outcome since it is mobilized as evaluation of competence, reliability, and trustworthiness.

Accounting systems are thus important intermediaries to the degree they support the relationship between localized organizational work, and broader institutional principles. Intermediaries act as media between lasting and unique practices and dramatize that 'institutions are constituted and reconstituted in the tie between the *durée* of the passing moment, and the *longue durée* of deeply sedimented time-space relations' (Giddens, 1979: 110). The intermediary is never 'merely' a formal technique but a technology that makes social relations durable (Latour, 1991). Accounting performance is neither formal/technical nor personal. It is neither the choice of subordinate nor of superior to discuss its relevance. They may disagree with it, but they cannot dispense with it; they may say that it is inappropriate, but they have to care about it and explain their position compared with it. It has to be discussed and as fully as possibly be integrated into the explanations reached at any episode of accountability. Accounting performance is an *obligatory passage* whose effect is 'stable relations of episodic power' (Clegg, 1989: 225). As an obligatory passage accounting performance reproduces in stable form the general agendas, issues, and concerns that go into and come out of contextual, situational episodic accountability.

Although accounting performance is repaired in and through talk, talk has an institutional dimension that gives superiors the right to be heard when they talk. Subordinates may attempt to reconstruct accounting through excuses and justifications, but the superiors – by virtue of their position within a hierarchy – have the right not to listen, or to raise their voices to end the debate. However, the superiors are also located in a situation that deems accounting performance important and are unable to avoid talking about it.

Accounting performance reappears constantly in fixed format. It breaks the evanescence of talk in accountability situations. Accounting is written by accountants but in situations that de-emphasize the writer (the accountant) as the author of the text.[4] The accounting text outlives the individual budgeter, budgetee, and accountant, and thus spreads in time and space beyond the individual and is written more for Danco than for the subsidiaries.

For example, Danco's management control system is not only applicable to all subsidiaries, but it is also seen as an important element in building the firm's competitiveness. The management control system, Danco insists, dramatizes the nature of modern management practices in paying extraordinary attention to, as Danco suggests, 'decentralized decision making authority that entails tight control' and has the effect that 'competition between subsidiaries alerts them to improve'. The accounting is related to, if not absorbing, the concerns modern managers should have; accounting is a broad cultural object that links situated practices to the social conditions of modern management work.

Accounting is therefore more than a means to compare different organizational spaces and to alert managers to learn from each other. It is deeply part of *managers' social qualifications* as the skills necessary to read, debate, and interpret accounting's accounts. Accounting performance is not a set of ad hoc scribbles on a piece of paper but systematic, if abstract, inscriptions of business issues and concerns. The consumption of accounting texts is undertaken in situated organizational episodes. This presupposes that managers can read 'accounting-scribbles' on the one hand, and not only understand but also accept their practical implications for decision making on the other (e.g. firing Cansub's CEO).

Between Cansub and Danco three issues are never debated as conditions of accountability, and although sometimes included in explanations they have an air of inevitability: common acceptance of the right of Danco to construct the accounting inscription; common acceptance of the view that profits should control actions;

common acceptance of the centrality of costs. Accountability, irrespective of the fragility of interpretation of accounting performance, is anchored in relations of domination that underscore the needs for business enterprises to be profitable. This institutional trait suggests the link between power, ownership of capital, the firm's resources and its spending. It legitimates explanations and the construction of possible appropriate measures. As Cansub's management suggests, not as an excuse but as an active self-disciplining procedure, Danco's intervention is seen as legitimate because 'it's their money we are spending'.

Conclusion

The space for accounting is an effect in two ways. It is produced as a set of calculations that pertain to and define the responsibilities accounting performance carves out and dramatizes. It is also an effect in its mobilization where it is part of an ongoing production and consumption of explanations that question the basis for a specific accounting performance. The space for accounting thus both resides in the production of an intermediary that makes a particular management control strategy durable. It also resides in the mobilization and consumption of this intermediary to explain, justify or excuse surprises. The space for accounting is an effect of the dialectic between production and mobilization of accounting systems in systems of accountability.

In this chapter this theme has been illustrated with case-material from a Danish multinational. The subsidiaries are constructed as profit centres and aligned with headquarters' strategies. The space for accounting is constructed more as a means for headquarters to monitor and intervene into subsidiaries' affairs than as a means to map them according to their own logic. The space for accounting is produced to overcome geographical distance and transport the subsidiary so that it becomes a supplement to headquarters' interests. This alignment attempts to conquer the friction of space and make subsidiaries 'directly supervisable' through an informational mode of management. The specific visibility constructed for profit centres is one which facilitates comparisons with budgets, over time or with other subsidiaries' performance. Performance is decoupled from sales and production activities, as these concerns are suppressed in profit centre accounting.

This space for accounting has its counterpart in situated explanations that contextualize accounting performance. The work of manufacturing products, selling, shipping and ensuring payments are arguments in explanations that connect to accounting performance.

Accountability exists as talk to justify or excuse a demand from a superior to explain. In producing explanations people challenge accounting performance and demonstrate their ability to criticize it, to deconstruct it, and to align it with other 'reasons' for variances than those formally modelled. Explanation refers beyond accounting performance and suggests that a 'proper accounting' would not have identified an accountability problem.

Explanation is talk. Talk refers to talk. The possibility of an unending spiral of explanation through talk makes it difficult to put an end to it. Superiors have, to a certain degree, the power to end talk. Theirs is the power to decide, to a certain degree, what to talk about and when to end it. Explanations are not an unlimited tour into talk. However, it is not only because superiors, by virtue of their being superior, can decide the timing and framing of talk. It is also that they are also controlled by accounting performance. They cannot dispense with it, as it – in modern firms – very dramatically points out relations between work and financial effect that cannot be dispensed with. Part of the superiors' social qualifications is the knowledge of accounting performance and the acceptance of mobilizing it. Although accounting performance is crude and sometimes borders on being foolish, it sets agendas and priorities managers cannot dispense with if they want to be managers.

Notes

1. The evidence is collected primarily through interviews in Danco and Cansub. As accountability is difficult to study generally, three 'focal issues' were selected to be debated in interviews: the problem of a rented warehouse, the problem of introducing a new sophisticated product, and the issue of new production technology. Of these, only the warehouse affair enters directly into this chapter. These focal issues were selected on the basis of their importance to people. They all wanted to refer to them in interviews and they all constituted exemplars of what management is in and for Cansub.
2. The loss was in the order of 10–12,000 CAD per month + labour + transport, adding up to approximately 30,000 CAD per month. The total loss incurred before Cansub could be released from the contract was approximately 110,000 CAD.
3. A distinction may be made between visibility as a strategy and its tactical implementation. As shown, in Danco visibility is a strategy as it maintains a sense of tight control. This has to be separated from the tactics by which managers from Danco employ numerous other means – e.g. telephone, visits etc. These tactics, however, serve to underscore the strategy of visibility and makes it even stronger.
4. 'Accountants are linked to their observations through accounting principles' (Morgan, 1988: 482) and have no direct access to the 'truth' about things. Rather, they are involved in producing a 'truth' which is dependent on the power-relations that make it up: '"Truth" is linked in a circular relation with systems of power which produce and sustain it, and to effects of power which it induces and which extends it. A "regime" of truth' (Foucault, 1977: 133).

References

Argyris, C. (1990) The Dilemma of Implementing Controls: The Case of Managerial Accounting. *Accounting, Organizations and Society,* **15** (6) pp. 503–11.

Bruner, J.S., Goodenow, J.J. and Austin, G.A. (1956) *A Study of Thinking*, John Wiley & Sons, New York.

Clegg, S. (1989) *Frameworks of Power*, Sage Publications, London.

Cray, D. (1990) Control and Coordination in Multinational Corporations, in *Global Organisational Theory Perspectives* (eds J. Sheth and G. Eshgi) Southwestern Publishing, Ohio.

Deetz, S. (1992) Disciplinary Power in the Modern Corporation, in *Critical Management Studies*, (eds M. Alvesson and H. Willmott) Sage Publications, London.

Dermer, J.D. and Lucas, R.G. (1986) The Illusion of Management Control. *Accounting, Organizations and Society,* **11** (6) pp. 471–82.

Foucault, M. (1977) *Discipline and Punish*, Penguin Books, Harmondsworth.

Giddens, A.G. (1979) *Central Problems in Social Theory*, Hutchinson, London.

Giddens, A.G. *A Contemporary Critique of Historical Materialism Volume I: Power, Property and the State*, Macmillan, London.

Giddens, A.G. (1984) *The Constitution of Society*, Polity Press, Cambridge.

Goffman, E. (1959) *The Presentation of Self in Everyday Life*, Penguin Books (1990).

Hedlund, G. and Zander, U. (1985) *Formulation of Goals and Follow-up of Performance for Foreign Subsidiaries in Swedish MNCs*, Institute of International Business, Stockholm School of Economics.

Horngren, C.T. and Foster, G. (1991) *Cost Accounting. A Managerial Emphasis*, 7th edn, Prentice Hall, Englewood Cliffs.

Hulbert, J.M. and Brandt, W.K. (1980) *Managing the Multinational Subsidiary*, Holt Rinehart and Winston, New York.

Latour, B. (1987) *Science in Action*, Harvard University Press, Cambridge, MA.

Latour, B. (1988) The Politics of Explanation: an Alternative in *Knowledge and Reflexivity: New Frontiers in the Sociology of Knowledge* (ed. S. Woolgar) Sage Publications, London.

Latour, B. (1991) Technology is Society Made Durable, in A Sociology of Monsters? Essays on Power, Technology and Domination (ed. J. Law) *Sociological Review Monograph,* **38**, MIT-Press, Cambridge, MA.

Law, J. (1994) *Organizing Modernity*, Blackwell, Oxford.

Loft, A. (1986) Towards A Critical understanding of Accounting: The Case of Cost Accounting in the UK, 1914–1925, *Accounting, Organizations and Society,* **11** (2) pp. 137–69.

Lyman, S.M. and Scott, M.B. (1970) *A Sociology of the Absurd*, Meredith Corporation, New York.

Macintosh, N.B. and Scapens, R.W. (1990) Structuration Theory in Management Accounting. *Accounting, Organizations and Society* **15**, 5 pp. 455–77.

Miller, P. (1992) Accounting and Objectivity: The Invention of Calculating Selves and Calculable Spaces. *Annals of Scholarship* **9**, (1–2), pp. 61–86.

Miller, P. and O'Leary, T. (1987) Accounting and the Construction of the Governable Person, *Accounting, Organizations and Society,* **12** (3) pp. 235–65.

Miller, P. and Rose, N. (1990) Governing Economic Life, *Economy and Society*, pp. 1–31.

Mouritsen, J. (1995) Accounting in Global Firms, in *Issues in Management Accounting* (eds D. Ashton, T. Hopper and R. Scapens) 2nd edn, Sage, London.

Munro, R.J.B. and Hatherly, D.J. (1993) Accountability and the New Commercial Agenda. *Critical Perspectives on Accounting,* **4**, pp. 369–95.

Roberts, J. and Scapens, R. (1985) Accounting Systems and Systems of Accountability – Understanding Accounting Practices in Their Organisational Contexts. *Accounting, Organizations and Society,* **10** (4) pp. 443–56.

Roberts, J. (1991) The Possibilities of Accountability. *Accounting, Organizations and Society,* **16** (4) pp. 355–68.

Robson, K. (1992) Accounting Numbers as 'Inscription': Action at a Distance and the Development of Accounting. *Accounting, Organizations and Society,* **17** (7) pp. 685–708.

Sewell, G. and Wilkinson, B. (1992) Someone To Watch Over Me: Surveillance, Discipline and the Just-In-Time Labour Process. *Sociology,* **26** (2) pp. 271–89.

Sheth, J. and Eshgi, G. (eds) (1990) *Global Organisational Theory Perspectives*, Southwestern Publishing, Ohio.

Part Five

Centres of discretion

The final unit of account deals with a more hybrid set of accountabilities, with a particular focus on centres of discretion. The emergence of these can be contrasted with the previous section, where the authors acknowledged the presence of intermediaries, but saw these as imposed by centres of calculation. Once positioned as 'agents', participants could not prevent their accounts from being aligned with those of intermediaries in the form of accounting numbers. So the story emerged very much as one of humans resisting machines.

The chapters in this last section deal with similar issues, but in rather different terms. Without setting up a drama in which humans seek to resist machines, and their product, they introduce what seems at first a counterintuitive twist. That is, they assume machines to be key participants in the social. They imagine the social as networks of heterogeneous materials, which may also include networks of 'members', such as a management team, and an alignment of 'intermediaries', such as is offered by a management accounting system. So the argument is that all of this material – people, devices and figures – helps to perform the social. In terms which, in mathematics, is called recursion, these all help to reproduce the organization, themselves, and even the orders in which they are participating. So if we begin with material in the form of dispersed networks, we can think of what is being performed as a recursive networking. One that has the end effect of distributing both 'obligatory passages' and 'discretion'. Consequently, we think of the analysis foregrounded in this chapter as the distribution of discretion and obligatory passages. This is a complex formulation, requiring a careful reading of all the different chapters before it can be fully understood.

In the first chapter of the section, Keith Hoskin charts accountability as a relatively recent irruption in modes of organization and government. Linking it to the rise of modernity, he differentiates accountability from earlier practices, especially stewardship. Although stewardship involved measurement techniques, these tracked only the movement of objects. What makes accountability so different – and its effects so pervasive – is that not only does it incorporate people into the measurement process, but it does so by producing measures that constitute, for the first time, a form of 'human accounting'. It accomplishes this by bringing together a number of practices. First, the performance of people is inscribed upon the movement of intermediaries, bringing them together as joint objects of accounting; and, thus, rendering them calculable. Second, persons are examined and ranked according to the 'outcomes' of the objects in their charge. Third, participants in the processes of accountability are treated as if each, individually, were centres of discretion. Although none of these practices was in itself new, it was not until the advent of accountability in the early part of the 19th century, that this particular constellation of practices was brought together.

In the next chapter, John Law draws in a variety of 'stories' from his ethnography of the managing of a prestigious scientific research laboratory. He sees managers' accounts as proceeding from the creation of 'virtual objects', such as the reality which the manpower planning system is supposed to be representing. However, when juxtaposed, these accounts appear as constructed around a slipping in and out of different modes of representation. So managers never are only pragmatists, getting by with less than full accuracy; and never are only empiricists, insisting on measuring real objects. In one reading, this might suggest the existence of a post-modern manager, one who embraces a relativism that is abroad today in the formula of 'anything goes'. But to argue that managers can switch epistemologies at will is to hang onto a story of humanism that is terminally ill. For anything doesn't go. Law is quite clear about this. Only certain discretions are performable; and even these are constrained in particular ways. The standard picture of managers as the flesh and blood that 'exercise discretion', he suggests, cannot 'be detached from the technologies or practices of accounting'. Each mode of accounting, 'panopticanism run riot' and 'due process' works in ways that discipline the subjectivities and objectivities they both demand and help to create. Further, in that there are multiple modes of accounting, these also suggest accountability is always decentred. So matters like power, or discretion, never can collapse and 'come together' at a single point.

In the final chapter Barbara Czarniawska-Joerges takes us to the laboratory of Sweden. Here, agendas once associated with the private sector, are sweeping aside institutionalized practices that were pre-

viously the hallmark of Sweden's envied welfare state. Like Hoskin and Law, she links accounts to the question of epistemologies. However, in the accounts she examines, it is the public sector officials, not the researcher, who turn to a 'logic of justification'. In their raising examples of a misalignment in accounts, her informants blow the cover on manoeuvres that require multiple membership. Governments are exposed as having 'several fish to fry'. Czarniawska-Joerges suggests this explicit examining of accounts in terms of consistency is indicative of an epistemological crisis, a crisis brought about by participants having to abandon the taken-for-granted notions that support and sustain a 'logic of appropriateness'. So in terms of members (not) being able to follow accounting rules, the cornerstone 'turns out to be fluid and temporary', obligations are a matter of 'negotiation and alliance forming', and identity is a 'result of process rather than its premise'.

The authors in this section of the book accept that a participation in the social goes beyond a matter of machines working alongside people. As is argued by the authors in the previous section, identity work can be understood as being inter-penetrated through and through by machines; sometimes in the form of pieces of paper, sometimes accounting numbers; often both. But, in that these hybrid processes also offer material for manoeuvres and forms of extension for identity, the authors in these chapters want to argue that the effects should not always be viewed negatively. In this respect, it is important to be clear that what is being argued is not just a message of reality being socially constructed. For Czarniawska-Joerges's interlocutors in the field would not 'bat an eyelid at the shocking news that reality was socially constructed'. Rather Czarniawska-Joerges is, like Law, examining the logics-in-use that usually delete such awareness from accounting processes. As she adds, for the public sector official, 'alternating between "essentialism" and "constructivism" and between "action" and "reflection" is sometimes tiring and always costly, but it happens to be their job'.

14 The 'awful idea of accountability': inscribing people into the measurement of objects

Keith Hoskin

Introduction

'Goodhart's Law' – that every measure which becomes a target becomes a bad measure – is inexorably, if ruefully, becoming recognized as one of the overriding laws of our times. Ruefully, for this law of the unintended consequence seems so inescapable. But it does so, I suggest, because it is the inevitable corollary of that invention of modernity: accountability.[1]

Accountability is more than, indeed systematically different from, responsibility. The latter entails, literally, being liable to answer for duties defined as yours. Responsibility implies stewardship, the proper conserving and use of those things charged to you, whether by an owner, a sovereign, or a metaphysical authority such as God, or the people. Responsibility entails the discharge of one's charge: it demands a reckoning, and in that sense an accounting for how you have conserved and used the things with which you have been charged (whether they be goods, money or powers). Its technical accounting form is therefore the ancient charge/discharge system of stewardship, which can be found as far back as ancient Egypt (Ezzamel, 1994).

Accountability, on the other hand, is in its operation and scope more total and insistent. Not only are duties specified, but the means of evaluating the level of their performance is already prescribed, in implicit or explicit norms, standards and targets of performance; wherefore surveillance over and judgement of performance is vastly widened and deepened. One is no longer just a steward of goods, monies or powers, answerable for past performance and present circumstance. Accountability ranges more freely over space and time, focusing as much on future potential as on past accomplishment, connecting and consolidating performance reports to plans and forecasts. As it does so, accountability in all its processes engages the self more insistently in the successful accomplishment of what is demanded over time and space.

The difference, one might say, is that with accountability there is no longer a simple relay of charge and discharge. Its reach runs both vertically and horizontally, up hierarchies and across boundaries: its presence is more extensive and continuous.

For example, in the modernist accounting world, this reach operates through the linked apparatuses of management accounting, financial reporting and auditing, in all their variants. Accountability therefore subsumes much that goes under the label of responsibility, but goes further. If responsibility entails being answerable to questions, then accountability does not so much dispense with questions as provide implicit answers to questions not-yet-dreamt-of. The constant mutual implication of standard, actual and forecast measures of performance means that what is currently invisible may subsequently become visible. Not only new targets but new *kinds* of targets may at any moment get constructed out of the debris of past success and failure. The 'awful idea of accountability' as one of the first recorded usages of that term, around 1800, presciently names it, is therefore a system threatening continual potential failure, even for those who are consistently successful.[2]

There are two implications that I draw from this initial reflection. First, since the noun-form only emerges so recently, I suggest that its formation is not accidental. Instead, the invention of accountability is one sign of a profound transformation, beginning from around 1800, in ways of seeing, of knowing, and of exercising power – a transformation one of whose consequences is indeed the modern system of financial reporting, management accounting and auditing. I shall reflect further below on how this transformation took place; it is an educational story. However, I am more centrally concerned here with the 'why' question – not least because, while Goodhart's Law elicits a wry smile of recognition, its specific formulation may tend to obscure *precisely* why this transformation took place. For the Law suggests that it is in *becoming* targets that measures become bad, which implies that measures in themselves are not bad. In this logic, measures are presumably either subverted from their course by human frailty, or not yet developed to a sufficient pitch of perfection to pre-empt subversion.

This perception, if understandably widely-held, is unfortunate. For it confirms people in ways of seeing which presume that 'the target' is the problem. So for system designers and managers, the Holy Grail is taken to be either better targets, or better ways of anticipating and handling a presumed natural-born predilection for beating the target system. In the vocabulary of constant improvement, targets must be designed to forestall the suboptimal behaviour of individuals, and so promote goal congruence with the greater good. So, for example, in order to deal with shopfloor workers who pace activity to depress production 'standards', managers produce slack-adjusted norms. Or to deal with divisional managers who suboptimally maximize Return on Investment by holding back on investment, top managers develop Residual Income as a means of promoting investment in line with corporate objectives. Or, again, to counter the obsession of financial analysts with earnings per share, company directors develop better product cost measures to stop management accounting systems being driven by financial accounting demands.[3]

Now certainly Goodhart's Law by illuminating the inherent futility in regimes of constant improvement, provides a healthy corrective to these calculative fantasies of managerialism. Yet my concern is that it fails to reveal to us why that futility is so inherent. Here I suggest that we return to consider the time, about two centuries ago, when the 'awful idea of accountability' first took linguistic shape. What we will find is that there was *never* an idyllic moment when measures of human performance existed purely as measures, neutral and dispassionate. So there is no need to presume a subsequent fall from grace into a modernist target frenzy.[4] Instead, the measures *themselves*, in their very genesis, already embody the principle that there should be, and necessarily are, targets.

As such, they are a new kind of measure, both formally and conceptually. Formally, they would seem to constitute a first form of 'human accounting', i.e. an accounting which looked beyond the valuing of objects and services, or the stewardship of goods and monies, to the quantified evaluation of human performance. At the same time, they engineer something that Hume, earlier in the eighteenth century, had attempted, in the name of logic, to proscribe: the conceptual overlap between 'is' and 'ought'. Hume's argument on this point is logically impeccable: no logical conclusion concerning what we ought to do can be drawn from what we do. In other words, there is a logical gap between 'is' and 'ought'. Yet measures that are targets precisely and systematically embody a conflation of the 'is' and the 'ought'; for their nature is simultaneously to describe and prescribe. Therefore – so long as they are produced via a scrupulous and sound method – they purely report what is, and so can hardly, in reason, be objected to. Yet measures as targets also prescribe what ought to be. And in so far as they do so, dispassionately and objectively, on the basis of what truly is, they can, the argument runs, surely be only for the best.

How, though, did such new measures come about? Furthermore, how have they come to be so pervasive? What, in other words, was there that could make accountability so awful, and yet so apparently irresistible? What is so seductive, what so difficult to gainsay, about measures that are simultaneously targets? My answer to the first question is, perhaps deceptively, simple. At the practical level, these new measures came about from a conjunction of certain already-existing practices which had never been systematically conjoined before. These practices included: *examination*, as the formal testing of human activity, *quantification*, the putting of numbers on the activity tested, and *writing*, in the sense of producing an archive of activities, tests, results, and judgements. To the other questions, I suggest that what also took place was a major redefinition of the rational self. Such measures, together with the results they generated, moved from being virtually non-existent to being seen as something both reasonable and self-evident. All this, despite the logical proscription articulated by Hume. Both developments, furthermore, took place almost without notice, despite the transformation that they wrought.

I shall discuss both these issues in more detail below. However, what is significant here is the conjunction of new forms of writing and numerical measurement together with a new definition of the rational self as *self*-examining, not just as something examinable. In this regard, Foucault once referred to a transition, around 1800, 'from historico-ritual mechanisms for the formation of individuality to the scientifico-disciplinary . . . thus substituting for the individuality of the memorable man that of the calculable man' (Foucault, 1977: 193). That is the transition which I now address in more detail in order to show how essential were *both* aspects of the transformation – the conjunction of the new practices and the reconstitution of the self.

Pedagogy, human accounting and the doubling of the self

Necessarily, such a brief programmatic statement leaves much as yet unresolved. Even at this stage, however, it should be clear that the approach I am adopting is not likely to discover accountability's genesis within the world of business as such. This is an additional, more literal, reason for describing this as an educational story. For the kind of human accounting I have just described, these writing, grading and examining practices, were inventions not of business but of the educational world – first developed, it seems, within elite eighteenth-century institutions of higher education. Yet how could such pedagogic practices have engineered a discourse which now has grown to have such global economic, organizational, and also psychological significance? And how might they relate to a fundamental reconstruction of the self? It is to these issues that I turn in this section, before going on to consider the wider issue of how these forms of accountability then penetrated into the business world, to supplement and then replace an older gentler regime of responsibility.

My explanation, like other late-modern approaches that have begun to focus on the power of practices, begins from the observation that, since around 1800, we have entered into a world peopled by certain new institutional and economic forms – such as the modern governmental state and the corporate business enterprise – and equally peopled by selves who partake in a new self-fashioning project, wherein identity and success are putatively self-defining and self-defined, whether evaluated along objective or reflexive lines. But I would further suggest that such transformations are linked aspects of one change, in which case, again in late-modern vein, my argument is that they must have their genesis neither purely at the social level nor within the self (for then either the self would become purely socially constructed, or the social purely a superfluous projection of the self, either of which explanations becomes self-refuting). In other words, *practices*, being neither purely social entities nor properties of individuals, are the sole means through which such a double form of transformation may be effected.[5]

Yet, more particularly, why should it be such obscure *pedagogic* practices that engineered such change, practices whose adoption was hardly noticed even in their own time? My answer here is in part that it is precisely their invisibility which made such practices so tranformative. But also, the significant social point is that these practices were encountered, and internalized, by that elite who were in the privileged position to remake the fields of intellectual knowledge and social power; and there is an equally significant epistemological point: that it was only members of that self-same elite who were concerned enough about the epistemological status of the rational self (a self so close to their own hearts) to engage in a debate which would result in the redefinition of that self as self-examining.

Historically, then, a pedagogic revolution took effect in the second half of the eighteenth century. Fairly abruptly, and without any apparent direct cross–fertilization, it appears that, in different European countries, students were suddenly brought under an insistent practice of being closely examined, having to write for the purpose of examination, and being evaluated rigorously on the basis of their writing (Hoskin, 1993: 280–95). Such demands were made, in different specific configurations, but with certain underlying regularities: for instance, in Germany, with the reform of the university 'seminar', beginning at Gottingen from around 1760: in France, with the introduction of examined laboratory practical work in some of the *Grandes Ecoles* from the 1770s: in England with the development of written examinations for the Mathematical Tripos at Cambridge University, again from the

1760s; and in Scotland at Glasgow University, where demanding *extempore* examining of students in the classroom was introduced, also from around 1760.

What I would then suggest is that this new conjunction of pedagogic practices had a double effect. First they exerted a 'psycho-pedagogic' power in the way that, as part of everyday schooling, they could get inside those who learned under them, constituting a new regime of 'learning to learn'. Both as students and teachers, an elite group internalized the idea that real learning was the getting of written, examined knowledge; they could subsequently translate that assumption into the various fields of knowledge they colonized, developing a new power for knowledge, as intensive research-based expertise. [It is noticeable (Hoskin, 1993, ibid) that the various distinctive forms of modern disciplinary knowledge emerge from within these sites. From the Seminar comes the first modern Arts discipline, philology, from the Laboratory comes modern 'big science'; from the world of the reformed Mathematical Tripos come those apostles of mathematical and computing reform, Peacock and Babbage (cf Schaffer, 1994); and from a teacher in the Glasgow classroom world, Adam Smith, comes the quintessential social science, economics. In the latter case, it is worth pointing out that the internal coherence of modern economics crucially depends on the conceptual adequacy of a new version of the rational self long familiar as 'rational economic man': as we shall see, what Smith developed was a pure psycho-pedagogic invention, the self-examining self: a new form of the rational self which brilliantly, if problematically, transformed the idea of self-interest from a process with wholly negative connotations into 'an acceptable and eventually into a highly commended drive for modern man' (Myers, 1985: 2).]

At the same time these practices exerted a 'socio-organizing' power. For in a parallel process of translation, members of the knowledge elite began to restructure a whole range of social settings into the disciplinary image. The social world became populated by new entities where writing, examining and grading were endemic: and it was not just that such entities could be run via these practices, e.g. in those modern managerial systems exhibiting what Alfred Chandler describes as 'administrative co-ordination' (Chandler, 1977); they could also be made visible representationally as integrated, almost-living wholes, endowed with quasi-organs, in 'organ-ization' charts. It was a transformation which could then appear almost natural, particularly as more and more of the individuals in these organizations became reconstructed, through their own learning to learn, as rationally self-examining and 'organized' selves (cf. Hoskin, 1995). Herein surely, prisons, schools, hospitals, factories, universities, state bureaucracies and corporate oligopolies most resemble each other, as both the social world and the self become more and more subject to a writing, grading and examining which together ensure the meticulous and continual circulation of plans, examinations, reports, feedback and feedforward evaluations – knowing me, knowing you, in our respective truths.

This, I suggest, is the context in which the 'awful idea of accountability' could suddenly emerge and become so irresistible. This transformation, whereby the pedagogic arena suddenly became flooded by numbers combining 'is' and 'ought', and wherein we became selves whose rational identity was constructed through a mix of external and internal examination, produced a context where 'accountability', to self and to others, could become a self-evident rational good. Precisely how this came about is the subject of my next section.

The self-examining self and the miscegenation of 'is' and 'ought'

'When I endeavour to examine my own conduct . . . it is evident that, in all such cases, I divide myself, as it were, into two persons and that I, the examiner and judge, represent a different character from that other I, the person whose conduct is examined into and judged of.'
(Smith, *The Theory of Moral Sentiments*, Part III, 'Of the Foundation of our Judgements concerning our own Sentiments and Conduct, and of the Sense of Duty', chapter I, section 6)[6]

This formulation of the self, as rational through being divided into two, appears to be unprecedented in western history, violating a previously presumed unity of self. It does not emerge, of course, in a vacuum. I have suggested (Hoskin, 1995) that it be understood as a step beyond a prior construction of the rational self as immobile 'viewing self', an apparent unity that looks out on the world as through the perspectival window, a way of seeing most powerfully captured in fifteenth-century Italian art.

Again this self, I have argued (Hoskin, 1995: 145–55), is not what it seems, since it is a product of prior practices of writing and examining that emerged in the medieval period, from around 1200 on. In effect, it is a self that occupies a zero point, which had been introduced with the development of the zero as '0', first found following the combination of alphabetic and arabic numerals in the medieval west, and it is also a self which, from that zero point, puts the world under critical examination, in a way developed first in the medieval university.

In other words, it is not purely an artistic production, this self. On the contrary, the artistic is one particularly compelling version of a self, which is equally predicated in such (earlier) breakthroughs as double-entry bookkeeping. Here, in the same way, debits and credits are observed from a zero point, whence they stretch out to record transactions in mirror entries, kept systematically with cross-references in ledgers and supplementary books; so that the form of entries, properly observed, ensures that every incoming and outgoing is located in an order that permeates the whole and is thus always available to inspection from the zero point.

Further the apparent unity of this self is as much an illusion as the all-in-focus view produced by the process of geometrical perspective: for technically it is the fusion of two viewing points, the fixed view from in front (which looks to the 'vanishing point' of infinity within the picture), along with an equally-perspectival view from sideways on (the 'distance point' operation). Only the combination of these two views makes it possible to chart both the vertical and horizontal coordinates (the orthogonals and transversals) of everything located within the two-dimensional pictorial space, in such a way that everything appears in proportion and focus (in a way that is of course impossible in viewing the three-dimensional world, where only one aspect will be in focus at any one time).

Epistemologically, the significant thing is the way that this new 'unitary' viewing is then internalized as the way of seeing the thought-world. We enter the era of what Richard Rorty has described as the 'representational' view of language, language as 'mirror' of the world: but such a view of language crucially depends on the assumption of a fixed and focused place to view both language and the world, in other words viewing as through a window onto a thought-world where everything is, when understood, captured clearly and in focus, as in the orthogonals and transversals of the perspectival painting.[7]

Such a way of seeing, inevitably and reflexively, came to affect the way of viewing the problem of the self as well. Most significantly for our concern here, this way of seeing was deployed by Thomas Hobbes, in the 1640s, to raise the ethical problem of self-interest, and how to reconcile the destructive tendency to selfishness with the good of all. This problem is so significant for our purposes here, because it was in confronting the problem of the relation between reason and self-interest posed by Hobbes that Hume focuses on the problem of the relation between 'is' and 'ought'. Hobbes, the great theorist of the State, had looked out (from his rational viewing-point) on the problem of the selfish self, and perceived the necessity for labile self-interested individuals to be constrained within the orthogonals and transversals of Absolute Rule and Law (Hoskin, 1995: 156). Since, for Hobbes, self-interest could not be curbed by reason, selfishness would always win out. Hence the need for the absolute power of the state, in order to counteract self-interest, for the good of all.

Hume, like other Scottish Enlightenment thinkers, wished to re-establish the ethical basis of individual life, and rescue the self from this bleak domination by irrationality: hence the importance, for him, of discriminating 'is' from 'ought', on the way to establishing a rational basis on which individuals could be shown to be capable of developing a moral sense without degenerating into selfishness. To this end Hume, before Smith, proposed that the self becomes ethical by considering how one's actions are viewed by an 'impartial spectator': in such a way, what 'is' becomes subject to an independent ethical touchstone of what 'ought' to be.

Yet, paradoxically, Hume's proposal opens the way to a new miscegenation of is and ought, since it fails to solve the Hobbesian problem, being open to the objection that the self could always ignore any Other, even the impartial spectator, and so succumb to selfishness once more. The subsequent 'resolution' of the dilemma is that proposed by Smith in the quotation that heads this section. Here it is made impossible for the self to ignore the Other by redefining the Other as part of the self, and so producing a new form of rational self as a split, two-sided unity, the self which acts and the self which examines those acts.

In a sense this is a continuation of the kind of viewing that Hobbes and Hume had already undertaken. Where Hobbes had looked out, through his perspectival window, onto the foolish and selfish selves in the thought-world beyond, Hume had attempted to construct a sort of reverse viewing, from the thought-world beyond, back on to the self who views. Hume's formulation of the impartial spectator paints a picture wherein I become ethical by looking through my window on the world and seeing there some moral Other, the impartial spectator, whose surveillance of me ensures that I develop moral sentiments. On this reading, what Smith achieves is a step beyond this, by discovering on the far side of the 'window' a mirror self, the self that examines, which stands in for and replaces the Other as judge of self.

Yet in fact, what he has done is expose the illusion in the idea that the self was ever a unitary immobile in-focus rational viewer, while replacing it with a new illusion, of the split unity, the rational because self-examining self. In art-historical terms, this was by then nothing new. For as Svetlana Alpers has memorably shown, the initial Italian form of producing perspective, viewing as through a window, had been technically superseded by 1500, by a technique which effectively framed *both* the vanishing point *and* distance point operations in a more global overview, thus producing a way of seeing wherein the viewer is no longer situated in front of a window, but is already *within* the space viewed. It is, as she describes in *The Art of Describing* (Alpers, 1982), the archetypal viewing disseminated in Dutch art, where it is as if the viewed world comes out to envelop us within its space, as what is depicted 'seems to extend beyond its bounds as if the frame were an afterthought' (1982: xxv). Henceforward the viewing self is liberated to view in focus not just as through a window but from any point in the viewing space.

The self can even self-knowingly acknowledge the nature of the perspectival game, producing pictures where the artist paints himself within the frame of his picture, but looking out at where he, the artist painting, must be. In the extreme reflection on this *faux-art* of representation, Velasquez, in his painting of around 1650, *Las Meninas*, depicts himself in the act of painting a canvas whose back alone we can see: so he is both without the frame and within, caught in the act of painting and looking out, as examiner of his act: but he also, by means of a mirror placed on the rear wall depicted in the painting, enables us to see the subjects of the canvas whose back alone we can see from in front of the picture – the King and Queen of Spain, who must be occupying the same space before the picture as Velasquez, as painter, and us, as viewers. . . . (Hoskin, 1995: 154–5).

It is this type of viewing that Smith now introduces to the thought-world. Yet this is not just an 'artistic' achievement. For Smith's new ethical double-self is a self-examining self. With Smith, examination penetrates to the very marrow of the soul. In other words, Smith solves the problem that Hume could not, by changing the rules of self-construction via an audacious double play. First, although there must still be a logical distinction between is and ought, there is no longer the absolute distinction that Hume could maintain, by keeping a separation between the self representing what is and the impartial spectator representing what ought to be. Smith has deconstructed that absolute separation by turning the Spectating Other into the Examining Self. Simultaneously, by introducing this idea of examination, he has turned the Other from passive observer into active judge. It is the two aspects of the change together that solve the Hobbesian dilemma. For now self-interest can now be *guaranteed* to be rational, thanks to the practice of self-examination undertaken by the two-sided perspectivally viewing unity.

In effect, Smith has constructed the first self with its own auto-pilot (and so, by way of an afterthought, has established the basis for the invention of rational economic man). At the same time, he is aware that there is some level of sleight-of-hand involved, some unstable fulcrum to this supposed superior rational self.[8] In that respect (Hoskin, 1993: 294): 'Smith's solution was no solution at all. For it did not overcome the Hobbesian problem; instead it defined it out of existence by moving the goalposts.'

Yet, by the very fact of being invented, this new version of the rational self became internalizable. What I would then suggest is that this began to happen as more selves became subject to the kind of rigorous examination that Smith invokes here. Here, in one fell swoop, is the explanation why Smith came up with this new formulation – it was to hand for him in his everyday life, since he was in the Classroom world of Glasgow University a teacher who deployed examination as a practice for making students learn (Hoskin, 1993: 289) – and the explanation why increasing numbers should have then internalized it – as they became subject to increasingly rigorous forms of this examination. For me the deciding moment is when students become subject to numerical grading, and so part of a regime of quantifiable human accounting, where the numbers both describe your actual performance and imply a truth about your underlying 'ability'. Here the confusion between 'is' and 'ought' which Smith has initiated by the miscegenation of Self and Other takes on a more insistent dimension. For here we have measures that tell a double truth about the self, and which engender a new two-sided concern with getting good marks, as the blazon of success, yet we know that always there lurks the possibility of the total zero, the mark of failure, humiliation and total non-identity. It is this emergent feature of this educational story to which I turn next.

From number one to total zero: success and the fear of failure

What is so compelling about the invention of these new pedagogic practices is the way in which they take over selves, in just the awful yet irresistible way that marks all accountability systems: even where people are aware of the logical and psychological dangers, like Smith, this miscegenation of is and ought cannot be thought or wished away. Here was an apparatus that embodied the means for measuring human profit and loss, producing measures that simultaneously defined your actual 'worth' and provided a valuation of the truly virtuous, successful, or passing performance (while equally defining the crime of failure): an apparatus therefore fit, as Foucault once put it, to judge individuals 'in their truth' (1977: 181).

Let me give just one example from the reformed world of elite education: the innovation of rigorous written examination at Cambridge and then at Oxford Universities between 1760 and 1810 transforms the psycho-pedagogic field within which selves operate. At first, there is a new culture of success, as at Cambridge where the few very 'best' students vie to become Number One, i.e. Senior Wrangler in the Tripos Examination (the terms betray an older examining world, here superseded: Wrangling was the practice of spoken disputation on set topics, i.e. oral examination of a type first developed in the medieval university, the Tripos was a stool that one occupied in order to claim the right to dispute). Quickly this becomes a mark of personal and institutional success, a sign of inborn virtue which reflects well on the Cambridge college of which the Senior Wrangler is a member: equally quickly, now that this measure is explicitly a target, college tutors begin trying to beat the system by finding ways to 'prove' that their candidate is best and that feared challengers are less good. This, of course, is not difficult since the examination structure is still fluid, and semi-oral. Examiners set questions orally to individual students as they finish a previous written anwer; individual examiners can set particularly hard questions to particular targets. And answers are evaluated in qualitative terms, as excellent, very good, X is better than Y, etc. It is in fact in consequence of the induced failure of the measure to be a good measure that in 1792 one Examiner proposes that all questions shall henceforward be marked numerically, so that is and ought will be brought into proper alignment, and the best candidate will be declared Number One (Hoskin, 1979).

We now know what would ensue: the never-ceasing procession of attempts to produce valid and reliable measures of an underlying ability, which always just eludes perfect capture. But equally what ensues, psycho-pedagogically, is the full impact of accountability: not just the glory of success but the fear of failure. This phenomenon, now something treated as virtually endemic, is something marked virtually by its absence before the examining change. It emerges indeed even before the introduction of numerical grading, at the earliest stage of reform. In the case of Oxbridge, it has been particularly studied by Sheldon Rothblatt, who notes the eruption of this new dynamic. As early as the 1770s, the Cambridge student Isaac Milner, who would go on to be Lucasian Professor of Mathematics and Vice-Chancellor of the University, and who was indeed Senior Wrangler and 'so superior to all his competitors that the Moderators put the word *Incomparabilis* after his name', already was infected. He recalled years later that 'he had been in a very desponding mood and had feared, till the result was known, that he had completely failed' (Rothblatt, 1982: 6).

The pressure intensified once all students became subject to the system, once it was both written and graded. Such future luminaries as Robert Peel, as a student at Oxford around 1810, just after written examinations were introduced, 'contemplated bowing out of the competition' under the pressure, and was only dissuaded for fear of letting down his father: Peel became the first student to get a Double First Class, in classics and mathematics. Rothblatt gives a number of other instances, including one of an attempted suicide from the 1830s: a case where the behaviour cannot be explained instrumentally, by a need to succeed in external social or economic terms, for this was still an elite world of young men predestined to succeed in those terms. The pressures were intra-familial and psychological: the numbers were a measure-target that could no longer be ignored. Identity, honour and self-esteem were at stake, and there is no ultimate touchstone of success that is impregnable. We enter a world where even external success can be seen as failure internally: Rothblatt mentions a future Bishop of Calcutta, Middleton, who leaves Cambridge 'bemoaning the circumstances that prevented him gaining the Chancellor's Medal', and bemoaning it all his life (1982: 10).

All this goes to show how easily both a new psycho-pedagogic and socio-organizing dynamic was set in train, once these pedagogic practices had become taken for granted as fundamentals of our everyday reality. Of course, in different cultures they could be taken up in different specific ways, and one such distinctive difference that I have concentrated on in previous work concerns the way in which, in the USA, these practices were translated into an effective new economic form, managerialism. The point of this is not to claim that there was some special genius about the American approach to deploying these new numbers that ensured that managerialism and its associated accountability in the workplace would triumph where in other countries they languished unrecognized. It is apparent, on a number of grounds, that similar initiatives were attempted in other countries. For instance, Simon Schaffer has recently pointed to the way in which one of the new Cambridge examination successes, Charles Babbage, a successor to Isaac Milner as Lucasian Professor of Mathematics, and one whose father was a wealthy banker, not only worked on his calculating engines for their inherent mathematical pleasures, but saw them as a site of 'intelligence', which could transform manufacture and the factories in which manufacturing work was undertaken. Babbage, as 'philosopher of manufacture' (Schaffer, 1994: 206), was as eager to apply the calculating machine to the development of successful mass interchangeable-part manufacture, and thus to an associated form of labour discipline, subject to the intelligence of the machine, which now became the 'site of intelligence', as any of the US managerial reformers.

The significant difference in the US context, something that marks it off from all prior approaches to handling workforces and work, is the continued absence elsewhere of an effective technology of human accounting. It is this that marks, in the economic world, the transition from responsibility to accountability.

Translating responsibility into accountability

The claim that accountability was absent from work organizations before the nineteenth century is undoubtedly, to the perfect empiricist, unprovable. For it is always possible that there was some earlier system, which operated with perhaps implicit standards or targets and systematic measurements of human performance, before this historical moment. However, if one goes over the available historical record, the evidence for such a system is not forthcoming. There appears to have been an absence of systematic shaping and controlling activity up and down hierarchies; and there was no quantified accounting for human performance – though there was much accounting for goods and objects, which took place frequently in systems where people were answerable for the discharge of certain charges, and in that sense were subject to *responsibility*.

Under such systems, down through the eighteenth century, the dominant form of operative power relation was that of stewardship, and the form of one's responsibility was to be answerable after the fact and grosso modo. So, for instance, on ancient and medieval estates, the steward (or bailiff or reeve) would be called every so often to account (perhaps annually, perhaps more sporadically), and made to answer for the detail of their stewardship. There would typically be some inspection of receipts and payments of money and produce, a form of information which is already found on estates in Greco-Roman antiquity (Macve, 1985). There might be an elaborate formal ritual, as in the medieval audit, the solemn and detailed hearing and examining of these accounts.

But this was hardly modern accountability. First, the whole temporal orientation of the process was focused on what had or had not been done. It faced the present to the extent that the accounts were a record kept up to date, but principally it faced the past. This applies even where we find a form of prescriptive judgement being exercised, as happened in many medieval audits. Here the evidence shows (e.g. Drew, 1947) that the auditors, in drawing up their final account would enter:

> not merely the actual transactions, but those which the auditors considered *should* have occurred. They would rewrite the entries in the accounts to reflect, e.g. the 'expected' yield of a field or a flock, and thereby surcharge the bailiff or reeve for the additional amounts due to his lord.
>
> (Hoskin and Macve, 1986: 115)

Two observations stand out here. First, the grosso modo nature of the control exercised is evident, as soon as one realizes that the 'expected' yields inscribed by the auditors were often so much higher than the actuals recorded that the surcharges then levied might be two or three times the official's annual salary (cf Drew, 1947). This is assuredly a use of knowledge to enact power, but it suggests a system where both sides operated on a presumption of considerable slack in reported 'actuals', and where the problem for the steward lay in estimating how frequent and rigorous audits were likely to be, and so how much one needed to secrete in advance.

Second, the ex post nature of the control, the focus on what has been done, is clear. The auditor, in quantifying expected yields, did not apparently do so as a target for the future; what was being compared was the actual performance recorded against what should have been expected, given what was now, ex post, known concerning labour and raw materials employed, and other relevant circumstances (e.g. the weather). What is signally absent is any focus on the control of future events, along with any deployment of human accounting measures on the steward's performance (for the accounting focuses purely on materials and objects).

Now an argument can be made that, from this medieval period on, a more insistent kind of 'control' was exercised over stewards – 'control' itself being a medieval invention, referring to a new textual form, the counter-roll, or in French the contre-rolle, a text that for the first time excerpted and abridged books of primary record, thus providing a new way of exercising power at a distance through writing (Hoskin and Macve, 1986: 114). However, even in later cases where business and economic historians have found evidence of advanced forms of exercising control and using accounting information, e.g. in Britain at the Crowley Iron Works (c. 1710), the Wedgwood pottery (c. 1770), the Boulton and Watt manufactory (c. 1800), as also in Italy at the Venice Arsenale, in Spain at the Seville Royal Tobacco Factory (c. 1770), or in the USA in certain textile mills (c. 1800), the argument is not easily made that accountability was exercised.[9]

Even recent re-evaluations of the evidence (e.g. Fleischman and Parker, 1991) fail to find the extension of managerial control types of initiatives over time. Cost experiments, such as those at Wedgwood, were not utilized to co-ordinate production, control costs and maximize productivity on a regular basis into the future. Even in cases such as Boulton and Watt, the Venice Arsenale and the Spanish Royal Tobacco Factory, where there is evidence of measuring worker performance and the establishment of cost data on products, it does not appear that standards of labour performance were effectively imposed and utilized over time to ensure productivity was maintained into the future. Such cases show that modern techniques could be envisaged: the problem lay in constructing a work regime where they could successfully be implemented.

What is lacking is 'any approach which simultaneously analysed both financial and human performativity, rendering the interrelated but separable values of products and persons jointly calculable' (Hoskin and Macve, 1994: 80). Instead, such managerial breakthroughs, and with them the deployment of technologies of accountability, appear to have first developed in the USA from the 1830s, as Alfred Chandler details in *The Visible Hand* (1977). However, my argument here has been that this did not happen as the 'response' to some ex post imputed 'need', the demands of the Industrial Revolution for example. It only transpired when a new constellation of disciplinary practices were jointly established, operating psycho-pedagogically and so making possible new forms of socio-organizing. In this respect, what first took place was a re-writing or re-constructing of the self, as a self-examining, infinitely calculable construct. The point that I have made in previous work is that this was successfully engineered in the US, not by businessmen (for they were too busy defending short-term profits and keeping costs low), but by men equivalent to Babbage in their background and pedagogic training. The sole difference was that in the US case, these men were given the direct and extensive financial and institutional support of the State in implementing their disciplinary innovations.

The men involved, as rehearsed elsewhere (e.g. Hoskin and Macve, 1993), were not businessmen but certain ex-cadets, who had first learned under the practices of writing, examining and grading, in the extreme disciplinary regime introduced into the US Military Academy at West Point from 1817. In terms of the successful development of the modern factory, the key figure is an ex-cadet from West Point, Daniel Tyler, who graduated in 1819, and introduced these practices into the Springfield Armory in 1832, undertaking a time-and-motion study. Here 'is' and 'ought' were brought into the most explicit and close symbiosis. For Tyler spent 6 months 'watch in hand' examining every aspect of production not just to establish averages of what *was* done, but to calculate norms of what *could* be done by the good worker working properly, and so to establish fair prices for standard performance. [This, be it noted, is 50 years before F.W. Taylor deployed the same approach and called it 'scientific management'.] The new approach, at first resisted by the work-force, was only introduced in 1842. As soon as it was, targets both for production and unit cost were both set and enforced (for instance in the barrel-welding department productivity doubled while unit costs halved). Now the workplace game of modern disciplinarity and resistance could begin. At the same time, it was the then-proven *economic* superiority of this new disciplinary approach, in enabling the increase of productivity while cutting unit costs, a pay-off which came about because of the State support for the men like Tyler, which ensured that theirs, rather than the parallel efforts of a Babbage, became the breakthrough to modern managerialism: which now, as Chandler rightly points out, dominates the global oligopolistic economy, whatever the particular form the managerial organization may take.

Modernity, post modernity and the self-accountable self

With formulations like Goodhart's Law, we now have a strong ironic awareness of the futility of measures that are targets. For this reason, I want to conclude this reflection on why accountability should have emerged around 1800 with a reflection on its status today.

The question arises as to whether we have here an epoch that has almost run its course? Whether this essentially modernist 'self-examining self' may now be giving way to a more reflexively aware and postmodern self that may transcend these dour, calculative pedagogic practices? It may, of course, be so. But what must be taken as given is that the practices that produce accountability have not as yet been superseded. We still learn under the regime of writing, examining and grading, and we still continue to be known in our truth via these practices. Accordingly, there is a 'regime of truth' at work here, to which we have to be committed. We are calculable, and yet also calculating selves, even while we recognize the systematic weaknesses, not to say untruths, that the regime produces.

I would offer just a brief reflection on this, taking as my starting-point one of Foucault's last observations on the nature of modernity and of the self within it. The question he poses, in the late paper 'What is Enlightenment?', is whether we should 'envisage modernity as an attitude rather than as a period of history' (1987: 39). In part, he is aiming a subversive shaft at the possible metaphysical trap which lies in invoking 'an enigmatic and troubling "postmodernity" ' as a temporal period (ibid). But he is also, in line with his emergent concern with the way practices produce discursive regularities, wishing to reflect upon the way we may be saying one thing, yet still be constrained to do quite another. So today we seek liberation, and envisage ourselves as postmodern selves, but obtain only hard work as our means of self-realization. Perhaps this is something that is becoming increasingly clear with the inbuilt accounting-driven push to delayering and unemployment: so that without work we encounter a fundamental threat to identity. In Foucault's own words: 'Modern man . . . is the man who tries to invent himself. This modernity does not "liberate man in his own being"; it compels him to face the task of producing himself' (1987: 42).

There are many modern sites where we might find this exemplified. The one I would choose to reflect on here is particularly poignant, because it has such a postmodern profile – Lloyd's of London. For here we have a highly visible example of (architectural) postmodernity, in the Lloyd's building of Richard Rodgers. Yet, in line with Parkinson's (Other) Law concerning organizations and buildings, which states that perfection of planned layout is achieved only by institutions on the point of collapse (or you move into a new building at your peril), Lloyd's exhibits a beautiful conjunction of the postmodern with the modern, which suggests that the power of the latter still dominates. For Lloyd's has combined its architectural renaissance with an accounting and managerial reformation which has in effect moved the institution from a premodern form of accounting control, where agents ran syndicates with minimal formal accounting systems and a very personal face-to-face style of decision-making, to a strongly managerialist one (Gwilliam, Hoskin and Macve, 1992). Over the past few years, not only have syndicate accounts been made subject to standard reporting requirements, but new forms of financial reporting, which shadow as far as possible the Return on Investment and Earnings Per Share measures familiar in other business sectors, have been adopted, as a means of giving visible evidence of financial probity and reform. Now arguably such reforms were politically and organizationally prudent, following the financial scandals of the early 1980s, and the still-unquantified costs of asbestosis claims that have emerged more recently. So behind the postmodern facade, it is rational to adopt the implantation of the kind of financial and managerial systems of accountability which first emerged in the US over a century ago.

But the unresolved question, as with all these measures from the outset, is whether they actually provide what they claim to, a truer, more reliable and valid perspective on 'what is'. It is the problem perceived in one way by Smith as he invented the self-examining self; the lurking problem of the logical contradiction at the heart of the whole accountability exercise. And this problem is perhaps now perceived even more clearly by people in general, given that we inhabit the would-be-postmodern era of late modernity. Accountability emerged as breakthrough in power-knowledge relations, a new technology that was manifestly incredibly powerful and apparently reasonable (self-evidently so, to the modernist self-examining self). Yet it is still open to the fundamental Humean objection that there is something inherently illogical in combining the 'ought' with the 'is'.

Conclusion

Hume's logical gap, I suggest, is precisely what shows up in the extended version of Goodhart's Law. It is not just system-beating, degenerate or unethical self-interest that keeps the law in place as a fundamental principle of modernity. It is the logical contradiction within which we are all placed by being subject to measures that are also targets, regardless of our degree of individual willingness to adopt system-beating practices.

So what do we do when we confront an 'unfair' is/ought contradiction? Where the inherent illogic shows through clearly, what we are bound to do is find some way of redefining the self, a means of self-preservation, which will handle the injustice produced by the measures of self-examination. In the interplay between practices and ourselves, as self-examining selves, many possible relations then obtain. We may become defined, as is evident in the chapter which follows, as 'centres of discretion', by the action of the existing centres of calculation that obtain in a given organizational setting.

As centres of discretion, however small and however focused, we are required to make ourselves visible in our judgement, backed wherever possible by appropriate and plausible calculations. In this fashion we are required to make our conduct (and our selves) self-evident. Yet we are well aware that we are not doing so as pure rational selves, revealing the truth as such. Accordingly, we may find tactics to maintain our self-respect from having conducted ourselves in line with this compelled, and compelling, self-evidence. We may resist identifying ourselves with what we do by, say, redefining a real self in opposition to this self-examining self (thus perpetuating a division between the 'is' and the 'ought').

Alternatively, we may define our self as the only rational one able to see through the truth regime, and its untruth, thus imputing to other agents various levels of stupidity and self-delusion. We may look for a reaffirmation of identity in forms of resistance, overt or covert. For the crisis of confidence engendered by accountability is one shared equally by the shop floor and those at the top of organizations. All who administer and experience these numbers are equally as aware of their in-built futility.

This, then, is the one form of truth that seems inescapable about this particular regime of truth. Born of a fundamental irrationality, it is something that is not directly resistible. This is not simply because its institutional apparatuses now dominate the whole social world. Nor is it because the logical weakness that inheres within the self-examining self, and within these measures as targets, means that its power is never total. Rather, in so far as we still occupy a world of modernity, (as I suggest we do), we must recognize that the practices of accountability remain our practices; and that such practices, even as they fail, continue to have their own form of success.

So accountability may remain trapped by its illogic: which is why it remains such an 'awful idea', in one sense of the word. At the same time, the more it fails, the more it succeeds. This aspect of accountability is attested and exemplified by such cases as Lloyd's of London, where managers, even though they may be in no better position to act more wisely on behalf of syndicate holders, at least now have an identity as modern managers. They can join the modern world, no longer sensing their practices are quaintly out-of-date. And, additionally, they have the means of accountability available, which will, period on period, make visible that what they 'are' doing is what they 'ought' to be.

Notes

1. 'Goodhart's Law', as originally defined by Goodhart, referred only, it must be said, to the money beloved of monetarists, stating that, as soon as a particular instrument or asset is

publicly defined as money in order to enable monetary control, it will cease to be used as money and replaced by substitutes which will enable evasion of that control (Goodhart, 1989). No matter: the susceptibility of the initial formulation to such more general redefinition only confirms the truth of the underlying insight.

2. The *Oxford English Dictionary* gives examples of the adjective 'accountable' dating from the sixteenth century, but of the noun form 'accountability' only from around 1800. Johnson's 1754 *Dictionary* does not have the noun, but Webster's *American Dictionary* of 1828 does, with the 'awful idea' phrase as its sole citation.

3. I mention this last possibility, as it is one of the arguments proffered for introducing Activity Based Costing as a means of re-engineering management accounting 'excellence', in Thomas Johnson and Robert Kaplan's *Relevance Lost* (1987). We await definitive proof, some with less-than-bated breath, as to whether ABC will have this desired target-refocusing effect.

4. This is not to deny the importance of exposing the existential dilemmas posed by targets to humans within the modernist world: e.g. the ever-presence of the means-obsessed desire for some advantage that will guarantee the required result: the openness to the post-Faustian bargain (post-Faustian since one trades not for lasting power but for next period's, and next period's, and next period's, success). Nor is it to negate the further implication of Goodhart, that each time some new unanticipated edge has been discovered, it can at best be countered, until, Hydra-like, the next new system-beating process sprouts forth. My point is that even such dilemmas do not prove that measures only generated them when they *became* targets.

5. My own view is that change ensues when a new 'order of practices' begins to operate both socially and within the self. The idea of such an 'order' is modelled in part on Foucault's idea, set out in his inaugural lecture at the College de France, that there is an 'order of discourse', i.e. an historically specific but overlooked level of language which lies between the deep structure of *langue* and the surface form of *parole* and which is in fact the guarantor and genesis of both (Foucault, 1981). At the same time, it draws on the emerging recognition that Foucault himself was becoming in his late works a 'theorist of practices' (cf McNay, 1992), who therefore carefully and deliberately describes his last major project on the 'care of the self' as a cross-breeding (*croisement*) of 'an archaeology of the problematics of, and a genealogy of the practices of, the self' (Foucault, 1984: 19). It now seems to me that, like the 'order of discourse', the 'order of practices' is something which has been overlooked: located, as it is, between the social and individual levels of action, it is similarly the guarantor and genesis of both (Hoskin, 1994).

6. The citation comes from the second edition of the *Theory of Moral Sentiments* (Smith, 1976: 109–12). As I have explained before (Hoskin, 1993: 290–2), Smith does not reach this solution all at once, having attempted in the first edition to retain Hume's idea of the outside impartial spectator, until he is driven to realize how it is self-defeating. He is, in this, excruciatingly aware of the importance of not violating Hume's is-ought distinction, arguing in this edition that we validate our moral judgments by 'some secret reference either to what are, or to what, upon a certain condition, would be, or to what, we imagine, ought to be the sentiments of others'. At the same time, he sets up the examinatorial wherewithal for his new solution, for he already states that, if we are genuinely rigorous in our moral judgement, we 'endeavour to examine our own conduct as we imagine an impartial spectator would examine it' (Smith, 1976: 110, 1st edition variant).

7. Such a way of seeing arguably reaches its highest expression in the Cartesian view which, whether looking outward to consider the *res extensa*, or inward to the *res cogitans*, views like the perspectival artist – as a unitary viewer, who supposedly sees everything dispassionately and in correct proportion. In the Cartesian '*cogito ergo sum*', the thinking 'I' must be as one, a unity, with the 'I' who am.

8. In the very passage where he invents this new self (cf Hoskin, 1993: 302, note 28), he is

already aware of the danger to reason posed by such splitting. Note the nuanced use of 'I divide myself, as it were, into two persons'; and how he immediately goes on to state that the Agent is 'the person whom I properly call myself'. As he concludes (Smith, 1976: 113): 'But that the judge should, in every respect, be the same as the person judged of, is as impossible, as that the cause should, in every respect, be the same with the effect.' Here he as good as acknowledges that he has, in constructing this new form of self that is rational through being double, uncovered the fact of its rational impossibility. But this does not mean that he has not re-written the self thus.

9. See for instance Thompson (1967), McKendrick (1970), Fleischman and Parker (1991), Hoskin, Zambon and Zan, (1994), Carmona, Ezzamel and Gutierrez (1994), and the discussion in Hoskin and Macve (1988), Appendix A. These organizations all exert forms of time and work-discipline, often with clock-regulated days and the use of overseers, fines, blacklists and beatings: i.e. direct surveillance and punishment, corporal or financial, for transgressions. But this is not a positive shaping of activity for the future. Proposals might be made along such lines, as in Venice where the proposals of the chief accountant, Bartolomeo Taduri, included setting targets for the construction masters, ranking them for promotion, and demoting those who failed to produce quality vessels. But such proposals regularly failed to overcome workforce resistance, as in fact happened in this instance.

References

Alpers, S. (1982), *The Art of Describing*, University of Chicago Press, Chicago.

Burchell, G., Gordon, C. and Miller, P. (eds) (1991) *The Foucault Effect: Studies in Govern-mentality*, Harvester Wheatsheaf, London.

Carmona, S., Ezzamel, M. and Gutierrez, F. (1994), *Control and Cost Accounting Practices in the Spanish Royal Tobacco Factory*, Discussion Paper, Carlos III University, Madrid.

Drew, J. (1947) Manorial Accounts of St. Swithun's Priory, Winchester. *English Historical Review*, **62**, pp. 20–41.

Ezzamel, M. (1994) The Emergence of the Accountant in the Institutions of Ancient Egypt. *Management Accounting Research*, **5**, pp. 221–46.

Fleischman, R. and Parker, L. (1991) British Entrepreneurs and Pre-Industrial Revolution Evidence of Cost Management. *Accounting Review*, **66**, (2) pp. 361–75.

Foucault, M. (1977) *Discipline and Punish*, Allen Lane, London.

Foucault, M. (1981) The Order of Discourse, Untying the Text: A Poststructuralist Reader (ed R. Young), Routledge and Kegan Paul, pp. 48–78.

Foucault, M. (1984) *Histoire de la Sexualite: vol.2, L'Usage des Plaisirs*, Gallimard, Paris.

Foucault, M. (1987) What is Enlightenment?, in *The Foucault Reader* (ed P. Rabinow) pp. 32–50, Penguin Books, London.

Goodhart, C. (1989) *Money, Information and Uncertainty*, Macmillan, London.

Gwilliam, D., Hoskin K., and Macve, R. (1992) Financial Control in the Financial Services Industry: the Case of Lloyd's of London, *Perspectives on Financial Control* (eds M. Ezzamel and D. Heathfield) pp. 203–28, Chapman and Hall, London.

Hoskin, K. (1993) Education and the Genesis of Disciplinarity: the Unexpected Reversal, in *Knowledges: Historical and Critical Studies in Disciplinarity* (eds E. Messer-Davidow *et al.*) pp. 271–304 University of Virginia Press, Charlottesville.

Hoskin, K. (1995) The Viewing Self and the World We View: Beyond the Perspectival Illusion. *Organization: The interdisciplinary journal of organization, theory and society*, **2**(1) pp. 141–62.

Hoskin, K. and Macve, R. (1986) Accounting and the Examination: a Genealogy of Disciplinary Power. *Accounting, Organizations and Society* (**11**) 2, pp. 105–36.

Hoskin, K. and Macve, R. (1988) The Genesis of Accountability: The West Point Connections. *Accounting, Organizations and Society*, **13**(1) pp. 37–73.

Hoskin, K. and Macve, R. (1994) Writing, Examining, Disciplining: the genesis of accounting's modern power. *Accounting as Social and Institutional Practice* (eds A. Hopwood and P. Miller) pp. 67–97, Cambridge University Press, Cambridge.

Hoskin, K., Zambon,S. and Zan, L. (1994) Management and Accounting at the Venice Arsenale in the Sixteenth Century: A Case Study. Paper presented at the 17th Annual Congress of the European Accounting Association, April 1994, Venice.

McKendrick, N. (1970) Josiah Wedgwood and Cost Accounting in the Industrial Revolution. *Economic History Review*, pp. 45–67.

McNay, L. (1992) *Foucault and Feminism: Power, Gender and the Self*, Polity, Cambridge.

McReynolds, P. and Ludwig, K. (1984) Christian Thomasius and the Origin of Psychological Rating Scales, *Isis* **75**, pp. 546–53.

Macve, R. (1985) Some Glosses on 'Greek and Roman Accounting'. *History of Political Thought* **VI**,(1/2) 233–64.

Rothblatt, S. (1982) Failure in Early Nineteenth-Century Oxford and Cambridge. *History of Education*, **11**, pp. 1–21.

Schaffer, S. (1994) Babbage's Intelligence: Calculating Engines and the Factory System, *Critical Inquiry*, **21**, pp. 203–27.

Smith, A. (1759/1976) *The Theory of Moral Sentiments*. Clarendon Press, Oxford.

Thompson, E. (1967) Time, Work-Discipline and Industrial Capitalism. *Past and Present*, **38**, pp. 56–97.

15 Organizing accountabilities: ontology and the mode of accounting

John Law

The origin in physical anthropological discourse is ever receding, not only because new fossils are found and reconstructed, but also because the origin is precisely what can never really be found; it must remain a virtual point, ever reanimating the desire for the whole.

(Donna Haraway, 1992: 193)

Introduction

This paper is about representation. And accounting. And it makes a strong claim. The claim is that representation is not about describing something which is already there. Rather, it is about *making* the knower and *making* what is known. By *creating the distinction* between knower and that which is known. And then concealing the connection.

To be sure, this sounds counter-intuitive. For most of the time we work on the assumption that there is a world out there. A world that may be known. A world that may be more or less satisfactorily described or pictured. That is, we ask only *epistemological* questions about our knowledge. About the quality of our accounts. About how well we know the world. About how our accounts might be improved. But the story about representation that I want to press is different. It is counter-intuitive. It is a story that pushes us in the direction of *ontology*. That is, it pushes us to ask questions about the nature of being, about what there is in the world, about the conditions which lead to the creation of objects in the world.

Very abstract. But I don't want to be abstract. I want to be practical and down to earth. I want, in particular, to be empirical: to practise 'empirical philosophy'[1]. The exploration of philosophical issues through empirical material. So I will explore these issues of accounting by ethnographic means. Accordingly, my story is of an organization. Of the way in which that organization worked upon its management information systems at the beginning of the 1990s. And, in particular, of the way in which it introduced a new management accounting system. And so created new forms of knowledge, of representation. But at the same time created a new organizational world or *object*. And a new kind of knowing *subject* or manager.

The paper falls into a number of parts. After some ethnographic scene-setting, I spell out and explore three understandings of representation or accounting: empiricist, instrumentalist, and poststructuralist. First, I show that the managers are at different times: empiricists (when they assume that what they know does or could correspond to organizational reality); and instrumentalists (when they work on the assumption that what they know is, or could be, a workable tool for handling organizational problems. Then I adopt the poststructuralist argument (which is also an ontological argument) that representation and accounting are about the creation of knowing subjects and known objects to explore two different and contrasting ways in which subjects and objects, knowers and known, are created in the organization. I argue that the first is closely linked to management accounting systems, and to the creation of a management-subject with those lionized attributes of foresight and discretion. The second is linked to bureaucratic paperwork such as agendas, and leads to a modest and much less fashionable subjectivity which reflects a concern with legal and bureaucratic due process. These, then, are two 'modes of accounting' which are quite different, and which generate subject-object distinctions in quite different ways.

Finally, I touch on three implications of the ontological approach to accounting. First, I argue that empiricist and instrumentalist approaches to knowledge operate to conceal the ontological character of representation. They do this by explaining any failure in accounting as a technical matter, thereby preserving the assumption that there is, behind that failure, a reliable entity that can be reliably known. I call this entity a 'virtual object'. Second, I explore some implications of coexistence of multiple modes of accounting. In particular, I consider the way in which technologies, like subjects, are constituted differently within different modes of accounting. And finally, I note that any given mode of accounting rapidly exhausts itself. Which means that the only way of creating an organization is to slip between different ontological regimes. That unless we adopt an idea of the organization as (essentially) incoherent we have to accept its ontology as heterogeneous, recognizing that the effect of organization is generated by continual displacement between ontological regimes.

Story 1

I spent most of 1990 as an ethnographer in a large scientific laboratory. I followed people around the Laboratory, watched their experiments, listened to them as they talked, and collected their paperwork. I also interviewed them, and attended innumerable management meetings. Indeed, I spent more time with the managers than I did with any other group. This was deliberate. I had been commissioned to study the practice of the management of science, and in particular to explore the ways in which managers use performance indicators in the course of their decision making.

1990 was a difficult year for the Laboratory. Employing over 600 people in a series of large facilities which were used for both basic and applied research, the Laboratory was under considerable financial pressure. Economies in science funding, a move towards diverse customer-client relations, a requirement to respond to opportunities in a competitive marketplace, combined together with the growing maturity of some of the basic scientific instruments in the Laboratory to generate the sense, at least amongst higher management, that it was important – indeed urgent – to make hard decisions. For instance, it was, or so the senior managers argued, not possible to carry on supporting all the activities that had traditionally been undertaken in the Laboratory. Choices – choices that would hurt some people both within and beyond the Laboratory – were unavoidable.

I arrived in the middle of this period. A new management team had recently been put in place, and was in the process of tackling these perceived difficulties. But what did this mean for the activities of the Laboratory? The new team found itself asking a series of questions. Which commercial Laboratory activities were profitable? How much did different projects cost? And what should stay and what would have to go? The answers to such questions were very far from obvious. The reason for this was that the character of the financial difficulties confronted by the Laboratory was clear only at a global level. Too little cash was coming in to cover outgoings, at least in the long run: this much was obvious. But where the cash was going, what it was paying for in terms of scientific results, where economies might best be made or new income generated – none of this was particularly clear. And the difficulties were exacerbated by an intensification of concern about financial accountability. Thus clients and funders, who were increasing in number, wanted to know that their payments were realistic. And they also wanted to know that their cash was being spent on their own contract work rather than in some other and inappropriate way.

The system of accounting used in the Laboratory was poorly adapted to these kinds of demands. It was primarily intended to provide figures about the income and expenditure of very large divisions, and to ensure that funds were spent in conformity with legal and bureaucratic rules about the appropriate uses for different classes of income. Accordingly, the accounts offered little information about the costs incurred by particular projects – and nowhere was this more true than for 'manpower'.[2] When the new management team was appointed there was no formal way of tracking the cost or the quantity of manpower being used on particular projects. Accordingly, it was argued that the 'true' costs of projects were unknown, and that it was only possible to arrive at 'approximations' from existing figures: for instance, by guessing the number of 'man-years' devoted to a project, and multiplying this by the notional average salary of all the people employed in the Laboratory.

It is important not to accept the notion of 'true cost' at face value. This is because what counts as an 'approximation' and what is taken to be a 'real' figure is a matter of convention, and that convention may change. Or, to put it a little differently, 'true costs' may be imagined as a phantom – like Donna Haraway's 'origin fossils'[3] – that can be endlessly mobilized to argue for a particular organizational reality, and so to effect particular organizational changes: as, for instance, in the reworked relationship between costs, manpower effort, and projects that I have just mentioned. In the Laboratory this process of reworking led to the creation of a 'manpower booking system'. Thus there had been accounting systems in the past, but these were deemed 'primitive'. But for the first time in the history of the Laboratory, all its employees were asked not simply to record the number of hours they worked, but in addition to use a new manpower booking form to book their time to one or more of a large number of different projects. They did this by coding up their activities in half-day blocks: half a day to this activity; half a day to that project; and so on. Then, at the end of each month, they were required to return this form to the Finance Office which summarized the returns, and issued these summaries to the relevant managers. For the first time, then, managers could look to see how much manpower was being booked to particular projects. This met a part of the concern with audit mentioned above. But further, and just as important, it meant that managers could compare the manpower 'actually' booked with the manpower that had been budgeted.

Commentary 1: theories of representation

A representation shows what it represents. Perhaps – it depends on the representation – it tells a story.[4] But what does this mean? And how does it do this? Different philosophers tell us different stories. Let's mention three of these:

First, there are *empiricists* who are committed to one form or another of correspondence theory. These writers tell us that representations have a referent: that is, they refer to something that is out there, in the world and they report on it; they report on it more or less adequately. Several metaphors are possible. But one is optical. It is to imagine that a technology of representation is a set of optics. This works well if it does not distort: if it is transparent; if what it tells *corresponds* to whereof it tells; if it allows the viewer to see what it reports without intervening, without distortion, or opacity.[5]

Second, there are *instrumentalists*. These authors tell us more practical stories, stories for which optical metaphors work less well. They say, for instance, that a system of representation is a product, a product of interaction between the viewer and the viewed. For, or so this story runs, the world could tell us many stories. It could be represented in indefinitely many ways. So the issue is not whether or not a representation 'corresponds' to reality. Indeed, the notion of correspondence is unclear even if it is not meaningless. Rather, the issue is: why do we want to interact with the world? What do we want to know about it? And how does it interact with our concerns? This, then, is an instrumental view of the character of representations: these are instruments or tools; they are the products of interaction. And these interactions are guided by interests and cognitive presuppositions carried by the narrator. Here, then, the test of a good representation is practical: the question is, *does it serve?*[6]

And third, there are *poststructuralists*. Writers of this kind tell stories about – other stories tell about – creation. They say, counterintuitively, that:

1 representations and their referents are generated together. In a process of doubling. At the same moment. So the story is one of creation *and* separation: the two *necessarily* go together.
2 that as a part of the making of a *relation* there is also separation – for a representation needs a referent (an *object*) and a *subject* if it is to tell a story about anything. And
3 very important, there is *deletion*. In particular, there is deletion of the process of separation and creation, deletion of the process that leads to the generation of the subject and the object-referent.

In 'post structuralist' stories of the *origins* of representation are shrouded in mystery. Though a secure referent and a secure object are indeed achieved. Once again, here the test of a good representation is practical. But it is practical in a more radical way than is found among the instrumentalists. For the issue is not only: does it serve? It also has to do with the deletion that serves to distinguish subject from referent-object. The question is: can the deletion be sustained? And how is this done? And what would happen if it were undeleted?[7]

I will say that all three theories of representation are carried, performed, or assumed in the Laboratory: *is it true? Does it work? Can the necessary deletion between subject and object be sustained?* The managers are going to wrestle with all three questions. But we will find that they wrestle with them in different ways under different circumstances.

Story 2

The manpower booking system was introduced shortly before I arrived at the Laboratory. As a result, I was not able to trace the discussions that led to its initial design. I did, however, listen to the managers as they debated the adequacy of the system after it was put into operation. In general they were reasonably pleased with the results. But there were also teething troubles to do with the accuracy of the system. For instance, quite a number of employees did not fill in their forms and return them at the end of the month:

Peter[8]:   [The manpower booking system] is still not very successful. For the month of August we still had 40-plus cards outstanding at 3.00 pm. today [the 10th of September]. This is about the norm. The people vary, [though] there are one or two persistent offenders.

Jim: That's about 10 per cent.

Adrian: All the cases I've investigated have been due to legitimate absence from the Lab.

Brian: But that's not an excuse. The cards are out a long time in advance, and we've asked supervisors to fill them in.

Adrian: It's difficult to find a way of operationalizing it.

Sometimes the failure to return the forms was said to be deliberate:

Adrian: If someone [refuses to fill their card in] send it to their supervisor.

Fraser: Even that doesn't work! Or people make 'protest bookings' – for instance to Finance and Supply, because they say they don't understand it.

Whether deliberate or not, the incomplete character of the returns was held to create a gap which affected the accuracy of the results. But how could this gap be plugged? People were chased up. And, as I've mentioned above, supervisors were contacted. But this still left gaps, and the only plausible way to deal with these was to make an estimated booking, usually based on the previous month's return. Most but not all managers agreed that this was reasonable:

Nigel: I've discovered that if manpower booking forms are handed in later than 2.00 pm on the first day of the month [the Finance Department] allocate that manpower to any project they fancy . . . !

Peter: I think that's a bit of an exaggeration!

Nigel: Okay, well, maybe it is a bit.

Peter: I have a lot of sympathy [with them]. They wait for a period. They send round a note. And only then do they allocate a booking.

Nigel: Well, at least at the Electricity Board they do it on a basis of last year's booking!

Another endemic problem was that of inaccurate bookings. This was more difficult to police, for failure here did not announce itself. So why did people book their time wrongly, and what could be done about it? Again, various reasons and possible remedies were offered:

Jim: People don't book clearly because the [booking] heads are not clear. They have now been clarified.

People also tended, as one manager put it, to 'lemming together' if they were uncertain how they should code their time. And although it was thought to be important to check the bookings made, managers also knew that this took both time and effort – time and effort that might be better spent elsewhere. Furthermore, even with policing there was always the possibility of resistance:

> Jim Smith phoned someone up and said, 'You didn't work *there* last month!' He got a very frosty response. 'You're not telling *me* where I worked! I *know* where I worked.' It is certainly true that in the Lab there are quite a lot of people who take a flippant or a cynical attitude to these forms. They aren't clear what they are for.

Commentary 2: empiricism and its limits

Here are some of the assumptions that seem to be built into the exchanges I report above. A first assumption is that there are real activities out there, activities that pre-date the manpower booking system. Second, these activities fit into certain kinds of organizationally relevant categories. Third, it is possible to represent these activities – to find ways of inscribing them on sheets of card such that the organization of these inscriptions corresponds to the organization of activities. In other words, everything proceeds from the taken-for-granted assumption that a reasonably *accurate* system of manpower booking is possible. Fourth, by the same token, it is accepted that error might creep into this process, noise which distorted the relationship between referent and representation. And fifth, by examining the origins of this error, it is possible to imagine improving the system, of finding ways of increasing the level of correspondence between the organization of activities and the organization of traces.

So the issue is one of accuracy. If the booking codes fit organizationally-relevant categories it is possible to ask about the accuracy or otherwise of the returns. This is the major question for the empiricist theory of representation. And it is the crucial step for the managers. Thus here the managers are empiricists. The object – a more or less achievable object – is to render the optics of the system transparent, indeed invisible. To ensure that the system generates not artefacts but rather represents organizational activities. That it, as it were, deletes itself in the space between the organization and its managers.

Except that this stress on accuracy is too simple. For there are other considerations. Pragmatic considerations. For instance, there are questions to do with cost-effectiveness:

> It is difficult to police the manpower bookings; the problem is to decide how much hassle it is worth.

So what did the managers do? I guess that it varied. I am not certain. But, though it might take time to 'police' the bookings by looking through these, the managers also considered this to be important:

> ". . . scrutinize the manpower bookings carefully,' one manager urged, 'because [it] makes a hell of a difference to costs. . . . Totally by mistake I found 89 man days booked to the project [that should have been allocated elsewhere].'

This, then, was the purpose of the manpower-booking procedure, and indeed all the other features of the management accounting system that were laboriously being put in place: to determine the 'real' costs of the different projects, rather than having to make do with 'approximations'.

But this had implications for the theory and practice of accuracy. Yes, the bookings and other indicators of costs should, so far as possible, correspond to the real costs. But this was unrealistic, for there were also limits – limits defined by pragmatics. So, between the non-quite-achievable 'real' bookings and those actually reported there would always be a gap. And the character of this gap, the dividing line between 'accurate approximations' and those that would not do, between the (reparable?) fluidity of the daily round and the adequacy of the manpower booking system with respect to criteria of accountability – this division was defined by the reasons for mounting the exercise in the first place.[9] This, then, is the place where the second theory of representation first comes into its own, the theory that works from pragmatism or workability. For the managers were also instrumentalists.

Story 3

I started off by saying that the issue was one of control. The managers felt they needed to know about the 'real' costs of the different projects. They wanted to know which projects had overspent, and which underspent. And they felt they needed to know this because, in extremis, they might cut budgets in order to save costs or bail out other projects. So it seemed important to collect data – for instance to generate workable and accurate representations of the way in which employees had spent their month. But the way in which data such as this was presented was also important. Indeed, this was a source of endless discussion. So what was the problem here?

Often managers expressed themselves as being unable to see what they were supposed to be seeing. This was a problem that cropped up in one form or another at almost every management meeting:

> Am I alone in finding Part 4 not transparent? I find it confusing. Every time there is a change I have to read everything, and all the footnotes. Can we ask [the Accounting Department] to look at this?

And again:

> What happens is that we have these things in bits and pieces, but I have never had the chance to look at it as a whole.

The object, then, was to find ways of summarizing – to develop what Cooper (1992) calls an 'economy of convenience'. Managers wanted to see things as a whole and during the year I was in the Laboratory they spent much time and effort trying to move the accounting system in the direction of visibility. Partly this was a matter of organization. The problem was to try to ensure that the appropriate representations were grouped together:

Fraser: [. . .] so we will get a different format *to* [that of] Paul Amies, and it will be printed out to fit estimates. It's a massive job. But things will be blocked together.

John: So we are sort of moving towards our own accounting system.

Fraser[?]:   The [projects funded by the European Community] will be blocked together. Staff costs *and* requisitions. We've never done that before.

. . .

Fraser: At present you get random lists of numbers. In future these will appear in a block, manpower, requisitions, and overheads – not just requisitions.

Sean: Paul Amies's system could do this? Could it?

Fraser: [Yes], but we have to tell Paul Amies what to do. I am doing it because we need to get cost-centres related to the science basis.

John: Yes. We have to do it. It is difficult to use Paul Amies's printout. You have to spend a morning ploughing through it. Anything which makes it easier to do is a good move. At present you have to jump through from [one part to another].

So the question was one of organizing – about how best to juxtapose the representations. But this was only a part of the problem. For assimilability also had to do with the amount of information presented to the managers. And this was huge. Typically, those who were trying to control spending came to meetings with 'Paul Amies's' computer printout – but this was often an inch thick. If the concern was with detail – with the minutiae of spending on minor items of equipment within a particular project – then this was the indispensable bible. However, if the concern was with the general state of the project, the printout was almost unusable. So the managers, partly in combination with the Finance Office, began to create alternative summaries:

John: Let me ask you a question. Do you get *this*? [He gestures at a substantial computer printout.]

Paul: We *don't* get a summary.

Fraser: That is the Andy Fraser special summary. I think it would help if you did. That gives you the global view.

Commentary 3: pragmatic focus

Now we move one step deeper into the pragmatics of representation, one step further into the theory and practice of instrumentalism. For, if we follow the managers, we see that the 'transparency' of the optics is not given. It is not even taken. Rather, it is a cunning artefact. Thus if we take the argument in stages, first we learn that it is not simply an empiricist matter of generating 'accurate' representations, or distinguishing between what is 'real' and 'approximations'. Neither is it simply a question of distinguishing between 'approximations' that will serve, and those that will not – though, as we have seen, this distinction is indeed deployed. Instead, and in addition, simplicity is achieved in an active process of blocking, summarizing, simplifying, and deleting. Which means that visibility is an effect, generated in part by pre-determining what is to count – and what, therefore, becomes counted.

Look back at the exchanges reported above: time and time again the metaphors are drawn from optics. There is talk of global views, of looking at things as a whole, of transparency. And there is talk of seeing things:

Terry: You don't give us a printout of the actual receipts received on this chart.
Andy: I could do.
Terry: That would mean we could *see* what expected receipts we needed to worry about.

So the metaphor is, at any rate partly, optical. And it is, in particular, about focus. About the need for a *focal point*.

But what defines a focal point? How can one tell that a representation has been properly drawn together, is properly in focus? There is no principled way of answering these questions. They are practical in import. Or, as Annemarie Mol and Marc Berg argue, multiple principles and multiple practices are located, as it were fractally, inside one another, and become distinguishable only for local purposes[10]. A set of representations which serves one purpose may turn out to be quite inappropriate for another. This is why I say that we are one step further into a pragmatic or interactive theory of representation. We learn, or relearn (for this is standard instrumental philosophy of science) that representations are tools. They either work, or they do not. And correspondence? Well, again, the only way of giving meaning to the notion of correspondence is again to ask whether or not a representation works.

Story 4

One day the Managing Director, Andrew, called six of his top managers to an emergency meeting. This was about the major new Laboratory project – the so-called 'Second Wiggler' project. The reason for calling the meeting was that things appeared to be falling behind schedule. And if this was so, then it was a very serious state of affairs.

Andrew: I'm trying to nip the problems in the bud, if there are any problems. Let's just review the situation. . . If we look at the last report [of six months ago, this is] okay except for the experimental [instruments]. Jimmy Smith says that the superconductor itself is okay. So the problem is with the experimental instruments. The manpower used was low, [but] it was said that it would pick up. We aimed to use nineteen in-house man years, but we [actually] used seven in-house man years.

At this point one of the other managers interrupted to say that Andrew's figure of seven was too low, and the correct figure was nine:

Andrew: Okay, [but we wanted] nineteen, not [nine]. And next year we *planned* to use twenty-nine. So we'll have to use thirty-nine. So there is a big gap developing. I think that this means that we've got a problem. Is this right?

Some discussion followed which rapidly reached a conclusion:

> **Andrew**: . . .I'm going to say that we are four to five months behind on effort. This is what drew my attention to it. So there *is* a problem.

But why had there been delay? How had the problem built up?

> **Tim**: [One of the reasons] is that we have changed the specifications of the [experimental instruments]. They have become more expensive, and more complicated.
>
> **Andrew**: Okay. So [as a consequence] you've accepted a change in the [interim] schedules, with the end date the same.
>
> **John**: The *chart* [with the new schedules] says that there is not a problem. But there *is* a problem. It is harder to stick to [the new schedule]. Then in eighteen months or two years it will become apparent.

But what about catching up? Nigel offered a diagnosis:

> **Nigel**: If we can resolve it quickly, with an increase in man years, then we can recover.

But when would this happen?

> **Andrew**: When was the manpower surge anticipated?
>
> **Nigel**: We are having a step function [increase in manpower now].

So things were starting to look less gloomy. The lost time might be made up.

> **Andrew**: So why are we having this meeting?
>
> **Nigel**: Because there will be consequences. . . .
>
> **Andrew**: So what were you doing?
>
> **David**: I called a [senior management] meeting. And we agreed in the past month . . . that we would address priorities.
>
> **Andrew**: I am much relieved. You are addressing priorities! You are already doing that.

So why, then, *were* they having this meeting?

> **David**: Okay. But *you* have to take decisions.
>
> **Andrew**: Fine.
>
> **Colin**: For instance, [another major contract] will have to be downgraded in priority.
>
> **Andrew**: The superconductor is top priority. . . . Nothing is as important as the superconductor.

So this was the bottom line: there were decisions, hard decisions, to be taken. They were hard decisions because they would have major consequences for other important projects. And the responsibility for taking those decisions lay on Andrew's shoulders.

Commentary 4: a discretionary mode of accounting

In the last commentary I talked about transparency and focus. But other things were going on too. For instance, though I did not bring this out, the concern with optics suggested a link with Foucault's analysis of panopticism and discipline[11]. Foucault, it will be remembered, describes Bentham's nineteenth-century design for the perfect prison – the 'panopticon' – in which inmates, and so their behaviour, would all be visible from a central point of surveillance. And the same Foucauldian metaphor – that of making multiple activities visible to one controlling place – may be appropriate here again. Perhaps, then, we would say that this meeting constitutes itself, or perhaps better is constituted, as a managerial panopticon. Perhaps we could say that it is a kind of focal point where everything that is relevant is brought together, summarized and displayed.

So far so good. But what happens if we follow Foucault one step further? For Foucault, it will be remembered, argues against essences – and at any rate implicitly against the idea that there is such a thing as 'human nature', that agents have certain attributes (for instance reliability, genius, or managerial ability) by virtue of their natural attributes. The question, then, is what happens if we follow Foucault and detach our analysis of representation from such a 'humanist' theory of agency?[12] What happens, for instance, if we say, as I did at the beginning of this essay, that representation may be treated as a process in which subjects and objects are simultaneously created? Let me approach this by telling a story about Andrew.

People talk a lot about Andrew. After all, for them he is the boss. And generally they talk about him in approving terms. For instance, they say that he is a fine and entrepreneurially minded manager; that he's tough and active; that he's good at drumming up business for the Laboratory, at finding new contracts and new work; and that he likes to perform well. So they say – he says so himself – that he hates 'cock-ups': if the Laboratory is given resources, then it is *responsible* for turning in a decent performance. Which means in turn that the managers – and Andrew himself – are trouble-shooters. They spot difficulties (or opportunities) as quickly as possible, they weigh up the options, and they choose the best of these, even if this means taking decisions that are said to be 'difficult', or have hard consequences for those on the receiving end.

This is a theoretically humanist story. But one doesn't have to be very deeply committed to non-humanism to see that it is at best incomplete. This is because Andrew's character as an effective entrepreneur, his character as an agent who can exercise effective discretion, cannot be detached from the technologies or practices of accounting. The evidence is in the story about the emergency meeting. Without the accounting and manpower figures he might not have been able to detach himself from the 'detail' of the project, its daily activity, and make the discovery that there was something wrong[13]. And it was precisely these accounting technologies that made the delay 'visible'. Which means that in their absence he would have also been unable to consider options, or generate priorities. The argument, then, is that Andrew as a managerial subject is, at least in part, the product of a system of managerial representation.

In looking at Andrew as a location in a network of representation I make an argument that is anti-humanist. And one that is also semiotic. That is, it assumes that the objects, subjects, representations, systems of accounting – indeed all the materials that are involved in management including Andrew himself – are effects that achieve their character as a consequence of the way in which they interact together[14]. My argument, then, is that to make sense of this story we need to consider the semiotics of representation. And we need in particular to explore the *performance* of a particular semiotic – that is how it is that relations of managing (and so the objects caught up in it including persons) recursively produce themselves in the course of interaction.

This is an important point. It is important because any such exploration takes us a long way beyond Andrew and his meeting with its papers and its printouts. It takes us to a much more general concern with what we might think of as the 'syntaxes of representation' or the 'modes of accounting'. By which I mean: the possibility that we may be able to impute ordering logics to sociotechnical relations. Ordering logics that are embodied and performed in many different places: in ordered texts; in the practices of people; in devices of all sorts; in interactions and habits; and in architectures[15].

And it is this ordering, the arrangements of all these diverse materials, which *together* provide for and perform: subjects, seeing subjects, places from which there is a global view; and, in the same moment, objects, or better a disciplined series of objects that are available to be seen. Seer and seen: they are constituted together in a 'semio-technical hierarchy'[16]. And they are constituted in a series of processes embodied and recursively performed in many different materials, many different times, and many different spaces.

All of this can be treated as an affirmation of post structuralism – of the process that has sometimes been called 'doubling'[17]. But in the present context it can also be seen as a much more specific claim about a mode of accounting and, to be sure, a mode of management. For the semiotics of this specific system of representation generate a very particular form of subject-place or panopticism[18]. There is, to be sure, surveillance, but it is one form of surveillance among many. So what is specific about this one? The answer has to do with the way in which it generates options. This is my proposal: that here we are witnessing a syntax of representation which generates that most lionized mode of being, subjectivity as *discretion* – for, as we will see in the next section, other forms of subjectivity are possible [19]; and, at the same time, that creates that most celebrated form of organization – the flexible and 'pro-active' enterprise which is capable of efficiently deploying its resources in order to respond to the opportunities presented by the environment. For the object that is created – this discretionary space which presents Andrew with the possibility of responding and redeploying resources – is an *array* of (thereby created) elements. It is an array of normalized elements, inserted into an exceedingly well-defined space[20]. So it is a set of elements that stand in specific and calculable relationship with one another. And the fact of that normalized specificity and the fact of that calculability – it is these that generate the options that are necesary for a subjectivity that rests upon the 'bold' and 'responsible' exercise of discretion.

Story 5

James Lawson is a junior manager who deals with a wide range of administrative tasks: he talks with visiting scientists, he liaises with outside bodies, but he also organizes much of the administrative paperwork in one part of the Laboratory. And as a part of this task, he prepares the agendas and writes the minutes of several important management meetings. Look carefully, now, at this example of his work:

RESEARCH PROGRAMME MEETING

The next meeting is to be held on Friday 21st December 1990 commencing at 9.00 a.m. in Conference Room 3.

AGENDA ** *(Please advice JBL of any amendments)* **

1. Apologies: J Bennett – *(F G Thomas to chair mtg.)*
2. Notes of 25th meeting on 30th November 1990
3. Revision of Estimates for 1991–92   *(F G Thomas)*
4. Family Trees
5. Follow-up from SRFC on 10/11 Dec (including ideas for
    membership of the committee)
6. Safety Matters
7. Any other matters or actions arising from the last meeting:
    (i)   Engineering – *(B Ayer)*
    (ii)   Computer Systems and Technology – *(J H Bridges)*
    (iii)   Miscellaneous
8. Agendas and dates of next meetings:
    (1)   Wednesday 23rd Jan. 1991, at 9.00 a.m.
    (2)   *(Proposed)* Wednesday 13th Feb., at 9.00 a.m.

J B Lawson 17.12.90
Secretary

Circulation: J Bennet   J H Bridges   R King   D B Crane
                 B Ayer   F G Thomas   J B Lawson   E Saxon
(For information)   T Fuller   J Law

Commentary 5: an administrative mode of accounting

Like the manpower booking figures, this agenda is another approach to accounting, another overview. It tells of a set of objects: people, dates, family trees (that is, organizational charts), computer systems and the rest. It tells us something about their putative relations, about how things ought to be[21]. And it also constitutes a subject, or a set of subjects. And again it is the product of more or less deleted work, the organization of all kinds of hidden materials including the work of James Lawson as he tries to collate the actions of other managers. So much we can take for granted. So why is it important?

The argument I want to make is that the agenda may be understood as a performance, an instance, of an *alternative mode of accounting* or organizational syntax. One that may be constrasted with the discretionary and panoptical accounting mode described above. Indeed, I want to argue that it generates a quite different form of representation, and with it, a different form of subjectivity and objectivity. And this (contrary to what might be expected from the standard literatures on the control of agendas) does not necessarily lead to the concentration of discretionary power – or if it does then it also effects a deferral of it[22].

Note first that, the document is self-referential or reflexive; it does not distinguish so clearly between subjects and objects; or, to put it a little differently, the subjects, the readers, that it constitutes, are also constituted as objects. For instance, there is the circulation list. And again, there is the note: 'F G Thomas to chair mtg.' So F G Thomas will read the agenda; but he will also, or so it tells, *perform* a role that has been designated by that agenda. Indeed, the relationship between subject and object is crucial to the performance of the ordering story told by the agenda. F G Thomas will have to weave the two together, jumping between them, acting both as subject and as object, if the business of the meeting is to be successfully completed.

Now note another feature of the document. The readers can sit back in their chairs and read it through. So they can take a distanced or 'distal' view and see what is included in the morning's business at a glance[23]. But unlike the 'overall' view offered to the management meetings by means of the production of statistics, first it does not report on matters past; and second, it does not generate options.

Representations such as the Andy Fraser 'special summary' generate an object, or a set of objects, through a process of blocking and simplification. In this respect the agenda is no different. But as I've already noted, what is distinctive about discretionary panopticism is that it seeks to constitute the objects it generates within a normalized space. In principle everything is brought to a point location precisely by virtue of the fact that there is a calculus for comparing and contrasting what would otherwise be incommensurably distributed. Indeed, this is precisely the point of the exercise: it seeks to generate the centred subjectivity of an informed, control-relevant and luxurious discretion. We saw this in the case of Andrew's emergency meeting about the superconductor. Here it meant that a small group of people sitting round a table were able to play simulation games: 'If we do this, then that; if we do that then the other; so let's do this, and avoid doing something else'.

But nothing like this is going on in the case of the agenda. Yes, it generates representations of items that are gathered together on a single sheet of paper. But it does not obviously draw things together. The items, blocked and ordered though they are, are not located within the normalizing grid of a manipulable calculus except in the most restricted sense. One might, for instance, imagine spending more time talking about 'Family Trees' and less on the 'Revision of Estimates'. But that is the limit: at best the calculus attaches to time or to the order of business. It does not relate in any calculative manner to the objects cited in the agenda. There is no question of trading these off against one another.

So that is one point. And the other? To return to where I begin, in this instance the subjects are not constituted as if they were separable from the objects that are represented. They cannot stand back and take an overview. They are not distant from what they are looking at. Instead, they have to get their hands dirty. So in this politics, a politics of involvement rather than of command, the very character of subjectivity is linked with the appropriate performance by the subject as an object. Here, then, is an accountably self-reflexive form of semiotics. One, that is, that is visibly self-reflexive. One in which the deletion of the work that makes subject and object as separate is (accountably) incomplete. It is a logic or a strategy or a mode of accounting that strains to perform proper administration, legality, and due process[24].

Conclusions

Epistemology, ontology and the virtual object

In this chapter I've touched on three theories of representation: *naïve empiricism*; pragmatism or *instrumentalism*; and the post structuralist concern with *representation as constitutive of subject and object*. My object has been to explore and inform aspects of these theories by looking at data drawn from a management ethnography. The argument has been that parts of what goes on in the Laboratory can be understood in empiricist or pragmatic terms. Indeed, the managers often express their commitment to these theories of representation, though their allegiance to empiricism is moderated by the 'realism' that comes with pragmatism.

Why are they so committed? One answer is that notions of accuracy or approximation serve. They serve, for instance, to warrant a commitment to particular representations. And so they serve both to justify particular courses of action and to provide, recursively, for their workability. Which means, in practice, that managers are able to justify themselves – to offer accounts for their actions – to their paymasters. While at the same time generating the kind of discretionary space described, albeit ambivalently above. A discretionary space that makes it possible – one might, perhaps add necessary – to redeploy resources in a manner that will be justifiable to 'head office'.

This is an analysis consistent with the pragmatism of the contemporary sociology of knowledge[25]. But there is a further possibility. This is that the processes of forming a knowing subject and the objects to be known by this subject are *necessarily* concealed by theoretical humanism and its counterpart, transcendental realism. And that such empiricist or pragmatic understandings of the relationship between knower and known precisely serve, in that function, to efface the question of ontology. To conceal the way in which knower and known are made together. And might, indeed, be made in quite other ways.

The argument is that uncertainties and doubts come in different sizes and shapes. Let me explain. It poses no fundamental problem for theoretical humanism to discover that particular representations are flawed. Given the various distortions that may affect transparency this is only to be expected, and can (or so it is imagined) be remedied by 'technical' improvements. Neither is there a basic difficulty for pragmatism if it turns out that whole modes of knowing are unsound. Such a discovery might raise serious epistemological questions about the adequacy of current belief, but within the humanism/realism space it can be safely assumed that such problems may be overcome by some analogue of paradigm shift[26]. However, uncertainties about ontology are profoundly threatening. And these become real if the status of the dualism of subject and object is put at risk: if, for instance, it is said (as it is in the writing of authors such as Foucault, Baudrillard or Cooper) that the division is a product rather than something that is given in the order of things. That the division, for instance, between managers and organizational realities is a process, something that is created, brought into being, negotiated. Which is, to be sure, what I have tried to suggest above.

So the argument I want to make echoes that of Donna Haraway. I want to say that the object/origin remains outside, a virtual point that reanimates the subject/object distinction (Haraway, 1992 p. 193). Or, to put it a little differently, that a notion such as 'real costs' works as a *virtual object*. That is, it is an object that appears to be real, to be solid, and to be out there. But is, in fact, something that has been created in the process of representation and accounting. An object that is both created, and at the same time warrants the process of representing within which it is created. Supplies it with its rationale.

I am saying, then, that the realist performance of a virtual object such as 'real costs' is crucial to the creation of the subject/object distinction. And to the erasure of the work that generates that distinction. For the apparent fact of an outside object, its 'out thereness', its reality independent of the knower, its value and character, its ontological unassailability – this is what warrants any process of inquiry. The search for truth – for instance in the form of real costs. Or (more modestly) the pragmatic search for a workable account of reality – here an adequate approximation to those costs.

But if the virtual object ('real costs') warrants these inquiries, the subject/object distinctions which they perform, and the work of doubling that is involved, then this suggests a different view of empiricism and pragmatism. These, though they are representational regimes in their own right, may also be understood as methods for reasserting the foundational (but virtual) character of the subject-object dualism – as members 'methods' for concealing the uncertain and reversible processes that generate and sustain these foundations. They may, in other words, be understood as *methods for effacing ontological doubts*[27]. Indeed for effacing the question of ontology. For defusing it by turning it into epistemology.

Technology and multiple accountability

The semiotic or post structuralist view of empiricism or pragmatism is counterintuitive from the standpoint of theoretical humanism. But it also offers a counterintuitive lever for thinking about technology. Simply stated, the problem is that technology – including the technology of representation – often appears in sociological stories as a 'thing'. Admittedly, the character of its thingness varies as a function of the story that is told. It may play the role of demon, undermining democracy, gemeinschaft or autonomy[28]. It may, alternatively, feature as a *deus ex machina*, liberating human potential and democratizing the world[29]. Or yet again, it may take on the role of a social chameleon, for better or for worse adopting the shape of its surroundings. But these appelations are unsatisfactory. They are unsatisfactory because they are simply too general, for technology is not a single 'thing'. It is, if we insist on using object-language, best seen as a self-generating array of things – things which interact with the social in many different ways. And, indeed, there is a sophisticated sociology about the interactions that take place between the social and the technical – a sociology that tells complicated and heterogeneous stories about the character of those interactions[30].

But commitment to semiotics, to various modes of accounting and performance, suggests a different and much more radical way forward. This is because, if we choose to press it home, it dissolves not only the social and the human, *but also the technological*. So 'technologism' as well as humanism also disappears, and with it the possibility of a sociology of interactions between technology and society. Instead the picture is one of subtle effects, of relations, of links in which the 'human' and the 'non-human' interweave and perform themselves in a monstrous and creative hetero-geneity[31]. This is the kind of heterogeneity that leads us to say that Andrew is not simply flesh and blood, nor even a set of socialized roles, but is (also) a dispersed network of materials that generates a specific form of discretionary subjectivity[32]. Semiotics thus dissolves essences in favour of relational effects – effects which tend to look messy and impure if we are committed to any particular version of the order of things[33].

So my argument is this. Semiotics avoids technological determinism, just as it avoids humanism. Like agents, technologies, including the technologies of representation, are dissolved by the aqua regia of structuralism. And this dissolution is important. But what should we put in its place? The semiotic answer is surely this: that we might look for multiple syntaxes, for different orderings in those relations, orderings which may perhaps create varying *modes* of subjectivity, objectivity or representation. So where should we look?

A possibility, but one which I believe we should resist, is to look for simple answers in the technologies of representation: to embrace McLuhan's adage that the medium is the message. The reason for resisting this is quite straightforward. It is that it is technological determinism by semiotic means: the attempt to read off the character of subjectivity from the supposed specific features of a technology of representation[34]. Negatively, then, I want to assert that it is *not* the case that 'literacy', 'print', or 'television', or any other medium implies one particular form of knowing subject[35]. And positively, like Cooper (1993), I want to press the view that technologies, texts, agents and social relations are all, and simultaneously, constituted in recursive and strategically heterogeneous syntaxes: which means that technologies have no special status.

The message, then, is that we might look at the way in which both medium and message are performed. Or, to put it differently, we might understand, as did such writers as Foucault, that the medium is more than a technology of representation in the narrow sense of the term. And this is precisely why I have chosen to tell ethno-graphic stories about managers *and* their representations. I wanted to suggest that managerial subjectivity is not determined by anything as simple as their literacy, or indeed by the xerox machine, that modern version of print. The existence of repro-ducible texts is, to be sure, important. But it is no more important than the existence of managers, organizational arrangements, meeting rooms, or devices of all sorts. All, so to speak, come together within a semiotically organized package – a particular mode of accounting. Or, to be more precise – and this is the further point of the empirical stories – these different materials come together as two rather different modes of accounting or organizational syntaxes.

Thus, as I have tried to show, there is one mode of accounting that is all to do with discretion. It is about panopticism run riot, the consistent attempt to divorce subject from object, the formation of a point-subjectivity constituted by normalized options. It is about a particular version of accountability: about what it is that counts as a 'proper' description, a 'proper' form of reporting, on the activities of people or the progress of projects. And it is also, as a part of this, about the strategic character of subjective intervention in the object. For this is a mode of intervention that is occasional but consequential, precisely because it is strategic and discretionary. Intervention can only come after the collecting, the calculating and the weighing up of options. After the accounts – both numbers and otherwise – have been made.

But there is another. As I have tried to show, this does not aspire to the lofty distinction between subject and object that is the strategic object of the first. So the extent to which the subject is constituted as a discretionary point is much more limited. Rather the concern is with due process and proper administration. Which means that the mode of accounting is quite different. It has to do with rule-following. With legality. With *showing* that proper procedures have been followed. With showing that no laws or conventions have been breached. Which implies that subjects endlessly turn themselves into objects – objects of the rules and procedures which, for instance, take the form of the standing orders or conventions which are performed in meetings. While, at the same time, objects are similarly constantly turning themselves back into subjects so that they may judge whether or not the rules have been properly followed. This, then, is a syntax or mode of accounting that is told and performed in documents such as agendas and minutes. And it is something which demands the performance of a constant weaving to and fro between subjectivity and objectivity. The former is not distant, strategic, and occasional. Rather, together with its interventions, it is continuous, reflexive, iterative, unfolding and tactical, distributed across time in ways that cannot be predicted or told in any detail at a single time or place[36].

Shifting accountability

So here is the claim. There are several ordering syntaxes, strategies or tactics, discourses, modes of accounting (the language that we use to talk of these does not really matter). That is, there are several ordering arrangements that recursively generate, and perform themselves in different materials, But if this is so then we have to confront the possibility that these experience their limits, that things escape them, that they run out. This then, is my final suggestion: that accountability (like the subject) is *decentred*. That it does not, cannot, 'come together' and collapse to a single point.

Consider the following exchange at the main management board. The managers were discussing a request for cash to sort out Laboratory archives:

Andrew: What archives? I didn't know that we had any. Where are they?

Tim: In the basement . . . it's full of them, box after box, that people have put down there when they ran out of space in their offices.

Andrew: What's the problem with just chucking them out?

Tim: The law says we can't destroy them. We have to keep organizational records.

Terry: I've often wondered about that. When my filing cabinets get full, I go through my files and take things out, really as I think best. Even my secretary doesn't know what I'm throwing away.

Andrew: Who actually *uses* these files? I've never looked at them – I didn't know they were there. What use are they?[37]

Though he is going to arrive at a different view, the comments by Andrew cited above start from the assumption that the matter is one of discretion. They also imply the possibility of standing back, of weighing up matters. Like the earlier discussion about the Second Wiggler, the matter is one of gathering information, and of representing it in an overall way that creates strategic discretion. 'What use are they'? This is the 'bottom line'. It is a distanced, a distal, view. Practical. Removed from the object with which it is concerned. But there something else is going on too. Tim reports that 'The law says we can't destroy them.' And this, or so I suggest, is a different syntax. A version of the second syntax explored above. For this is a comment that blurs subject-object boundaries. It is a form of words allied to due process and proper administration. And it is something that can only be performed if persons oscillate between subjectivity and objectivity. First subjects. And then objects.

The argument, then, is that the management meeting performs and embodies several syntaxes. And that there is *movement between them*[38]. The character of that movement, and the occasions on which it takes place, remain unclear. Perhaps it is that, when accounting in a particular mode gets blocked, there is a leap to an alternative, one that might move the meeting past the place that cannot be successfully represented in the original syntax. Perhaps it is that, when accounting in a particular mode appears inconsistent with a second syntax, that the second mobilizes itself. (This would be consistent with the second intervention by Tim above.) But, whatever the character of such displacements between different sets of syntaxes, it would appear that neither the managers as subjects, nor the meeting as a process, can be understood unless one allows for the play between different versions of subjectivity and objectivity. And it also suggests another 'virtual' mechanism by which the character of the object sustains itself – that of deferral of one mode of accounting and entry into an alternative.

The argument, then, is that both subjects *and* representational structures are necessarily decentred. Such that when they discover their limits and incoherences, these are not to be overcome in some new mode of representation which brings them together in a higher synthesis. But rather that that is how it is: that knowing is limited. Which means, if it is right, that knowing is a process. Or better, many different processes. Processes of deferral. Processes that involve perpetual displacement from one mode of knowing to another. So it is in this view that the managers and committees of Daresbury Laboratory are decentred. Necessarily decentred, slipping between discourses, places and times. Running into impossibilities which they 'solve' by jumping somewhere else – by thinking in alternative ways. So the committees (or so I'd venture to suggest) make impossible combinations, linked together through partial and elusive connections. Never to be brought together[39]. Never to be united in one vision. Never to make a single epistemology. Or a coherent ontology.

Acknowledgements

I am grateful to all who work at the Daresbury SERC Laboratory for allowing me such open access to their day-to-day work. I am also grateful to the Economic and Social Research Council, and to their programme managers, the Science Policy Support Group, for generous financial support within the 'Changing Culture of Science' research initiative. Without this support, an extended period of fieldwork would not have been possible. In addition, I am grateful to the participants and organizers of the 'Technologies of Representation' meeting at Warwick University in December 1992, where I first explored the issues considered in this paper. Finally, I would like to thank Michel Callon, Bob Cooper, Bruno Latour, Annemarie Mol, Rolland Munro and Marilyn Strathern for continuing encouragement and dialogue about things that can only be elusively known.

Notes

1. A term which no doubt has a long genealogy, but which I learned from Annemarie Mol.
2. Following Laboratory practice, I will use this gendered term.
3. See Haraway (1992: 193).
4. For one account of the ambivalent relationship between 'seeing' and 'telling' see Foucault (1983); but the subject is a large one in the theory of art. See, for instance, Alpers (1983), Bal (1991) and for a recent survey Mitchell (1994).
5. One has to go some way back in writing in the history or philosophy of science to find examples of straightforward optical correspondence theory. For a sociological version, see Merton (1957). For an account of the limits of optical metaphors, and the importance of understanding the 'consumption' of control technologies see Munro (1993). Munro's argument is related to the critique of technological determinism discussed below.
6. There are many interactive versions of the character of representation. See, for instance, Hesse (1974) and Kuhn (1970). I suspect a similar notion also underpins Jameson's fascinating analysis of the Frank Gehry house (1991), though he also shows an ambivalent link to the third and ontological version of representation discussed below.
7. As I have indicated, this is a characteristically poststructuralist position. See, in particular, Foucault (1970; 1983) Derrida (1976), Baudrillard (1988) and Cooper (1993) on the space between the tellable and the untellable, and the way in which this is (or alternatively is not) deleted. This is worked through empirically for scientific texts in Latour and Woolgar (1979), and for religious and management experience, in Law and Mol (1995b). But ethnomethodology is predicted on a similar notion of the relationship between referent and representation. See Garfinkel (1967) and Munro (1994).
8. The Daresbury SERC Laboratory is real, as are the managers and others whom I mention. But when I mention people I use pseudonyms. The conversations reported were not taped, but recorded by hand. Words added are included in square brackets.
9. Munro argues that competent local performance of the gap between the 'social' and the 'technical', or (my words) that which is fluid and that which is accountable, is also a performance of competent membership. See Munro (1994), and on the fluid and the accountable, see Mol and Law (1994a) and Law and Mol (1995b).
10. Which means that their contrast as opposed pairs is far too simple. See Mol and Berg (1994). Note that a fractal is a mathematical expression whose recursion generates a pattern of values that are broadly similar at different levels of scale. For a popular introduction see Gleick (1987). For an application to anthropological material see Strathern (1991).
11. See Foucault (1979).
12. Though there is a large literature on theoretical humanism and its alternatives, the methodological and political implications of the distinction are particularly well illustrated in Mol and Mesman (1995).
13. I place quotation marks around the term 'detail' because I want to avoid the implication that size or scale are given in the order of things. For exploration of this see Strathern (1991), and Mol and Law (1994b).
14. Semiotics draws on a linguistic metaphor, first developed by Ferdinand de Saussure in his 'synchronic linguistics'. In the latter de Saussure argued that signs are arbitrary – that they depend for their significance on the relationship that they have with one another. Though semiotic approaches to social analysis vary, sometimes they have argued that social life may be treated, in this way – that is by the method of synchronic linguistics – as if they were a language. Note that this is not at all the same thing as saying that social life *is* a language. Thus the 'discourse analysis' of such writers as Foucault is concerned not simply with talk, but also with action and other, inanimate materials. Materials of all kinds perform

themselves recursively as an expression of a particular ordering logic. See Foucault (1979). For further discussion see Law (1994) and Law and Mol (1995a) and Mol and Mesman (1995).

15. I explore this possibility at some length in Law (1994) by developing the notion of the 'mode of ordering'. Here (and there) it is my assumption that it is possible to impute several – indeed perhaps many – different ordering modes to the relations making up any organization. Here let me simply add that when I speak of 'logic' I do not intend to refer to the formal logics developed in mathematical philosophy, but rather to coherent and persistent features of social relations. One test of that coherence would, I think, be their recursive propensity: that is, their tendency to reproduce themselves.

16. See Cooper (1992: 266).

17. The 'doubling', that is, of the object that is represented, and the representation itself. See Cooper (1993).

18. There is a link between the panopticism explored by Foucault, and the notions of the 'centre of translation' or the 'centre of calculation' developed by Latour (1990). Latour's analysis (indeed like the present approach which borrows from it) considers the way in which translations are precariously put in place to produce (though equally precariously) a panoptical syntactical effect. Foucault is less concerned with the elaboration of translation (a term which he does not use), than with the syntactical limits and logics within which such elaboration takes place.

19. The notion of discretion – the exercise of externally unconstrained choice, usually made on the basis of information – is developed by Barnes (1988), and in slightly different terms by Callon (1991) where he distinguished between actors and intermediaries. For a somewhat sceptical commentary see Law (1991b).

20. For a discussion of the topologies implicit in sociality see Mol and Law (1994a).

21. In this respect it is a scenario. See Callon (1986).

22. Agenda setting is discussed, though not specifically in an organizational context, in Lukes (1974).

23. On the relationship between distal and proximal views of organization, see Cooper and Law (1995).

24. The notion that semiotics are also politics is developed in different ways by such writers as Barthes (1973) and Foucault (1979). For an interesting application to advertising see Williamson (1978). For a comparison of the politics of semiotics and that of *verstehende* sociology see Mol and Mesman (1995).

25. See, for instance, Barnes (1977).

26. See Kuhn (1970).

27. This is doubtless why those who question conventional ontology can easily be made to appear ridiculous. For discussion of the ontological question in a post structuralist mode see, in particular, Foucault (1983), Baudrillard (1988), Mol and Mesman (1995) and Benschop and Law (1995); and in a quite different idiom, the reflexive and recursive concern with local ordering called 'ethnomethodology' by its inventor, Harold Garfinkel (1967). For an overview which links post structuralism to a number of other literatures which grapple with the same point, and in particular considers the character of technology, see Cooper (1993).

28. See the superb analysis of 'technics out of control' by Winner (1977).

29. This is a genre of writing usually found amongst utopians.

30. For a useful discussion see MacKenzie and Wajcman (1985), together with the case-studies assembled in Bijker, Hughes and Pinch (1987).

31. See Law (1991) for a series of essays that explore this theme. And the metaphor of the 'cyborg' used by Haraway (1991).

32. Note that these networks therefore sometimes (only sometimes) generate the products or effects that we choose to call technologies, societies, agents, or representations.
33. See Latour (1993).
34. Thompson (1990) calls this kind of reading the 'fallacy of internalism'.
35. A number of otherwise most appealing authors are clearly attracted by this possibility. See, in particular, Baudrillard (1988) and Poster (1990). As a post structuralist antidote, see Derrida's (1976) comments on Lévi Strauss. As non–structuralist antidotes, see Eisenstein (1980), Ong (1988), and Goody (1977). See, also, the important essay by Latour (1990).
36. This argument is developed more fully in Law (1994).
37. This data is taken from Law (1991), and is reproduced with kind permission of the Board of the Sociological Review.
38. Compare this with the argument about multiple language games and play developed by Lyotard and Thébaut (1985).
39. I draw the term 'partial connections' via Marilyn Strathern's decentred study of complexity (1991) from Donna Haraway's (1991) call for a cyborg politics.

References

Ahonen, P. (ed) (1993) *Tracing the Semiotic Boundaries of Politics*, Mouton de Gruyter, Berlin.

Alpers, S. (1989) *The Art of Describing: Dutch Art in the Seventeenth Century*, Penguin, London.

Bacharach, S., Gagliardi, P. and Mundell, B. (eds) (1995) *Research in the Sociology of Organizations*, Studies of Organizations with European Tradition, 13, JAI Press, Greenwich, Conn.

Bal, M. (1991) *Reading Rembrandt: Beyond the Word-Image Opposition*, Cambridge University Press, Cambridge.

Barnes, B. (1977) *Interests and the Growth of Knowledge*, Routledge and Kegan Paul, London.

Barnes, B. (1988) *The Nature of Power*, Polity, Cambridge.

Barthes, R. (1973) Myth Today, in *Mythologies* (ed. Roland Barthes), pp. 109–59, Paladin, St. Albans.

Baudrillard, J. (1988) *Selected Writings*, Polity, Cambridge, MA.

Beniger, J.R. (1986) *The Control Revolution: Technological and Economic Origins of the Information Society*, Harvard University Press, Cambridge, MA.

Benschop, R. and Law, J. (1995) *Representation, Distribution and Ontological Politics*, paper presented at Workshop on the Labour of Division, 23rd–25th November, 1995, Keele University Centre for Social Theory and Technology.

Bijker, W.E., Hughes, T.P. and Pinch, T.J. (eds) (1987) *The Social Construction of Technological Systems: New Directions in the Sociology and History of Technology*, MIT Press, Cambridge, MA.

Callon, M. (1986) The Sociology of an Actor-Network: the Case of the Electric Vehicle, in *Mapping the Dynamics of Science and Technology: Sociology of Science in the Real World* (eds M. Callon, J. Law and A. Rip) pp. 19–34.

Callon, M. (1991) Techno-Economic Networks and Irreversibility, in *A Sociology of Monsters? Essays on Power, Technology and Domination*, Sociological Review Monograph 38 (ed J. Law) pp. 132–61, Routledge, London.

Callon, M., Law, J. and Rip, A. (eds) (1986) *Mapping the Dynamics of Science and Technology: Sociology of Science in the Real World*, Macmillan, London.

Chia, R. (ed.) (1995) *In the Realm of Organisation: Essays for Robert Cooper*, Routledge, London (forthcoming).

Cooper, R. (1992), Formal Organization as Representation: Remote Control, Displacement and Abbreviation in *Rethinking Organization* (eds M. Reed and M. Hughes) pp. 254–72, Sage, London.

Cooper, R. (1993) Technologies of Representation in *Tracing the Semiotic Boundaries of Politics* (ed P. Ahonen), pp. 279–312, Mouton de Gruyter, Berlin.

Cooper, R. and Law, J. (1995) Organization: Distal and Proximal Views in *Research in the Sociology of Organizations: Studies of Organizations with European Tradition* (eds S Bacharach, P. Gagliardi and B. Mundell) **13**, pp. 275–301, JAI Press, Greenwich, Conn.

Derrida, J. (1976) *Of Grammatology*, John Hopkins University Press, Baltimore.

Eisenstein, E.L. (1980) *The Printing Press as an Agent of Cultural Change: Communications and Transformations in Early-Modern Europe*, Cambridge University Press, Cambridge.

Foucault, M. (1970) *The Order of Things: an Archaeology of the Human Sciences*, Tavistock, London.

Foucault, M. (1979) *Discipline and Punish: the Birth of the Clinic*, Penguin, Harmondsworth.

Foucault, M. (1983) *This is Not a Pipe*, University of California Press, Berkeley, California.

Garfinkel, H. (1967) *Studies in Ethnomethodology*, Prentice-Hall, Englewood Cliffs, New Jersey.

Gleick, J. (1987) *Chaos: Making a New Science*, Sphere Books, London.

Goody, J. (1977) *The Domestication of the Savage Mind*, Cambridge University Press, Cambridge.

Haraway, D. (1991) A Cyborg Manifesto: Science, Technology, and Socialist-Feminism in the Late Twentieth Century in *Simians, Cyborgs, and Women: The Reinvention of Nature*, (ed D. Haraway) pp. 149–81, Free Association Books, London.

Haraway, D. (1992) *Primate Visions: Gender, Race and Nature in the World of Modern Science*, Verso, London.

Hesse, M.B. (1974) *The Structure of Scientific Inference*, Macmillan, London.

Jameson, F. (1991) *Postmodernism, or the Cultural Logic of Late Capitalism*, Verso, London.

Kuhn, S. (1970) *The Structure of Scientific Revolutions*, Chicago University Press, Chicago.

Latour, B. (1990) Drawing Things Together in *Representation in Scientific Practice* (eds M. Lynch and S. Woolgar) pp. 19–68, MIT Press, Cambridge, MA.

Latour, B. (1993) *We Have Never Been Modern*, Wheatsheaf/Harvester, Brighton.

Latour, B., and Woolgar, S. (1979) *Laboratory Life: the Social Construction of Scientific Facts*, Sage, Beverly Hills.

Law, J. (ed) (1991a) *A Sociology of Monsters? Essays on Power, Technology and Domination, Sociology Review Monograph 38*, Routledge, London.

Law, J. (1991b) Power, Discretion and Strategy in *A Sociology of Monsters? Essays on Power, Technology and Domination, Sociological Review Monograph* (ed J. Law) pp. 165–91, Routledge, London.

Law, J. (1994) *Organizing Modernity*, Blackwell, Oxford.

Law, J. and Mol, A. (1995a) Notes on Materiality and Sociality *The Sociological Review* **43**, pp. 274–94.

Law, J. and Mol, A. (1995b) On Metrics and Fluids: Notes on Otherness in *In the Realm of Organization: Essays for Robert Cooper*, Routledge, London (forthcoming).

Lukes, S. (1974) *Power: a Radical View*, Macmillan, London.

Lynch, M. and Woolgar, S. (eds) (1990) *Representation in Scientific Practice*, MIT Press, Cambridge, MA.

Lyotard, J.-F. and Thébaut, J.-L. (1985) *Just Gaming*, Manchester University Press, Manchester.

MacKenzie, D., and Wajcman, J. (eds) (1985) *The Social Shaping of Technology: How the Refrigerator got its Hum*, Open University Press, Milton Keynes.

Merton, R.K. (1957) *Social Theory and Social Structure*, Free Press, New York.

Mitchell, W.J.T. (1994) *Picture Theory*, University of Chicago Press, Chicago.

Mol, A., and Berg, M. (1994) Principles and Practices of Medicine: the Co-existence of Various Anaemias. *Culture, Medicine and Psychiatry*, **18**, pp. 247–65.

Mol, A., and Law, J. (1994a) Regions, Networks and Fluids: Anaemia and Social Topology. *Social Studies of Science*, **24**, pp. 641–71.

Mol, A., and Law, J. (1994b) Impurity: about the Fractal Distribution of Anaemias, mimeo, University of Limburg and Keele University.

Mol, A., and Mesman, J. (1995) Some Questions of Method: About Neonatal Food and the Politics of Theory, *Social Studies of Science*, forthcoming.

Munro, R. (1993) Just when you thought it was safe to enter the water: Accountability, Language Games and Multiple Control Technologies. *Accounting, Management and Information Technologies*, **3**, pp. 249–71.

Munro, R. (1994) Calling for 'accounts': Monsters, membership work and management accounting, paper presented to the 4th Interdisciplinary Perspectives on Accounting Conference, 11–13th July 1994, University of Manchester, Manchester.

Ong, W.J. (1988) *Orality and Literacy: the Technologizing of the Word*, Routledge, London.

Poster, M. (1990) *The Mode of Information: Poststructuralism and Social Context*, Polity, Cambridge.

Reed, M. and Hughes, M. (eds) (1992) *Rethinking Organization*, Sage, London.

Strathern, M. (1991) *Partial Connections*, Rowman and Littlefield, Savage, Maryland.

Thompson, J.B. (1990) *Ideology and Modern Culture: Critical Social Theory in the Era of Mass Communication*, Polity Press, Cambridge.

Williamson, J. (1978) *Decoding Advertisements: Ideology and Meaning in Advertising*, Marion Boyars, London.

Winner, L. (1977) *Autonomous Technology: Technics-out-of-Control as a Theme in Political Thought*, MIT Press, Cambridge, MA.

16 Changing times and accounts: tales from an organization field

Barbara Czarniawska-Joerges

Introduction

In several European countries, a change is being heralded. The art of running public sector organizations, 'public administration', has abdicated in favour of 'public management' (see e.g. Humphrey and Olson, 1995). However, 'management', as any dictionary will instruct, is a synonym for 'administration'. So, although traditional usage attributes 'administration' to the public services and 'management' predominantly to business organizations, it might also be claimed that a change from 'public administration' to 'public management' is no change at all.

An alternative interpretation, espoused in this chapter, suggests that this alteration in designation from 'administration' to 'management' indexes a change in ethos.[1] Of course, changes to the area of practice (organization field) known as public administration have been, in part, orchestrated and are, in part, emerging from a loose coupling with a variety of planned interventions. However, as there is no necessary link between interventions and ethos, I do not intend to present a mere chronology of interventions. Instead, I will go on to show how a shift in ethos can be understood in terms of changing accountability rules.

This article scrutinizes an example of this shift in ethos, drawing on events which occurred in the Swedish public sector in the early 1990s. An interesting situation had arisen, in which everyone seemed to agree that the old rules were obsolete, but nobody seemed to have a clear vision of what the new rules might be. All parties, therefore, busied themselves with promoting their own ideas about what was of crucial relevance to such rules, such as justice or rational action. But before the reader is transported to Sweden, it might be appropriate to examine what is meant by 'accountability rules' in this text.

Accountability and its rules

Accountability can be seen as a central concept in the understanding of social action. The ethnomethodological tradition – inspired by Alfred Schütz (1953/1971), developed by Garfinkel (1967, 1988), Sacks (1966–67), and Cicourel (1974), and carried over into the context of organizations by Bittner (1965), Silverman and Jones (1977) and Boden (1994) – postulates that accountability is the main bond in human interactions, indeed the main social bond altogether. Participants, usually called 'members', make the world 'reportable' by continuously accounting for what they do in the imaginary or real presence of other people, who serve as auditors. The point of such accounting is to display the (situational) rationality of one's action, and thus of one's social competence.

Ethnomethodological thinking is directed towards the task of understanding the social world; the world, that is, which we construct and yet take for granted. It does not mean that this construction is forever lost from our attention – it can be traced in and through the accounts which we give to each other. These accounts are of special interest to ethnomethodology, making it increasingly congenial to researchers inquiring into the process of reality construction. One of the points in which ethnomethodology distinctly differs from other approaches is that it locates theorizing about practice within the realm of practice, thus removing the pretences to a special status demanded earlier by science on the ground of a supposedly superior access to knowledge (Garfinkel, 1967).

There are some facets in most ethnomethodological thinking which need to be questioned and extended, however. For instance, accounting is often assumed to occur only in situations where the social tissue seems likely to break, as a means for mending it. As Scott and Lyman put it in their seminal article, 'An account is a linguistic device employed whenever an action is subjected to valuative inquiry' (1968, p. 46). They assume that people account for their actions only when they have to justify them, and then do it in the form of explicit reasons.[2] There is no such need when everybody is doing what they should, because nobody (except ethnomethodologists, that is) would think of asking them to do so, because of the risk of actually rupturing the social tissue. For Scott and Lyman, questions like 'Why do people live at home with their children?' are not asked, 'because they have been settled in advance in our culture and are indicated by language itself' (p. 47). This line of reasoning has also been taken up by Alasdair MacIntyre. MacIntyre points out that it is *the structure of normality*, invisible to the actors but possible to reconstruct by an observer, which forms the basic interpretive framework for action. He argues:

> Acting in accordance with those structures does not require the giving or the having of reasons for so acting, except in certain exceptional types of circumstance in which those structures have been put in question. (. . .) It is departing from what these structures prescribe which requires the having and the giving of reasons.
>
> (MacIntyre, 1988: 24–5)

Here MacIntyre repeats Scott and Lyman's point about accounts being called for by a departure from 'normal' conduct.

But what interests MacIntyre, and the author of this chapter, are those exceptional types of circumstance which subsequently lead to a change in the structure of normality. So this is where I depart from many ethnomethodologists. In the philosopher Richard Rorty's terms, these are instances when what was considered an 'abnormal discourse' becomes 'normal' and vice versa (Rorty, 1980).

In order to tackle these exceptional circumstances, the notion of accounts must be extended to include not only accounts which justify deviations from the structure of normality, but also those which explain conformity to it. Such a notion can be found in Rom Harré's analysis of action in which accounts – an interpretation of a behaviour in intentional terms, relating it to social convention – are what transform a behaviour, or a movement, into an action (Harré and Secord, 1972; Harré, 1979; 1982; Davies and Harré, 1991). Conduct can be treated as action when it can be *accounted for* (a priori, simultaneously or a posteriori) in terms which are acceptable in a given social setting. Accounts, so understood, may simply refer to the structure of normality, or they may take the structure of normality up for scrutiny.

Ethnomethodology, on the contrary, seems to assume social and cultural stability: things are as they are. And, rather than be able to change things, incompetent members become socialized or withdraw. Although this is no longer Durkheim's consensual rule-governed society, it is a society consisting of a vast but stable repertoire of fragmented micro-rules. And yet one could wish for another state in between: i.e. one which assumes the possibility of consensus, however fragile and temporary, and which therefore admits the possibility of its breaking or remaking, in situations that have nothing to do with 'anomie'.

This lack of concepts for the ongoing ordering of the multiplicity of alternative and competing accounting rules may be connected with another feature for which ethnomethodological thinking is criticized. Namely, it does not seem to see the need for explaining the connections between the various rules of accounting. This tendency suggests a hidden naturalism, a tacit assumption that all people share the same 'basic' normality structure, something akin to the Universal Mind (Lynch and Bogen, 1994). Latour (1994) observed in this context that ethnomethodology explains sociality; but not society: there is nothing (but 'universal human nature') to fix various actions and accounts, and to make situations repeatable and relatable to one another.

Latour regards technology as such a fixing and connecting device. Pursuing this line of thought a little further, one could say that one of the common uses of technology is the fixing and stabilizing not so much of particular accounts, but of whole sets and systems of accounting rules, otherwise known as *institutions*. A good illustration is provided by Thompson (1991), who shows that it was printing technology which allowed Luca Pacioli to turn the practice of accounting, already known for 200 years, into a modern and durable institution. If it had not been for this, the practice could have vanished altogether – if, say, all the Venetians had been wiped out by the plague.

This realization impels yet another comment – that the conventional ethnomethodology lacks a historical reflection. The 'natural attitude', or the 'structure or normality', is not only culturally produced but is also temporally and spatially bound. Accountability, says Mary Douglas (1992), is the founding stone of *modern* institutions, in accordance with the dominant 'forensic' model of the human being. Individual persons must be able to account for themselves – both in the human court and on Judgement Day. What is more, adds Meyer (1986, 1987), such accountable persons are necessary to make possible both the market and the state. Thus the invention of the 'legal person', which makes organizations accountable – as citizens, producers and consumers. This invention in turn requires a set or sets of rules of accounting, of collectively accessible means for creating appropriate accounts. Such rules concern both the method and the logic of accounting, and are synonymous with what is often called 'a social context' (Czarniawska-Joerges, 1992a).

The double logic of organizing

In the context of modern organizations, one can usefully speak of what March and Olsen (1989), inspired by MacIntyre (1988), call the *logic of appropriateness* and the logic of consequentiality. Here, following Rorty (1980), I shall call the latter the *logic of justification*, which seems to me to better capture what is meant. It is the logic used by the actors to justify their action when these are challenged by an observer. In 'normal' situations observers just assume appropriateness, while – as I shall try to show – in situations when the 'structure of normality' is shaking, appropriateness is a logic that can be used by organizational actors as an alternative or a complementary mode vis-à-vis the logic of justification. In other words, when the logic of justification fails to gain acceptance, its tacit grounds – the logic of appropriateness – is taken up for scrutiny.

The logic of justification claims rationality as its method, or rather as its rhetoric: competent members account for their action, presenting them in terms of rationality (Garfinkel, 1967). When complementing a member's competence, we should therefore speak of *rational accounts* rather than rational actions (Czarniawska-Joerges, 1992b).

What accounts are considered rational? In Pitkin's ironic summary, a rational account has premises which all can accept (without necessarily agreeing with them), steps which all can follow and conclusions which must all be universally accepted (Pitkin, 1972). Pitkin displays the paradox built into accounting which uses the logic of justification. This logic is grounded in the universalistic assumption, so central to rationalist thinking, while a moment of reflection makes it obvious that there is nothing which can be accepted by 'all', as there are many rationalities at all times. What unites these disparate rationalities in our times and at our place, is a relatively shared belief that rationality is universal. By contrast, the logic of appropriateness emphasizes local negotiations and agreements which, although temporary and fragile, can last for a long time (as long as a given institutional order or parts of it). Such local and temporal ways of understanding can of course still claim universality and refuse reflection on their historicity, in an attempt to obfuscate their origins. Thus the logic of justification assumes rationality as a universal principle and allows for local deviations, whereas the logic of appropriateness assumes local and temporary conventions, one of which is a belief in the universal value of rationality.

The logic of appropriateness can perhaps best be explained as based on a required congruence between act, actor and scene (Burke, 1945/1969): how should a person like me (her, him) act in a situation like this? While the justificatory set of accounts assumes universality, the set built on appropriateness requires a specific and strong set of definitions about the identity of the actors and characteristics of a situation (Meyer, 1986; March and Olsen, 1989). Once again, however, a paradox is evident: what sounds like an application of emotivist ethics (MacIntyre, 1980), that is to say, a subjective judgement of what is 'appropriate', in fact depends on a collective repertoire of categories. 'Obligatory' conduct is dictated by obligations to a given community (MacInyre, 1988; March and Olsen, 1989).

In the field

In the tales from the organization field below, I will try to show that both kinds of logic are used to form accounts in organizations that are experiencing identity crises

(Czarniawska-Joerges, 1994). The tales illustrate the two paradoxes mentioned above. First, that what is supposedly universal relies on a collective consensus. Second, that what is supposedly individual and particular relies on a collective repertoire of classifying devices. These paradoxes are not evident in times characterized by a stable structure of normality, when accounting occurs smoothly and automatically.

But imagine a time, and a place, when actors are no longer sure what 'everybody else' is doing and thinking, when they are no longer certain of their own identity, and are finding it impossible to categorize events as they happen. Such was the situation I found during a study I conducted over a period of 14 months in 1989–1991, applying a method which I have been using with some success for more than two decades and which makes it possible to grasp some vital aspects of large and complex organizations (Czarniawska-Joerges, 1992a).[3]

What organizations were studied? The definition of an 'organization' is in itself problematic. March and Simon acknowledged this, saying that '[i]t is easier, and probably more useful, to give examples of formal organizations than to define the term.' (1958: 1). I tend to see organizations as nets of collective action, distinguishable from one another by the kind of products (including meanings and symbols) attributed to them, which makes it possible to draw borderlines according to those who are making the attribution. For the purpose of the study reported here, I created an entity called a *constellation* of organizations, to give a name to a grouping of nets which are perceived as separate but belonging together.[4]

In what follows, I am using excerpts from original accounts[5] as they were given to me in the regular conversations I had with the people who had agreed to make systematic observations. For the background text I have used a conventional realistic style ('This is how it went'), trying to follow the typical reporting mode (slightly ironic and distancing, alternating with deeper commitment), and to preserve key figures of speech and typical expressions. The issues chosen are those considered perennial to the welfare state: negotiating wages and setting taxes.

Tale 1: solidarity or merit? Local pay negotiations

One of the most dramatic changes in Sweden during the period of the study was the new possibility of conducting pay negotiations locally in the public sector (as opposed to the previous central bargaining). The reason behind this measure was connected with the emergence of an employee labour market, in which the public sector was forced to compete with private companies so as not to lose its most competent people and to be able to attract young well-educated personnel.

Salaries and perquisites were of course an important part of that attraction, but they were also an important part of the difficulties that arose. 'Somebody who wants to be well paid cannot possibly work here. We cannot offer anything like that, alas'. This interlocutor, a Big City manager, calculated that his subordinates earned about SEK 3–5,000 a month (£250–450) less than people employed in similar positions in private companies, something which is generally typical of the kind of operations which do not produce profit. Sometimes, however, it was possible to offer a good salary, but not other perquisites. One interlocutor from Northtown summarized the results of the head-hunting for the top position in the Industrial Relations Office in the local authority as follows:

> Both candidates have their own consulting companies. What they demand is private pension insurance, pension guarantees, free use of car and telephone – and we don't have that, not usually . . .

Negotiations thus ground to a halt, and when it seemed that a new recruitment process was about to be initiated, the politicians demanded that an internal candidate be employed instead.

Interestingly, although the usual sets of accounts are present here, they are being swapped around. It is the councillors who are using the economic argument, saying that the recruitment campaign is too expensive and would take too long. Considering the time it would take for a candidate to work out the necessary notice period at a previous workplace and to be trained for the new job, they argue, it is very uncertain when possible positive effects would actually appear; whereas the costs loom large and there is no uncertainty about them. But officials have a strong argument against: the internal candidate does not have the right profile. That is, although the candidate has long and appropriate experience, he does not have the external network needed for this position.

Councillors are not the only group who can put a stop to the sophisticated recruitment procedure: very often it is the personnel department. In the Big City government offices, it was forbidden to offer a raise in connection with an interdepartmental transfer. This led to the practice of writing job descriptions that made positions sound more qualified than they really were. The personnel department learned about this too, and invented its own measures to prevent it. When someone was approached with an offer by another department, the personnel people could give the former boss the right to impose a salary freeze. Thus the person in question had the choice of staying in the old job with no salary change, or moving to a new position without a raise. In this way, the comment ran, those responsible for recruitment and mobility were dedicating themselves to the prevention of active recruitment and mobility, in the name of higher things.

> The only certain result of all this is that individuals are deprived of the possibility of a more satisfactory existence at the workplace. In the short run this way of punishing a specific person works beautifully, but in the long run it works against our own interests if people are prevented from self-development. . . . The normal alternative, for young and talented people, is to quit public employment simply to be able to get a higher salary. And then all the investment, all the training and coaching goes to waste . . . From the point of view of personnel policy the best thing to do would be to eliminate personnel departments: all department heads should be able to decide such questions for themselves in ways which are the most advantageous for a given office . . .

But the most important partners in all these questions were of course the trade unions. All the previous quotations come from the municipalities; the insurance offices had a different and very clear dilemma. How much is a good education worth compared to long experience?[6]

Quotation 3

> It turned out that two unions had two completely different opinions on the matter, of course. SACO [the university educated employees' union] took for granted that insurance offices should employ people with a good education, whereas FF [the insurance employees' union] took it equally for granted that we must invest, totally and completely, in the people who are already employed, who do not have to be trained, who can be sent directly into production. I [the office director] suggested something in-between, and the result was this kind of ambiguous job ad which could be interpreted both ways . . .

In Northern County the parties reached a compromise, but the situation was not equally calm everywhere. One of the regional social insurance offices started a wild strike in an attempt to influence the central salary negotiations which had run into a dead end. Although no news about it appeared on radio or TV, the information reached all the other government offices. Here is a commentary from the Big City County office:

> – The parties involved have obviously adopted very distant positions . . . which results from the fact that FF only want central negotiations resulting in an average pay increase, whereas the employers want local individual adjustments, so that Pelle can be given 2,000 and Olle 200 kronor. If, let us say, everybody gets 700 kronor, for instance, this means that those with lower salaries will benefit more from it. And this is exactly what FF wants. If you get a percentage raise for example, then those who earn more get more. If the raise is to be decided locally, then the employer will divide everything and say, OK, now Ulla is so good she must go up two salary levels compared with before.
>
> – And what's so difficult about that?
>
> – The problem is that . . . let's say there are 18–19,000 people who work in insurance offices. The difference lies in whether it's centrally decided that everybody's to get an X kronor raise, or whether it's decided that a certain sum of money, Y, is to be divided locally. The second means that you're giving up the possibility of controlling how it's going to be divided. The local distribution can be more unfair than the central one.
>
> – Why should that be?

> – I'm not saying that it will be, but it might, and in any case the point is that FF and the employer do not see eye to eye on this issue. FF insists that the main sum must be divided equally, possibly with higher raises for those who have lower wages. But the employer's wage policy is different; that is, they're trying now to do more to reward those who seem to be the most deserving . . . or whatever I should call it. At any rate, now we have a wild strike in N office as of yesterday, and the rumours are spreading like wildfire through our place.
>
> – And what are people saying?
>
> – Well, that we should do the same, maybe not for pay, but for the working conditions . . .

Quotation 4

I pressed my interlocutor toward an evaluative judgement, which she refused, even if the tone and the narrative indicated which side she was on. We need not speculate further about the motives of that particular person in that particular situation. I chose to include this quotation as a further indication of the fact that the basis for judgements becomes unclear.

Summarizing, Quotations 1 and 2, both from people representing the employer in municipalities, report a change of attitude: perquisites and job mobility are no longer unthinkable in the municipal administration. On the contrary, traditional thinking on these matters is perceived as impoverishing organizational resources and hurting individuals. Quotations 3 and 4 illustrate an observable split between the two unions and between the employers and the unions, something which is very typical in labour relations – but not when the employer is a public sector organization. The white-collar union used to show solidarity with the blue-collar union, and the employer tried to meet union demands. Now their relationships are becoming identical with those in the private sector. What do the employees think about it? They do not know – yet. When the rules seemed to be changing, it was difficult to know who to ally oneself with – all of a sudden the employers appeared to be on the side of the employees against the unions and the personnel departments – but did it only seem to be like that? 'Obligations' seem to have been temporarily disconnected from any particular group of community, making the notion of 'obligatory action' suddenly meaningless.

This series of accounts shows how the 'old' and the 'new' ethos visibly clashed. While public administration managers were trying out the alternative way of thinking about recruitment and promotion, albeit tentatively, the other two organizations stood for the 'old' set of accounting rules and invented ingenious ways of defending it.

In saying this I am making 'another organization' out of the personnel departments, and quite intentionally so. My insistence on calling organizations 'action-networks' and delineating their borders in a way which depends on the purpose of the delineation, only confirms what is common practice in the field. It is often the actors' decision to be part of a given action-network, to disengage themselves from one network and to join another. They might fail in their attempt, but they can always try. Thus a personnel department might constitute itself as the competitor or collaborator of other departments, rather than as a unit serving them. Similarly, a group which goes out in a wild strike in fact constitutes a new temporary organizational unit, which is not a part of the union or of the work organization.

In both these cases of attempts at assuming a new identity, a new set of accounting rules is being tried out in interaction with the other actors in the field. The relationship is clearly mutual: a personnel department establishes itself as an antagonistic unit, dedicated to the defence of the old order, but in reaction to other departments it tries to establish itself as a pioneer of the new ethos. Both sides, obviously, need the other's acceptance to maintain the new identity, and in the examples given above such acceptance was neither given nor earned. When repeated, it must be taken as a general recognition that 'the structure of normality' has been shaken. In everyday talk, such situations are labelled as crises. Let us then consider this particular crisis in more detail.

Organizational accounts in times of crisis

The circumstances surrounding what has become known as 'the demise of the Swedish model' could be described in these terms: it is a legitimacy crisis in which the received notion of the welfare state is being questioned. Although beginning in the early 1980s, the crisis of the welfare state has been felt most keenly in the early 1990s, and although it concerned the society as a whole, it has been most acute in the Swedish public sector organizations. I am obviously using here a bit of media rhetoric ('the crisis'), but without any intention of joining the chorus lamenting (or celebrating) 'the demise of the Swedish model'. I propose to see the present crisis in the Swedish public sector in terms of an 'epistemological crisis' necessary to the development of a viable tradition (MacIntyre, 1988).

According to MacIntyre, an epistemological crisis occurs when a tradition is no longer capable of answering questions, removing inconsistencies or solving problems simply by referring to its authoritative texts. While history shows that such crises can indeed bring a tradition to an end, it also provides many cases in which they generate a tradition-constituted and tradition-constitutive inquiry, which produces numerous innovative re-interpretations and creative solutions, strengthening rather than weakening the tradition in question. The Catholic Church is the most frequently quoted example of successful tradition, while North American liberalism, says MacIntyre, is just now in the grip of an epistemological crisis, in much the same way as its leftist cousin, the Swedish social democracy.

Recreating history is always a fictive enterprise, but the problem of the beginning is always a real one. Perhaps one should start with what became known as the 'People's Home', the Swedish modern project which aimed to set life right (Hirdman, 1989). The societal education programme inherent to that project led to the construction of a consensus as to what was good and what was bad (for society); what was progressive and what was reactive; what values were important and what phenomena were to be eliminated. All this was more or less taken for granted, until it came up for inspection when the societal agreement between capital and labour (which can perhaps be said to go back to the 'historical compromise' in Saltsjöbaden in 1938) was called into question.

Nowhere was this so evident as in the public sector which for all those years was both the bearer, the guardian and the implementor of the main values in Swedish society. Solidarity and equality, progress and care, were all incorporated in the doings and preaching of the public administration. But, after the beginning of the crisis (around 1978 or so, about the time of the first oil crisis) the public administration became identified as the source of evil and corruption (Czarniawska, 1985). It had lost the right to propagate the societal values because, in the eyes of the public, it did not conform to them. In part it was the values that had changed; in part it was the perception of the conduct which was to be evaluated – the interpretation of accounts – which had changed. It was no longer possible to explain deviations by referring to the 'basic principles'.

An epistemological crisis assumes the form of an identity crisis on the individual (organizational) level. If the previous world's description does not hold, and reality isn't what it used to be, who am I? Who are the others? What community am I supposed to oblige by my 'obligatory action'? If these questions sound as if they are addressed to people rather than organizations, it is because the institution of the legal person makes organizations accountable in the same way that individuals are. However, organizations cannot account for themselves; only people can do that. Thus organizational actors regularly account not only for their own action, but also for the action of others. A member of a team accounts for the action of the team, a manager accounts for the dealings of the management group, a subordinate accounts for peers when reporting to the supervisor etc.

How did people employed in public sector organizations react to the crisis? As we have seen above, with confusion and uncertainty; with attempts to find new ways and to defend the old. What they were most uncertain about, though, was the validity of the social agreement which up to then had been legitimating their action and steering their choices.

The first premise of the logic of appropriateness in the Swedish public sector before the crisis could be said to be simple and straightforward: 'It is right to do so and so, because we have agreed to do so – according to our legitimate way of reaching such an agreement'. In times of crisis, like the one they were experiencing, the reasoning acquired a questioning note: 'I thought this was right because we had agreed that it was – but do the others still think the same? Is there any 'we' left? And had we really reached an agreement about *this* specific situation?'

Reflective accounts like these reveal the breach in the normality structure by making the usual logic of justification insufficient. Indeed, the second tale shows the actors consciously analyzing the nature of this rupture.

Tale 2: is tax planning fraudulent or economic?

A special state commission investigated the rationale and possible effects of a proposed tax reform. The Finance Minister made known his intentions about the ways municipalities would be affected by the reform. The team within the commission which dealt with indirect taxation suggested that local governments should be released from the obligation to pay VAT on their purchases (they would be able to reclaim VAT already paid), while the general applicability of value-added taxation would be extended. The local comments insinuated, however, that this generosity of the state would be evened out by reduced subventions.

Quotation 5

> They [in orig., 'man', close to the English 'one'] launch this phantom debate about state and municipal taxation, whereas the greater part of the planned taxation is in fact state taxation. They always push off everything. They say, 'We're lowering the state taxes' but in reality they push the problems over onto the local governments, saying 'You must handle all that within the unchanged minicipal taxation frame, you mustn't expand your operations, and you'll get smaller subventions.' Sure thing, there'll be a tremendous commotion! You can't give and take with the same hand. A large portion of the money which we receive as state subventions was already taken from the municipal taxes by way of various fancy models, so that in reality one could stop all this shuffling back and forth and tell the municipalities to use their money freely.[7]

Nevertheless, the state regulations still existed, and local governments began, albeit grudgingly, to make preparations to face the consequences of the tax reform. Numerous unanswered questions arose. Should one prepare a gross budget or a net budget? The tax experts were in favour of net budgeting, as the VAT paid would be refunded at any rate. The apostles of internal decentralization in local government recommended gross budgeting, so that the newly created 'accountability areas' really would be able to use the money coming to them with the recently established budget responsibility.[8] The tax refunded could in this case become their income.

All this produced technical difficulties, as the existing accounting system was not sensitive to value added tax and did not specify it. What added to the gravity of the situation was the fact that speedy reaction is crucial in terms of tax refunds. If the municipalities were not to pay VAT on their purchases in future, it made sense to wait to acquire whatever was needed. But how to cope with present needs? As it turned out, the municipalities were not left alone to cope with all these new problems, they were offered help and support from various quarters.

Quotation 6

> We receive now, daily, whole heaps of suggestions from banks and finance companies who all believe that we absolutely must introduce all these fantastic solutions, leasing and all that. It turns out . . . that the state decided on a standard sum which municipalities will have to pay back from their VAT refunds. And this means that a local government can appropriate more money from VAT than had been assumed, and can make money on it. Thus several municipalities have already decided to put a freeze on all purchases until 1991, when the tax reform takes effect, and in the meantime to lease or rent.

After some investigation it was decided in Big City that different administrative departments must make up their own minds. Previously the municipal government's attitude towards leasing had been ambiguous, and leasing was generally considered more expensive than renting or purchasing. All this might have changed as a result of the reform, but it still did not automatically make leasing an attractive alternative. What could be done with money saved by leasing, if buying and investing were to be generally prohibited? Some of the alternatives considered as being possibly profitable, were 'investo-leasing' (at low interest rates compared to ordinary loans) and leasing of certain items only, for example computers. Finally, Big City decided to 'soften up' the clause in the city statute which prohibited leasing.

Quotation 7

– Before, it was considered immoral when certain business firms planned what was regarded as tax evasion.

– But what prevents anybody from using the same argument now?

– Exactly . . . that's exactly what the crux of the matter is. . . . After all, it is obvious that all this is going to hurt taxpayers, somewhere. It will either be the taxpayers in Big City or the taxpayers in Sweden who will bear the cost of it all. Although if all municipalities in Sweden do the same thing, the result will be neutral. After all, even the state leases. . . . The moral aspect isn't very interesting any more. Now the thing is to look out for oneself as best one can. We had a meeting in the large cities' group and were all of the same opinion: we must do whatever we can to cheat the state, because the state is cheating the municipalities out of a great deal of money the way things are today. All this is a bit comical. One would think that we'd all co-operate to do the best thing for the economy. But no, the thing now is to put spokes in one another's wheels whenever possible . . .

A conference was arranged between the Association of Local Authorities, the Association of County Authorities and the top officials at the Ministry of Finances, where it had been publicly announced that the tax reform should lead to a balanced result for both state and municipalities – a resolution which, after all, only repeated what had already been stated in the Budget Bill. Central government and SALA experts initiated a discussion about the best ways of centralizing the VAT reform, while at the same time the mass media reported to the public that many local governments were planning tax evasion.

Sweet Hamlet was well advanced in the process of corporatizing its real estate administration when the council decided not to sign the contract with the newly formed company until the end of 1990, and thus to be able to appropriate the VAT at the beginning of 1991. But before the decision was made, advice and help had been sought from one of the Association's auditors. Consequently, people working in the company were classified as 'loaned' from the municipal office, whereas managers were formally counted as employees of the local government on a 'special assignment' to the company.

> – I think the whole thing is idiotic, but it is a legal loophole, no doubt about that. Still, I don't like such subterfuges, but what can I do, other than say how things are.
>
> – Do the taxation authorities know about all this?
>
> – Sure they do, I have talked personally to the head of the sales tax department at the County Council . . . We're certainly not the only ones to do it, but it is so . . . opportunistic, I think.

Quotation 8

This is not the only dilemma into which the taxation reform pushed municipalities like Sweet Hamlet and many others. During one of the conferences organized by the Association, one of the Association's lawyers encouraged the delegates from the municipalities to ask the municipal water company to pay their fees in advance (that is, before the tax reform came into effect).

> – Some local governments refused to do so, because they thought it unfair towards Feldt [the Finance Minister at that time]. He fell into a rage about it, and threatened to withdraw the state subventions from the municipalities who did do it. In our municipality we had spent some thought on it – we did not know what to do, but we took the money eventually.
>
> – Do you think Feldt is going to punish you?
>
> – It would be most peculiar if he were able to.

Quotation 9

My interlocutor added that he was surprised himself at his council's lack of loyalty. Their argument is that, if the Association encourages its members to act against the instructions of the central government, it must mean that 'the government had not thought it through, not just yet, not this part at any rate'. In the meantime the Association was reinforcing its tax expertise, as queries and requests for advice came in every day. Consultants were careful to point out, however, that organizations which depended on public funds must be very cautious about what might be seen as tax evasion, but they still explained all the technical details about how to go about it.

Finally the government decided that it was illegal to pay water and energy dues in advance. The decision did not apply retrospectively, but as the energy charges – which were the highest – were to be paid only three months later, this put an end to the whole procedure.

Rumours circulated about which municipalities had accepted the advanced dues (among others, Sweet Hamlet and Big City) and which had refused to do so. My interlocutor from Big City, who lived in another municipality which, unlike the social democratic Big City, had a right-wing majority (at a time when the social democrats were in power) told me what happened there:

Quotation 10

> – My home municipality did not accept the payments. If somebody sent them in, they were returned.
>
> – On moral grounds?
>
> – On moral grounds, although this is a kind of moral which is difficult to understand . . . one would imagine that it would be the social democratic municipalities who would refuse on moral grounds, but it was the other way round. It was the municipalities with a right-wing majority who refused the payments, and yet they are the ones who oppose most other taxation. All of a sudden tax evasion was beneath their moral level. It has been said that we have to loyally support a parliamentary decision. When it comes to Robin Hood taxation [richer municipalities pay more tax to the state], we have to loyally oppose it instead – but this is also a parliamentary decision, so I'm getting really confused . . .

Big City managed to pay its water and garbage charges before the law against advance payments came into effect. However, it was not the advance payments but the leasing deals which attracted most attention in the Big City council and offices. Thus, when the next law came in – this time prohibiting the appropriation of tax paid on leasing deals – the municipal actors were a bit rattled.

Quotation 11

> – Even an idiot would have understood that if people know something in advance, they are going to prepare themselves for that, call it tax evasion or not. The Ministry of Finance could have guessed that all these moves were going to be made. Also, it would be easy to build up a defence against all this, as there would anyway be discounting rules so the municipalities wouldn't be able to discount whatever they wanted to. Or, the state could compensate itself through a proportional reduction in subventions . . . Oh well, right now there is a lot which happens without having any lasting effects, but it's amusing in a way. After all, one always learns something . . .

On my reading, the local actors here are prepared and willing to participate in an experiment, but are having continuous and repeated problems in interpreting all the different events. One popular account puts the state in the position of a player in a zero-sum game, who like many inexperienced players, however, is getting angry about losing and is therefore trying to change the rules again. The following dialogue reflects the ambiguity in the nature of the accounting rules and in the question of what rules applied to whom:

Quotation 12

> – But if all the steps taken by both state and municipalities lead to results opposite to those intended, isn't it better to quit the game?
>
> – Well, on our municipal side we still believe that they can't hamper everything we do and that there are still opportunities for advantageous actions. It is just that nothing is known for certain. After all, it's just an investigation whose results won't be considered before May 1990 [it turned out to be June as a result of the government crisis], so we're out and trying to paddle in unknown waters . . . Maybe it will all come to nothing, but then at least we can say we tried . . .

The actors' accounts and interpretations above, although illustrating the same phenomenon as the one reported in Tale 1, throw a slightly different light on the same process. In the remuneration case, two types of ethos clashed head on. The present tale shows a new set of accounting rules emerging, in pain and ambiguity, from within the old one: advancing, retreating, encouraging experiments and tentative accounts.

In Quotation 5, the account is framed mainly in terms of competence, or rather the lack of it. The central government is seen as trying to achieve various (presumably positive goals) but ruins it by a lack of understanding of the basics. 'You can't give and take with the same hand'. There is a tone to this aphorism which ridicules anyone who overlooks this basic rule. The tone could be interpreted as suggesting that repeated incompetent action may lead to mistrust. It is difficult to be loyal to an incompetent partner. What is more, a suspicion may have grown that the incompetence was really due to the fact that the central government had several fish to fry – it wanted, above all, to appear liberal and tolerant in the eyes of the press (hence the expression 'a phantom debate'). The local units found it difficult to account for the central government's action in what would seem to be the commonly agreed terms.

With time the accounts of both governmental and municipal action changed. Quotation 6 contains an ambiguous utterance 'a local government can appropriate more money from VAT than had been assumed' and one is led to wonder whether it was central government's ignorance or benevolence that permitted this. But the next quotation (Quotation 7) from the same respondent is very clear: central government is excepting itself from the rules of loyalty that it established a while ago. 'Before, it was considered immoral when certain companies – among those operating on market conditions – were planning what was regarded as tax evasion'. Earlier, the rules of justification that were obligatory in the public sector were grounded in the idea of the public good as represented by the services to the tax-payer. That was where the obligations of civil servants lay: with the citizens. Now things seemed to be the other way round: loyalty is due to the government, which demands efficiency in the name of the citizens but at their expense. Citizens are no longer the auditors – other organizational actors are. Playing the game of economic competence and competition attracts the players' attention so much that they tend to forget that the game was supposedly initiated in the name of the citizens. Striving to save the taxpayers' money leads, absurdly, to its greater waste. On the one hand, this cannot be sorted out by referring to the original premises, or in the media's catch phrase, by going 'back to basics'. On the other hand, assuming alien grounds for justification leads to an identity crisis.

The Big City representative was not alone in his opinions. His colleague at Sweet Hamlet used words like 'idiotic' and 'opportunistic' (Quotation 8). Indeed, the reactions were not only verbal. On the one hand, some municipalities refused to play the game. On the other, the Finance Minister was furious and threatened sanctions (Quotation 9). The situation acquired another twist.

Were municipalities governed by the opposition parties refusing to cheat the state because they had a sudden attack of loyalty, or because they wanted to boycott the whole reform? (Quotation 10). Here the logic of appropriateness is spotlighted by its negation: it used to seem appropriate for municipalities with the right-wing majority to do the opposite to whatever was appropriate for municipalities ruled by a social democratic majority. Now, their attitudes varied between one event and the next – on what grounds, then? And how to explain the Finance Minister's reaction? Is his anger caused by the revelation of his own dishonest intentions (of cheating the local governments), of his own or his partners' incompetence, or is it because he feels misunderstood and lacking moral support? Or again, is the Finance Minister angry on the grounds of incompetence (his own or others') or of disloyalty? Is anger an appropriate reaction on the part of a Minister of Finance? Quotations 11 and 12 reveal some ambivalence also among the respondents. It seemed as though various actors were trying out some new accounting styles, and either did not stick to them or found that such styles did not meet with approval.

De-institutionalization observed

One theme emerges: a major change in accounting rules has been announced, but it was – during the fourteen-month period under scrutiny – uncertain just what this change was going to be. The general idea was to make public administration more economical and effective. On the one hand this invited a series of actions which had previously been considered immoral, and on the other led to punishment administered by those who apparently wanted to encourage experimentation.

The former justification rules, which could be used in situations just like these, do not seem to be working any more. They may all have been based on rationality, but rationality of a formal kind – the best means for reaching the goal – clearly depends on what kind of goal it is. Thus it is possible to suggest here that a change in substantial rationality has taken place: from collective interest to individual (organizational) interest; from a public administration ethos to a business ethos, as captured in the expression 'public management'. The moral criterion of 'solidarity' has been exchanged for the criterion of 'efficiency' (see also March and Olsen, 1976; March, 1978; Gustafsson, 1983). Here it becomes evident how the logic of justification depends on the logic of appropriateness: an account whose premise everybody accepts, which encompasses steps everybody would have taken, and which arrives at a conclusion that everybody would accept – that is, everybody like us in a situation like this. It was not the conflict between efficiency and solidarity which caused uncertainty – the thinking of the great economists' morals and virtue combine very nicely (albeit in various configurations) with commerce and money (Ignatieff, 1984). Rather, it is the shift in both accounting rules and identities that is difficult. If what used to be taken for granted is no longer self-evident, what is to be taken for granted now? The various accounts which have been reported in this chapter suggest that the rules were changing, but that nobody knew or could decide beforehand what the future rules would be.

What I had the chance to witness and what I have tried to describe in this text, is an incredibly powerful process of deinstitutionalization (Røvik, 1996). Due to a more or less forced, and more or less general, consensus about the end of the old consensus, the old rules of accounting for the conduct of the public administration actors appear as being no longer valid. New rules are being sought and constructed.

In times of transformation, the construction of the old rules becomes visible. This visibility of the rules is what sustains the epistemological crisis. For once the rules are visible, they are also more easy to challenge. Their destruction reveals that, behind the rules of formal rationality, so important to the logic of justification, were hiding the rules of substantial rationality, which by definition cannot be universal ('Whose justice? Which rationality?'). In much the same way as formal rationality and formal logic may be valid for anybody ('all'), these rules make sense only when there is an agreement about what is supposed to be said; what is 'appropriate' in the first place. To give an obvious and exaggerated example, a person devoting her time to reciting syllogisms in the centre of a street market would be considered not supremely rational, but mad.

However, if agreement on the type of substantial rationality appropriate to a given person (organization) and situation forms the cornerstone of the logic of justification, then this logic seems to be subordinate to the logic of appropriateness. It is necessary to know who you are and where you are to be able to try to convince people of the rationality of your action and in order to be able to know who you are it is necessary to know what group or community you are supposed to serve or represent, whose demands you have to meet.

Where do identity and situation labelling come from when they are no longer taken for granted, and are no longer given by a clear relation to a distinct community? They are forged, say Davies and Harré (1991) through and in the process of positioning, which can be seen as ongoing negotiations about who are the partners in the interaction and what the interaction is. The cornerstone thus turns out to be fluid and temporary, obligations are a matter of negotiation and alliance forming, and identity is a result of a process rather than its premise.

It is not enough to say that times of transformation show that the giants of the past had feet of clay. This is all right, so long as it is not assumed that future giants will have feet of steel (this assumption, now being painstakingly corrected, was typical of the East European countries after the fall of the Berlin Wall)[9]. What I am trying to say is that the paradoxical character of the basic set of accounting rules is nothing exceptional or specific to Sweden. In times of transformation, the daily de-paradoxifying attempts (Luhmann, 1991) that are so characteristic of modern organizations become suspended; the paradoxicality of everyday life is made apparent and becomes the engine of renewal and change (Lyotard, 1987). Similar phenomena occur in England and Germany, Italy and France – all within their specific context, of course, but still associated with this uneasy amalgamation and exchange of the ethos of business and public administration.[10] In times when the fundamental dualism of the modern era seem to have lost their fundaments, the world appears as populated by hybrids (Latour, 1993).

There is another way of showing that this phenomenon is by no means specific to Sweden. The accounting rules constituting the western culture are far from homogenous. As MacIntyre points out, they are the sediments of different religious traditions (Puritan, Catholic, Jewish) and of different stages and local variations in the development of modernity (MacIntyre, 1988). All these bits and pieces exist not only in the 'culture', but in each one of us in various combinations and collages. Altogether, they produce at least three meta-accounts of rational action based on three different theories of justice: the collective pursuit of individual interests, the collective pursuit of collective interest, and the disinterested pursuit of formal rationality for its own sake. All three have been involved in the events related here, with those concerned heeding the first two and trying to conscript the third on their side.

And yet, continues MacIntyre, '[o]ne of the most striking facts about modern political orders is that they lack institutionalized forums within which these fundamental disagreements can be systematically explored and charted, let alone there being any attempt to resolve them' (1988: 2). Perhaps MacIntyre is looking in the wrong place. Such forums are created, of necessity, at the ground level of concrete organizations, where people try to fashion their accounts in experimental ways and now and then reflect upon the ways in which the 'old' and the 'new' accounts were constructed. Thus a situation involving crisis and a forced transformation leads not only to a public debate but to many small conversations in which different standpoints can be confronted and scrutinized: a tradition-constituted inquiry, not in academia or at party headquarters, but on the shop-floor, as it were.

I want to stress this point because it goes against the well-established idea of practitioners as the dupes of social reality. Mary Douglas, for instance, ironizing about the social scientists' radical skepticism, contrasts such egg-headed doubters with 'those crude officers of public administration, whose minds such complicated doubts would never cross. They have a vested interest in legitimacy and so in the possibility of rational discourse. It is only the excluded elite who seriously entertain radical doubt and allow it to subvert the enterprise of communication' (1986: 83).

With all due respect, it is only the self-excluded elite which can produce such a picture of public administration. The noble savage has now become the noble public servant. The people I met in 'the field' would not have batted an eyelid on hearing the shocking news that reality was socially constructed. They should know; after all, they play an important role in it. Alternating between 'essentialism' and 'constructivism' and between 'action' and 'reflection' is sometimes tiring and always costly, but it happens to be their job.

It is actually the social scientists who have a not-so-vested interest in holding the 'rational discourse' sacred and keeping it away from inspection, who wave the terrifying flag of 'relativism' and all the nihilism that this implies.[11] This is not to deny that the existing social order, of whatever kind, tends to react negatively to any public reflection, glossing over it as quickly as possible (totalitarian orders simply prohibit it). Certainly, while the social-democratic tradition is being forced to submit to self-inquiry, the rival position is busy shutting itself off from any inspection and solidifying the 'first premises' of Market and Management. The press, while waving the flag of 'independent inquiry', is in fact discouraging any soul-searching or serious reflection and rewarding simplification and gloss. Meanwhile the inquiry in process on the organization floor is being censored from inside and outside, in the struggle to restore the 'structure of normality'.

It is therefore likely that this scrutiny and the accompanying public debate will cease when the present epistemological crisis is over. Whatever the new social agreement is like, it will sink into people's consciousness like its forerunner, and everybody will be accounting in an orderly manner, taking for granted the new premises as they did the old ones. Another possibility, though, is that this fragmented state of affairs will permanently replace the former stable societal consensus (if it ever really existed). This may lead to the existence of permanently reflective societies, in which the epistemological crisis has become institutionalized – a state of affairs that neither ethnomethodologists nor institutionalists thought to be possible. This state of affairs will most certainly require a change in the accounting rules in the social sciences themselves.

Acknowledgements

The author wishes to thank the Swedish Council for Research in the Humanities and Social Sciences for financial support, and Jan Mouritsen and Rolland Munro for intellectual support. Special thanks to David Silverman, who however disagrees with many of the tacks followed in this article. Nancy Adler has done the exasperating (for her) job of setting the English straight.

Notes

1. Here I use 'ethos', that is a code of conduct in a given community, as synonymous with a set of accounting rules for a community created by a common activity.
2. To be more exact, Scott and Lyman, following Austin (1962), introduce a further distinction between excuses and justifications, which will be treated together in this text.
3. While the study contained an element of conventional participant observation and interviewing, the main bulk of the material comes from an 'observant participation': regular contacts with organizational actors who told me in detail about actions and events taking place at their workplace over the past two to three weeks. This involved 10 to 20 visits to each one of the organizations studied, and resulted in a rich description of events structured along the line of a dramatist analysis (Czarniawska-Joerges, n.d.).
4. One of the constellations studied was composed of the government (ministries), the Swedish Association of Local Authorities (SALA) and local governments (here called Big City, Northtown and Sweet Hamlet). This, then, was the municipal constellation with its local, central, and federative components.

   The other, the social insurance constellation, was composed of the National Social Insurance Board (NSIO), the Association of Social Insurance Offices (ASIO), and social insurance offices located at the county level (Big County, Northern County and Middle County). It should be added here that social insurance in Sweden covers medical care, rehabilitation in case of accidents at work, and so on. Although the resources are administered centrally by NSIB, the handling of applications and delivery of payments are dealt with by the County Social Insurance Offices (CSIO). The local origins of social insurance are still sedimented in its former federative organ, ASIO.

5. In translation. This in itself creates a vast variety of problems, which are not taken up in the present context (see MacIntyre, 1988). It is worth noting, however, that main technique of ethnomethodology, conversation analysis, seems to assume complete translatability, or at least does not pose questions concerning its use across different linguistic contexts.

6. But even in local government offices people complained that it takes an incredibly long time to get people who come fresh from the university sufficiently trained to be able to perform satisfactorily.

7. All accounts in this section come from Finance Directors in two municipalities (Big City and Sweet Hamlet) and are quoted in the order they occurred, over a period of about four months.

8. An important point to make is that, in Swedish, 'accountability' and 'responsibility' are covered by the same word, *ansvar*. Interesting etymological possibilities open up in this context. One possibility is that there is no word in Swedish which means 'to answer by counting'. 'Accounting' is translated either as *redovisning*, as in the accounting profession, or *redogörelse*, as in everyday speech. Both mean 'show (or make) something ready'. Another possibility, however, is that this is a case of a historical paronomasia, with the same sound in the words *rede* as number, account, and even reason, and *rede* as ready, prepared (Hellquist, 1989: 822), so that *redovisning* might in fact mean not 'show something as ready' but 'show something by counting'.

9. See the special issue of *Industrial and Environmental Crises Quarterly*, 1994, 1.

10. See for example the interesting analysis of the Berlusconi phenomenon (Diamanti, 1994).

11. See Levine (1993) and Ashmore *et al.* (1994) on the 'rhetoric of reality demonstration', focusing on two themes: table (the banging of it) and death.

References

Ashmore, M., Edwards, D., and Potter, J. (1994) The bottom line: The rhetoric of reality demonstrations. *Configurations*, **1** pp. 1–14.

Bittner, E. (1965) The Concept of Organization. *Social Research*, **31** pp. 240–55.

Boden, D. (1994) *The Business of Talk. Organizations in Action*, Polity Press, Cambridge.

Burchell, S. Clubb, C., and Hopwood, A.G. (1985) Accounting in its social context: Towards a history of value added in the United Kingdom. *Accounting Organizations and Society* **10**(4) pp. 381–413.

Burke, K. (1945/1969) *A Grammar of Motives*, University of California Press, Berkeley.

Cicourel, A.V. (1974) *Cognitive Sociology. Language and Meaning in Social Interaction*, Free Press, New York.

Czarniawska, B. (1985) The ugly sister: On relationships between the private and the public sector in Sweden. *Scandinavian Journal of Management Studies*, **2**(2), pp. 83–103.

Czarniawska-Joerges, B. (1992a) *Exploring Complex Organizations*, Sage, Newbury Park, CA.

Czarniawska-Joerges, B. (1992b) Rationality as an organizational product. *Administrative Studies*, **11**(3) pp. 152–62.

Czarniawska-Joerges, B. (1994) Narratives of individual and organizational identities, in *Communication Yearbook 17* (ed S. Deetz) pp. 193–221 Sage, Newbury Park, CA.

Czarniawska-Joerges, B. (n.d.) *Narrating the Organization. Dramas of institutional identity.* (Manuscript)

Davies, B. and Harré, R. (1991) Positioning: The discursive production of selves. *Journal for the Theory of Social Behaviour*, **20**(1) pp. 43–63.

Diamanti, I. (1994) Politik als Marketing. Das Phänomen Berlusconi – Markt, Werbung, Kommunikation. *Lettre International*, **36** (Autumn), pp. 34–7.

Douglas, M. (1986) The social preconditions of radical scepticism, in: *Power, Action and Belief. A New Sociology of Knowledge?* (ed J. Law) pp. 68–87, Routledge and Kegan Paul, London.

Douglas, M. (1992) Thought style exemplified: The idea of the self, in: *Risk and blame* pp. 211–34, Routledge, London.

Garfinkel, H. (1967) *Studies in Ethnomethodology*, Prentice-Hall, Englewood Cliffs, NJ.

Garfinkel, H. (1988) Evidence for locally produced, naturally accountable phenomena of order, logic, reason, meaning, method, etc. in and as of the essential quiddity of immortal ordinary society, *Sociology Theory*, **6** pp. 103–9.

Gustafsson, C. (1983) Efficiency and related rules for organizational action. *International Studies of Management and Organization*, **19**(3) pp. 34–48.

Harré, R. (1979) *Social Being*, Basil Blackwell, Oxford.

Harré, R. (1982) Theoretical preliminaries to the study of action, in *The Analysis of Action* (eds M. von Cranach and R. Harré) pp. 5–34, Cambridge University Press, Cambridge.

Harré, R. and Secord, P.F. (1972) *The Explanation of Social Behaviour*, Basil Blackwell, Oxford.

Hellquist, E. (1989) *Svensk Etymologisk Ordbok*, Liber, Malmö.

Hirdman, Y. (1989) *Att Lägga Livet Till Rätta*, Carlsson, Stockholm.

Humphrey, C. and Olson, O. (1995) Caught in the act. Public services disappearing in the world of 'accountable' management? in *Issues in Management Accounting* (eds D. Ashton, T. Hopper and R. Scapens), Prentice-Hall, Exeter.

Ignatieff, M. (1984) *The Needs of Strangers*, Chatto and Windus, London.

Latour, B. (1993) *We Have Never Been Modern*, Harvard University Press, Cambridge, MA.

Latour, B. (1994) On technical mediation. *Common Knowledge*, **3**(2) pp. 29–64.

Levine, G. (1993) Looking for the real: epistemology in science and culture, in *Realism and Representation. Essays on the Problem of Realism in Relation to Science, Literature, and Culture* (ed G. Levine) pp. 3–23, The University of Wisconsin Press, Madison, Wisconsin.

Luhmann, N. (1991) Sthenographie und Euryalistik, in *Paradoxien, Dissonanzen, Zusammenbrüche. Situationen offener Epistemologie.* (eds H. Gumbrecht and K-L. Pfeiffer) pp. 58–82, Suhrkamp, Frankfurt.

Lynch, M. and Bogen, D. (1994) Harvey Sack's primitive natural science. *Theory, Culture & Society*, **11** pp. 65–104.

Lyotard, J-F. (1979/1987). *The Postmodern Condition. A Report on Knowledge*, Manchester University Press, Manchester.

MacIntyre, A. (1980) *After Virtue*, Duckworth, London.

MacIntyre, A. (1988) *Whose Justice? Which Rationality?* University of Notre Dame Press, Notre Dame, Indiana.

March, J.G. (1978) Bounded rationality, ambiguity, and the engineering of choice. *Bell Journal of Economics*, **9** pp. 587–608.

March, J.G. and Olsen, J. (1976) *Ambiguity and Choice in Organizations*. Universitetsforlaget, Bergen.

March, J. and Olsen, J. (1989) *Rediscovering Institutions. The Organizational Basis of Politics*, The Free Press, New York.

Meyer, J.W. (1986) Myths of socialization and of personality, in *Reconstructing Individualism: Autonomy, Individuality and the Self in Western Thought* (eds T.C. Heller, M. Sosna and D.C. Wellbery) pp. 208–21 Stanford University Press, Stanford, CA.

Meyer, J.W., Boli, J. and Thomas, G.M. (1987) Ontology and rationalization in the Western cultural account in *Institutional Structure: Constituting State, Society and the Individual* (eds G.M. Thomas, J.W. Meyer, F.O. Ramirez and J. Boli) pp. 12–37, Sage, Beverly Hills, CA.

Mouritsen, J. (1994) Rationality, institutions and decision making: Reflections on March and Olsen's Rediscovering Institutions. *Accounting, Organizations and Society*, **19**(2) pp. 193–211.

Pitkin Fenichel, H.M. (1972) *Wittgenstein and Justice*, The University of California Press, Berkeley.

Robson, K. (1991) On the arenas of accounting change: The process of translation. *Accounting, Organizations and Society,* **16**(5/6) pp. 547–70.

Rorty, R. (1980) *Philosophy as the Mirror of Nature,* Blackwell, Oxford.

Røvik, K-A. (1996) De-institutionalization and the logic of fashion in *Translating Organizational Change* (eds B. Czarniawska and G. Sevón) De Gruyter, Berlin (forthcoming).

Sacks, H. (1966–7/1992) *Lectures on Conversations* (vol.1 2). Blackwell, Oxford.

Scott, M.B., and Lyman, S.M. (1968) Accounts. *American Sociological Review,* **33:** pp. 46–62.

Silverman, D. and Jones, J. (1976) *Organizational Work,* Collier Macmillan, London.

Thompson, G. (1991) Is accounting rhetorical? Methodology, Luca Pacioli and printing. *Accounting, Organizations and Society,* **16** (5/6) pp. 572–99.

Index